NORWICH CATHEDRAL CLOS

THE EVOLUTION OF THE ENGLISH CATHEDRAL

GW00361088

Studies in the History of Medieval Religion

ISSN: 0955–2480

Founding Editor
Christopher Harper-Bill

Series Editor
Frances Andrews

Previously published titles in the series
are listed at the back of this volume

NORWICH CATHEDRAL CLOSE

The Evolution of the English Cathedral Landscape

Roberta Gilchrist

THE BOYDELL PRESS

First published 2005
The Boydell Press, Woodbridge
Paperback edition 2016

ISBN 978 1 84383 173 0 hardback
ISBN 978 1 78327 096 5 paperback

The Boydell Press is an imprint of Boydell & Brewer Ltd
PO Box 9, Woodbridge, Suffolk IP12 3DF, UK
and of Boydell & Brewer Inc.
668 Mt Hope Avenue, Rochester, NY 14620–2731, USA
website: www.boydellandbrewer.com

A CIP catalogue record for this book is available
from the British Library

This publication is printed on acid-free paper

Designed and typeset in Perpetua by
The Stingray Office, Chorlton-cum-Hardy, Manchester

Contents

List of Illustrations

Colour Plates

between pp. 148 and 149

between pp. 180 and 181

Preface

THE background to this volume stretches back to 1993, when I received an opportune telephone call from the chapter clerk of Norwich Cathedral. I was invited to an interview for the post of Cathedral Archaeologist, to serve as the archaeological curator of the cathedral church and precinct, under the Cathedrals Measure 1990. A long and busy association began, with my appointment coinciding with a series of major new developments and conservation programmes. Over the subsequent twelve years, these included comprehensive survey and recording of the historic fabric, and assessment and excavation in advance of new developments on two of the former monastic ranges. The pace and extent of change at Norwich Cathedral has been remarkable, and perhaps more rapid than at any time since the Reformation! The post of Cathedral Archaeologist is concerned principally with matters of heritage management, but the position also complemented my personal research interests in medieval monasticism. Over time, it provided an ideal opportunity for the detailed, contextual study of a major medieval monastery, one that survived the Dissolution as a reformed secular cathedral.

Background research for this volume began with a study funded by English Heritage to provide a strategic archaeological assessment of Norwich Cathedral Close (Gilchrist 1998); I am grateful to Richard Halsey and English Heritage Cathedrals Team for supporting this initiative. A period of research leave provided time for final research and writing, funded by the Arts and Humanities Research Board and the University of Reading (2003). The publication costs for this monograph have been subsidised by the Gatsby Charitable Foundation, the Chapter of Norwich Cathedral, and the School of Human and Environmental Sciences, at the University of Reading. Drawings have been prepared by Margaret Mathews, Philip Thomas and Sue White; Terence Burchell provided photographs for figure 41 and plates 4a and 8a/b. Chris King has assisted with preparing digital images for the final manuscript. For permission to reproduce images, I would like to acknowledge the Chapter of Norwich Cathedral, Norwich Castle Museum, Norwich Record Office, Norfolk Landscape Archaeology, the Norfolk Archaeological Unit, the Society of Antiquaries of London, Philip Thomas, Robert Smith, Roland Harris and Steven Ashley.

Cathedrals have attracted long and diverse study, and inevitably this volume draws upon the work of many researchers. In particular, I would like to acknowledge the influence of Eric Fernie, Veronica Sekules and Carole Rawcliffe, and to thank each of them for their personal support. The numerous recent projects at Norwich Cathedral have involved many archaeological and historical specialists, and their work has brought new insights to this study. I am especially indebted to Philip Thomas, clerk of works to Norwich Cathedral (and formerly archaeological surveyor), and to the research assistants who were employed on the archaeological assessment of Norwich Cathedral Close that was funded by English Heritage (1996–7). Jonathon Finch compiled the database and researched post-medieval documents and plans; Claire Noble translated medieval obediential accounts; and Robert Smith conducted rapid surveys of sixteen standing buildings. Owen Thompson contributed to the study of many areas of the close through his personal knowledge of the post-medieval illustrations of the cathedral. The Norfolk Archaeological Unit, and particularly Heather Wallis and John Percival, have conducted several excavations and watching briefs in the close that have informed this study.

Numerous scholars have been generous in sharing their knowledge of Norwich Cathedral and other related subjects, and I would especially like to thank Ian Atherton, Paul Cattermole, John Crook, David Gaimster, Richard Gem, Roland Harris, Maurice Howard, Barney Sloane, David Stocker and Tim Tatton-Brown. Comments on the manuscript were kindly provided by Eric Fernie, Chris King, Philip Thomas, and particularly David Stocker, whose observations helped me to refine several arguments. I would like to thank past and present members of the Chapter of Norwich Cathedral and the Norwich Cathedral Fabric Advisory Committee, for their positive support of my research into the cathedral's archaeology. Special thanks are extended to Stephen Platten, Colin Pordham, Tim Cawkwell, Henry Freeland, John Maddison, Sandy Heslop, Hugh Feilden and the late Keith Darby.

Finally, I would like to thank my colleagues and postgraduate students at the department of Archaeology, University of Reading, for the stimulating research environment in which we work. Greatest personal thanks are reserved for my husband, John Preston, for his continued support and patience for research projects that sometimes dominate our lives, and certainly my time — anniversaries, birthdays and holidays have been diverted regularly to Norwich. Sharing Norwich with him has been a great delight, and it is fortunate that the city provides such a rare mix of historic architecture, good shopping and the exceptional hospitality of 'By Appointment'!

Abbreviations

NRO	Norfolk Record Office
DCN	Dean and Chapter of Norwich Cathedral (in NRO)
DN	Diocesan Records of Norwich (in NRO)
MC	The Papers of Arthur Bensly Wittingham (in NRO)
NNAS	Norfolk and Norwich Archaeological Society
RCHME	Royal Commission on Historical Monuments of England
SMR	Sites and Monuments Record
VCH	Victoria County Histories

1

Introduction:
Norwich Cathedral in Context

ENGLISH cathedrals have enjoyed extensive study for nearly two centuries, and yet the broader physical and social landscape in which they sit has largely been neglected. With notable exceptions, even recent scholarship has focused on the cathedral church, generally excluding the precinct from consideration.[1] This monograph aims to redress this imbalance, by interpreting the development of Norwich cathedral close from its foundation c.1096 up to c.1700. The cathedral landscape permits a long-term, interdisciplinary perspective: Norwich cathedral will be studied in terms of the creation of the landscape of the close and transformations in its use and meaning over time. In contrast with all other categories of medieval monastery, cathedral-priories weathered the Reformation, emerging after the Dissolution as reformed, secular establishments (1539–42). Monastic archaeology has directed considerable effort to examining the dissolution process at individual religious houses, and architectural historians have examined the ways in which former monasteries were transformed into courtier and gentry houses (e.g. Doggett 2001; Howard 2003). The cathedral-priories offer unique potential to study the experience of change and continuity through the eruptions of the Reformation and beyond.

In 1996, Richard Morris remarked that 'the extension of cathedral archaeology to embrace considerations beyond those of building form and development is overdue', calling for study of a cathedral community with regard to its buildings, society and economy (Morris 1996, 4). The present volume contributes to this research objective, offering an holistic study of Norwich cathedral that draws on archaeological, architectural and historical evidence to examine the changing social and economic functions of the cathedral landscape. The evidence of Norwich cathedral will be assessed against patterns recorded for other cathedrals and monasteries. This comparative approach attempts to counter the fragmentation that sometimes accompanies historical archaeology; analogues will also be drawn from appropriate categories of secular settlement, including castles, palaces and manor houses. Although Norwich cathedral close is not the most celebrated

---

[1] For example, see papers on individual cathedral churches in Tatton-Brown and Munby (eds.) 1996, and volumes of the *British Archaeological Association Conference Transactions*. For broader consideration of aspects of cathedral closes, see Hall and Stocker (eds.) 2005, in press; Stocker 2005, in press; Rady et al. 1991; Tatton-Brown 1994; Crook 1984; Heighway 1999.

or best-preserved of England's cathedral landscapes (see Canterbury: Willis 1868; Tatton-Brown 1984), the extent of its survival and significance has generally been underestimated. Comparative, interdisciplinary study of Norwich cathedral close has the potential to identify typical and singular experience in the development of the English cathedral landscape. The story of Norwich cathedral close deserves telling, and it provides an opportunity to stretch the conceptual boundaries of cathedral archaeology.

The English Monastic Cathedral

In contrast with continental cathedrals, which were served by communities of secular canons or priests, England developed a hybrid system of monastic and secular cathedrals. The monastic cathedrals were a unique institution that grew from the process of ecclesiastical reform in tenth-century England. By the end of the ninth century, monastic life had been decimated by a combination of Viking attack and internal decay. It was revived under the patronage of King Edgar and through the energies of Abbots Dunstan, Ethelwold and Oswald, who resurrected ancient monastic sites and converted cathedrals from secular colleges of priests to monastic communities of monks (Knowles and Hadcock 1971, 12). The mother church of the diocese was served by monks who were ruled by a monk-bishop, rather than by an abbot. By the time of the Norman Conquest, there were monastic cathedrals at Canterbury, Winchester, Worcester and Sherborne. Rather than suppress this distinctively English institution, Archbishop Lanfranc encouraged its survival. Communities of monks replaced secular clergy in the dioceses of Rochester (c.1080), Durham (1083) and Norwich (c.1096) (ibid., 17).

The resulting diocesan structure was an equal mix of monastic and secular cathedrals. Monastic communities of Benedictine monks were established at Bath, Canterbury, Coventry, Durham, Ely, Norwich, Rochester, Winchester and Worcester, with Carlisle served by Augustinian canons. Secular communities of priests governed by cathedral statutes were installed at Chichester, Exeter, Hereford, Lichfield, Lincoln, London, Salisbury (replacing secular Old Sarum), Wells and York. The secular cathedrals also housed 'vicars choral', the communities of lesser clergy who sang the services and represented the canons in the choir. The endowments of the secular cathedrals were divided into prebends, held by individual canons or prebendaries. The secular establishments developed independence from their bishop, who required permission to enter the cathedral (Edwards 1967). In contrast, the bishops were the titular abbots of the monastic cathedral-priories, and their endowments were common property held under the Rule of St Benedict (Crosby 1994). The monastic cathedrals drew from the rich tradition of coenobitic religious experience (from the Greek *koinobion*, meaning communal life) and followed the Rule of St Benedict. The Rule was composed by Benedict of Nursia c.530–40 at the Italian monastery of Monte Cassino (McCann 1952, ix). In the formulation of his Rule, Benedict strove for a well-organised ascetic life, one that achieved sanctity through the elevation of the principle of community and the renunciation of the individual (discussed below).

The cathedral-priories were distinctive in their commitment to the monastic concept of community and in their relationship to the bishop as titular abbot. At the time of their foundation, the monastic cathedrals differed in one further crucial respect. Monks took vows to observe a celibate life, in an exclusively male community that was distanced from female company. In contrast, it was acceptable for secular priests to marry until the mid eleventh century, when the Gregorian Reform promoted clerical celibacy as a mark of the priest's separation from lay society (Elliott 1999, 82) and in an effort to address nepotism and the transfer of hereditary benefices through clerical families (Brooke 1956). In continental cathedrals, canons' wives played diverse liturgical roles right up to the eleventh century (McNamara 1999, 17), and in England some cathedrals tolerated married clergy well into the twelfth century. For example, one quarter of the canons at St Paul's cathedral in London were married, according to a prebendal catalogue covering the years 1090–1127 (Brooke 1956, 18). The English clergy accepted celibacy only gradually from c.1050: clerical marriage was not fully stamped out until c.1130 among the upper clergy, and by the end of the twelfth century among the lower clergy that served parish churches (ibid., 16).

The Norman cathedrals were established precisely during this period of social transformation: the peculiarly English institution of the cathedral-priory may have been favoured for its promise of monastic celibacy. The spectre of priests' wives brought considerable anxiety to the church, and their exclusion from secular cathedrals could not have been guaranteed during the period of Norman cathedral foundations. The introduction of clerical celibacy was accompanied by an increased emphasis on the regulation of sacred space: the maintenance of holy places required the ritual purity of the clergy and the exclusion of women as potential polluters (Elliott 1999; McNamara 1999; see p. 240). Such gynephobia was institutionalised through monastic spatial practices, for example at the cathedral-priory of Durham, where women were barred from entering the cathedral church itself and a western galilee was specially constructed to accommodate female visitors.

The respective cathedrals of monks and secular canons differed also in the physical plant that was required to sustain them. In the thirteenth century, some secular cathedrals provided the vicars (the junior priests) with quasi-monastic dormitories (e.g. York from c.1250, Lincoln from c.1270) (Stocker 2005, in press). By the 1350s, however, smaller lodgings were provided within the precinct for them to live individually, often grouped in a close and provided with a common hall, for example at Chichester and Wells (Tatton-Brown 1994; Hall and Stocker (eds.) 2005, in press). Hierarchical distinctions between the canons and vicars were manifest in the quality of housing for the respective groups, as shown at Salisbury (RCHME 1993), and in the separate areas set aside for their burial (see p. 96). The cathedral-priories were monasteries, designed at their outset to minimise elements of individuality and hierarchy and to practise a high degree of self-sufficiency, in keeping with the Rule of St Benedict. They were provided with the usual range of monastic buildings grouped around a cloister (see Chapters 4 and 5), together with domestic and agricultural appurtenances in the inner and outer court (Chapter 3) (Figure 1; Plate 9). By the later Middle Ages, it is evident that the cloister had become symbolic of the superior status of a cathedral church, whether it was served by monks or secular canons (see p. 68). All but two of the medieval secular cathedrals developed cloisters, perhaps suggesting that monastic tradition was valued by cathedral communities of both types.

The Reformation impacted with greater severity on the monastic cathedrals, involving the suppression of the communities of monks that served them, while the secular cathedrals simply experienced a reduction in resources and numbers of prebends. In the reorganisation that followed, the long-standing distinction between the medieval secular and monastic cathedrals disappeared, and national cathedral provision was reformed. The cathedrals of Bath and Coventry were made redundant, and six new cathedrals were formed from previous monastic foundations at Gloucester, Peterborough, Chester, Bristol, Oxford and Westminster, the last soon transformed into a royal peculiar (Lehmberg 1988, 80–86). The key roles of a cathedral following the Reformation included the provision of sermons and education, alongside the more traditional functions of administering the sacraments, hospitality and poor relief (Lehmberg 1996, 215).

Appraising Norwich Cathedral

Historiography

Cathedral archaeology has advanced through two significant periods of development. The first wave of archaeology accompanied the major schemes of church restoration c. 1850–90, involving recording and scrutiny of church fabric. The second peak has encompassed both excavation and buildings archaeology and has occurred alongside conservation and new developments over the past forty years, more particularly since provision for archaeology was established by the Care of Cathedrals Measure 1990 (Gem 1996).

Antiquarian study of Norwich cathedral began with the observations of Sir Thomas Browne (1605–1682), a renowned physician and natural philosopher, who leased a meadow in the close; its historical study began with the work of the Norfolk historian Francis Blomefield c. 1745. The first scaled drawings were completed by John Adey Repton c. 1794–1804, remarkable for both their accuracy and their early date (Figure 2).[2] Repton produced a series of elevations and sections and a ground-plan of the church and cloisters, recorded elements of the infirmary shortly after its demolition and depicted details of the precinct gates and fabric of the cathedral

---

[2] J. A. Repton was the son of the landscape designer Humphrey Repton. For 200 years, Repton's drawings of Norwich cathedral were used for the practical purposes of architectural repair, until a digital measured survey was completed by Roland Harris and Philip Thomas in 1998.

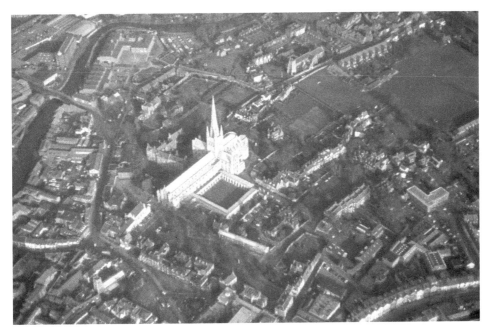

FIGURE 1. Norwich cathedral from the air. The buildings of the bishop's palace can be seen to the north of the church, and beyond them the meander of the River Wensum. To the east are the Great Hospital and playing fields of the Norwich School, stretching towards the Wensum's eastern arm. Photograph by Derek Edwards, reproduced with permission of Norfolk Landscape Archaeology (TG 2308).

church (Pierce 1965). Illustrations of the close survive from the late eighteenth century onwards, with more numerous engravings of the church published in volumes such as Britton's and Winkles's series on cathedral churches (Britton 1817; 1836; Winkles 1838).

The most prominent name in the antiquarian study of cathedrals is the Reverend Professor Robert Willis (1800–1875), who held the Jacksonian Chair of Engineering at Cambridge and contributed to the study and recording of ten English cathedral churches (Thompson 1996). In 1847, the *London Illustrated News* reported on a lecture given by Willis on the site of the former monastic west range at Norwich. He examined the cathedral closes of Canterbury and Worcester in detail, and according to the Norfolk and Norwich Archaeological Society (NNAS) he had planned a monograph on Norwich cathedral and precinct (*Norfolk Archaeol* 3 (1850), 421). Sadly, this work remained incomplete at his death, and only a short article based on Willis's notes was published posthumously (Stewart 1875). With no major proponent of Norwich during the 'golden age' of cathedral archaeology, the precinct of Norwich cathedral has remained little known and only partially understood.

During repair to the nave in 1899, the dean expressed the desire to locate the bones of the supposed boy martyr William (d. 1144). Another prominent figure in

FIGURE 2. Longitudinal section of Norwich cathedral by John Adey Repton, c.1794, from
west to east and looking north. Reproduced with permission of the Society of Antiquaries
of London.

the history of ecclesiastical archaeology, William St John Hope, conducted small-
scale excavations (St John Hope and Bensly 1899). He published the results together
with William Bensly, the cathedral's chapter clerk, who seems to have inspired
an entire family's antiquarian interest in Norwich cathedral (Bensly 1908). Close
family associations with the cathedral were not unusual in the nineteenth century:
one family contributed three successive surveyors in John Brown (1834–69), John
Henry Brown (1869–91) and C. J. Brown (1891–1932). Bensly passed the mantle
of chapter clerk to his nephew, Leonard G. Bolingbroke, who conducted important
but previously unacknowledged work on the close. Bolingbroke was active as an

officer in the NNAS and developed his own collection of antiquities, bequeathed to the Norwich Castle Museum. In 1899, he saved a medieval merchant's house from destruction: he established Strangers' Hall, Norwich, as a folk museum and gave it to the city in 1922 (Wood 1965, 190).

Bolingbroke was the first to give explicit attention to the study of the post-medieval close, although the published result is just a short summary of a longer, anecdotal lecture to the NNAS (1922). He made observations during building works in the close and studied post-medieval leases to establish the date of the buildings and their historical associations. This work was developed by his cousin, Arthur Bensly Whittingham, who published Bolingbroke's material in his own discussion of the buildings described in the Parliamentary Survey of Norwich cathedral in 1649 (1985). Whittingham was Bensly's grandson, and he served as surveyor to the fabric of Norwich cathedral from 1932 to 1963, after which he remained as an advisor until his death in 1988 (Fernie 1989b). Like his cousin, Whittingham was active in the NNAS, but he published little of his substantial knowledge of the cathedral. His two major contributions were milestones in the interpretation of the close, including an interpretative plan of the medieval precinct produced in 1938 (published 1949 and amended 1975) and a discussion of the development of the close since the Reformation (published posthumously in 1988). He left a substantial archive of notes on his excavations and watching briefs in the close, covering a period of fifty years (MC 186). Although these activities informed his 1978 plan of the precinct, they remain unpublished.

Recent years have seen a flourishing of scholarship on the cathedral church at Norwich, including Eric Fernie's meticulous analysis of the Romanesque cathedral (Fernie 1993) and a comprehensive, multi-author volume marking nine hundred years of the cathedral's history (Atherton et al 1996). Repair programmes on the north transept and tower and spire have been integrated with archaeological recording and interpretation (Gilchrist 1999; 2002). Since 1993, any developments within the close have been preceded by archaeological assessment, evaluation and recording.[3] New developments have required relatively small-scale excavations, designed to mitigate destruction of archaeological deposits. A number of such interventions have been conducted by the Norfolk Archaeological Unit, and together they increase our understanding of areas including the refectory, hostry and infirmary (Wallis 2002a; Wallis 2003; Percival 2001).

Methodology and sources of evidence
While scholarship on the cathedral church at Norwich has enjoyed a renaissance, synthetic study of the close has been limited to Whittingham's plans of the medieval precinct and the close in 1649. In addition to Bolingbroke's notes, Ian Atherton

[3] This policy pertains to the area of the close managed by the Dean and Chapter under the Care of Cathedrals Measure. Beyond the north wall of the cathedral church, the area of the bishop's palace is divided between the Norwich School and the Church Commissioners. An archaeological assessment of this area was conducted in 2002 (Gilchrist 2002).

published an excellent summary of the post-medieval history of the close (Boling-broke 1922; Atherton 1996). Whittingham's plans lacked any evidential discussion by which their accuracy could be evaluated, and his archive of notes and drawings is often indecipherable. As Fernie commented in his obituary of Whittingham, his attention to detail was 'liable to produce pieces of paper so covered with annotated, extended and corrected information that the surface of the paper was well nigh obliterated under the weight of script' (Fernie 1989b).

In order to appraise the precinct of Norwich cathedral, it was necessary first to put Whittingham's plans to one side and to return to the primary evidence. To inform both academic understanding and management of the cathedral's archaeol-ogy, a strategic archaeological assessment of the close was funded by English Her-itage and the chapter of Norwich cathedral (Gilchrist 1998). A database of over 1,000 records was established, encompassing all previous archaeological records and secondary sources, surveys of standing buildings and a sample of medieval and later documents and pictorial sources.[4] The data were included in the study only where their robustness and spatial provenance could be verified, with the aim of producing a series of maps that would assist with the management of the close. These included maps of archaeological interventions and subsurface deposits, historic building stock and evidence for the medieval precinct and post-medieval close. The plans in this volume derive from these maps as well as information from subsequent assessments and interventions, using a new measured survey of the church and cloister as the base plan. The strategic assessment was limited to the description and mapping of these sources, leaving broader interpretation to be pur-sued in this volume.

Archaeological sources for the close include those discussed above, in addition to building surveys conducted in the 1970s by the Norwich Survey and since 1993 by the author. Dating has been reliant principally on stylistic typologies, stratigraphic evidence and documentary sources.[5] The medieval documents provided little infor-mation that could be mapped, but they offer insights to the physical character of the medieval precinct. An unusually large collection of obediential accounts (dated 1262–1538) survives from Norwich cathedral-priory, numbering approximately 1200 rolls (DCN 1/1-13). These allow an appraisal of the priory's economy and a good understanding of its internal workings, including the regular repair of build-ings (Saunders 1930; Dodwell 1996b; Virgoe 1996; Noble 1997). Particularly useful

---

[4] The database was constructed by Dr Jonathon Finch, who served as research assistant to the project. Robert Smith carried out rapid surveys of sixteen standing buildings, including descriptions of historic roof structures. Dr Claire Noble sampled medieval records in the NRO, covering five periods each of ten years' duration (1329–40, 1349–60, 1470–81, 1525–36). These periods were chosen in order to include years with most comprehensive coverage and critical periods before and after the Black Death; 195 manuscripts were studied. The survey of pictorial sources benefited from the personal research of Owen Thompson, which was shared generously with the project. The database was deposited with the Norwich Urban Archaeological Database.

[5] There has been no dendrochronological study of the historic roofs of the close, and those of the cathedral church and cloisters were replaced comprehensively in the twentieth century.

for this study have been the inventories that were made when officers changed, including the refectorer (1393 and 1411), the sacrist (1438) and the hostiliar (1534). The priory's *First Register* assists in dating the construction of the earliest buildings. This document is based on two manuscripts of c.1300, which were most likely compiled after original documents had been lost in a great fire in 1272 (Saunders 1939). Rolls of the communar and pitancer provide a detailed account of the rebuilding of the cloister after the fire (Fernie and Whittingham 1972).

Life in the precinct can be glimpsed from narrative sources, including the *Life of St William of Norwich*, written by the monk Thomas of Monmouth c.1172–3 (Jessopp and James 1896). Twelve-year old William was murdered in Thorpe Wood in March 1144, and his body was discovered in a shallow grave in the woodland. Rumours quickly circulated that he had been crucified, and in the prevailing anti-Semitic fervour the story grew. It was alleged that he had been ritually murdered by the city's Jews during Passover. This young corpse was exploited by the monks of the cathedral in their dubious effort to manufacture a local saint. The second source is Bartholomew Cotton's *Historia Anglicana*, c.1290, which provides an account of the riot and destruction of the cathedral in 1272 (Luard 1859). Monastic observances can be reconstructed from the Rule of St Benedict and from the Norwich *Customary* (Tolhurst 1948), augmented by comparative reference to sources produced at other monasteries, such as the *Rites of Durham*, a record made in 1593 of customs that had prevailed before the suppression of the cathedral-priory at Durham (Fowler 1902). Transgressions from these ideals are communicated in the records of bishops' visitations to the priory, surviving from the years 1308, 1347, 1411, 1492, 1514, 1520, 1526 and 1534 (Cheney 1936; Carter 1935; Jessopp 1888).

The extended life history of cathedrals has yielded sources that have proved crucial in mapping the close, most notably leases dating shortly after the Reformation (DCN 47;[6] Williams and Cozens-Hardy 1953), and the Parliamentary Survey of 1649, made when dean-and-chapters were suppressed and their property confiscated (Metters 1985). The physical character of the close can sometimes be gleaned from audit and estate papers, records of the chapter and the personal papers of successive deans. The post-medieval sources offer abundant spatial evidence, but until 1909 properties were identified by the name of the tenant, making it difficult to link documentary references with specific buildings on the ground. To address this matter, a well-documented period was studied in some detail: late-eighteenth-century leases, chapter books, timber accounts and so on were examined in relation to cartographic evidence. It was then possible to locate earlier buildings by comparison with property abuttals on leases, by reference to former occupants.

Three maps are of major significance in the cartographic history of Norwich: William Cunningham's perspective of 1558, Thomas Cleer's formal plan of 1696, and Anthony Hochstetter's measured plan of 1789 (Chubb and Stephen 1928, 192,

---

[6] I have used Bolingbroke's notes and commentary on the earliest ledger books, which unfortunately are not consistent in their use of folio numbers.

plates XVIII, XXI and XXIV respectively). In addition, a useful and little-known colour drawing of c.1630–50 shows the cathedral from the north. This map was discovered in the archives of the Great Hospital, Norwich, by Walter Rye (Rye 1906). It is signed by Richard Wright, who is considered to have been a local cartographer, and clearly depicts the shape and approximate boundaries of the close (Plate 1). The impression given by this drawing is broadly supported by Cleer's map of 1696 and by a perspective drawing by Thomas Kirkpatrick of 1723 (Chubb and Stephen 1928, plate XXII). More accurate maps for tracing historic features in relation to the present landscape are Hochstetter's map of 1789, J. Dallinger's of 1830 (surveyed by W. S. Millard and I. Manning), and the Ordnance Survey maps of 1883/5. Dallinger's and the Ordnance Survey first editions have been combined as the basis for mapping the precinct.

These sources complement the evidence of archaeology and standing buildings, allowing an accurate reconstruction of the medieval and early modern close to c.1700. It is satisfying to report that Arthur Whittingham's plans and interpretations have been found to be broadly reliable, where they can be checked against supporting evidence. There is potential for future study of the buildings and topography of the close in the eighteenth and nineteenth centuries, a period beyond the remit of this volume.

Interpretative approaches
Art-historical studies of cathedrals have given priority to the evaluation of aesthetic innovation in medieval architecture, while traditional archaeological studies have been descriptive of surviving fabric with little concern for cultural context. For example, Eric Fernie assesses Norwich cathedral as

> a building of the first rank, not in a sense that it engendered a series of experiments or a host of followers, but in being a classic statement, the work of a knowledgeable and sensitive architect making use of all the sources available to him to produce an object which works as well aesthetically as it does liturgically and symbolically (Fernie 1993, 154).

In considering the contrasting approaches of archaeology and architectural history, Fernie concluded that archaeologists were more concerned with unravelling the techniques of medieval building, while architectural historians were engaged in discerning subtleties of meaning (Fernie 1989a, 20). A new generation of medieval archaeologists has moved beyond the parameters of description and technology to consider the social use and meaning of medieval buildings. A more anthropological approach is now prevalent, in which archaeological and historical evidence is interrogated with ethnographic aims. Recent studies of medieval monasteries, churches, guildhalls and castles, for example, have considered how men and women created and experienced these medieval spaces (e.g. Gilchrist 1994; Andrén 1999; Giles 2000a; Graves 2000; Johnson 2002). These studies tend to elevate spatial and social approaches, concentrating on the physical, visual and sensory experiences of medieval life. In contrast, monastic historians frequently prioritise economic, biographic and institutional themes (e.g. Harvey 1993).

Monastic studies have often judged medieval communities by modern standards, nowhere more evident than in Augustus Jessopp's searing indictment of Norwich cathedral-priory.[7] Like Blomefield before him, Jessopp was disappointed by the literary and political achievements of the monks of the cathedral. In contrast, modern historians including Barbara Dodwell (1996c) and Joan Greatrex (1991) have assessed the monks' standing in comparison with their medieval contemporaries, based respectively on the priory's book-ownership and the high rate of attendance of Norwich monks at Cambridge and Oxford. The Whiggish tendency to interpret the past with moral prejudice is increasingly challenged by modern scholarship. For example, Megan Cassidy-Welch has confronted the prevailing model in Cistercian studies that detects the *decline* of the Cistercian ideal. She argues instead for a greater appreciation of the historical context of change in monastic life (Cassidy-Welch 2001).

This study adopts a contextual and anthropological approach, evaluating the experience of medieval and early modern life in Norwich cathedral, rather than judging the success or progress of its aesthetic or cultural achievements. The emphasis is placed on sacred and social space, examining the development and change of Norwich cathedral over six centuries. This long-term perspective encourages a more holistic approach to historical archaeology, uniting evidence from across the traditional medieval/post-medieval divide. The meaning and significance of patterns observed at Norwich are explored through comparison with other cathedral-priories and appropriate urban and rural sites.

In addition to outlining the development of the cathedral landscape, Norwich is used as an exemplar for the contextual study of changing sacred space in a single institution. Four spatial themes are interwoven in the chapters that follow and drawn together in a final chapter addressing sacred and social space. The first theme is *'boundedness'*, describing how the community is defined spatially by boundaries and by the control and regulation of access to, and throughout, the precinct. Consideration is also given to the *degrees of sanctity* that were perceived within the monastic precinct. The belief that the sacred could be located precisely at the high altar of the cathedral church led to a web of spatial hierarchies. Although any altar represented the sacred, the high altar of a cathedral-priory embodied the most holy space of an entire diocese, one wrapped within a Benedictine monastery and the bishop's see. The result was the ranking of buildings and people according to their appropriate proximity to the divine. The third theme considers *metaphorical space*, the iconographic meanings of particular spaces that affected the placement

---

[7] 'The priory of Norwich has nothing to boast of in its history. It was not set down in the wilderness, it had no fabulous past to look back upon it. No saint had come forth from it, no martyr or hero had ever shed the lustre of his name upon its annals . . . From first to last it had been a singularly useless institution as compared with any other great English monastery with equal resources.' (Jessopp 1888, xvi)

and embellishment of buildings and patterns of movement through them. The final issue is that of *change and the renegotiation of spatial rules*, including transformations in spatial practices in the later Middle Ages as well as the spatial iconoclasm of the Reformation and the Civil War, and the gentrification of the close from the later seventeenth century.

MONASTIC LIFE IN THE CATHEDRAL-PRIORY

The Rule of St Benedict provided the cornerstone of western monasticism (McCann 1952). Its seventy-three chapters address the spiritual and practical details of communal religious life, reinforced through daily readings to the assembled monks in the chapter house. The emphasis on community was achieved by the practised and repeated rejection of individuality. Separation from the world was demonstrated by the formulation of physical boundaries that contained the monastic community and signalled their shared withdrawal from secular company. The monastery was not merely segregated from external society; the monks engaged in a distinct life-style that stimulated particular sensory experience. The cathedral church was an opulent setting, where services were choreographed to the aroma of incense, the glow of candles, the timbre of bells and the cadence of melodic chant. Ideally, this sensory splendour was tempered by the frugal asceticism of life in the cloister. By the twelfth century, however, some religious perceived that monastic life had grown too luxurious. The new reformed monastic orders set out to regain the simplicity of the apostolic life, notably the Cistercians, who sought withdrawal to marginal wilderness. In contrast, the Benedictines retained the tradition of urban life, which in a cathedral-priory included a commitment to hospitality, education and charity alongside the ceremonial roles of the mother church of the diocese.

Induction to the monastery required private property to be relinquished, and demanded the monk to give up 'disposition even of his own body'. Personality and sensuality were masked by the common clothing of the monastic habit and the shaved tonsure. The monks were vowed to obedience and committed to self-denial, demonstrated by their adherence to celibacy, a regulated diet and a gruelling time-table of monastic offices, spread throughout the day and night. Clothes, diet and sexual abstinence represented important aspects of identity in medieval life, and religious communities used them to signal their distance from seculars. They also demonstrated their distinctiveness through more abstract discourses of time, sound and space. The monastic timetable, or *horarium*, strictly controlled the periods during which the monks could worship, study, work, eat, speak and sleep. Careful regulation of the timetable led to an early monastic concern with bell-ringing and clocks, with mechanical measurement bound up with cosmological values of time (see pp. 255–6).

The monastic timetable determined when the monks were allowed to speak, and, unless specifically permitted, they were expected to maintain silence in the cloister. The Rule required silence as evidence of humility:

Let us do as saith the prophet: *I said, I will take heed unto my ways, that I offend not with my tongue. I have set a guard to my mouth. I was dumb and was humbled, and kept silence even from good words.* . . . Therefore, on account of the great value of silence, let leave to speak be seldom granted to observant disciples. (McCann 1952, 36–7)

The monks communicated through a monastic language of signs, and some medieval sign-lists survive, indicating common signing for eating implements, articles of clothing and areas of the cloister (Meyvaert 1973, 56). The *Life of St William* confirms that sign language prevailed in the twelfth-century cloister at Norwich: the author recorded that, when he witnessed a vision of the cathedral's founder, he could not communicate this adequately until he had received permission to speak (Jessopp and James 1896, xx). Outside services, the monks became accustomed to silence; on one occasion described in the *vita*, an unexplained noise in the chapter house was the source of great terror to the sacrist (ibid., 187). Urban noise pollution was also an unwelcome irritation. In the fourteenth century, one of the monks of the cathedral penned a poem of complaint against the smiths working in the areas bordering the precinct:

> Swart, smoky smiths smirched with smoke
> Drive me to death with the din of their dints (Myers 1969, 1055).

Monastic ceremony

The Rule set out general principles on how the monks should lead their lives, but supplementary guidance was required to direct them through the increasing complexity of later medieval liturgy. A surviving *Customary* from Norwich cathedral is devoted almost entirely to liturgical observances, setting out the sequence of services and meals, with day to day variations 'being brought about by the nature of the day, feast or fast, and by the seasons both liturgical and solar' (Tolhurst 1948, xxv). The liturgy of the *Customary* borrowed heavily from the abbey of Fécamp in Normandy, where Norwich cathedral's founder-bishop Herbert de Losinga had been professed. The bishop wrote to Fécamp asking if monks could be sent from Norwich to observe liturgical practice, implying that the liturgy was demanding enough to require written instructions, additional notes and the experience of first-hand observation (Chadd 1996). The extant copy of the *Customary* dates from the second half of the thirteenth century but was amended in a series of later hands as local practice evolved.

The Rule of St Benedict established the routine of daily choir offices, from Matins to Compline, and the time at which meals should be taken. Later monasteries varied practice according to season, taking into account the amount of daylight and the temperature in which services would be conducted. The length of night services was determined by the nature of the day, with Sundays and feast days accorded longer versions with twelve lessons, in contrast to shorter forms with three lessons in winter and one in summer (Tolhurst 1948, xxv). During summer (from

Easter to 13 September) two meals were allowed, but only one on fast days and vigils, and in winter the mid-day siesta was omitted. In Lent, only a single meal, in the evening, was allowed (ibid., xxiv).

The monastic officers and their duties
By the thirteenth century, specific functions and physical complexes within the precinct were the responsibility of particular officers of the priory. These obedientiaries, as monastic officers are known, received the income from specified parts of the estate to fund their offices (Virgoe 1996, 349). The obedientiaries included the cellarer, who was at first responsible for the provision of all food and had purview over dining activities. By the late thirteenth century this role was subdivided, with the cellarer retaining responsibility for the purchase of all foodstuffs (except corn), the upkeep of kitchen utensils and the payment of kitchen staff, while a refectorer was established to oversee the requirements of dining in the monastic refectory. The most influential office became that of 'the master of the cellar', who was in charge of the prior's chamber, the entertainment of lay visitors and the payment of lay officials, the provision of corn to the entire community, and oversight of the kitchen, brewhouse and stables (Dodwell 1996b, 241–2). Important roles were fulfilled by the infirmarer, who cared for the sick and elderly, and the hostiliar, who maintained the guest hall. Further housekeeping roles were those of the chamberlain, with responsibility for the monks' clothing and bedding, and the minor office of the gardener, who tended gardens and orchards within the precinct. Church services and books were organised by the precentor, and the sacrist was responsible for the upkeep of the church and perhaps the cemetery. Finally, the almoner distributed alms and maintained the almonry in the precinct.

All these officers were associated with particular physical spaces of the precinct, but from the rolls it can be surmised that only the almoner was exclusively accountable for the maintenance of the buildings connected with his position. In contrast, the fabric of other offices was addressed variously by the allocated obedientiary, together with the office of the communar and pitancer. The precise role of this obedientiary is unclear, but he seems to have dealt with matters relating to all in common, with the exception of the specific tasks of other named officers, such as the master of the cellar (Fernie and Whittingham 1972, 10). At Norwich, the communar was linked with major rebuilding projects, such as the reconstruction of the cloister following the riot of 1272.

Although the bishop was the titular abbot of the priory, the community, its lands and its finances were the actual responsibility of the prior. The bishops and priors of Norwich remained essentially rooted to the concerns of the secular world, and each day this world pierced the tranquillity of the precinct, as secular visitors and servants crossed its thresholds.

The Population of the Precinct

The medieval cathedral precinct housed both monastic and lay populations, and its landscape was designed to cater for the communities of both the living and the dead (see pp. 248–51). The foundation of the cathedral-priory had been intended to support sixty monks, but the first reliable census in 1348/9 recorded sixty-seven. Their number was halved by plague in the later fourteenth century, but in the fifteenth century it continued at between fifty to sixty monks, and at the Dissolution their number was thirty-eight (Dodwell 1996b, 231). The social origins of the monks in the later Middle Ages can be suggested on the basis of the place-names that they adopted upon entry to the monastery; they came principally from Norfolk villages, and especially from the priory estates. Norwich families were also represented, predominantly from two parishes within or bordering the precinct, St Mary in the Marsh and St Martin at Palace. While some elite families were recorded, most Norwich monks derived from the brewing, victualling and building trades (Noble 2001, 230; 260). There was also a college of six secular priests in the precinct: the chantry college of St John the Evangelist was established in the western part of the lay cemetery (Saunders 1932a). Religious personnel were adult males over the age of nineteen (the minimum age of monastic profession), although two years of probationary training and novitiate preceded the formal profession. Although children were prohibited from monasteries by 1215, a school for boys was founded in the precinct in the thirteenth century. This school was associated with the almonry and had thirteen resident pupils at the suppression of the priory in 1538 (Harries et al. 1991; Greatrex 1994).

Other residents and visitors can be calculated from the records of the monastic officers. The number of servants supporting the monastery can be reconstructed from details of stipends paid to servants, and the records of the daily distribution of bread permit an estimate of guests and their servants staying in the monastery. From this information, H. W. Saunders estimated a population in the precinct of perhaps 270 people in the thirteenth and fourteenth centuries, only fifty to sixty of whom were actually monks (Saunders 1930, 160–62). The remainder of those fed daily in the monastery were '*famuli*' (guests in the hostry hall), visitors, workmen, men from the manors, boys in the school, poor visiting the almonry, and some 150 staff of the cathedral officers. The servants in the prior's household numbered 51, with the cellarer employing 26 staff, the sacrist 25, the almoner 15, the chamberlain 15, the infirmarer 2, the hostiliar 4, the precentor 1, the refectorer 4, the pittancer 1 and the gardener 2 (ibid., 163).

These servants were seculars, and they could be married men who were resident in the precinct with their families. For example, the twelfth-century *Life of St William* records the case of 'Botilda, the wife of Girard who was the monks' cook', who reserved a piece of fern from William's funerary bier to bring her relief in childbirth (Jessopp and James 1896, 78). In the later Middle Ages, the monastery's tailor and barber lived with their wives in the precinct (Jessopp 1888, xvii). The *vita* of William also refers to 'Gerard who took sanctuary in the Church of Norwich, fleeing from the tyranny of his lord . . . so long as he lived, he remained a servant in the Church' (ibid., 198–200). A chamber for 'the sanctuary men' was located over St Andrew's chapel in the north transept of the cathedral church. It was documented from 1404 onwards (Whittingham 1949) and may have accommodated men who sought sanctuary in the church.

In common with arrangements in predominantly masculine households of medieval castles and palaces, there was one task that frequently fell to female servants. The cellarer and the infirmarer both employed a laundress or washerwoman (*lotrix pannorum*) (Saunders 1930, 99, 132); such a woman was immortalised in a comic boss in the cathedral cloister, depicting a thief stealing the laundry (Plate 2A). The precentor, in contrast, employed a washerman to launder the textiles used in the performance of the services (ibid., 136). This discrepancy may be explained by the medieval understanding of sacred space, which regarded seculars, and women in particular, as potential polluters and prohibited their access to parts of the church and cloister (see p. 240).

The ambiguity with which women were regarded is emphasised by the position of another female inhabitant of the precinct, the anchoress. These highly esteemed religious women took vows of solitude and were enclosed permanently in cells attached to monastic or parish churches. Norwich cathedral records an anchoress in 1305, and anchorites of unknown sex were accommodated in the monks' cemetery and at the parish church of St Helen's in the precinct (see pp. 97–8). Women also lived in the precinct as corrodians, secular lodgers who were funded by a pension or annuity, such as Magdalen, together with her husband William Bauchon, in the 1290s (Atherton 1996, 636). In general, however, corrodians at Norwich were men who were former royal servants, nominated by the king for comfortable retirement in a monastery. By the later Middle Ages, lands on the edges of the precinct were leased to seculars of both sexes, and eminent patrons were permitted to establish town houses within the precinct, adjacent to the monks' cemetery (see p. 59). The upper part of the inner court included houses rented to professionals, such as the Cambridge physician Master Conrad in 1471 (Rawcliffe 2002, 48), while the space surrounding the bell-tower was developed as shops for lease to craftworkers (see pp. 189–91).

There were frequent visitors to the cathedral precinct, for the purposes of worship, commerce, special religious occasions and social interactions. The cathedral-priory was on the doorstep of a major city, with the population of Norwich averaging between five to ten thousand inhabitants in the medieval period and then burgeoning in size between the years 1500 and 1700, until the first reliable census of 1693 recorded a population of twenty-nine thousand people (Campbell 1975, 10, 18). Seculars entered the precinct as pilgrims, to worship at the cathedral church and at the parish churches within the precinct, to seek penance or sanctuary, to tend the graves of loved ones (or their remains in the charnel house) and, from the fifteenth century, to hear sermons preached in the green yard. Although Norwich was never a major cult centre, pilgrims were drawn to visit the remains of St William in the twelfth century and again in the later fourteenth century, when the pelterers' guild revived his cult (Shinners 1988, 136). Visitors attended the regular fairs and markets held in the lay cemetery, and guild members met near the west end of the cathedral church; the barber-surgeons convened in the Carnary chapel, while the Guild of St Luke had their own hall in the lay cemetery. Patrons of the monastery were received in the cloister and chapter house, and relatives of the monks conversed with religious in the outer parlour. High-ranking guests received the hospitality of the prior's household, bestowed with special gifts and entertained by players and minstrels. Ecclesiastical and secular guests lodged in the hostry or guest hall, and charity was dispensed daily to the poor at the almonry by the Ethelbert gate.

Following the Reformation, the population became more diverse, as former monastic buildings and lands within the cathedral close were leased to secular tenants (Chapter 8). The cathedral fought to retain the exclusivity of the close, barring women from some areas until the acceptance of clerical marriage (between 1549 and 1553, and again after 1558). In common with the corporation of Norwich, the cathedral sought to exclude nonconformists, Catholics and the poor and to control social recreations such as alehouses. Their attempts at social engineering resulted in a population that was skewed in terms of age and gender. Within the close, there were far more women than men, with a high proportion of wealthy widows as heads of households; the city shared this bias, with a substantial proportion of households headed by single women, mostly widows (Atherton 1996, 644; Pound 1988, 134–6). In reconstructing the landscape of the close, the physical spaces, occupations and interactions of a variegated population must be considered.

2
Norwich Cathedral:
Defining the Medieval Landscape

T HE medieval cathedral church and priory were at the centre of a substantial precinct, a monastic landscape carved out of a significant portion of medieval Norwich (Figure 3). The lands of the precinct were gained primarily during the first decade of its foundation, and expanded in the fourteenth century eventually to cover the area of approximately forty-two acres that represents the modern close. All monastic communities were separated to a greater or lesser extent from the secular world around them. This separation was both symbolic and real: the boundaries of the precinct marked the distinction between the secular and religious spheres (see p. 241), but also established the ownership and jurisdiction of the prior's lands. The precinct had to be large enough to support the needs of the monastic community. This followed St Benedict's desire that it should 'be so arranged that all necessary things, such as water, mill, garden, and various crafts may be within the enclosure, so that the monks may not be compelled to wander outside it, for that is not at all expedient for their souls' (McCann 1952, 152–3). Benedict envisaged a principle of self-sufficiency, a basic tenet of monastic life that would allow religious communities to be free from potentially corrupting ties with the outside world.

This chapter sets out the background to the foundation of the priory and its precinct, and traces the evolution of its boundaries, making comparisons with the precinct development at other cathedrals. Within the precinct there were several other religious foci, and the parish churches and religious satellites of the priory are introduced. Monastic exploitation of the landscape is explored through the requirements and design of the system of water supply, and the acquisition and use of building materials. First, the 'prehistory' of the precinct is explored in its Roman and Saxon heritage. In contrast with all other Norman cathedral-priories – Bath, Canterbury, Carlisle, Coventry, Ely, Durham, Rochester, Winchester and Worcester – only Norwich was established on a 'new' site. It lacked the tradition of a holy landscape that was provided by association with earlier Christian monasteries, their saints and relics. Norwich was instead a Saxon 'brown-field' site, at which a monastic landscape and tradition were cultivated.

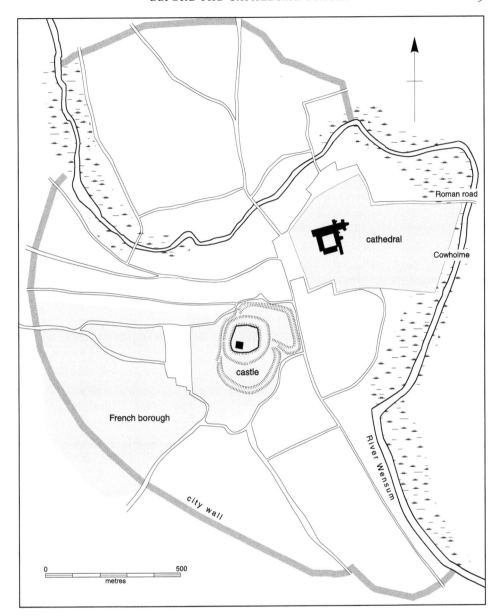

FIGURE 3. Location of Norwich cathedral in the City of Norwich. Drawing by Margaret Mathews.

BEFORE THE CATHEDRAL-PRIORY

The cathedral was established within a meander of the River Wensum, with the river bounding the precinct to the east and turning westward to snake north of the bishop's palace. The river and its fording places were key determinants in the settlement of the city of Norwich. The cathedral precinct was located adjacent to the site of one of only two fordable places on the River Wensum (which later became Bishop's Bridge), the other being the site of Fye Bridge, to the north. The area of the precinct is relatively flat and low-lying, and easily accessible from land and water routes. Its position is typical of that chosen for a monastic settlement; the river and its productive meadows were components of rural and urban monastic precincts, such as Cistercian Rievaulx (N Yorkshire) (Coppack 1999), Benedictine York (Norton 1994) and the secular cathedral of Salisbury (RCHME 1993). The underlying geology of Norwich cathedral comprises well-draining sand and river gravels,[1] sloping steeply towards the River Wensum to the east. This strategic location is likely to have tempted prehistoric, Roman and Saxon traffic, and eventually attracted permanent urban settlement.

Norwich has yielded relatively little archaeological evidence of prehistoric or Roman activity (Ayers 2003, 17–22), with human focus during early periods concentrating instead on sites south of the city, such as Arminghall and Caistor. Prehistoric and Roman finds have been recorded in the precinct, including a chipped flint axe head recovered in 1844 from the meadow in the east of the precinct, probably Neolithic in date, and perhaps deriving from the river bed (Norfolk SMR No. 552). Three sherds of pottery of Bronze Age date were excavated from the site of the cathedral refectory in 2001, recorded in a possible feature or buried soil horizon (Wallis 2002a). Roman evidence is more abundant, but represented only by residual material, such as two coins from the recent refectory excavations, and Roman tiles reused in the foundations of the first setting out of the eastern end of the Romanesque cathedral church (Wallis 2002a; Cranage 1932). It is generally agreed that a Roman road passed east–west through Norwich, just to the north of the medieval cathedral precinct (Campbell 1975, 2).

It was proposed by the archaeologist Alan Carter that the site of Bishop's Bridge was used as the crossing for the Roman road (Carter 1978), corresponding with the route of a street known in medieval and later documents as Holme Street, which would later become Bishopgate (Figure 4). Bishopgate crosses the floodplain of the River Wensum on a low causeway, which may be Roman in date. The Roman road's conjectured route departed from the present line of Bishopgate to enter the precinct at the east (sextry) gate (towards St Giles' hospital), passing beneath the location of the crossing of the cathedral church, and westwards through the line of the present Erpingham gate (Carter 1978, figure 7). Originally, it was predicted to exit the precinct further north, but excavations in the area of the Carnary college in 1975 found no evidence for this (Norfolk SMR No. 280; *Medieval Archaeol* 20 (1976), 167, 191). Carter also proposed the former existence of a north–south road, that would have created a junction with the Roman road, and suggested that they overlapped at the point of the crossing of the later cathedral church.

[1] Alluvium and first terrace river gravels (British Geological Survey sheet 161, 1:50,000 series, 1975).

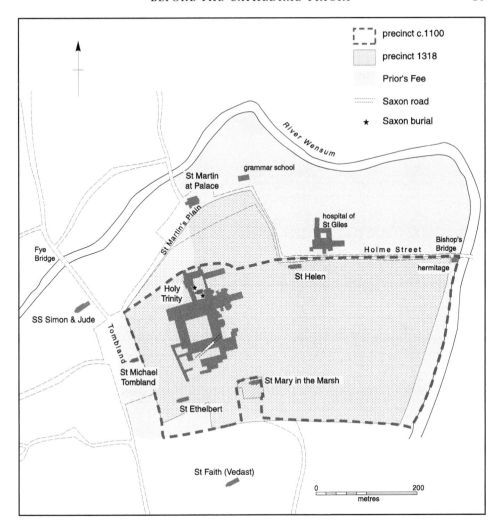

FIGURE 4. Development of the precinct, showing the locations of Saxon churches, the precinct boundaries c. 1100 and after 1318, the Prior's Fee, and excavated Saxon burials and road. Drawing by Margaret Mathews.

The existence and approximate line of the east–west Roman road is fairly certain, and it would have continued to attract use in later periods. Excavations in the grounds of the bishop's palace in 1955–6 produced Ipswich-type ware of Middle Saxon date, in addition to late Saxon Thetford ware pottery, a Saxon bronze buckle and smelting slags (Norfolk SMR Nos 44–45; *Medieval Archaeol* 1 (1957), 148). On the basis of this evidence, Carter postulated an embryonic urban settlement, focused on the crossing point of the two conjectured Roman roads (Holme Street, crossing a proposed north–south road). Others have been more tentative in assigning this area urban status before the tenth or eleventh centuries, and there is general concurrence that the main Saxon nucleus of the town was further north than the precinct, to the north of the River Wensum (Atkins and Evans 2002; Ayers 1996, 62). The evidence on the site of the bishop's palace could also be indicative of an early religious settlement: the Ipswich ware and iron slag, and their location in relation to a prominent causeway, suggest the possibility of a pre-Viking church. David Stocker and Paul Everson (2003) have discussed the significance of causeways in the landscape of the Christian conversion, noting that early monastic sites in the Witham Valley (Lincolnshire) were located at the ends of the fenland causeways. They argue that such locations were prompted not by ease of transport or communication, but in order to 'convert' the ancient ritual associations of rivers and pools.

The Normans arrived in Norwich to find a thriving Saxon town, one of the three or four most important urban communities in England. It was large and densely settled, with a population of between five to ten thousand people (Campbell 1975, 1, 3), and perhaps twenty-five churches and chapels at 1066, rising to forty-three by 1086 (Carter 1978, 195). For decades, archaeologists have been concerned with determining precisely how and when Norwich boomed into a Saxon city. Its size and shape, with separate named quarters of Needham, Conesford, Westwick and Coslany/Northwic, suggested that distinct settlements had merged together to form an urban nucleus (Carter 1978). More recent excavations have challenged this 'polyfocal' model of nuclear development, revealing evidence instead for ribbon development of settlement on both banks of the River Wensum, above well-drained gravel terraces (Ayers 2003, 24–7). The confluence of the Wensum with the Yare provided the opportunity of an inland port, reached by a river system easily navigable from the coast. The coincidence of different soil types meeting at this location provided a fully balanced range of natural resources, with alluvial flats to the east meeting the chalk beneath the city, overlaid by sand, gravel, clay and loam. It appears that the area was settled in the ninth century, with occupation intensified in or by the tenth, and that by the eleventh century Norwich was a thriving port.

The topography of the city as it was known from the eleventh century onwards has allowed archaeologists to reconstruct the probable plan of its Saxon precursor (Carter 1978; Ayers 2003). Alan Carter believed that the precinct was a main focus of urban settlement in the ninth and tenth centuries (Carter 1978, 204). Certainly, the establishment of the precinct eclipsed a number of Saxon churches and their local neighbourhoods. It has also been proposed that the precinct interrupted a well-ordered street plan, not dissimilar to the gridiron patterns familiar from Saxon burhs established in Wessex. Brian Ayers has offered a reconstruction of the Saxon townscape preceding the cathedral, based on the proposed Roman road, known locations of Saxon churches, and the later street plan (Ayers 2003; 1996).

Saxon churches were placed typically on street intersections, and Ayers uses the known and conjectured positions of Saxon churches to propose a well-developed gridiron street plan for Norwich by the eleventh century (2003, 40). At least three Saxon churches are known to have been located on land given over to the cathedral: St Mary in the Marsh, Holy Trinity (or Christ Church), and St Michael, Tombland

(Figure 4). Two further churches formerly in the close are believed to have had Saxon origins, St Helen and St Ethelbert. Additional Saxon churches were sited near by: St Martin at Palace, to the north of the precinct, St Vedast to the south, and SS Simon and Jude to the west. St Mary in the Marsh survived at least into the sixteenth century, and its precise plan and location can be reconstructed from documentary evidence and standing remains encased in later structures (see Figure 7).

Holy Trinity was once considered to have been located beneath the eastern end of the cathedral church, but recent opinion places it beneath the cathedral crossing (Fernie 1993; Ayers 1996).[2] It is suggested here that the position of the Saxon church of Holy Trinity can instead be estimated by the incidence of Saxon inhumation burials that have been recorded in two places in the close. Burials were excavated to the north-west of the north transept in 1989 (Bown 1997), and were observed to the east side of the Norman wing of the bishop's palace in 1960 (Norfolk SMR No. 441). In both cases the burials were described as being below the Norman fabric, of the transept and palace respectively. These inhumations can be given Saxon dates on stratigraphic evidence, and are therefore likely to be associated with the site of a former church: Holy Trinity is the best candidate. Ayers follows Carter in suggesting that a north–south street intersected with the east–west line of Holme Street at the point of the cathedral crossing. He suggests that the proposed north–south road ran directly through the close, linking the churches of St Mary in the Marsh and Holy Trinity with St Martin at Palace to the north and St Vedast to the south. However, the positions of the burials suggest a location for Holy Trinity to the north of the north transept, and not beneath the crossing. Further, new analysis of the bishop's palace draws attention to the shared alignment of the primary tower (c. 1096) and the chapel of St Mary (see p. 150). Excavations in 1859 confirmed that an earlier chapel was located on this site, although description of the remains does not allow close dating (Harrod 1864, 36). It is suggested here that the site of the bishop's chapel is a strong candidate for the location of the Saxon parish church of Holy Trinity.

While the specifics of the late Saxon gridiron street plan remain hypothetical, recent excavations on the site of the cathedral refectory have contributed significant new evidence. Late Saxon deposits were extensive, including gravel-surfaced roads, post-holes and beam slots of structures, and rubbish pits containing pottery and animal bone. The twelfth-century refectory appears to have sealed a late Saxon urban landscape, revealing conclusive evidence that this part of the precinct area was a densely settled, urban space immediately prior to the establishment of the cathedral.

[2] Excavations by Dean Cranage in 1930, prior to the construction of the Regimental chapel over the site of the former Lady chapel, uncovered partial plans of two successive apses at the east end (Cranage 1932). While Cranage believed the small, earlier apse to be a Saxon church, Eric Fernie has interpreted the feature as contemporary with the building of the cathedral. Fernie considers the smaller apse to have been abandoned as the result of error, or changes in plans for setting out the cathedral church. He reached this conclusion on the basis of the three factors: the composition of the foundations, which are very similar to those of the cathedral; the degree of integration of the masonry of the two apses; and the overall shape of the lower apse, which is typical of the eleventh century (Fernie 1993, 19–22).

The excavator suggests that there was a road crossing the site diagonally on a north-east to south-west alignment, and therefore departing from the route conjectured by Ayers and Carter. The gravel-surfaced Saxon road had buildings adjacent to it on both sides, and an area behind the buildings for disposal of domestic rubbish. These late-Saxon features were sealed by a distinct soil horizon, interpreted as the clearing and levelling of the site in preparation for the building of the cathedral (Wallis 2002a). Excavation of test pits on the sites of the west and east ranges has added further weight to the conclusion that the whole area of the precinct was urbanised before the foundation of the cathedral-priory. Two Saxon pits were located beneath the hostry (Wallis 2003) and two Saxon pits were identified beneath the later chapter house (Voisy 2003). Although truncated by later activity, these features were identified with Saxon occupation by sherds of Thetford-type ware. Excavations in the Lower Close in 1975 suggested evidence of a Late Saxon field system to the north of St Mary in the Marsh (Atkin and Evans 2002, 50–65), indicating that the range of urban occupations may have embraced agriculture.

The Establishment of the Monastic Precinct

The foundation of the cathedral was one of three major initiatives to impress Norman authority on the Saxon town. From c.1075, the castle was founded together with a market area to the west, known as the New (or French) Borough. The castle provided a new social and topographical focus, placed on a prominent spur above the town, and located c.365m from the site of the cathedral (Figure 3). These Norman footprints absorbed massive tracts of land and rerouted streets, altering the heart of Saxon Norwich and forever moulding the subsequent topography of the city. A large strip of the Saxon waterfront served as the eastern boundary of the cathedral precinct, with incipient commerce replaced by monastic agriculture. The area of the precinct remained a semi-rural space, forcing suburbs to develop along the city's main north–south arterial routes.

The Saxon diocese of Norwich was headed by the bishop's see at Elmham,[3] with a second minor see at Hoxne in Suffolk. The see was moved to Thetford c.1071, under Bishop Herfast (1070–84). This seems to have been intrinsic to a Norman policy that transferred rural sees to protected centres, for example shifting Dorchester to Lincoln (1072), Selsey to Chichester (1075) and Sherborne to Old Sarum (1078) (Knowles and Hadcock 1971). The relocation of the East Anglian see to Thetford may have been intended only as a temporary solution, since Herfast nurtured ambitions to move the see to Bury St Edmunds, in a plan to usurp the abbey's exemption from episcopal control (Dodwell 1957; Dodwell 1996a). His plan

[3] Debate continues as to whether the bishop's see was located at North Elmham or South Elmham, both of which were major estates of the bishop by the eleventh century. Both have evidence to suggest an important ecclesiastical status, including a ruined Saxon church and early cemetery at North Elmham and a fragment of ninth or tenth-century tombstone built into the church at South Elmham, in addition to Saxon settlement at South Elmham Hall (see Campbell 1996).

would also have secured a Saxon monastic lineage for the see, appropriating Bury's associations with St Felix (c.633), and the tenth-century foundation that focused on the relics of St Edmund, King and Martyr (d. 870). Not surprisingly, the plan was resisted strongly by the abbey at Bury, and by c.1081 Herfast was forced to relinquish his claim. Plans were eventually progressed to move the see to Norwich, and in 1086 the Domesday Book recorded that William I had granted a block of property in the eastern part of the Saxon town to Herfast: '14 dwellings which King William gave to E(rfast) for the principal seat of the Bishopric' (Brown 1984, 117a). No further progress was achieved under the succeeding bishop, William Beaufai (1085–c.1090), leaving the ambitious Herbert de Losinga (1091–1119) to fully develop and execute the move to Norwich.

The timing of the move, and the scale of the cathedral complex, seem to have been bound up closely with de Losinga's personal circumstances. The apocryphal story is that the cathedral's foundation was motivated by de Losinga's need for penance to absolve his sin of simony. For the princely sum of £1000, he had purchased from William Rufus preferment for both himself and his father, the latter of whom became the abbot of Hyde (Winchester). This action seems to have shocked his contemporaries, and Herbert was moved to seek absolution from Pope Urban. He failed to seek the king's permission before travelling to Rome, resulting in a period of stalemate between de Losinga and Rufus in the early 1090s (Dodwell 1957; Dodwell 1996a). De Losinga's choice to establish a monastic rather than a secular cathedral may have stemmed partly from accusations of simony and nepotism that must have surrounded his own clerical family. The installation of Benedictine monks would demonstrate celibacy (see p. 3), and guard against dynastic succession, as occurred at the bishoprics of St David's and Llandaff in the late eleventh century, and at St Paul's cathedral up to c.1130 (Brooke 1956, 11, 18).

Having chosen to found a monastic cathedral on a new site, the bishop faced a symbolic disadvantage. Every other cathedral-priory in England enjoyed the traditional setting of a Saxon monastery. De Losinga countered this lack of tradition through the design of the church, cloister and bishop's palace at Norwich. All of these incorporated archaic iconographic elements (see pp. 251–3), perhaps in a conscious programme to create a sense of continuity and legitimacy for the new see. Most telling in this context may be the carving that adorned the bishop's entrance to the north transept from his palace: this appears to represent St Felix (Fernie 1993, 83–7). Although the actual site of Bury St Edmunds had eluded the bishops of Norwich, its monastic heritage was appropriated for their see palace.

Barbara Dodwell has estimated that in the year 1095, Herbert sought the king's permission to implement the plan to move the see to Norwich, and sought additional lands on which to build (Dodwell 1996a, 39). Between 1096 and 1106 he had obtained three further parcels of land to create a vast cathedral landscape, more in keeping with continental episcopal cities than with English cathedral precincts. It was common for the new Norman cathedrals to reuse the consecrated sites of existing churches, as had occurred at Lincoln and Chichester. At Norwich, the king's original grant of land had given the bishop two churches: Holy Trinity (or Christ Church) and SS Simon and Jude. Given the dedication of the cathedral to the Holy Trinity, it seems likely that the parish church of Holy Trinity was selected to form the focus of the new foundation. As proposed above, this Saxon church was located near the north transept of the cathedral church, suggesting that de Losinga reused its precise location to form the core of the bishop's see palace, perhaps reusing the church of Holy Trinity for the bishop's chapel. This move, together with the retention of Saxon parish churches in the precinct, reveals the strong impetus to demonstrate ecclesiastical continuity for the new cathedral.

The cathedral's *First Register* records how further land was acquired. Between 1096–1100, Herbert traded land with Roger Bigod, the Earl of East Anglia, to obtain the site of St Michael's church and its lands (Saunders 1939). This extended the original block of land to the south and west, to take in part of Tombland, to the west of the precinct. Tombland, thought to be from Old English *tōm*, meaning empty, seems to have been the site of a market (Carter 1978, 191 n. 4). The land was extended significantly to the east by a grant from Henry I in 1101, of the manor of Thorpe and the water meadows called Cowholme (Tillyard 1987, 135). Finally in 1106, Henry granted 'the land from the bishop's land to the water, and from the bridge of St Martin to the land of St Michael' (ibid., 136). These grants consolidated the greater part of the precinct, and provided satellite areas outside the precinct that remained under the prior's jurisdiction (the Prior's Fee) throughout much of the Middle Ages (Figure 4).

Within the boundaries of the precinct, the natural topography was harnessed to best effect. Archaeological excavations and augering have shown that the natural geology slopes steeply towards the River Wensum on the east, resulting in a low-lying marshy region adjoining the river. This marshland area was prone to flooding, a phenomenon that increased in the late thirteenth century as the climate changed, and some lower-lying parts of the city became uninhabitable (Hallam 1984; Campbell 1975, 11). The higher ground to the west was reserved for the main monastic complexes, with the cathedral and cloister located on the highest natural ground. However, de Losinga was determined to obtain the best vantage point over his cathedral landscape, and he created a raised platform to the north of the cathedral on which to build his palace (see p. 144). The lower-lying area was also raised through the creation of an artificial terrace that coincides with the monastic lower inner court. Approximately 1m of deposits was dumped as part of the initial planning of the precinct, and the area was later raised a further 1.5m, with a total of 2.7m of deposits laid down between the eleventh and the sixteenth centuries (Atkin and Evans 2002, 65).

Construction of the main monastic ranges addressed the issue of the pronounced sloping ground. In order to establish a level terrace for the cloister, it was necessary to reduce the ground-level in the area of the west range and to increase that of the south and east ranges. Excavations have demonstrated that soil was dumped in the refectory to increase the level, while the hostry site was reduced to the level of naturally derived sands (Wallis 2002a; Wallis 2003). Treatment of the foundations also differed for the monastic buildings of the south and west ranges. Those of the refectory battered away from the walls and were constructed in bands of flint alternating with chalky clay; those of the hostry were remarkably shallow (c.200mm), sitting directly on natural sands. The sloping ground required the design of different foundations in order to maintain a common floor level between the refectory and hostry. The sloping site may also have facilitated the provision of the sunken cloister, which was built c.1m below the floors of the medieval monastic ranges, and may have held specific iconographic meaning (see p. 253).

The approximate order of construction can be discerned from surviving archaeology and the cathedral's *First Register*. The earliest masonry construction focused on the fortified tower of the bishop's palace (see p. 151), and the eastern end of the cathedral church. The cloister was planned integrally with the church, and would have been in construction by the time the crossing was completed (by c.1119, according to the *Register*). It is likely that construction of the monastic ranges commenced with the east range, working around the cloister towards the west. The dormitory and refectory of the monks were essential components, while the guest accommodation in the west range was a less urgent consideration. Work on the refectory (the south range) was completed by c.1125, and the hostry (west range) would have been erected once the nave of the church had been completed (estimated by c.1140). Excavations on the hostry site have confirmed a pause in construction between the levelling of the site for the building of the cloister and the subsequent erection of the hostry (Wallis 2003). The gradual build-up of material in this area would have accumulated over several decades. In common with other monasteries, the cathedral-priory at Norwich is likely to have provided temporary accommodation in timber buildings, while the monastic cloister was built over a period of approximately fifty years. A possible candidate is a timber structure that was excavated in the area of the Lower Close green (see p. 56).

The evolution of the precinct at Norwich closely parallels the experience of other urban monasteries, such as Worcester and Gloucester. The precinct of the latter expanded west and northwards over three stages, between the tenth century and 1218 (Holt and Baker 1991). At forty-two acres, the size of the precinct at Norwich compared favourably with premier urban sites such as Westminster (forty acres) and St Augustine's, Canterbury (thirty acres) (Morant 1995, 3), but was eclipsed by the thirteenth-century secular foundation at Salisbury (eighty-three acres: RCHME 1993, 7), or rural houses such as Cistercian Rievaulx (Yorkshire) (ninety-two acres: Coppack 1999, 177).

TRACING THE BOUNDARIES: THE PRECINCT, THE PRIOR'S FEE AND THE ESTATES

The boundaries of the precinct at Norwich can be discerned with some degree of confidence, but they shifted during the later medieval period, and did not coincide precisely with those of the liberty of the Prior's Fee (Campbell 1975, 24; Tillyard 1987). Even maps of the late eighteenth and early nineteenth centuries are contradictory in relation to some areas of the precinct boundaries, although they allow an approximation of the extent of the later medieval precinct. Earlier sources, such as thirteenth-century court records and fourteenth-century patent rolls, allow some medieval changes to be identified (Figure 4).

The eleventh- and twelfth-century boundaries can be reconstructed from Domesday Book and details given in the cathedral's *First Register*. From the wording of the 1106 grant from Henry I, Margot Tillyard has suggested that the northern boundary of the precinct extended to Palace Plain in its north-west corner, and right up to the River Wensum in the north-east, taking in the full bend of the River. Contradictory evidence suggests that the northern boundary of the precinct lay immediately to the north of the Norman buildings of the bishop's palace, and was not extended until 1318 to follow the line of Palace Street (formerly St Martin's) and Bishopgate (formerly Holme Street). The palace grounds were expanded in the early fourteenth century, as detailed in a patent roll of the twelfth year of the reign of Edward II (1318). This document was discussed by Henry Harrod in relation to his archaeological investigation of the garden of the bishop's palace in 1859. The patent confirms that Bishop Salmon sought enlargement of the site by the addition of two pieces of land measuring 47 perches by 4ft, and 23 perches by 12ft (Harrod 1864, 29). Harrod marked this line on his plan of the palace, and concluded that any episcopal buildings north of the line must date later than 1318. It is not clear whether Harrod's line of 1318 was conjectural, but walls are marked on his plan that seem to indicate that he had located the junction of the original precinct wall around the palace. Foundations were also observed at this spot by Arthur Whittingham in 1943, when a new water pipe was laid near the north-west corner of the bishop's palace (MC186/48). Whittingham suggested that subsurface foundations survived of a twelfth-century structure, and a later wall abutting it on the north. He dated the secondary wall to the fourteenth century on the basis of characteristic masonry and tool marks. Up to 1318, it appears that the northern boundary of the precinct was close to the northern termination of de Losinga's wing of the bishop's palace.

The land within the bend of the river to the north-east may have been obtained in 1106, but was not incorporated into the precinct. This marshy area was put to good use by Bishop Walter Suffield (1244–57), who established the hospital of St Giles on the site c.1249 (Rawcliffe 1999). The adjacent Cow Tower, an artillery tower constructed in stone with brick facing, was in the city's control by the late fourteenth century, but may have been constructed by the prior of the cathedral (Ayers et al. 1988, 191). The later medieval boundary seems to have corresponded with that shown on Hochstetter's map of 1789: from Bishop's Bridge following the line of Bishopgate (south of St Giles, or the Great Hospital), skirting the bishop's palace via Hospital Lane (now a continuation of Bishopgate), and following Tabernacle Street, St Martin's Plain and St Martin's Street westwards (now Palace Plain and Palace Street).

The wording of Henry's grant of 1106 suggests that the precinct may have originally extended up to the River Wensum on the east. However, a thin strip of land between the river and the east precinct wall became common land (Ewing 1849, 6). Certainly the colour perspective made c.1630 shows the east precinct wall stopping short of the river, allowing a narrow ribbon of land at the waterside (Plate 1). The precinct was bounded to the west by Tombland, which has remained a fixed boundary from c.1100 to the present day. The precinct's original limit to the south is least certain, but it seems to have skirted around the churchyard of St Mary in the Marsh, which was absorbed into the precinct between 1250–65, and enclosed behind a wall (Tillyard 1987, 136). Until the later thirteenth century, the boundary to the south may have corresponded with the line of Horse Fair. Land in the south-west corner was given up to the precinct of the Franciscans: the Greyfriars moved to this site after 1226, when they were given land 300 yards south of the cathedral (Knowles and Hadcock 1971, 227). In 1292 they obtained nineteen grants of land to enlarge the site, including a gift from the prior and convent of Norwich. In 1297, the Franciscans were granted leave to enclose a lane on the north side of their plot, providing a space 100ft by 10ft for the enlargement of their dwelling (VCH Norfolk II (1906), 430). The sharp dog-leg corresponding with the present St Faith's Lane (formerly Seven Coal Row) is shown on all early maps, perhaps representing the triangle of land given over to the Franciscans in the 1290s.

Certain lands outside the precinct were under the prior's jurisdiction. The Prior's Fee originally included Spitelland (the pre-Reformation parish of St Paul's), Holme Street, and land north up to St Martin's and Whitefriar's Bridge. Land to the south corresponded roughly with the later precinct boundary but reached as far as King Street to the west, turning northward to include all of Tombland (Campbell 1975, 24). De Losinga is believed to have marked the western boundary of the fee by the erection of a cross in Tombland to act 'as a cautionary landmark' (Fernie 1993, 163). Within the fee the prior had view of frankpledge and claimed exemption from taxes and tallages owed by the city (Campbell 1975, 12). The exemption of the priory's tenants from contribution to taxes caused a great deal of tension between the priory and the city. Such conflicts were not unusual in cathedral cities, for example at Chartres, the cathedral's tax exemptions led to riots and violence in 1210, 1215 and 1253 (Hayes 2003, 48). At Exeter, the cathedral's poor relations with the city culminated with the murder of the precentor in 1283, after which the king gave permission for the erection of a substantial wall to protect the close (Orme 1986, 6–7).

At Norwich the tension came to a head in 1272. The citizens burned down the gates into the precinct and spent three days pillaging and burning cathedral property, in the process killing some of the priory's servants. According to Bartholomew Cotton's *Historia Anglicana* of c.1290 (Luard 1859), fire broke out after burning arrows had been shot from the tower of St George's parish church in Tombland. The cathedral church and claustral buildings were devastated by the fire, and a massive programme of rebuilding was required. This damage is evidenced by the internal masonry of the cathedral church, which is calcined to a pink hue. Further evidence was suggested at Number 71, adjacent to the *clocher*, which was a target of the attack, where a burnt layer containing fired daub was recorded in 1955 (Norfolk SMR No. 43). The city was taken into the king's hands and put under interdict until a settlement in 1276, in which the citizens were forced to pay three thousand marks (£2000) to repair the damage to the priory, and thirty townspeople were hanged in punishment (Rye 1883). Clashes between the priory and city remained frequent and escalated again in 1443, with 'Gladman's Insurrection'. This violent occupation of the precinct was also motivated by objections to the prior's liberties in the suburbs, and may have been modelled on the riot of 1272. Although no one was killed in 1443, the city again paid massive fines. Eventually in 1524, the priory surrendered its jurisdiction in Holme Street (to the north of the precinct), Tombland (to the west) and Ratten Row (the southern limit of Tombland) (Tanner 1996, 266–7). Disputes continued into the 1630s, however, with these areas being reabsorbed into the liberty (Lehmberg 1996, 202; Atherton and Morgan 1996, 550).

The lands and assets of the cathedral-priory extended well beyond the precinct. There were five dependent monastic cells, St Leonard's in Thorpe Wood, Lynn, Yarmouth, Aldeby and Hoxne (Suffolk), and sixteen manors belonging to the prior.[4] Like any monastery, Norwich possessed an estate of dispersed holdings that had been donated principally at the foundation, and with further gifts and acquisitions made up to c.1300 (Virgoe 1996, 343). These holdings included lands, rents, mills, timber and tolls, physical resources that were recorded as 'temporalities'; and tithes and offerings from parish churches appropriated to the cathedral, income recorded as 'spiritualities'. Within Norwich, for example, half of the city's parish churches owed their tithes to the cathedral, a situation that may have increased tensions between the city and priory (Tanner 1996, 269). On the rural estates, barley was the most frequently recorded crop, with specialisation according to farming regions. Wheat was grown in central and eastern Norfolk, and sheep were kept on manors in the north and west of the county (Virgoe 1996, 352). The estates were sufficiently profitable to support a community of sixty monks and its servants easily, making the cathedral a principal landowner and extending its influence widely. The first historian of its archive, H. W. Saunders, likened the cathedral to 'some octopus with its head and heart in Norwich, the monastery stretched its tentacles over the length and breadth of this big county, drawing from some one hundred and fifty villages' (Saunders 1930, 3).

TRADITIONS OF LAY WORSHIP: THE PARISH CHURCHES OF THE PRECINCT

De Losinga began building in 1095, requiring the closure of the churches of Holy Trinity and St Michael's (Dodwell 1996a); the latter was located near the western

---

[4] The manors were located at Trowse Newton, Plumstead, Monks' Grange, Eaton, Catton, Hindolveston, Hindringham, North Elmham, Gateley, Thornham, Hemsby, Martham and Taverham.

boundary of the precinct, and had been the most important church in Saxon Norwich (Campbell 1975, 8). Three other Saxon churches were retained within or
adjacent to the precinct, although only one, St Mary in the Marsh, was definitely
pre-Conquest, having been documented in two Anglo-Saxon wills (Whitelock 1930,
nos. xxvi and xxxviii). St Mary's, in addition to St Ethelbert's and St Helen's, apparently continued to have the right of burial as parish churches. It is likely that their
existing churchyards were within the line of the precinct boundaries, but contained
within separate enclosures (Figure 7). In the case of St Mary in the Marsh, court
records indicate that it was absorbed into the precinct between 1250–65 and enclosed behind a wall (Tillyard 1987, 136). Certainly its cemetery and its walls are
referred to in fourteenth-century accounts of the communar (DCN 1/12/20),
and burials are recorded in the fifteenth and sixteenth centuries (Blomefield 1745
[1806], 53). Post-medieval leases refer to the churchyard lying on both the north
and south sides of the church of St Mary in the Marsh, and to 'the church stile'
(DCN 47/1, 1563).

The presence in a monastic precinct of three parish churches with independent
burial rights was unique to Norwich, and resulted from its circumstance as a new
cathedral foundation in an area of established parochial provision. The situation can
be compared with that of other post-Conquest monastic foundations, in which an
earlier parish church was retained adjacent to an abbey or priory, such as St Margaret's parish church at the refounded Benedictine abbey at Westminster. The secular
cathedral of Exeter is a close parallel: a number of early chapels were located in the
close, and three of these survived into the thirteenth century as parish churches: St
Martin, St Petrock and St Mary Major (demolished 1971) (Orme 1986, 3). Some
other cathedrals had parish churches convened within a discrete area of the cathedral building, and a small number had a single parish church located in the monastic
cemetery. At Ely, the parish church of Holy Trinity was constructed against the
north wall of the cathedral, to serve parishioners who had previously worshipped
in the nave. It was consecrated between 1362 and 1366, and demolished in the later
sixteenth century (Holton-Krayenbuhl 1997, 123). A similar situation developed
at Rochester, where the surviving parish church of St Nicholas was built immediately to the north of the cathedral church. It was dedicated in 1423 for the use of
parishioners who had previously worshipped in the nave (Newman 1976, 489). At
Worcester, the church of St Michael Bedwardine was located in the lay cemetery
to the north of the cathedral-priory by the mid thirteenth century. A detached
bell-tower was added to St Michael's, sharing the west wall of the church (McAleer
2002, 57). It has been said that this served as the parish church for people living in
the precinct, perhaps evolving from a cemetery chapel (Holt and Baker 1991, 14).
However, Joan Greatrex has noted that there is no evidence for either the origins or
functions of St Michael's church in medieval sources (Greatrex 1998, 16).

Two of the parish churches at Norwich disappeared in the thirteenth century.
St Helen's, roughly opposite the site of St Giles' hospital, stood in the cathedral
precinct until c.1270. After a jurisdictional dispute the church was appropriated

to the hospital by the bishop and demolished, but the grant exempted the existing burial ground and an anchorhold (Rawcliffe 1999, 46, 49). Fragmentary remains of St Helen's may survive within later structures. These include a substantial medieval wall forming the north face of a seventeenth-century building on the approximate site of the church (Number 44), and possible medieval foundations observed when a modern conservatory was added to the west of Number 60a, in the early 1990s. St Ethelbert's, just within the west precinct wall (in front of Number 6), was absorbed into the precinct with the exchange of land between de Losinga and Bigod in 1096. Bartholomew Cotton's *Historia Anglicana* (c.1290) records that it was deliberately burned in the riot of 1272 (Tanner 1996, 260), and not rebuilt.[5]

The parish church of St Mary in the Marsh continued in existence through-out the Middle Ages, and received tithes from seculars living within the precinct (Blomefield 1745 [1806], 50). Its last rector, John Toller, was appointed in 1559, and shortly afterwards the parish was amalgamated with those of St Vedast and St Peter Parmountergate (ibid., 52). The parishioners of St Mary in the Marsh were to use a chapel in the south aisle of the cathedral for their services (St John the Baptist, later transferred to St Luke's chapel), and to adopt the cloister garth for burial. With evident disapproval, the antiquary Francis Blomefield recorded that the dean of the cathedral then stripped the church of its lead roof, while the chancellor of the diocese gutted the interior and much of the stonework. After the bells had been sold, the parish church 'stood useless for some time, till it was turned into a dwelling-house' (ibid., 53).

It has been reported that the church survived until shortly before 1564, by which time it had been converted and leased as two separate properties (Whit-tingham 1985, 118; Bolingbroke 1922, 14). The church is shown on Cunningham's plan of Norwich of 1558, although its precise form is not discernible (Chubb and Stephen 1928, plate XVIII). The earliest Minute Book of the dean and chapter, dated 1564, refers to the 'late dissolved parish church of Sanct Maryes in ye Mar-ysehe', confirming its closure before this date (Williams and Cozens-Hardy 1953). Remarkably, however, the outline of the church is shown on a plan accompanying leases dated 1761–75 (DCN 127/11). This previously unreported document shows the clear outline of the church, comprising a rectangular structure with a typi-cal East Anglian round tower at its western end, adjoining a narrow west porch, and a buttressed transept or chapel extending from the south wall. By the eight-eenth century, the former churchyard had been subdivided into small tenements in a property known as Gascoin and Lines. The plan accompanies leases discussing the lands of spinsters Ann and Rachel Brigham, shown to the north and south of the church, and the purchase of the remaining period of the lease by George Sandby, chancellor of the diocese. Sandby also acquired adjoining properties including sta-

---

[5] It is reported that geophysical survey undertaken in the 1970s suggested that the remains of St Ethelbert were located beneath almary green (Ayers 2003, 78). It has not been possible to locate any report on the geophysical survey.

bles, shops, tenements and a public house, some of which refer to land adjoining the churchyard of St Mary in the Marsh.

By mapping the abuttals noted on the leases for Gascoin and Lines, it is possible for the first time to reconstruct the extent of the cemetery of St Mary in the Marsh at the end of the Middle Ages (Figure 7). This took in a considerable area of approximately two thousand square metres on the south of the brewery green (Lower Close green). Although the church had been dissolved before 1564, its cemetery walls remained known or standing, and parts of the church itself were evidently extant. New houses built by Stephen Moore in 1775 incorporated the remains of the pre-Conquest church, and continued to be known as 'St Mary's Chant' (Bolingbroke 1922, 14). Although the present terrace of Numbers 10–12 appears ostensibly Georgian, its central spinal wall reuses the north wall of the Saxon church of St Mary in the Marsh (Figure 5). There is also evidence surviving of later medieval additions to the parish church. The wall inside Number 12 has a blocked sixteenth-century window visible from the present cellar stairs, and at first-floor level there is a large sixteenth-century window with transom and lozenge mullions.

The incorporation of three parish churches within the monastic precinct, complete with their parochial cemeteries, was highly unusual. Again, this may reflect the desire to promote ecclesiastical continuity at the new cathedral site. But perhaps de Losinga also needed to court the affections of local people, having acquired such an

FIGURE 5. The Georgian terrace that fronts onto the lower close conceals the remains of the Saxon parish church of St Mary in the Marsh (Number 12). Photograph © Roberta Gilchrist.

expansive tract of their city's lands. While this diplomatic move may have eased local relations at the time of the cathedral-priory's foundation, it proved detrimental in the longer term. It seems that burial within the cathedral cemetery was never popular with local people, nor was it easily achieved (Tanner 1996, 278). Without this vital connection, the role of the cathedral in the city's popular devotions gradually diminished in the later Middle Ages. The space available for both lay and monastic burial at Norwich cathedral was extremely restricted. Perhaps de Losinga expected lay burial to continue within parochial cemeteries (both within and without the precinct), with interment in the cathedral church or cemetery reserved for a very few of the elite. More generally, burial of the laity in monasteries was a rare privilege until the mid thirteenth century, when the friars extended the practice more broadly (Postles 1996, 622). This omission was at least partly addressed by Bishop Salmon in 1316, when he established a charnel house in the precinct for the bones of people who had been buried in the churches of Norwich.

RELIGIOUS SATELLITES

The college of St John the Evangelist was established in the north-western corner of the precinct, nestled between the Erpingham gate and the lay cemetery (see p. 100). The college was a chantry foundation established by Bishop Salmon, and in 1316 given by him to the prior and convent of the cathedral. He referred to the 'Chapel of St John the Evangelist with its buildings which we have founded . . . for four priests . . . dwelling in the buildings erected by us'. The purpose of the college was to pray for Salmon's soul, and for those of his parents and of the other bishops of Norwich, and to serve as a 'repository for human bones, buried in the City of Norwich and clean of flesh, to await the general resurrection' (Saunders 1932a, 50–61).

In addition to this second religious foundation within the precinct, three hospitals located in the Prior's Fee were connected with the cathedral, although two were independent institutions. A grammar school was also established just to the north of the precinct, adding to the two schools maintained within the priory (one in the almonry of the inner court, the other at the college of St John).

The priory also supported a hermitage located on the edge of the precinct (Clay 1914, 235). The gardener later leased 'the hermit's house at Bishopgate' for a small rent (Saunders 1930, 130). Whittingham suggested that the remains of this hermitage were located near Bishop's Bridge (1985, 118), an apt location. In discussing the fenland landscape of the Witham Valley, David Stocker and Paul Everson have drawn attention to the symbolic significance of bridges and causeways in the creation of the Christian landscape. The sacred quality of such sites was harnessed to ensure that 'rituals formerly centred on the river and its pools became focused instead on the monastic causeway that now led straight to it' (Stocker and Everson 2003, 285). In the later Middle Ages, hermits were found most often at bridges, highways and ferries, maintaining routes of communication to provide service to the community while retaining some degree of solitude (Clay 1914, 49).

The medieval hermit was a solitary religious man who lived at the margins of society, eschewing material comfort and companionship. His liminality was emphasised by the topographical siting of hermits' dwellings, on the physical and psychological margins created by boundaries, rivers, roads, coasts and cliffs (Gilchrist 1995, 162–75). Bridge-hermits were at times responsible for raising revenues through alms and tolls to assist in the construction of the bridges in their care (Clay 1914, 58–9). A bridge-hermit would have been particularly appropriate for the patronage of the cathedral-priory. Eamon Duffy has suggested that the Christian symbolism of bridges and bridge-building appealed to learned patrons, invoking imagery that likened bridges to bishops and popes (Duffy 1992, 367–8). The priory seems also to have supported a bridge-hermitage in St Mary at Newbridge parish (Tanner 1996, 277), and there were anchorites' cells attached to both the cathedral church (see pp. 97–8) and the parish church of St Helen within the precinct (Rawcliffe 1999, 49).

The hospital of St Mary Magdalen, Sprowston, was set up on priory land approximately half a mile to the north of the city, outside Magdalen Gate. Herbert de Losinga established this leper hospital before his death in 1119 (Rawcliffe 1995, 163), and the infirmary hall survives today (Gilchrist 1995, 45, 47). A second hospital was set up by the cathedral-priory early in the twelfth century, on land in the north-east of the city which was part of the Prior's Fee. St Paul (or Norman's) hospital was intended for fourteen poor men and aged residents of both sexes. By the early fifteenth century, only sisters were admitted on a permanent basis. The master of the hospital was a Benedictine monk from the cathedral-priory, who was a senior obedientiary (Rawcliffe 1995, 164). A third hospital had close connections with the cathedral, but was fully independent. St Giles (later the Great Hospital) was founded in 1249 by Bishop Walter Suffield, located on Holme Street just to the north of the precinct, and within the bend of the River Wensum (Figure 6). St Giles was established to provide thirty beds for the infirm poor and some accommodation for elderly or sick clergy. By the late fourteenth century the hospital had assumed the status of a college of priests, with considerable emphasis placed on liturgy and music (Rawcliffe 1999).

Adjacent to St Giles' hospital was the episcopal grammar school. The earliest reference to this school was 1156, although it is thought to have been founded by de Losinga (d. 1119). This grammar school educated boys in Latin and accounting, to serve the church and the merchant community (Harries et al. 1991, 11).

MATERIAL CONSIDERATIONS

In comparison with the occupants of the city, the monks had very refined ideas about the need for fresh water, the regular disposal of refuse, and the symbolic and comfortable benefits of building in stone. The priory was well located in relation to water supply and building materials, with the local vicinity providing flint, lime, sand, gravel and clay for building materials, and the riverside providing a source

FIGURE 6. To the north of the precinct is the Great Hospital, formerly the hospital of St Giles, founded by Bishop Suffield in 1249. Photograph © Roberta Gilchrist.

of reeds and willows for roofing and wattle. The major omission was the substantial amount of freestone required for the construction of the church and claustral buildings.

Water supply

Water for cleansing the monastic buildings was diverted from the River Wensum, while the river gravels on which the priory was located were ideal for sinking wells. Today, the water table is approximately 5m below the level of the monastic ranges (c.o OD). The surrounding chalk would have acted as an effective water filter for a drinking supply. In contrast with the medieval city of Norwich, there is no evidence to suggest that the ground-water in the precinct was contaminated by sewage.

Most monasteries were provided with elaborate systems of water supply, and greater care was taken to develop monastic water resources than in any other type of contemporary settlement (Bond 1989; 1993), including royal and episcopal palaces. The significance of water to the medieval cathedral-priory cannot be overstated. Water was needed for ritual purposes, for cooking, for flushing away waste, for cultivating gardens, for keeping fishponds, and for industrial use in the millhouse, laundry, bakehouse and brewhouse. The main requirements of the monastic cloister were threefold: the supply of water, its distribution to buildings in the cloister and courts, and the removal of waste. Especially for urban foundations, it was sometimes necessary to make great compromises in monastic planning to accommodate the water supply. This, for example, led to the siting of the dormitory at Worcester cathedral-priory in the west range, rather than the standard east range, and the rotation of its alignment to run east–west, projecting from the cloister.

A number of wells were documented in the obediential rolls, and they supplied many areas of the inner court, including the kitchen (DCN 1/2/101d), brewhouse (DCN 1/1/76), bakehouse (DCN 1/2/101h), hostry hall (DCN 1/7/6) and almonry (DCN 1/6/90). Further wells were sited to the west of the cathedral church, at the church doors (DCN 1/4/93), and in the garden of the *clocher* (DCN 1/4/57). Physical evidence for wells has been recorded to the north of the cathedral church,[6] and in the south transept, where the cathedral's gaol was located until 1828. A well in Number 64, formerly the chamber of the medieval infirmarer, was excavated by the Norfolk Archaeological Unit (Percival 2001, 13). This had a diameter of 1.5m and was constructed in flint rubble, with a lining of flints bonded with mortar. None of these surviving wells can be dated confidently, and they could be either medieval or early post-medieval. References to conduits and troughs in the obediential rolls suggest that water was cranked from wells using a rope and bucket, with pressure built up by filling tanks by hand. The making of a trunk (trough) with lead and brass for the hostiliar's well is recorded in 1359 (DCN 1/7/19), in addition to the mending of a conduit (*gondyt*) in the guest hall chamber with brass (*auricalco*) (DCN 1/7/18). These supplied brass basins in the hostry guest hall and common hall (DCN 1/7/106 and 110), delivered by a spout that was supplied by a conduit (DCN 1/7/147).

Archaeological evidence confirms that the monastic buildings were supplied by a culverted water source, in contrast with the wells that were provided for the service buildings and secular accommodation. It was previously believed that both Norwich and Ely cathedral-priories had been supplied entirely by wells, and recent archaeological findings at Ely have also displaced this myth (Holton-Krayenbuhl et al. 1989). At Norwich, a massive culvert flowed through the infirmary latrines and beyond them to the north, turning eastward before the refectory to flush the latrines of the monks' dormitory. Although it was not referred to explicitly in medieval documents, this has been located during recent excavations to the south of the infirmary hall. These revealed a twelfth-century stone drain, comprising a barrel vault constructed in rubble, c.1.2m wide and 2m high, with Caen stone arches supporting the monastic buildings above (see p. 177). The surviving fabric of the monks' latrine suggests that it was also flushed by flowing water (see p. 119). From the monks' latrine the culvert would have run directly eastward, to drain into the meadows of the outer court. Sewage could have been carried by ditches draining the meadows, or alternatively it may have been channelled to nourish the fishponds.

The water source supplying this system is uncertain, but the plan of c.1630 shows a great 'channel' running through Tombland, and 'the pumpe' located at the

---

[6] This was sealed c.1942, after an incendiary device was dropped into it during a bombing raid on the close.

northern end of the thoroughfare (Plate 1; Rye 1906, 50).[7] Investigations in the precinct of the Franciscan friary, directly south of the cathedral precinct, revealed evidence of another stone-lined culvert, running on an east–west alignment from King Street towards the river. The Greyfriars' precinct was also served by a stream, the Dallingfleet, although its alignment appears to be unrelated to the drain (Ayers 2003, plate 8). The cathedral-priory's water system may have been fed directly from the river to the east, or from the documented channel to the west of the precinct, supplied by the river after it had curved westward to run north of the precinct. The latter source would take advantage of gravity created by the natural ground of the precinct as it sloped downwards towards the River Wensum in the east. A source to the west of the precinct would also have allowed the buildings to be supplied in the appropriate sequence, according to the degrees of purity required for their ritual purpose.

A hierarchy of water supply is suggested by the famous medieval drawing of the water system at Christ Church, Canterbury, dated to the priorate of Wybert (1153–67) (Willis 1868). The colour plan from Canterbury distinguishes between the incoming supply, the distribution system, and the drainage system. It is possible to trace the route of the incoming supply, showing that the cleanest water was required for the *lavatorium*, outside the refectory, and for the infirmary. These features employed water for ritual purposes and for spiritual cleansing and healing; from this point, the water was redistributed to supply the kitchens and other buildings, and to flush the latrines. A source to the west of the precinct at Norwich would have facilitated the supply of purest water to the *lavatorium* (see p. 92) and the monastic kitchen, then to the infirmary (the likely location of medicinal bathing and bleeding: see p. 165), and finally, to the latrines of the infirmary and the monks' dormitory (Figure 7). The sloping site would have assisted in draining effluence into the fish-ponds and river to the east of the site. The monastery's canal (see pp. 48–50) may also have served as a central drain or sewer. In medieval sources this can be identified as *le Flette*, or the *flet*, which was periodically cleansed at the cost of the cellarer (DCN 1/2/70; 1/1/34).

Building materials

It was imperative to import building stone to Norwich, since there are few sources of freestone within one hundred miles (Ayers 1990). Flint rubble was used for the wall cores of the cathedral church and claustral buildings, which were faced in stone purchased from Caen in Normandy, and Barnack, Lincolnshire, as indicated by the rolls of the communar and pitancer (Fernie and Whittingham 1972). Petrological study has expanded the range of known stone types to include Quarr stone from the Isle of Wight, used up to c.1120 (Gilchrist 1999, 129), Roche Abbey stone from Yorkshire (Gilchrist 2002, 309), and Lincolnshire limestones including

---

[7] Recent oral history records the existence of a large tunnel running beneath Tombland (Tony Sims, pers. com.); throughout England, medieval monastic drains are commonly confused with tunnels.

Clipsham, Ancaster, Weldon and Ketton (Gilchrist 1999, 122). Stone was shipped via Yarmouth on the east coast of Norfolk, where it entered the local river systems of the Yare and Wensum, and arrived through the canal to be unloaded on the quay (Fernie and Whittingham 1972, 14). The lack of freestone may be one reason for the cathedral's adoption of ground-floor open halls, including the monastic ranges of the refectory and the hostry. Stone undercrofts were relatively rare in the city, making the fourteenth-century vaults that were inserted into the bishop's hall and tower all the more distinctive.

The obediential rolls detail construction and repairs, revealing that the roofs of all the claustral buildings were covered in lead, their interior walls were plastered, and their windows were glazed. Floors were paved by the later Middle Ages, and mats and rushes were purchased periodically as floor coverings (DCN 1/7/19; DCN 1/4/118). Specialist timber from the Baltic was obtained for multiple purposes, referred to as Riga boards and East Reich boards (DCN 1/1/33), perhaps for roof or door construction, when listed together with pitch and tar for weather-proofing. By the later Middle Ages, the buildings of the inner court were lined internally with wainscotting, to provide a measure of insulation by timber panelling (DCN 1/1/106).

The buildings of the inner court were constructed in flint rubble with stone dressings, and frequently incorporated brick for structural purposes. Brick was used very early in Norwich, and evidence from the Ethelbert gate suggests that its primary build of c.1120 incorporated some amount of brick (Macnaughton-Jones 1969). Brick was not used for exterior façades within the precinct until after the Dissolution, in contrast with secular construction patterns of the region. Buildings of the outer court are likely to have been of timber construction, with materials largely provided by the priory estates. There was a distinction in roofing fabrics between the inner and outer court; for example, in providing a lead roof for the main granary (DCN 1/1/74), and a thatched roof for the granary by the water (DCN 1/2/101g) and the granary of the almonry (DCN 29/4/44). Windows were similarly differentiated, with shutters provided for outer court buildings (DCN 1/1/77), rather than glazing. Roof tiles were regularly purchased for service buildings and some floors were boarded (DCN 1/11/1; DCN 1/4/118). The obediential rolls and standing fabric confirm that a hierarchy of building materials operated in relation to the status and location of buildings. A similar perspective is evidenced in Salisbury cathedral close, where flint rubble was used for major houses, and timber-framing was utilised for subsidiary buildings and the halls of smaller houses (RCHME 1993, 20). Comparison can also be made with an inventory of Cistercian Rievaulx abbey, suggesting that the buildings of the inner and outer court were roofed with slate or tile, in contrast with lead coverings of the claustral complex (Coppack 1999, 182).

Light and heat
Within the cathedral church, strategic lighting of particular images and altars was

achieved through the provision of large numbers of candles (consuming some 10–12 hundredweight of wax annually). The twelfth-century *Life of St William* confirms that a great taper was set at the head of the (supposed) martyr's tomb in the chapter house, 'to show reverence' (Jessopp and James 1896, 127). Safe progress through the cloister and precinct at night required mobile lighting, and lamp lockers survive at a number of major entrances, including the hostry porch, the porch to the prior's hall, and two in the dark entry. The *Life of St William* describes how servants of the church set lamps in the cloister every night, to guide the monks to the night services (ibid., 188). The obediential rolls detail the purchase of lighting for domestic areas: for instance, the hostiliar purchased candles, wicks, cotton and oil for the hostry; oil was used for lamps and for a 'chille' in the hostry hall (Saunders 1930, 129). In 1429–30, a new glass lamp was acquired to light the infirmary door (DCN 1/10/17). Heating was provided in the guest hall by brassiers, and it is likely that there would have been a central open hearth with a louvre above. Fireplaces were located in the outer parlour, warming house and perhaps also in the prior's hall. Fuel included bundles of wood (faggots) from Thorpe Wood (DCN 1/1/105) and elsewhere, charcoal (DCN 1/4/58), and peat stored in the turf house in the swannery (DCN 1/2/101e).

Having visualised the scale of the precinct and the materials of its construction, we can now consider the major zones of the monastery and how physical movement between them was controlled.

3
Entering the Monastic Precinct:
Zoning, Access and the Outer Court

THIS chapter introduces areas of distinct social and land use within the precinct, including religious, domestic and agricultural zones. Archaeological and textual evidence is employed to reconstruct the walls, gates, thoroughfares and greens, the planning features that continued to shape the character of the close in later centuries. Particular emphasis is given in this chapter to the outer court, for which little standing evidence remains.

THE MAJOR ZONES OF THE PRECINCT

The heart of the precinct was the cathedral church and the adjoining cloister of the monks, an inner sanctum that was sustained and protected by a series of overlapping zones extending outward to the edges of the precinct (Figure 7). These outer areas fulfilled specialist functions to ensure the self-sufficiency of the priory, but also acted as a buffer to regulate the access of secular people to the monastic areas. Discrete zones also resulted from the presence of the bishop's palace and the secondary religious foundations that were established both within the precinct and as satellites in the Prior's Fee (Figure 4).

The cloister
The cathedral church can be visualised as the centre of a series of concentric rings, with proximity to the church reflecting degrees of both sanctity and authority within the priory. Directly to the north of the church was the bishop's palace (Chapter 6), forming an independent enclave, and directly to the south was the cloister of the monks, under the direction of the prior. The lay cemetery was located to the northwest of the cathedral church, and the monks' cemetery took in the area to the east and south of the eastern arm of the church (Chapter 4). Around the cloister were the main monastic buildings: the dormitory on the east, the refectory on the south and the hostry (guest hall) to the west (Chapter 5). To the south of the cloister was the infirmary, which was an essential part of the workings of the cloister (Chapter 7). The claustral ranges and infirmary can be treated as the core monastic entity.

By the late thirteenth century, a prior's lodging had been constructed immediately to the east of the cloister. This was located in close proximity to the cloister of the monks, but formed an independent household with its own hall, chapel and

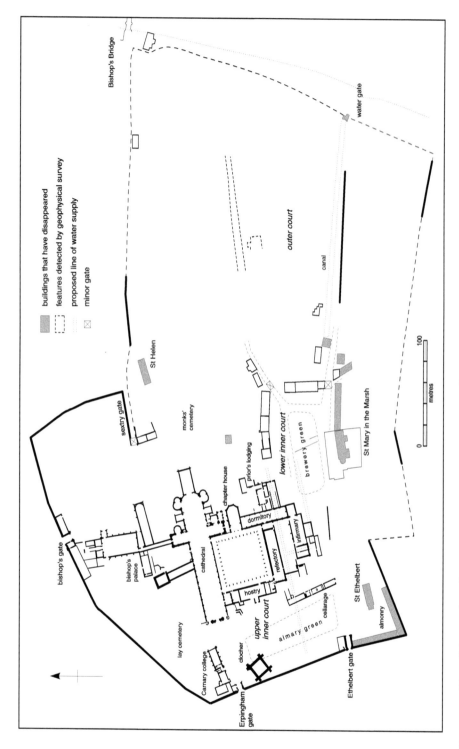

FIGURE 7. Plan of the precinct showing major zones, gates, greens and precinct walls. The reconstruction of St Mary in the Marsh is based on an eighteenth-century plan. Drawing by Margaret Mathews.

private chambers. The prior's complex balanced that of the bishop's palace to the north, and represented the real base of daily power within the monastery (Chapter 6).

The inner and outer courts

It is generally proposed that a monastic precinct was divided into an 'inner' and 'outer' court, both contained within the precinct walls. The inner court was closer to the cloister, and contained the guest accommodation, in addition to domestic functions such as a granary, bakehouse and brewhouse. The traditional monastic orders, including the Benedictines, Cluniacs and Augustinians, usually sited the inner court adjacent to the west front of the church, and at urban houses this court might provide all domestic facilities. This location afforded easy access for secular visitors to the nave of the church, and was close to secular accommodation in the west claustral range (Morant 1995). Rural monasteries also possessed an outer court at a greater distance from the cloister, which contained the agricultural and industrial buildings (Coppack 1990, 100). The Cistercians, in particular, clearly distinguished between the inner and outer courts, providing an inner and outer gatehouse through which visitors passed successively to enter the precinct. At the Cistercian abbeys of Roche and Fountains, Yorkshire, the river was used to divide the inner and outer courts and to provide greater separation between them (Coppack 1999, 178).

The standard model of the monastic precinct proposes an inner (western) court at urban monasteries, and both an inner and outer court at rural monasteries. However, it is apparent that the larger, urban Benedictine monasteries also possessed a separate outer court, including Chester, Bury St Edmunds, Gloucester, St Augustine's, Canterbury, and York (Whittingham 1951; Heighway 1999; Tatton-Brown 1991; Norton 1994). The same provision was made at cathedral-priories, such as Worcester and Durham, that shared the Benedictine commitment to monastic self-sufficiency (Atherton Bowen 1991; 1992). By contrast, planning for the secular cathedral of Salisbury in the early thirteenth century made no allowance for service buildings or agricultural facilities, suggesting full dependence on the urban market (RCHME 1993). In relation to the sites of other urban monasteries, the precinct at Norwich was exceptionally large and unencumbered. This facilitated a large outer court, located in the water meadows at the eastern edge of the precinct (discussed below), and an expanded inner court, with its offices split between two sites according to their function.

The inner court: subsistence and philanthropy

The inner court at Norwich cathedral-priory was distinctive in that it was subdivided into two spaces with separate functions. In order for the monastic community to be self-sufficient, an area was provided close to the cloister for baking, brewing and the storage of grain and other provisions. On the basis of surviving medieval buildings and post-medieval documents, it is possible to locate this area precisely. The service buildings of the inner court were placed to the south-east of the cloister, allowing easy access to the river, from which provisions could be landed, and to the agricultural resources of the outer court (Figure 79; see Chapter 7).

Monastic inner courts also included facilities for the accommodation of guests. Within a cathedral-priory the scale of hospitality required was very considerable, and it was combined with the need for charitable and educational activities appropriate to the mother church of the diocese. A separate area of the inner court combined the functions of the guest hall, cellarage, almonry and cathedral school. Again, the survival of medieval buildings and later descriptions allows the precise identification of this upper part of the inner court. The philanthropic area was located along the western strip of the precinct, from the boundary wall up to and including the west range of the cloister, the hostry. This area was organised to allow easy access for guests, pilgrims and secular visitors. This western area also became the focus of commercial activity in the fifteenth century (Figure 75; see p. 189). At Norwich this western area of the inner court has sometimes been referred to incorrectly as the 'outer court' (Fernie and Whittingham 1972, 29; Noble 1997, 3), which was instead the service area taking in the full eastern part of the precinct (discussed below).

The division of the inner court into two distinct halves allowed the careful management of both facilities and people. The servants of the monastery frequented the service area and outer court, while secular visitors were limited to the western margin of the precinct. The buildings in these two areas were arranged around open spaces or greens, which had crystallised approximately by the mid fourteenth century. The earliest post-medieval leases refer to the upper and lower greens as the almary green and the brewery green. This layout was to endure through successive medieval and post-medieval centuries, being reordered respectively as the upper and lower greens in the late seventeenth century, and surviving today as the Upper and Lower Close.

The Precinct Walls, Gates and Thoroughfares

Massive walls delineated the boundaries of the precinct at Norwich, substantial sections of which survive today to a height up to 5m (Figure 8). The precinct walls are well preserved at a number of cathedrals, including Canterbury, Chester, Winchester and Worcester. In contrast, urban monasteries that were suppressed at the Dissolution rapidly lost the boundaries that had defined their precincts. Such walls possessed symbolic and jurisdictional significance, together with real defensive capabilities. Their defensive character can be seen at the secular cathedral of Salisbury, where the close wall is c.4m high, with a walkway and battlemented parapet, lookouts and an external ditch (RCHME 1993, 38). The monastic cathedral at Norwich was provided at least partially with perimeter walls at its foundation, with the circuit extended in 1276. Secular cathedrals such as Salisbury, Wells and Exeter were given permission to erect defensive walls during the later thirteenth or fourteenth century (ibid.; Rodwell 2001, 5; Orme 1986, 6). While licenses to crenellate were sometimes sought as symbols of lordly status, hostile attacks on monasteries were

FIGURE 8. Precinct wall along Bishopgate. This section enclosing the bishop's palace is likely to date from the fourteenth century. Photograph © Roberta Gilchrist.

not uncommon in the thirteenth and especially the fourteenth centuries, providing a genuine need for such fortification (Thompson 2001, 105).

The precinct walls at Norwich are mixed rubble of flint and brick, and would have been constructed using a shuttering system to build in lifts that allowed the mortar between the aggregate materials to dry (see Rodwell 1986). The nature of their fabric makes accurate dating difficult, but a significant amount of fabric may survive from the twelfth or thirteenth centuries. Possible thirteenth-century lengths of wall survive near the water gate (parallel with modern Recorder Road), and a short section running west from the river, parallel with the cathedral's former canal (Ferry Lane). The earliest fabric survives at the Ethelbert gate, where the re-built structure incorporates the original Norman precinct wall.

The wall adjacent to the gate into the bishop's palace shows signs of arches that may have carried a wall-walk, indicated by a series of vertical rows of brick. Based on evidence for the expansion of the bishop's precinct to the north in 1318, a fourteenth-century date can be proposed for this section. The wall along Bishopgate survived in its entirety until shortly before 1904.[1] During conservation of the fabric in 2003, evidence was observed for a door from the Ethelbert gate to a wall-walk between the Ethelbert and Erpingham gates (Thomas 2003). This feature

---

[1] Photographs of its former appearance and its demolition were published by the antiquary Walter Rye, in a public shaming of the Dean and Chapter for their 'want of taste' (Rye 1904).

indicates that the walls were controlled from the main gates, and emphasises the defensive potential of the cathedral-priory's circuit of walls.

In common with many monasteries, the walls at Norwich were fortified some time after their construction: the map of c.1630 shows the complete circuit of walls as having been battlemented (Plate 1). In 1328, Bishop William Ayremynne (1325–36) sought a license to crenellate the walls of the bishop's palace (Thompson 1998, 167), and the cathedral precinct was also crenellated in the fourteenth century (ibid., 108). A fortified gateway was built on Bishop's Bridge c.1343, controlling entry to Holme Street (*Medieval Archaeol* 43 (1998), 269) (Figure 9).

It is likely that the zones within the precinct were also delineated by walls, such as that which survives along the edge of the former canal. It was customary to define the boundaries of the lay cemetery with walls, for example at St Augustine's, Canterbury, accessed through a cemetery gate (Tatton-Brown 1991, 79). The bishop's palace would also have been separated from the cathedral-priory by boundary walls, as at Christ Church, Canterbury (Rady et al. 1991, 3), and the inner and outer courts were sometimes distinguished by masonry walls, as they were at Gloucester (Heighway 1999, 19). Archaeological evidence has confirmed that internal boundary walls were provided at Norwich to define the area of the infirmary (see p. 178). The obediential rolls indicate that the hostry court was separated from the upper green by a wall, and that the Carnary college was walled off from the lay cemetery. The existence of former minor gates suggests that the outer court was walled off

FIGURE 9. The medieval remains of Bishop's Bridge, located to control access to Holme Street (Bishopgate). Photograph © Roberta Gilchrist.

from the remainder of the precinct (discussed below). It is most likely that the bishop's palace and cemeteries at Norwich were delineated by stone walls, although no evidence survives above ground. There are indications of a former gate into the lay cemetery, now incorporated into a sixteenth-century house that was constructed abutting the Carnary chapel, to the west of the cathedral church (Number 69).

The precinct walls were entered by a series of major and minor gates that controlled access into the enclosure. By the fourteenth century there were three gates providing formal and ceremonial access from Tombland and Holme Street, to the west and north of the precinct respectively, and a fourth receiving traffic from the River Wensum to the outer court. A series of at least three minor gates (and possibly five) controlled ingress from the outer court to the inner precinct, bringing the total number of controlled entrances to between seven and nine. This total was typical of the cathedral-priories and larger abbeys: Norwich, Ely and Gloucester had four major portals into the precinct, and Reading, Peterborough and Bury St Edmunds had five major entrances, which would have been supplemented by peripheral entrances and posterns (Morant 1995, 52–4).

These gates were the vulnerable points in the precinct's defensive circuit of walls. The walls at Norwich were breached during two separate conflicts between the cathedral and the townspeople. The account by Bartholomew Cotton of the riot of 1272 describes the burning of the main gate and church (St Ethelbert's), in addition to 'the gate of the church' (Tanner 1996, 260). The distinction drawn between these two gates implies that a second gate existed that led from Tombland to the west door of the cathedral church, pre-dating the later Erpingham gate. During a second conflict in 1443, known as 'Gladman's Insurrection', the townspeople dug under the gates of the precinct and successfully gained access to the priory (Tanner 1996, 262). The convent of Norwich was not unique in its turbulent relationship with the surrounding town: Thetford was attacked in 1313, and Bury St Edmunds in 1264, 1305 and three successive years from 1326 (Thompson 2001, 105).

Water routes and minor gates
The river provided convenient transport for people and goods entering the precinct, requiring a formal gate at the eastern boundary of the precinct. The water gate stands next to the seventeenth-century ferry house (known today as Pull's Ferry, and formerly as Sandling's). The gate itself can be dated to the fifteenth century, comprising a wide segmental archway for boats, and an adjacent smaller archway for pedestrians (Figure 10). It has a round tower on the north, which is polygonal internally. Pictorial evidence, such as a painting by Edward Dayes, dated 1793, indicates that this tower was originally taller, and that chambers were located over the water gate and in the roof space above.[2] The survival of a water gate is unusual, with

[2] The water gate was restored in 1948, after the ferry across the River Wensum was closed permanently in 1942, when the Norwich City football ground moved from a site opposite the cathedral to Carrow Road (Atherton 1996, 653).

FIGURE 10. The fifteenth-century water gate, showing the wide entrance for boats to enter the cathedral's former canal. Photograph © Roberta Gilchrist.

only two other examples extant at Waltham abbey, Essex, and at Worcester, both also two-storey structures (Morant 1995, 19).

A canal was created from the water gate towards the cathedral, stopping just short of the inner court (Figure 11). It is generally believed that the canal was dug to transport stone for the construction and later repair of the cathedral. Monastic canalisation of water courses for transport is relatively rare, but examples are known, including Glastonbury abbey (Somerset) (Bond 2001b, 103). The canal at Norwich may have been used initially for this purpose, but would have been a convenient way of supplying the inner court with general provisions, while at the same time serving as a drain to remove waste from the service buildings. A similar system is recorded in the fourteenth century at the adjacent hospital of St Giles, where goods were transported up a 'creke' to an unloading bay; the plan of c.1630 shows that this creek was diverted from the river to the north-east of the hospital (Plate 1). The bakehouse and brewhouse at St Giles were situated on or near a stone-lined canal (Rawcliffe 1999, 46, 56), perhaps modelled on the cathedral's facility.

The filling in of the cathedral's canal has generally been dated to c.1780, on the basis of later accounts. In his publication of 1815, Philip Browne claimed that the ditch 'was existing about thirty years ago but is now filled up' (Browne 1815). A later source may simply have restated Browne's assertion without reference, noting in 1842 that the canal was filled in fifty to sixty years ago (Blyth 1842, 104). Certainly the canal was maintained right up to the late eighteenth century: a series

FIGURE 11. Ferry Lane, adjacent to the former canal, with remains of the medieval wall that enclosed the canal (right). Photograph © Roberta Gilchrist.

of payments was made for cleansing weeds and emptying sluice gates at the head of the ditch, from 1745 to 1769 (DCN 11/9).[3] The infilling seems actually to have taken place in 1772–3, when over the course of a year, hundreds of loads of colder were carried from 'the Town to the Ferry Ditch' and spread over it (DCN 12/104–5).

When digging was carried out in 1898 for new drains in Ferry Lane, a stone wall was found 'some way below the surface and extending for some distance to-wards the river'. The workmen described what may have been a quay at the head of the canal, a structure '5ft high and 3ft wide' (Bolingbroke 1922, 25). The edge of the canal was detected further east in 1971, when a service trench opened in front of Number 24 revealed a flint and mortar wall running down the centre of Ferry Lane, at a depth of c. 2m from the modern road surface (Norfolk SMR No. 203). Cleer's map of 1696 and Blomefield's of 1745 show the position of the canal on the northern part of Ferry Lane, suggesting that a row of stables and coach houses dating to c. 1790 may partially straddle the infilled canal. The decision to build new stables here was taken in 1788 (DCN 24/5), and by 1795 a building in this position

---

[3] In 1769, a building over the east side of the ditch was 'laid on fresh mending' and the ditch thor-oughly cleaned: 'the Silth-Traps at the head of the Ferry Ditch to be emptied and the whole ditch from thence down to the River to be thoroughly clean'd and scour'd all the weeds and rushes and mud to be taken out and thrown on adjacent meadow' (DCN 57/1).

is confirmed by estate papers (DCN 57/7/2). The architectural date of the stables corroborates the evidence from other sources that the medieval canal survived until the late eighteenth century.

Beyond the canal and quay was a pedestrian gate to the inner court. This was opposite the gable end of Number 32, where a hinge pin still remains in the wall. In 1898, substantial foundations here of flint and hard mortar were interpreted as a medieval gatehouse (Bolingbroke 1922, 28). This is supported by descriptions in Chapter leases of 1568 and 1573 of 'the gatehouse next the brewery' and 'the gatehouse going down towards the ferry' (DCN 47/1). A lease to Joane Edwards in 1599 records the length of this gatehouse as 18ft 5in. A second pedestrian gate was located at the top of a lane to the north-east (now Hook's Walk), which ran parallel to the canal, and entered the inner court from the great garden. Its location is known from a recently rediscovered plan of 1805, which marks it for demolition along with several buildings abutting The Three Cranes public house (now Number 34). The gate stood between Numbers 50 and 51. Its position may be indicated by a blocked door in a wall that connects the two properties.[4]

A third minor gate was situated to control entry from Bishopgate to the monks' cemetery, and to the bishop's palace and its chapel. This gate was connected with the sacristy or sextry, and was known in medieval account rolls as the sextry gate (DCN 1/4/59), later described as having two towers (DCN 47/1, 1570). This seems to have been a cart gate, rather than simply a pedestrian postern. A buttress projecting from the north-west corner of Number 60 still retains a stone block which held the metal fixing for this gate. There is reference in these sources to a possible fourth minor gate, allowing access through the east precinct wall from the common land running along the eastern edge of the precinct. The almoner's account for 1472–3 records the cost of making gates next to the river within the meadows of the gardener (DCN 1/6/86). An eighteenth-century source refers to a fifth minor gate, a former postern entering the precinct from St Faith's Lane (formerly St Vast's, deriving from St Vedast's) (Blomefield [1745] 1806, 54).

Ceremonial gates

The main entrances at Norwich were provided with two-storey gatehouses typical of the form that was constructed at monasteries. In contrast with castle gates, these lacked overtly defensive features, and instead provided a prominent edifice for the display of arms, heraldry and iconography. Such gates were signposts to pilgrims and visitors, an exterior façade that advertised the spiritual and political status of the monastery within the walls. These were formal and ceremonial entrances, while the monastery's servants and provisions entered through minor gates. By the fifteenth century (and likely earlier), there were two gates into the precinct from Tombland, and, unusually, these portals seem to have held equal status. The outward faces of

---

[4] The doorway is a segmental arch formed by a double row of bricks (opening 2.4m high and 1.7m wide).

both gates were highly ornamented, the Ethelbert with elaborate and innovate flush-work, and the Erpingham with rich carving. Additionally, the tall single arch of the Erpingham gate allows the west front of the cathedral to be seen from Tombland. The arch frames the view towards the principal entrance to the cathedral church, perhaps indicating that the gate may have been intended as a grander 'west front' to the relatively plain western façade at Norwich.

Originally, the main ceremonial entrance from Tombland was the Ethelbert gate, which took its name from the Saxon church that stood nearby until the riot of 1272 (see pp. 29–30). The original gate was destroyed in the riot, and rebuilding was funded by the townspeople in compensation. A date of 1316–17 can be sug-gested for the commencement of construction, on the basis of entries in the com-munar and pitancer rolls (Fernie and Whittingham 1972, 96), with completion in the 1320s. In common with all the cathedral's gates, it is of flint construction with stone dressings. The gate has two storeys: its upper chamber was built as a chapel dedicated to St Ethelbert, reached by a north side-turret. The entrance of the gate comprises two bays of early lierne vaulting with carved bosses of c.1320–30 (Woodman 1996, 162). The Ethelbert gate has been assessed as perhaps the earli-est and most important example of flushwork (Sekules 1980; 1996), although the gatehouses at Burnham Norton (Norfolk) and Butley (Suffolk) are near contempo-raries. The Ethelbert gate is one of only nine surviving gatehouses decorated with flushwork, and is unusual in that flushwork was employed on all four elevations (Morant 1995, 83, 86).

The Ethelbert's public (west) front is highly ornamented with geometrical flushwork in the gable, above a storey of canopied niches interspersed with lancet windows, and a frieze of chequerwork below. The central niche of the top regis-ter was occupied by the figure of Christ displaying his wounds, replaced in 1964. A stringcourse of quatrefoils separates the upper storey from an entrance arch with carved spandrels, showing St George and the dragon, and flanked by canopied niches. The many niches would have contained carvings of saints, which together with the richness of the flushwork, must have presented an imposing and highly charged message to onlookers. Veronica Sekules has proposed that the symbolism of St George and the dragon – emphasising divine triumph – may have been intended as a moral commentary on the riot of 1272 (Sekules 1996, 202).

John Adey Repton recorded the Ethelbert gate in 1803 (Figure 12), showing its appearance before repairs by William Wilkins in 1815 altered tracery and modi-fied the gable. Repton's drawing shows the gate in a poor state, but he recorded important details that were subsequently lost, such as the crenellated coping. The original flushwork design was finer than the nineteenth-century replacement, com-prising a central rose of six spherical triangles around a concave hexagon, contain-ing five daggers. The central rose overlapped with the flushwork lights on either side, two small roses containing three spherical triangles (Thomas 2003). A major programme of restoration in 1963–6 replaced the important spandrel carvings, although these survive in the cathedral's collection of worked stone. The work in

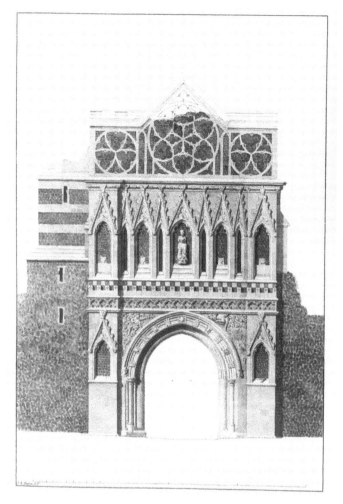

FIGURE 12. West elevation of the Ethelbert gate by John Adey Repton, c. 1803. Reproduced with permission of the Society of Antiquaries of London.

the 1960s included removal of plaster beneath the vault, revealing that the original Norman gate had been incorporated in the reconstruction. The early fabric has been dated to c. 1120, and consisted of coursed flints and areas of early bricks that had been badly burnt (Macnaughton-Jones 1969, 77). There were traces of shafting, suggesting that there were piers at each end of the gate, and a vertical row of blocks of ashlar with twelfth-century tooling remained *in situ* near the eastern arch. Putlog holes for the cross-beams for a wooden vault were recorded under the present vault. The Norman fabric was covered with a mixture of flint and plaster in the fourteenth-century rebuilding.

The Erpingham gate was sited to allow access from Tombland to the west door of the cathedral (Figure 13). Although an earlier gate may have existed on this site,

FIGURE 13. The fifteenth-century Erpingham gate provides a visual frame for the Alnwick porch and the main entrance to the cathedral church. Photograph © Roberta Gilchrist.

the present structure has been dated to c.1420 by associated heraldry (Tristram 1938, 41; Sims 1996), and to c.1435 on stylistic grounds (Sekules 1996, 206). The tall single arch is supported on either side by semi-hexagonal buttresses, and is richly moulded with carved figures of saints and ornamental and heraldic motifs. The saints sit in vaulted niches and stand on brackets: the inner order displays the twelve apostles, while the outer presents an equal number of female saints.[5] The buttresses are surmounted by two seated figures that were once easily discernible as

[5] Tristram (1939) identified those on the north side (reading from the top) as St Margaret, St Osyth, St Agnes, St Mary Magdalene, St Etheldreda and St Catherine; on the south are St Mary of Egypt, one unidentified saint, St Helena, St Barbara, St Withburga, and a final unidentified saint.

a secular priest holding a book and instructing a young boy, and a Benedictine monk also holding a book (Britton 1817, 31).[6] In the centre of the scheme is the shield of the Passion, with a niche above containing a kneeling figure. The Trinity, the Crucifixion and the Eucharist occur in the shields on the spandrels (Tristram 1938, 46). Sekules has proposed that these were symbols of religious orthodoxy, intended to challenge the Lollard heretics who were under investigation by Bishop Alnwick (1426–36) (Sekules 1996, 205–7).

The patron of the gate is considered to have been Sir Thomas Erpingham, veteran of Agincourt, whose arms are depicted in the carvings, together with those of his two wives. The prominent niche above the arch is now occupied by a statue of Erpingham, but there is considerable evidence to suggest that this is not original to the scheme. The rear wall of the niche has been extended to accommodate the statue, which is not fully carved on its right side. When Sir Thomas Browne described the gate in the late seventeenth century, the niche was empty, but the Erpingham effigy had been placed there by the time that Francis Blomefield wrote in 1745 (Blomefield 1806, 54). Until the 1750s, this gate was known simply as the church gate, and did not have the overt association with Erpingham that it enjoys today. Tony Sims has suggested that the niche may have originally contained a representation of the Trinity, part of an iconographic scheme linking it with the Agincourt chantry that was located beneath the Carnary chapel (Sims 1996, 455–6). The kneeling effigy of Erpingham may have been moved from the Alnwick porch on the west front of the cathedral, or from the chantry beneath the Carnary (Finch 1996). Original pigment has been detected on the gate, including red used for the lips of the figures and on the shield of the five wounds, and green on the armorial surcoat of Erpingham (Park and Howard 1996, 404).

The Erpingham gate was originally vaulted but there is now a plaster ceiling in place, inserted in the nineteenth century when a domestic wooden chamber was removed. On the eastern elevation, a stringcourse and central window were removed in the mid twentieth century. The chamber above the gate was approached by a door in its north wall, which is now partly blocked. It retains a timber roof with butt-purlins and collar that may be dated to the late sixteenth or early seventeenth century (Smith 1999). The Ethelbert gate was also modified for domestic use in post-medieval centuries, including the insertion of fireplaces and the blocking of the door to the wall-walk (Thomas 2003).

The bishop's gate, leading from St Martin at Palace Plain to the palace grounds, is the third and final great gate constructed into the monastic precinct (Figure 14). It is dated architecturally to c.1435, and is likely to have been begun by Bishop Alnwick (1426–36) and completed by Bishop Lyhart (1446–72). It has the more usual domestic gatehouse arrangement with two separate entrances, one for carts and one for pedestrians. It has two polygonal turrets and a wide archway with two-centred head, over a brick undercroft. On the upper story there is an image niche

---

[6] These figures were sketched in 1788 by John Carter (Norfolk Studies Library NC/A8).

FIGURE 14. The fifteenth-century gate to the bishop's palace, with cart and pedestrian entrances. Photograph © Roberta Gilchrist.

between two windows, and battlements with tracery and shields. There are tracer-ied spandrels and a tierceron-star vault in the archway, and both the outer doors are medieval (Pevsner and Wilson 1997, 226). A survey of the bishop's palace made in 1646 suggests that the tower to the east of the gate contained a porter's lodge, sited over the bishop's prison (Stewart 1875).

Lanes, greens and tenements
It can be estimated that by the mid fourteenth century, the monastic buildings of the inner court were organised around two open spaces, the brewery green and the almary green. There is archaeological evidence to indicate that before this date a different use of space had prevailed. Excavation in 1976 of a large trench in the

Lower Close green (the brewery green) revealed a series of late thirteenth-century road surfaces running in a north-west to south-east alignment (Norfolk SMR No. 300). These roads overlaid a twelfth-century building of post-hole construction, which contained a hearth and an oven, and has been interpreted as a possible smithy (Atkin and Evans 2002, 50). From this it may be proposed that service buildings were originally grouped more densely or irregularly in the eastern inner court, but were removed subsequently by roads cutting across the area. Following the fire at Norwich in 1272, there would have been a steady influx of stone and building materials arriving in the precinct, travelling up the canal and unloaded on the quay at its head. The direct route for this material would have taken it across the present Lower Close green, and the likely intensity of traffic may have required a series of road resurfacings.

A second lane ran northwards from the top of the canal, behind the brewhouse and bakehouse. Its route is fossilised in a hollow way behind Number 31. It must have been used to transport provisions from the outer court or quay to the monastic granary, incorporated into the present Numbers 54–55 (see p. 193). The rear of the building (its north elevation) retains blocked arches associated with an arcade, which can be dated to the thirteenth century on the basis of decoration on the piers of the arcade (Figure 77). The size of the arcade indicates that the building was once used for storage, and that a loading bay was provided on one side. The location of the loading bay on the north side of the building confirms that goods arrived via the hollow way running behind the brewhouse, rather than across the site of the present green. This suggests that by the thirteenth century, a specific route was set out to allow the transport of goods through the outer court, reserving the open space of the lower inner court for a more specific purpose, such as the unloading of stone for the rebuilding programme. When the intensity of building work lessened, the road leading from the quay was absorbed into the green.

Lanes developed to allow access to St Faith's Lane to the south, and Bishopgate to the north. The lane towards St Faith's was a southern extension to the hollow way behind Number 31, allowing access through the outer court of the precinct, without having to pass through the gates at the top of the canal or at Hook's Walk. Today, the lane runs directly to St Faith's, but previously it turned sharply westward on reaching Number 16 (as shown on Hochstetter's map). A lane or path can also be suggested through the cemetery, leading from the sextry gate past the sextry itself.

A lane leading to the outer court survives in the present layout of the close, and it retains a medieval building respecting its alignment (Figure 15). The lane known as Hook's Walk approached the brewery green from the outer court, and it perhaps provided access from Bishopgate via the line of the modern Gooseberry Garden Walk. Excavations in 1990 in Gooseberry Garden Walk, however, revealed no deposits of archaeological significance (Norfolk SMR No. 26332). A subsequent watching brief, conducted prior to the erection of a fence along the full length of the walk, recorded no archaeological features (Northamptonshire Archaeology 2004). This negative evidence suggests that the area to the north of Hook's Walk

FIGURE 15. The medieval lane known as Hook's Walk. Number 50 (left) was constructed in 1664, shortly after the restoration of the dean and chapter. Photograph © Roberta Gilchrist.

was occupied only by the great garden, rather than by a domestic lane. Instead, it may be suggested that Hook's Walk continued directly eastward through the outer court, perhaps to reach the gateway built by the almoner in 1472–3, next to the river within the meadows of the gardener (DCN 1/6/86). Geophysical survey in this area revealed a linear feature that appears to align with Hook's Walk and extend the lane eastward, possibly a former trackway formed by two closely spaced parallel ditches (Northamptonshire Archaeology 2002, 4).

Number 49 is aligned on Hook's Walk, a later medieval building known as 'the Gardener's Chequer' (Figure 16). Its south elevation retains two blocked lancet windows, possibly of late thirteenth or fourteenth century date. The position of this structure suggests that Hook's Walk could have been partly lined with medieval buildings. It is likely that the chamberlain's office was sited to the south of Hook's Walk, as indicated in a lease to Robert Stanton dated 1549 (DCN 47/1). This describes 'the Wardropers Office' as being to the south of 'a certain entry leading into the meadows' and near a chamber 'sometime called the Gardeners Chekker'.[7]

A contemporary lane seems to have run through the Upper Close green (the almary green), and was observed during excavations on the site of the west range by

---

[7] This evidence contradicts Whittingham's placement of the chamberlain's house at the site of Number 50, (1985, 114), which is to the north of Hook's Walk.

FIGURE 16. Number 49, located on Hook's Walk. This medieval building may have been the office of the monastic gardener. Photograph © Roberta Gilchrist.

Arthur Whittingham in 1934 (MC186/47). In his plan of 1975, Whittingham shows the line of the road as it approached the *locutory*, and dated the feature to c. 1200–1300. The *locutory* was the outer parlour of the monastery, where monks could talk with secular visitors. These guests would have entered the precinct through the Ethelbert gate, and followed the lane across the green towards the *locutory* or the west door of the church.

Tenements
The location of Hook's Walk in the remote region of the outer court would make it the ideal position for offices associated with minor obedientiaries, and perhaps for the accommodation of servants and corrodians of the priory. A corrodian was

a secular lodger housed within a monastery, funded by a corrody, a form of pension or annuity.

Male and female corrodians frequently purchased their own retirement in a monastery, including the provision of a dwelling in the monastic precinct, sometimes occupying a house together with a spouse and children (Harvey 1993, 182). As previously noted (p. 16), resident corrodians at Norwich included William Bauchon and his wife Magdalen in the 1290s (Atherton 1996, 636). Corrodians at cathedral-priories were more commonly older men maintained for life upon nomination by the king or prior (Lehmberg 1988, 43). This was certainly the case at Norwich, where corrodians were normally royal servants nominated by the king and maintained by the communar (Fernie and Whittingham 1972, 39 n. 4). For example in 1340, Master John de Stratford, the king's cook, was sent to Norwich cathedral to be maintained for life (ibid., 37), and John de Swanton relinquished his corrody at Norwich when he was made joint surveyor of the king's work at Sheen in the 1360s.

In the later Middle Ages, the precinct also attracted grand tenements, such as that of Sir Roger Townsend, located near the sextry gate. In 1558, a lease conveyed 'the lodgings, lately of Sir Roger Townsend, with free ingate and outgate at and by the great gates under the tower and at the great gates towards the hospital of St Giles' (DCN 47/2). Research on London's monasteries has indicated that tenements were established in monastic precincts in the later fifteenth and early sixteenth centuries, at sites including the hospital-priory of St Mary Spital, the Cistercian monastery of St Mary Graces, the nunnery of St Mary Clerkenwell, and the headquarters of the order of St John of Jerusalem at Clerkenwell. The London evidence suggests that organised 'closes' of such tenements developed, focusing on the cemetery or outer court areas, and often connected with gates into the monastic precinct (Sloane 2003). It has not been clear previously whether this process was unique to London, but the Norwich evidence confirms that the practice was also prevalent at provincial cathedral-priories. In common with the London pattern, Townsend's tenement was located near a minor gate leading into the monks' cemetery.

Some of the London monasteries indicate structured planning of tenements, such as St Mary Spital, where a roadway leading away from the cloister was 'lined with tenements that appear to have been built almost as a terrace' (Sloane 2003). This description could apply equally well to Hook's Walk, and provides an important comparative context for the development of lanes in the precinct at Norwich. Hook's Walk may have housed a combination of obediential offices, servants' and corrodians' houses, and tenements leased or built by prominent local families. The former lane extending to the east of Hook's Walk, indicated by geophysical survey, would have given access to properties at the north-eastern corner of the precinct. Two buildings by Bishop's Bridge contain extant medieval fabric, Numbers 54 and 70, Bishopgate, on the north and east boundaries of the precinct, respectively. These are likely to be survivals of tenements built or leased by secular tenants of the medieval priory, such as the widow Margaret, lately wife to Richard Nyseham, who in 1530 rented a tenement on Holme Street (Bishopgate) and the *ponyerd* next to *Fysshers Medowe* (DCN 1/2/99).

THE OUTER COURT

The eastern part of the precinct at Norwich formed the outer court, which was the agricultural and industrial zone, separated from the inner court by a series of gates and walls (Figure 17). In comparison with extensive rural precincts, outer courts at urban monasteries contained a relatively restricted number of facilities. For example, a survey of buildings at Benedictine St Mary's, York, c. 1545, recorded

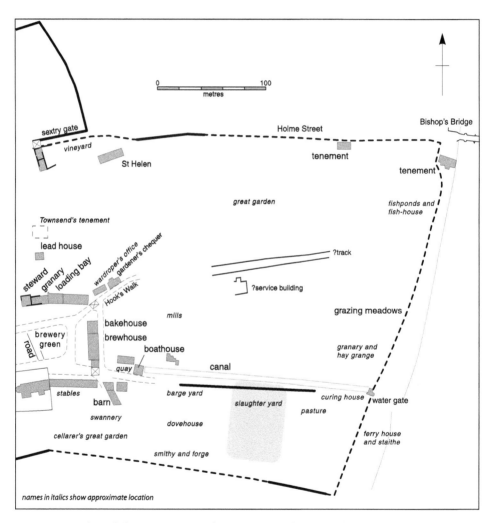

FIGURE 17. Plan of the outer court, showing extant features, the evidence of geophysical survey and approximate locations of buildings described in medieval accounts and sixteenth-century leases (in italics). Drawing by Margaret Mathews.

an outer court adjacent to the River Ouse, containing stables, a barn, garners, a cowper house, a bakehouse and brewhouse with an attached millhouse, and great and little gardens (Norton 1994). The large water meadows at Norwich allowed the cathedral-priory to develop features more usually associated with rural monasteries. Large parts of the outer court were taken up by grazing meadows, fishponds, gardens and orchards, but there were concentrations of buildings dedicated to milling and storing grain, preserving food, laundering sheets and clothing, iron-working, and animal husbandry. Geophysical survey of the area has indicated two features, one interpreted as a possible building in the area of the great garden, and the other a ditched enclosure in the meadow by the riverside (Northamptonshire Archaeology 2002).

The outer court was approached directly by the River Wensum, where the water gate to the precinct was located and survives today. A ferry house is mentioned in the cellarer's rolls (DCN 1/2/69), with a staithe next to it, where provisions could be unloaded and redirected for storage. Nearby was a moated area known as 'ferry close' (Noble 1997, 4). The canal was created from the water gates towards the inner court, allowing easy transport of landed goods. Boathouses and a bargehouse were documented by the master of the cellar's accounts (DCN 1/1/33; 106), and two boatmen were paid regular stipends of 7s by the cellarer (Saunders 1930, 99). A surviving house located at the top of the former canal may once have served as a boathouse. Number 29 retains features in its west wall which may be blocked vents for a boathouse.[8] The location of the barge yard can be suggested from a lease between the chapter and William Farewell in 1553, placing it to the south of the canal (DCN 47/1).

The inner court was ringed by a series of gardens to the east and south-east, with the priory's (the gardener's) great garden to the east of the church and cloister, and the cellarer's great garden to the south-east. These large gardens are likely to have been separated from the inner court by fencing. Smaller gardens were maintained by the sacrist, infirmarer, almoner and cellarer, adjacent to their offices in the inner court. The locations of the larger gardens were first suggested by Arthur Whittingham from his interpretation of two post-medieval sources: the earliest Ledger books (DCN 47/1–2), dating 1566–1649 (Williams and Cozens-Hardy 1953), and the Parliamentary Survey of the Close, made in 1649 (Whittingham 1985). These sources frequently record the dimensions of plots and buildings, and the features on to which they abutted. In the mid-seventeenth century, large areas of the precinct were still given over to agricultural functions, and a great deal of continuity with medieval land-use is implied. Further detail is provided by the medieval obediential rolls, including thirty-three accounts of the gardener, which have been studied by Claire Noble (1997). She conveys the impression of the precinct as a verdant patchwork, in which all spaces not occupied by buildings were cultivated

---

[8] These are two timber openings at the base of the wall, now blocked with brick (1.3m × 0.35m).

as orchards or gardens, enclosed with woven fences or palings (Noble 1997, 4). Gardens for contemplation and medicinal production were located near the Lady chapel and infirmary respectively. Those of the outer court were more utilitarian in purpose. Extensive garden spaces were common in monasteries, although pollen evidence has shown that suburban precincts could also include areas of grassland and scrub (Bond 2001a, 65).

The larger gardens of the outer court would have been given over to vegetable production, with crops recorded including garlic, shallots, porrets, leeks, colewort, beans and herbs, all typical medieval fare. Orchards provided important fruit and nuts, with apple, pear, cherry, walnut and hazelnut mentioned (Noble 1997, 5, 9); hazel and walnut plantations seem to have been particularly common monastic features (Bond 2001a, 67). Perhaps more surprising is the presence of a vineyard located between the sacrist's garden and the great garden (and therefore in the north-western corner of the outer court). The sacrist's account for 1335–6 records the purchase of vines, wands, and bindings for vines, and the making of an enclosure for the *arbutis* (DCN 1/4/31), which is a vineyard in which vines are trained around trees.[9] Monastic vineyards were also maintained at Bury St Edmunds (Whittingham 1951), Peterborough, Thorney, Beaulieu, Canterbury and Abingdon. English wine production decreased by the end of the thirteenth century, with the changing climate causing colder winters and wetter summers, but some vineyards survived until the Dissolution, such as that of Barking abbey (Bond 2001a, 68–9).

The meadow to the east of the garden was susceptible to flooding, a regular hazard for the priory's neighbours at St Giles' hospital, just to the north of Holme Street (Bishopgate) (Rawcliffe 1999, 43). Some of this meadowland would have been used for grazing animals, which would have required exclusion from any vulnerable gardens or orchards of the outer court. The great garden was surrounded by a moat that would have served this purpose. It was reorganised in 1483–4, involving an extension to the prior's orchard to its south-west (Noble 1997, 4). This large area of meadow is also the likely location for fishponds and fish-processing.

Despite its urban situation, the cathedral-priory maintained several fishponds, features more common at rural monasteries. Fish played a primary role in the monastic diet, since the Rule of St Benedict required the monks to abstain from consuming the flesh of four-footed animals (McCann 1952, Chapter 39). Exceptions had always been made for the sick monks staying in the infirmary, but by the later Middle Ages all monastic orders had relaxed their rules on the consumption of meat (excepting the vegetarian Carthusians). At Norwich, meat-eating became more common throughout the entire monastic community, with designated rooms in which carnivorous feasts were allowed (see p. 258). Fish retained a central place in the diet: it has been estimated that at Westminster abbey, fish was eaten at dinner on around 215 days each year, with the daily allowance per monk being about 1.25–

[9] Remarkably, an account of new building work along Bishopgate in 1904 referred to 'an old vinery' having been destroyed along with a section of the north precinct wall (Rye 1904, 6).

2lbs (Harvey 1993, 46, 51). Sea fish was more important in the diet than freshwater fish, and herring, cod and haddock were transported from the coast smoked, dried or pickled (Bond 2001a, 73). The inland waterways connecting Norwich with the east coast of Norfolk must have allowed the monks to regularly enjoy fresh sea fish. Freshwater fish could be obtained from the River Wensum, using basketwork fish-traps, and from fishponds in the outer court. Monastic fishponds were developed from the twelfth century onwards, and many rural monastic precincts had six or seven ponds, covering up to six to seven hectares. They were intended for the storage and breeding of bream and pike, and smaller fish like perch, roach and tench (ibid.). Additional facilities and larger ponds are likely to have been developed on the priory's outlying estates.

Within the outer court at Norwich, the cellarer's rolls referred to buildings in a 'pond yard' (DCN 1/2/75), and water being culverted to supply a fish pond, when a gutter was made with resin and boards for bringing water to the fish (DCN 1/2/75). Fish were purchased to stock the ponds, including eels to feed pike (DCN 1/1/30), and pickerel and roach for stock (DCN 1/11/1). The purchase of fish to stock ponds appears to have been quite exceptional, with comparable references known only for Abingdon and Peterborough abbeys (Bond 2001a, 74). It has been suggested that medieval monastic fishponds were not intensively managed, and that productivity would have been low (Currie 1989). It seems that the Norwich cellarer was unusual in making some effort to restock and manage the ponds, but it is unlikely that the outer court could have produced the quantities of fish required to feed the monks and guests. Nets and fishing equipment were obtained for use in the outer court: for example, one purchase totalling 15s included one dragnet with a rope, and three trammel nets with cord, bow nets, thread and floats (DCN 1/1/30). Fish was processed for longer-term storage at a fish-house (DCN 1/2/101h), perhaps comparable in form to the surviving example of Glastonbury abbey's fish-house at Meare. The cellarer's accounts also specified a curinghouse (DCN 1/2/101i) and a salthouse (DCN 1/216), for the preserving of pork and other meats. A regular stipend of 3s was paid to a curer of herrings (Saunders 1930, 99).

The records of maintenance in the obediential rolls alert us to the presence of many buildings in the outer court that cannot be mapped with any precision, but from which some locales of specialist activity can be proposed. The cellarer's accounts refer to buildings at the water's edge, evidently a complex of mills and grain stores in the meadow adjacent to the River Wensum. These included the 'granary at the water' and the 'hay grange at the water' (DCN 1/2/101g). A woolhouse referred to by the master of the cellar may have been a waterside warehouse sited to receive shipments of fleeces from the monastic estates (DCN 1/1/74).

There are references to mills at Norwich, including a mill in the court (DCN 1/2/101c), a horse mill (DCN 1/2/16), a malt mill (DCN 1/2/101f), a pounding mill (DCN 1/4/76), and the stipend of a miller in the precinct (DCN 1/2/21). References to a horse mill and the stable of the mill horse confirm that horsepower was used in at least one of the priory's mills. Other mills could have been powered either by wind or water, given the abundant river water available for channelling, and the frequency of windmills in the region. At the adjacent hospital of St Giles, wind and horse mills are recorded (Rawcliffe 1999, 54). Urban monastic water mills have been little studied, due to the rare survival of evidence, but stone fabric has been recorded from mills at Durham and Coventry cathedral-priories, and the medieval mill at Reading's Benedictine abbey survived until 1965. This seems to have been a twelfth-century mill with a single centrally-placed, undershot wheel (Bond 1993, 73).

There are references at Norwich to both a smithy (DCN 1/1/35–36) and a forge (DCN 1/1/44, 105), industrial features that would have been pushed to the eastern edge of the precinct in order to contain the smoke, noise and hazard of fire. A chapter lease of 1563 describes the 'Smith's Forge' as being near the cellarer's great garden and the dovehouse (DCN 47/1). The laundry would have been at the water's side, not just for convenience of water supply, but to limit pollution to the watercourses of the inner court, and to reduce the dangers resulting from boiling cauldrons of water. The chamberlain's accounts refer to 'le Washing house' (DCN 1/5/14), while the cellarer notes the 'scalding house' (DCN 1/2/16). The location of the documented piggery is not known (DCN 1/4/31), but on olfactory grounds one might suppose it was in the eastern area of the outer court. Pork was an important foodstuff to the priory, and a regular stipend of 10s was paid to the 'master keeper of the pigs' (Saunders 1930, 99). The site of the slaughterhouse (DCN 1/4/76) is fully documented in a chapter lease of 1563. It was located between the dovehouse yard on the west, and pasture on the east, abutting the canal on the north; its maximum dimensions were 77 yards by 29 yards (DCN 47/1).

Stables are mentioned for the cart horse and mill horse specifically (DCN 1/1/38b, DCN 1/2/45), work animals that would not have been accommodated in the stables of the inner court. They may have been housed just to the west of the church of St Mary in the Marsh, where stables were documented in the seventeenth century (Bolingbroke 1922, 14). These stables survived until 1794, and the houses on the site, Numbers 13 and 14, were built by William Wilkins a century later (Whittingam 1985, 106). Directly to the south of the brewhouse was the swannery, located with reference to a chapter lease of 1553 (DCN 47/1). This was an enclosed area (DCN 1/2/45), which included the facilities of the swannery itself, in addition to a dovehouse (DCN 1/2/101e), turfhouse, great barn and other buildings within the swannery (DCN 1/2/96), some of which were thatched (DCN 1/2/45). Swans were a luxury food consumed for their appearance rather than taste; they are likely to have been reserved for the prior's table and for eminent guests. The swannery may have included a swan pond and swan pit for fattening birds for the table, as at St Giles' hospital, where there was also a 'swanherde' for marking the swan pairs on the river and watching the cygnets (Rawcliffe 1999, 54). The swannery building itself later became the Garden House Inn. Part of it survives today in Number 14a, (Whittingham 1985, 118), although no fabric earlier than the seventeenth century can now be detected.

The outer court at Norwich cathedral-priory contained facilities that largely would have met the principle of self-sufficiency that was envisaged by St Benedict. There is no documentary or archaeological evidence, however, for the manufacture of items either for routine maintenance or sale, such as the tiles or bricks that were sometimes produced at rural monasteries, for example the Cistercian abbey at Bordesley, Worcestershire (Stopford 1993). Only the gardens produced surplus for sale, with the gardener marketing fresh fruit and vegetables and nursery plants and seeds, including madder, teasles and hemp seed (Noble 1997), water-lilies, apples, cherries, pears, walnuts, leeks, onions and garlic (Saunders 1930, 131). The production of industrial crops was relatively common in monasteries, particularly madder, hemp and flax (Bond 2001a, 65), but the sale at Norwich of vegetables and fruit seems to have been unusual, and reflects the very considerable size of the precinct and the quality of its management.

4

Monastic Memory and Meaning:
the Church, Cloister and Cemeteries

THE spiritual life of the priory focused on the cathedral church and the daily round of services that were performed by the monks in the choir. Their monastic vocation and communal life were represented in the architecture of the cloister. In functional terms, it integrated four ranges of buildings and provided efficient access between them. But the cloister was also a metaphorical space: it could represent the heavenly paradise that was the focus of monastic contemplation (Cassidy-Welch 2001, 48), or the earthly prison that was life confined in a mortal body (Meyvaert 1973, 57). The cathedral church and cloister were designed as a frame to contain and enhance the performance of the liturgy (Klukas 1984). Liturgical practice connected the central areas of the monastery as a performative space, with processions linking the cloister, church and cemetery, and uniting the living and dead brothers as a single monastic community.

The cloister is the most characteristic feature of a coenobitic monastery: the church and three ranges of buildings were placed around a central square, or courtyard (Figure 18). This enclosure is the cloister yard, comprising an open space, or garth, in the centre, flanked by the cloister alleys, or walks, which run concentrically within and provide access to the church and ranges. By the eleventh century, there was considerable uniformity in the way in which Benedictine monasteries arranged the buildings around their cloisters. The functions of the monastic ranges at Norwich can be predicted from comparison with other well-preserved or excavated monasteries, and from study of the plan of St Gall (Figure 37). This large vellum plan presents a line drawing of a Carolingian monastery, and is considered to have been a blueprint for the ideal monastery, drawn up for Haito, bishop of Basle, in his *scriptorium* at Reichenau, around the year 820 (Horn and Born 1979, vol. 1, xxi). This plan shows the two-storey buildings around the cloister, including details such as the placement of tables and beds, and the locations of all offices and service buildings in the precinct. In order to receive maximum light and heat from the sun, the cloister was normally placed to the south of the church, with the church forming the northern side of the courtyard. Exceptions to this rule were caused by local topography, requiring cloisters to be placed to the north of some churches to avoid existing buildings or burials, or to facilitate a water supply. The south cloister may also have come to be associated especially with male monasticism: in contrast, many nunnery cloisters throughout Europe were placed

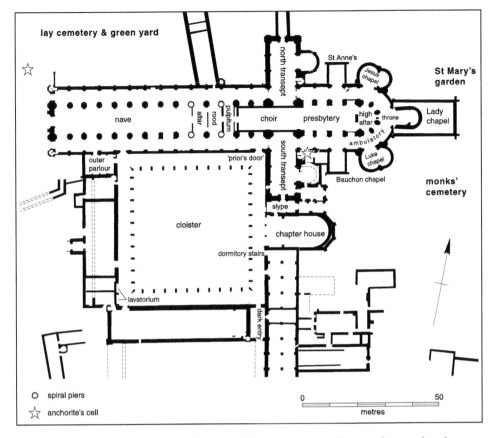

FIGURE 18. Plan of the cathedral church and cloister, showing features discussed in the text. See Plate 9 for full phased plan. Drawing by Margaret Mathews.

to the north of the church (Gilchrist 1994), and the domestic accommodation of secular clergy at French cathedrals was usually placed to the north of the church (Reynaurd and Sapin 1994).

The origin of the cloister as a concept in central planning is likely to have derived from classical and Late Antique influences, including Roman courtyard houses, the galleried atria of basilican churches in Rome, and the courts attached to Syrian churches from the fifth century (Horn 1973). It has been argued that the model of the Roman rural villa suited the feudal agrarian economy of early medieval Europe. Further, it has been proposed that common use of the claustral plan was consolidated with the Carolingian drive for uniformity in monastic practice (ibid., 242–3; Thompson 2001, 37). These functional conclusions have been countered by recent research that considers the cloister for its 'mnemotechnical' use, or its metaphorical meaning within monastic practice (Carruthers 2000; Cassidy-Welch 2001).

By the later Middle Ages, the English cloister had become significant in another respect: the presence of a cloister signalled the superior status of a cathedral church. Cloisters were integral to monastic foundations such as Norwich from their inception, but they were later developed at the secular cathedral foundations of Wells, Salisbury, Hereford, Chichester, Exeter, London and Lincoln. Of the medieval secular foundations, only York and Lichfield failed to develop cloisters (Rodwell 2001, 343). The impetus to provide a cloister adjacent to a secular cathedral may have stemmed from their mnemonic use for meditational purposes, together with their centrality to liturgical processions. The elaborate processions required by the Use of Sarum developed alongside the provision of cloisters at Salisbury and elsewhere (Cocke and Kidson 1993, 10). The sequentially arranged, historiated decoration of the cloister at Norwich emphasises the importance of physical movement in appreciating its medieval meaning (discussed below).

This chapter introduces the spaces of the church, cloister and cemeteries of Norwich cathedral-priory, including the buildings and chapel of the Carnary college, concentrating on evidence for their overall form and use. The reader is referred to detailed assessments of the construction and dating of the Romanesque and Gothic church and cloister (Fernie 1993; Heywood 1996; Woodman 1996). The emphasis here is more archaeological in its examination of the changing meanings and use of space from the twelfth century to the later Middle Ages.

THE CATHEDRAL CHURCH

The church and claustral buildings at Norwich were completed within fifty years of the priory's foundation, creating a coherent and closely integrated design (Figure 18). In this respect the cathedral-priories contrast with many monasteries, where cloisters were developed gradually over many decades, and with the secular cathedrals, where irregular cloisters evolved with little relationship to the planning of the church (with the exceptions of Wells and Salisbury). Eric Fernie has assessed Norwich cathedral to be 'a traditional rather than a revolutionary building' (1993, 154). He traces its stylistic origins to the Norman tradition exemplified by Saint-Étienne in Caen, by way of Lanfranc's cathedral at Canterbury (1070–77) and the contemporary rebuilding of St Augustine's, Canterbury (ibid., 118). Norwich cathedral seems to have drawn several features from St Albans (1077), including its simple west façade (in contrast with westworks such as Bury, Ely and Peterborough), the height of the lantern tower, and the arrangement of the choir stalls and screen. In several respects, Norwich follows Bury St Edmunds (begun 1095), and the two churches may have shared the same architect. Their characteristic features include exceptionally long naves, ambulatories with radiating chapels, and crossing piers of the same design (ibid., 119). The form taken by the clerestory is also significant. Fernie (1993) and Heywood (1996) have argued that the triple-arch clerestory with superimposed nook shafts is distinctively East Anglian in form, with Norwich or Ely serving as the innovator. An intriguing source for the clerestory has been proposed by John Crook and Roland Harris, who note that the closest parallel in date and form is the former 'clerestory' at Westminster hall, completed c.1099 (pers. com.).

De Losinga enjoyed close connections with the court of William Rufus, and it is highly probable that Westminster hall formed the bishop's inspiration for the eastern arm of Norwich cathedral.

Construction of the church began from the east end and proceeded westward, confirmed by archaeological evidence (Cranage 1932), and described in the cathedral's *First Register*. By the time of de Losinga's death in 1119, the cathedral church had been completed up to the *pulpitum* (Figure 18). This seems to have been a planned pause in the building programme at a strategic place. This junction is indicated by a visible break in construction (Fernie 1993, 44–6; Heywood 1996, 100–102), and by excavated evidence of a raft foundation of flint rubble, ending at the fourth pair of piers in the nave (St John Hope and Bensly 1901, 126). It is confirmed also by the use of Quarr stone in the eastern arm, north transept and nave aisles up to the fourth bay from the crossing (Gilchrist 1999, 130). Quarr stone, a freshwater limestone from the Isle of Wight, derived from a limited outcrop and was used in medieval construction for a maximum period of only fifty years, c.1070–1120 (Tatton-Brown 1993). The construction of the tower was also planned to allow a break in the building programme. Stylistic and archaeological evidence of the tower's interior and exterior suggests a break at the level of the roof ridge of the church, where an external band of arcading survives on the west elevation. The tower projecting above the roof line was built contemporaneously with the nave of the church (c.1121–40), and the distinctive tracery of lozenges and roundels appears from stratigraphic evidence to have been secondary to the main arcading of the belfry, suggesting a further phase of cosmetic work in the mid twelfth century (Figure 19) (Gilchrist 2002).

The walls of the church are flint rubble (with some reused Roman brick) faced with ashlar blocks of Caen stone, and are up to 2m thick. The foundations are c.1.8m below ground level, comprising whole flints laid in rows in mortar. This construction, together with the well-draining river gravels on which the church is placed, has successfully mitigated the subsistence experienced by many great churches. The piers of the nave arcade incorporate both fine Caen and coarser, darker Barnack stone, creating a striped effect to the modern eye. Some twelfth-century painting survives to confirm that originally the interior of the church would have been plastered and painted (Park and Howard 1996), and perhaps also the exterior, although no evidence for the latter practice survives at Norwich. The use of alternate stone types perhaps reflects medieval constructional methods, rather than a deliberate visual device. The fabric was erected in lifts, comprising horizontal bands of masonry that were placed in a single pour of mortar. Any change of material during the construction, for instance as a fresh cart of stone was unloaded, created the banded effect. Concentrations of Barnack stone can be seen in the third and fourth bays of the south aisle of the nave, together with twelfth-century scaffold holes and mortar breaks (Figure 20). The use of architectural ornament in the church is fairly spartan, relieved by the occasional use of chevron and billet moulding, interlaced arcading and some decorated capitals. Only the north transept was decorated with

FIGURE 19. West and south elevations of the tower, showing distinctive tracery of lozenges and roundels. The tower's fabric above the ridge level of the nave roof dates c.1121–40. Photograph © Roberta Gilchrist.

sculpture, signalling its close connection to the bishop's palace and his ceremonial route through the church (see p. 144).

The Romanesque form of the church is preserved almost in its entirety, excepting the roofs and the clerestory of the presbytery. Its plan is typical of Benedictine monasteries and cathedrals, with a long eastern arm (four bays plus the apse), a long nave (fourteen bays), a transept forming the crossing, aisles, and an eastern ambulatory with three radiating chapels. The medieval liturgical foci can be discerned easily today. Like all Benedictine monasteries, the nave was used by the laity, and the eastern arm was reserved for use by the priory. The apse contained the sanctuary, with the high altar in the next bay to the west. Behind the altar stood

0   Metres   5

FIGURE 20. Elevation of the third bay in the south aisle of the nave, showing blind arcading and putlog holes. A new door was created in the 1970s for access to the cathedral shop; further remodelling of this bay is planned to create the entrance to a new visitors' centre. Drawing by Philip Thomas, Cathedral Survey Services. Copyright Chapter of Norwich Cathedral.

the bishop's throne, in the most prominent position. The choir stalls of the monks occupied the crossing and the first two eastern bays of the nave. Immediately to the west of the *pulpitum* (the screen dividing the choir from the nave), was the nave altar in the third and fourth bays, dedicated to the Holy Cross.

The position of the nave altar was defined by the placement of four cylindrical piers decorated with spiral grooves; two of these still remain, and a third is partially visible beneath later casing (Figure 21). These piers are distinctive from the remainder of the arcade, which is composed of an alternating rhythm of two pier forms: a square core with attached pilasters and shafts, and a circular core with fewer

FIGURE 21. The location of the nave altar was framed by four cylindrical piers decorated with spiral grooves (left); behind the altar is the *pulpitum* screen. Photograph © Roberta Gilchrist.

attached shafts (Heywood 1996, 80). The use of piers with helical grooves to mark the sanctuary of the nave altar is paralleled at Durham cathedral (begun 1093), the crypt of Canterbury cathedral (begun 1096) and Waltham abbey (Essex) (c.1120s) (Fernie 1977; 1980). Fernie has proposed that up to the twelfth century, spiral piers were used to mark important places, suggesting an iconographic reference to Old St Peter's in Rome. 'Barley-sugar stick' columns had been reused in the shrine that was built for St Peter in front of the apse of the fourth-century basilica in Rome (eight of the original twelve now stand in the piers of the crossing in new St Peter's). These spiral columns were probably second-century in date. In the Middle Ages, it was believed that Constantine had brought them from Solomon's Temple and had installed them at St Peter's.

It is likely that the main vessel of the church was covered with an open timber roof. Parts of the roof space are painted and must have been visible through a timber roof structure, for example the eastern face of the crossing tower (Figure 22). The only parts that were vaulted originally would have been the aisles, the ambulatory, the ground floor chapels, the transept arms and perhaps the main apse. Externally, the church would have been characterised by its profusion of turrets, towers and pinnacles, conveying the Carolingian origins of its major design features (Fernie 1993).

The elevation consists of three levels: the main arcade on the ground floor,

FIGURE 22. View of the presbytery from the east, showing wall passages at gallery and clerestory levels, and fifteenth-century vaulting. The painted gable above the eastern face of the crossing suggests that an open timber roof structure was provided for the Romanesque church. Photograph © Roberta Gilchrist.

the gallery above, and the clerestory with its wall passage (Figure 22). Routes of circulation within the church and its upper levels can still be traced easily. There were three entrances to the church through the west front, two in the south aisle of the nave (leading to the cloister), one in the north transept (leading to the bishop's palace), and one in the south transept (leading to a slype in the east range of the cloister). Originally, there were no entrances in the eastern arm of the church, although a door to the north was added when the fourteenth-century chapel of St Anne was demolished in the eighteenth century. Four spiral stairs gave access to the gallery level, two positioned in the east walls of the transepts and two at the corners of the aisles at the west end. The gallery provided access throughout the entire church at the second level, and further stairs in the transept and west end led to the clerestory. In common with arrangements at Gloucester, Tewkesbury and Chichester, these spaces were incorporated in the cathedral's music and liturgy. The ambulatory with radiating chapels was repeated at gallery level, and these upper chapels were decorated for ecclesiastical use. The gallery conveyed processions to the upper chapels in the eastern arm, and the *Customary* confirms that lights were placed in the gallery and clerestory passages on the occasion of great feasts (Tolhurst 1948, 31). The nave gallery also provided a direct processional route to the bishop's palace at first floor level.

A unique feature of the church is its *cathedra*, the bishop's throne and the symbol of the cathedral church of the diocese. The treatment of the throne is noteworthy in several respects. First, the stones of the seat itself are weathered, yet they appear to be in their twelfth-century position (Fernie 1993, 29). Together, these two observations suggest that the remains of the throne are older than the cathedral itself, and may represent a feature that was translated from the Saxon cathedral at Elmham (Radford 1959; Whittingham 1979). Secondly, the position of the throne is unusual. It is sited in the central arch of the apse, directly behind the high altar, and along the main axis of the church; the more usual position would be to the side of the altar. The throne is also elevated, and directly below it there is a deep niche opening into the ambulatory behind the throne (Figure 23). Excavations in the 1890s revealed a curved base thought to represent an earlier set of steps to the throne (Cranage 1941), suggesting that it was not originally in this elevated position. Fernie has proposed that the present arrangement dates from the insertion of a raised floor into the sanctuary. Judging from the style of the capitals and arches of the niche positioned below the throne, this reordering would have taken place in the early twelfth century, perhaps for the enthronement of Bishop Eborard in 1121 (Fernie 1993, 28–9). Finally, there is a change in floor levels in the aisles and ambulatory surrounding the sanctuary that contains the throne. From the transept, the floors slope downwards towards the east end, with surviving Romanesque bases and plinths confirming that this was the twelfth-century arrangement. The sunken character of the ambulatory recalls the use of early medieval ring-crypts to house relics for their display to pilgrims. The niche below the throne at Norwich is likely to have held relics, and indeed the throne itself must have been regarded as a relic of the early church in East Anglia. Fernie has observed that the positioning of the throne follows that laid down in the fifth-century Syriac *Testamentum Domini*, a practice that would have been long outmoded by the early twelfth century (ibid., 66). He concludes that the nostalgic treatment of the throne was therefore an attempt to provide Norwich with a relic. This device may also have been intended to enhance the cathedral's sense of antiquity, and to lend greater legitimacy to its new site.

Norwich cathedral has been central to recent art-historical debates concerning the use of proportional planning in medieval buildings (Hiscock 1999; 2002). Fernie has argued that the dimensions of the ground plan and elevations of the

FIGURE 23. Relic niche located beneath the bishop's throne, accessed from the ambulatory. Photograph © Roberta Gilchrist.

cathedral were carefully planned according to the ratio of one to the square root of two, or the side of a square to its diagonal ($1:\sqrt{2}$, or $1:1.4141$).

> Starting with the overall layout, the side of the cloister relates to the length of the nave in this way, that is, the diagonal of the cloister square is the same as the length of the nave, and the length of the nave relates in the same way to the length of the church from the façade to the chord of the apse (Fernie 1993, 94).

He has demonstrated through a series of measurements that $\sqrt{2}$ was central to the proportions of the church, cloister and the original wing of the bishop's palace. Fernie proposes that this was a utilitarian device used commonly by medieval designers and builders, rather than a ratio that possessed inherent symbolic meanings. Alternatively, it may be argued that the ubiquitous use of $\sqrt{2}$ in medieval planning could relate to broader number symbolism. Medieval neo-Platonic philosophy used modular planning and biblical numbers to convey a sense of measurable order (Sekules 2001, 126). Whatever the meaning of such proportional planning, Fernie's observations confirm that a consistent design was in place before construction of the church and cloisters began. The whole complex was laid out to create a unity between the nave and the cloister, and between the nave and the eastern arm of the church. Each element of the twelfth-century plan was part of an integrated whole.

While essentially a twelfth-century building, later medieval additions also shaped the character of the cathedral church. Liturgical developments required greater space in the eastern arms of monastic churches, and Norwich followed others in extending eastward through the creation of a Lady chapel. In the mid thirteenth century, Bishop Suffield (1244–57) sponsored an extension four bays in length and slightly wider than the presbytery. The Lady chapel was constructed between 1245 and 1257, and was ruined by 1569 (DCN 47/2).[1] Its association with devotion to the Virgin is supported by the placement of St Mary's garden around it, an enclosed garden within the monks' cemetery that is likely to have been used for contemplation and meditation (Noble 1997). Two square chapels were added to the presbytery c. 1325–30, perhaps to serve as private chantry chapels (Woodman 1996, 179); the southern of these, known as the Bauchon chapel, survives today.

A timber spire was erected over the crossing tower in the 1290s, which was blown down by a great storm in 1361 or 1362, destroying the clerestory of the eastern arm. This was rebuilt with a tall wall passage supported on thin columns. The second spire perished in a fire caused by lightning in 1463, and was replaced with the present spire, c. 1472–85, which is an octagonal brick cone with a thin stone facing (Gilchrist 2002, 320). The presbytery was refaced c. 1480–90, the arches reshaped to a more contemporary four-centred profile, the walls resurfaced and topped with diamond-plan cresting (Woodman 1996, 194–6). The restyling of the presbytery was achieved with some degree of secular patronage, from the upwardly mobile Boleyns, but most building work at Norwich was funded by its bishops, who continued to represent the founder. Secular patronage was generally less common at cathedrals, due to the absence of founding families (Martindale 1995, 153). Secular sponsorship is evident in the renewal of furnishings, notably in the choir stalls that were funded by local gentry in the fifteenth and sixteenth centuries, perhaps the earliest example of lay patronage of choir stalls in a monastic cathedral (Tracy 1990, 32). The final spire is attributed to Bishop Goldwell (1472–99), and the remodelling of the west front to Bishop Alnwick (1426–36), entailing the addition of a shallow

---

[1] A new chapel was built on the site in the 1930s, when fragments of worked stone were recovered that are thought to have been associated with the thirteenth-century Lady chapel. Twenty-four large segmental mouldings survive (Norwich Cathedral Worked Stone Inventory), which formed a large arch of three orders. This former arch is likely to have been the entrance from the ambulatory to the Lady chapel.

porch with a massive window above it. The west front survived in this form until 1875, when the turrets were lowered, the porch was truncated and the pilasters were altered by the Victorians to what they erroneously believed had been their Romanesque appearance (McAleer 1993). It was alleged that a western transept had once existed or been planned, until excavations finally disproved the theory (McAleer 1966; Fernie 1974). The crowning glory of Norwich cathedral is its unsurpassed series of narrative bosses (discussed below). This innovation stemmed from the rebuilding of the cloister, but was extended to the church with the vaulting of the nave by Bishop Lyhart (1446–72), the eastern arm by Bishop Goldwell (1472–99) and the transept arms by Bishop Nykke (1501–35/6). The patronage of Goldwell and Lyhart can be detected iconographically in the golden wells shown on the bosses in the choir, and the recumbent deer on corbels in the nave.

THE CLOISTER

The monastic cloister was not merely a thoroughfare connecting the conventual buildings, but rather the centre of daily life outside the divine services. It was bound to the liturgy through processional routes and with monastic ritual through observances conducted at the *lavatorium*, the washing place at the entrance to the refectory. It was also a place of silent study and shared conversation for the monks. According to the *Customary*, on weekdays the monks of Norwich cathedral-priory were permitted additional time to talk in the cloisters, but on Sundays and feast days any extra time available was spent in reading (Tolhurst 1948, xxiv). The regular use of the cloister for conversation was a marked relaxation of the Rule of St Benedict (McCann 1952, 36–7). The space at the centre of the cloister, the garth, 'blossomed with roses' in the late twelfth-century *Life of St William* (Jessopp and James 1896, 66). The complete Gothic cloister survives at Norwich, together with substantial remains of the south and west conventual ranges.

Although rebuilt in the later Middle Ages, the cloister retains its original dimensions. At 56.5m by 56.5m externally, Norwich was the largest Romanesque cloister in England. It was surpassed eventually by the secular cathedral at Salisbury, where the cloister of c.1230 was planned at c.51.5m, but finally achieved 57.5m square (Cocke and Kidson 1993, 8–10). The twelfth-century cloister at Norwich was single-storey, in contrast with its later medieval successor. The outer walls over the cloister roofs were ornamented with blind arcading, and windows were provided to light the three monastic ranges from the cloister. The walls above the twelfth-century cloister, formerly external spaces, survive inside the rooms above the south, east and west walks. The space over the east walk retains fragments of blind arcading, and over the west walk interlaced arcading survives. The latter was modified sometime in the 1960s or '70s, when a false ceiling was inserted and the spandrels of the arcades were rendered to give the impression of a row of two-centred arches. Their original appearance was recorded by John Gunn in 1879, who also showed putlog holes in the east face of the wall, above the vaulting of the later cloister (Gunn 1879). These putlogs represent the roof height of the Romanesque cloister.

The west wall of the cloister also retains five circular, double-splayed windows, and the partial remains of a sixth (Figure 24). These were constructed using wickerwork centring, a technique commonly employed in the building of Saxon churches in East Anglia. Because of this provenance, earlier writers judged the west wall to be pre-Conquest fabric that had been incorporated into the Norman cloister (Gunn 1879; Taylor and Taylor 1965 I, 470–71). Given the prolonged use of this method in the construction of local parish churches, it is more realistic to date the wall to the early years of the Norman building programme (Heywood 1996, 107). Fernie has noted that the length and position of the extant west wall suggest a cloister size more in keeping with Norman than Anglo-Saxon standards, and has proposed that double-splayed windows would have afforded greater privacy in screening the cloister from guests accommodated in the west range (Fernie 1993, 23). It was common practice to construct the domestic ranges of a medieval monastery from east to west, leaving the non-essential accommodation of the west range to be constructed last. The west wall of the cloister was erected early in the building programme, in order to screen the cloister from public view, with the west range itself begun when the east and south ranges were complete. Archaeological excavations on the west range have confirmed that after the site had been levelled of Saxon occupation, it remained empty for a considerable time. Sediments gradually accumulated over a period of several decades, before the hostry was constructed (Wallis 2003).

The appearance of the twelfth-century cloister can be appreciated from a group of richly decorated sculptures that were discov-

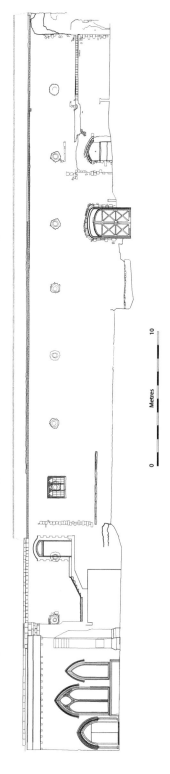

FIGURE 24. West wall of the cloister (east wall of the former hostry) dating c. 1100, showing surviving and reconstructed double-splayed windows. From the left, the second, third and eighth windows have been removed or blocked. Drawing by Philip Thomas, Cathedral Survey Services. Copyright Chapter of Norwich Cathedral.

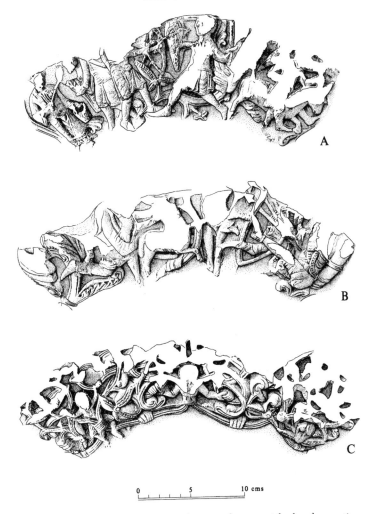

0   5   10 cms

FIGURE 25.Capitals from the Romanesque cloister, drawn with the decoration unwrapped
to show classical figures, perhaps including Circe (A), Odysseus (B) and Dionysus (C). Drawing by Steven Ashley. Reproduced with permission of Steven Ashley.

ered in the early twentieth century. Fourteen capitals and twenty-five voussoirs
had been reused as masonry in the later medieval cloister.[2] Their decorated faces
had been turned inwards, and some retain red, yellow and green pigments. Carved
decoration was wrapped around the capitals in the manner of a frieze (Figure 25).
When metaphorically unwrapped, these capitals reveal that the carving was used
to convey complex narratives. The Norwich capitals fall within the tradition of

___

[2] In total, eighty-three fragments of worked stone may be attributed to the demolished twelfth-
century cloister, including the capitals and voussoirs, and others including bases, nook shafts, imposts and
corbel heads (Norwich Cathedral Worked Stone Inventory).

historiated cloisters, such as Moissac (in the Pyrénées), completed c.1100 under
Cluniac control. Moissac is believed to be the earliest historiated cloister, with
forty-one of its seventy-six capitals narrating scenes from the life of Christ, the
Book of Revelations, the Old Testament and the lives of the saints. There appears
to have been no coherent plan in the spatial location or grouping of the capitals at
Moissac, although many held apostolic significance for the monastic cloister (Shapiro 1985). Historiated Romanesque cloisters are well known in France and Spain,
but evidence for the practice in England is fragmentary (for example, from Reading
abbey).

The capitals from Norwich are double in form, and only one member of each
pair has carved ornament, suggesting that the carved face would have been viewed
from the cloister walk. Some of the surviving capitals drew from classical authors
such as Ovid and Virgil, and portrayed characters including Circe and Dionysus.
Although the depiction of pagan themes may seem incongruous to a cathedral cloister, the classical tradition was valued by twelfth-century Benedictines. Jill Franklin
suggests that these capitals may have been placed to assist the boys of the cathedral
school in learning classical myths that formed part of their education (Franklin
1996, 134). The narrative capitals would have acted as a mnemonic, with their
thematic content reinforced during frequent movement through the cloister walks,
and use of the walks for study and contemplation. The voussoirs from Norwich can
be reconstructed to form an opening 2–3 m wide, most likely to have been the
entrance to the Romanesque chapter house (ibid., 126).

The setting out of the cloister at Norwich was unusual in the treatment of floor
levels. The cloister walks were sunken in relation to the four surrounding ranges of
buildings, by a depth of approximately 800–1000mm, creating a subterranean effect
(Figure 26). Excavations on the sites of the south and west ranges have confirmed
that their twelfth-century floor levels were elevated in comparison with the adjacent
south and west cloister walks.[3] The steps still survive that connected the cloister
with the higher levels of the church to the north, the guest hall to the west and the
refectory to the south, while on the east, the extant chapter house screen confirms
the higher level of the former east range (Figure 38). Although these steps date from
the reconstruction of the cloister in the fourteenth and fifteenth centuries, they respect the earlier floor levels. In common with the rebuilding of the cloister at Wells,
the procedure at Norwich seems to have involved the reuse of the lower parts of the
inner walls (Rodwell 2001, 255), and retained substantial parts of the superstructure. The floor level at Norwich was retained in the later rebuilding, although new
Purbeck flagstones were provided throughout the cloister.

The typical arrangement of a monastic cloister allowed level access between
the claustral ranges and the cloister alleys. The sunken cloister at Norwich may

[3] The level of the cloister walks is approximately 4.5–6 OD, while the level of the Norman floors
of the refectory and hostry can be estimated at c.5.3–4 OD, a difference of some 800mm. The difference
between the north cloister walk (4.65 OD) and the current floor level in the south aisle of the nave (5.87
OD) is 1022mm.

FIGURE 26. West walk of the cloister, showing sunken level in relation to the hostry door. The claustral ranges were elevated by c.800mm. Photograph © Roberta Gilchrist.

have been intended to cope with the difference in levels caused by the sloping site, although a more common solution was to build on terraces. The cathedral-priory at Coventry, for example, was constructed on a series of four artificial terraces, with the church on the highest ground and the refectory on the lowest (Rylatt and Mason 2003, figure 3). At Wells, the sloping site caused the east and west cloister alleys to be c.800mm lower than adjoining areas (Rodwell 2001, 245). The first cloister at Cistercian Rievaulx was 900mm lower than the later cloister, and may have been terraced or stepped to cope with a sloping site (Fergusson and Harrison 1999, 48). Surviving Cistercian cloisters at Le Thoronnet and Silvacane, Provence, demonstrate that the Cistercians dealt with sloping sites in this unique manner. Where it was necessary to construct parallel cloister walks at different levels, the two linking walks were stepped down in stages to bridge the gap. The sloping site at Norwich could have been conquered by use of terraced platforms or 'stepped down' cloister alleys. A sunken cloister was preferred, despite the need to raise the ground levels of the east and south ranges by dumping imported material.

The provision of a subterranean cloister is distinctive, and may have been intended to complement the sunken ambulatory around the presbytery. The cloister walks served effectively as ambulatories, providing access but also maintaining the separateness of the conventual ranges (Cassidy-Welch 2001, 57). The cloister was also a liturgical space, and was used for processions in which the monks were carefully spaced with four to five paces between them (Chadd 1996, 319). In common with the ambulatory, the sunken cloister may have been intended to recall Early Christian precedents. Rather than compensate fully for the sloping site, the topography was harnessed for symbolic effect. It is highly significant that Herbert de Losinga planned the cathedral at Norwich shortly after his visit to Rome to seek absolution from Pope Urban for the simoniacal purchase of his see (Dodwell 1996a). The sunken cloister was one element in de Losinga's scheme to embue the new cathedral landscape with a sense of antiquity, drawing on the Roman and Saxon past. The sunken cloister was used strategically to create 'an iconography of heritage', together with the treatment of the north transept, the bishop's throne and the nave altar, and the siting and landscaping of the bishop's palace (see pp. 143–4).

Old St Peter's in the Vatican was constructed by Constantine on the site of the necropolis that contained the tomb of the apostle. The terrain of the necropolis bore some superficial resemblance to the site at Norwich, sloping 'gently but steadily to the east and more sharply from the north to south' (Krautheimer et al. 1977, 183). The topography of the Vatican led to the basilica of St Peter's being constructed on a platform, with a lower atrium to the east, a rectangular courtyard (57.5m × 44.7m) which was lower than the church and reached by steps. When the atrium was torn down in 1608–9, its floor was level with the basilica, but an earlier mosaic floor was found '2 or 4 palmi, 45 or 90cm, below the flagstone pavement' (ibid., 266). Richard Krautheimer concluded that the atrium at Old St Peter's was planned to be either 450mm or 900mm lower than the basilica.[4] He argued that the lower floor extended the full width of the courtyard 'forming a sunken area to be reached from the higher levels both of the basilica and its narthex west and of the landing and entrance east' (ibid., 267). He proposed that the sunken floor level of the atrium at Old St Peter's was retained when roofed porticoes were added in the fifth century (resembling the ranges of a cloister), and until at least the eighth century. However, the date of its replacement with the level floor recorded in 1608–9 is unknown. When de Losinga visited the Vatican in 1094, the atrium of Old St Peter's is likely to have been a sunken courtyard to the east of the basilica. When the bishop began building at Norwich just two years later, he obtained a site with terrain reminiscent of the papal complex. De Losinga chose to reproduce the combination that he had seen at St Peter's of the spiral columns (discussed above) and a sunken cloister, with very similar dimensions and depth to that of the Vatican (for full discussion, see pp. 251–3).

The cloister at Norwich was rebuilt as part of the campaign of reconstruction that followed the fire of 1272. Although essential repairs to the church had been completed before its reconsecration in 1278, the ambitious programme of rebuilding stretched into the fifteenth century (Figure 27). The cloister itself seems not to have been sufficiently damaged to have merited rebuilding, but the opportunity was taken for its remodelling nonetheless. When work began in 1297, the bishop and prior could hardly have imagined that this particular project would take 133 years

---

[4] Both measurements were given in a seventeenth-century account by Grimaldi.

FIGURE 27. View of the cloister, showing decorated curvilinear tracery of the west and south walks (1314–56). Photograph © Roberta Gilchrist.

to complete. It was dogged by financial insecurity, management problems and a hiatus of two decades following the Black Death, in which two of its masons perished (John and William Ramsey).

The reconstruction of the cloister was documented in great detail in the obediential rolls of the communar and pitancer (Fernie and Whittingham 1972). Close study of these rolls has informed art-historical analyses and attributed dates to the construction of the cloister walks and their tracery (Fernie 1993, 170–9; Woodman 1996).[5] The slow progress of the construction programme is reflected in the contrasting styles of tracery in the cloister walks: the geometric work of the east cloister (1299–1314), the decorated curvilinear tracery of the south and west cloister (1314–1356), and the perpendicular style of the north cloister (1382–c.1400). The final product resembles a tracery catalogue, moving clockwise in a survey of developing English styles (Figure 28). From stylistic study of the cloister bosses, Veronica Sekules has suggested an alternative phasing (Sekules 2004). She argues that the major keystones of the arcades all date to the mid fourteenth century. On this basis, she proposes that the skeleton of the new, two-storey cloister was fully in place by c.1350. This would suggest that the basic structure of the new cloister

---

[5] The sequence of construction, costs, masons and styles can be consulted in Fernie and Whittingham 1972; Fernie 1993, 170–9; Woodman 1996.

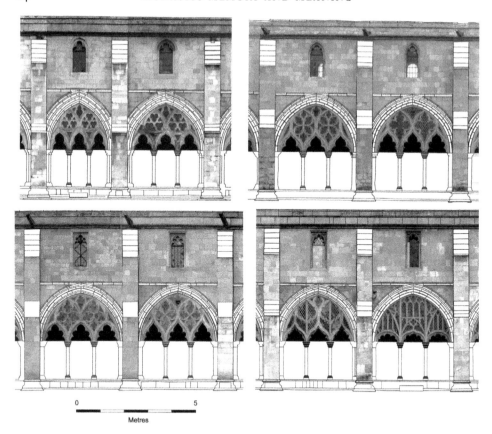

0   5
Metres

FIGURE 28. Cloister tracery, showing two sample bays from each side of the cloister. Top left: the east cloister, top right: south cloister. Bottom left: west cloister; bottom right: north cloister. Drawing by Philip Thomas, Cathedral Survey Services. Copyright Chapter of Norwich Cathedral.

was completed within fifty years, but that completion of the traceried windows and carved bosses took a further eighty years (Figure 29A).

The bays of the inner wall of the cloister are divided by stepped buttresses with a large overarch containing glazed tracery on slender colonnettes (Woodman 1996, 166). The upper storey is lit by a single window in each bay; these spaces were used for additional study carrels, and for storage used by the sacrist and other obedientiaries (DCN 1/4/76). The interior of the cloister has clustered Purbeck marble shafts, now severely eroded, dividing each bay, and benches lining the outer, perimeter wall. The rolls confirm that Purbeck marble was shipped from Corfe, limestone from Caen and Clipsham, and stone from Quarr in 1412–14. If the latter material came from the Isle of Wight, this must have been Bembridge limestone, since deposits of Quarr stone had been exhausted by 1120 (Gilchrist 1999 n. 65). The vaulting was erected after the construction of the bays. It was backed by brick (observed in 1965), and referred to in the accounts as tile bought for 'hidden parts'.

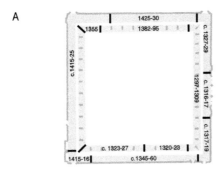

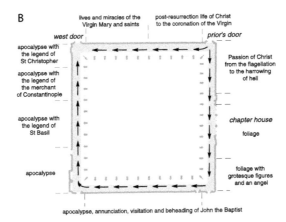

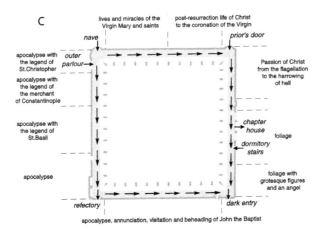

FIGURE 29. Plan of the cloister. Drawing by Margaret Mathews.

A: proposed dates of bays (inner) and vaults (outer).

B: iconography of the bosses, with arrows showing liturgical routes corresponding with sequential, biblical chronology.

C: iconography of the bosses, with arrows showing orientation of the bosses in relation to circulation routes through the cloister.

A layer of brushwood or heather backed the bricks. This method was used also in the Ethelbert gate and in the tower in the bishop's palace, presumably to serve as insulation, or to cushion the vaults when they were filled with rubble, to provide a level floor for the room above (Fernie and Whittingham 1972, 35).

The bosses

The treatment of the vaulting was unsurpassed, with the keystones that hold the ribs in place decorated with a unique series of 'historiated' bosses, dating approximately from c.1330–1430. The bosses were part of a narrative scheme in which each boss conveyed a story, or was one in a sequence of bosses telling a story. These iconographic narratives were interspersed with foliage, mythical beasts, green men, and folklore. The narrative bosses of later medieval cloisters, such as Norwich and Antwerp, are likely to have developed from the Romanesque tradition of historiated cloisters (such as Moissac, with its narrative capitals, mentioned above). The Norwich bosses represent the earliest series of historiated bosses known, and are by far the largest group to survive (Tristram 1935, 1936, 1937; James 1911; Rose 1996). Each Caen stone boss took two weeks to carve, after which it was painted vividly.[6] The completed cloister comprised forty-nine bays, with the vaulting of each bay requiring eight bosses (with two exceptions), totalling 394 bosses. The subsequent programmes of vaulting in the church developed the same technique, so that over one thousand stone roof bosses survive at Norwich cathedral, approximately seven hundred of which are historiated (Rose 1996, 363). Their significance is emphasised when compared with the next largest group of historiated bosses, a group of fifteen that survives at Tewkesbury abbey.

The earliest bosses in the cloister (in the east walk, outside the chapter house) represent foliage patterns, but as work progressed in the east walk 'storied' bosses appeared in the northern bays. These five bays were decorated with the Passion of Christ (the Flagellation, Carrying the Cross, the Crucifixion, the Resurrection and the Harrowing of Hell) (Plate 2c). In addition to the central narrative themes, there are bosses providing 'marginal' decoration, in the tradition of illuminated manuscripts. These include human, animal and hybrid figures, green men (Plate 2b), dragons and grotesques, such as the one placed over the door to the slype, depicted defecating over the entrance. The placement of such incongruous figures in a monastic setting was intended to shock: these monstrous creatures inspired reflection on temptation and spiritual deformity (Camille 1992).

The narrative bosses continued in the south walk with the Annunciation, the Visitation of Mary to Elizabeth, and the beheading of John the Baptist (Rose and Hedgecoe 1997). This walk saw the beginning of a remarkable series of bosses depicting the Apocalypse (Plate 3c), the Revelation of St John the Divine, told through

---

[6] Much of the painting visible today was restored in the 1930s by Professor E. W. Tristram, and the north walk is considered to be the best representation of the original medieval palette (Curteis and Paine 1992).

thirty-eight bosses in the south walk and sixty-four in the west walk (Rose 1999). The carver, Simon Hue, was mentioned by name in 1326–7, as chief 'gravour' of the bosses (Fernie and Whittingham 1972, 35). It is apparent that the images carved on the bosses were copied from illuminations, and in 1346–7 a history of the Apocalypse was purchased by the pitancer to serve as a guide (Fernie and Whittingham 1972, 38). Apocalypse imagery was prevalent in England from the mid thirteenth century, and the bosses in the south walk are consistent with traditional Apocalypse manuscripts (Alexander 1999). Those in the west walk deviate from orthodox imagery, and may have been inspired by more local sources, such as cycles of mystery plays (Rose and Hedgecoe 1997, 23).

Sekules has noted a number of scenes which are unique to the Norwich Apocalypse and which are not represented in the manuscript traditions. She argues that the Norwich series shows a strong concern with ecclesiastical authority and morality, perhaps reflecting the regular tension between Norwich cathedral and royal power. The west walk emphasises the themes of plague, the Whore of Babylon and the demise of earthly kings (Sekules 2004). Although idiosyncratic in its rendering of the Apocalypse, the choice of this theme at Norwich is consistent with later medieval preoccupation with the Last Judgement. Roughly contemporary Apocalypse schemes were commissioned for a number of cathedrals and Benedictine monasteries: these include wall paintings in the chapter houses at Coventry cathedral-priory, c.1360–70 (Rylatt and Mason 2003), and Westminster abbey in the 1380s (Binski 1995), and the east window glass at York minster, c.1405–8. The choice of Apocalypse imagery for Benedictine cloisters and chapter houses is significant: the chapter house, in particular, was a location imbued with values of ecclesiastic authority, discipline and the passing of judgement (Cassidy-Welch 2001).

The west walk bosses at Norwich also include the legends of St Basil, the merchant of Constantinople and St Christopher. The north walk continued the life of Christ, with thirteen post-Resurrection bosses, followed by the Death, Assumption and Coronation of the Virgin, and the lives of St John the Evangelist, St Laurence, St Martin, St Clement, St Nicholas and St Thomas of Canterbury. The bosses in the nave of the church continued this historical, sequential treatment. Reading from east to west, 250 bosses tell the history of the world in biblical terms from the Creation and Fall to the Last Judgement. The early-sixteenth-century bosses of the transepts move from the birth of St John the Baptist to Christ's ministry of healing (Rose 1996, 376).

When the bosses are considered in terms of the use of the cloister, it is clear that they were intended to be more than a visual confection, however fabulously crafted. The metaphorical meaning of the cloister was enhanced by the choice of narrative themes and their spatial relationships. In contrast with the small groups of historiated bosses at other cathedral cloisters, such as Worcester and Lincoln, the bosses at Norwich are arranged in a sequential pattern. Their placement is significant in relation to both conceptual and physical planes. They represent Christian time in a sequential manner, if not a consistently linear one, and are located to connect narrative sequences with physical movement through the cloister (see pp. 253–7). Consistent narrative sequences are ordered according to entrance points to the cloister, and particularly the doors from the north walk into the cathedral church (Figure 29B–C).

The pivotal point is the east door in the north walk, known today as 'the prior's door', which provides access from the south aisle of the nave to the cloister. The monks used this door both in the liturgy and as an access route to attend their daily offices in the church. Processions were made through the cloisters on Sundays, on all principal feasts and daily during Christmas, Easter and Pentecost. The usual route was clockwise around the cloister, finally entering the church at the west door in the north walk, making a station in front of the Rood at the nave altar, before returning to the choir by the door in the *pulpitum* (Tolhurst 1948, xxiv–v). Three canopied niches are located in the east cloister walk, to the south of the 'prior's door'. These served as *sedilia*, seats reserved for priests, and were usually sited in church chancels. Their position in the cloister suggests that the monks sometimes began their processions in the east walk, waiting at the 'prior's door' to commence. The east walk was also the route used by the monks to attend the night services in the church; they left the dormitory using the night stairs, and travelled northward through the east walk to enter the church through the 'prior's door'.[7] It is important to note that the bosses depicting the Passion read narratively from north to south, in a sequence moving southward from the church into the cloister. This suggests that their placement was guided principally by the formal liturgical use of the cloister, rather than for the routine passage of individual monks from the dormitory to the church.

A clockwise procession of the cloister would begin with the Passion of Christ, and move through the extended Apocalypse cycle, surveying the Judgement and ending with the siege of the Holy City, before re-entering the church through the west door in the north walk. The Apocalypse bosses are carefully orchestrated to lead the narrative back into the cathedral church: the church completes the Apocalypse cycle, representing the emergence of heavenly Jerusalem. The bosses in the north walk of the cloister also read narratively from the 'prior's door', moving westward. They resume the story that had been begun in the east walk by bosses carved several decades earlier. These show the events of Christ's life after the Resurrection, and proceed towards the life of the Virgin. Such images were particularly appropriate to the north walk, since Marian iconography and the Easter liturgy were associated with the northern regions of churches. At the cathedral church of Winchester, for example, the Holy Sepulchre chapel is in the north transept (Park 1987), and at Ely, the Lady chapel formed a northern extension to the cathedral church. From

---

[7] This route is suggested by a passage in the *Life of St William of Norwich*, which described events on the night following the translation of William's body from the chapter house to the church. The sacrist, 'who was sleeping as usual in the Church, got up in order to rouse the brethren in the dormitory at the hour of matins, as was customary' (Jessopp and James 1896, 187). Having reached the chapter house, he heard 'a terrible sound' and sat transfixed until 'the servants of the Church came after a while to set the lamps in the cloister'.

the iconography of the bosses, such as the three Marys at the Sepulchre (Plate 3B), it may be suggested that the north cloister walk would have been central to processions connected with the Easter liturgy. The cloister at Wells cathedral was also significant in Easter rites: the cloister garth was known as the Palm Churchyard (Rodwell 2001, 316), suggesting a link with the liturgy for Palm Sunday. This connection is evident also for Cistercian cloisters, in which the culmination of the liturgy for Palm Sunday took place in the north cloister walk (Cassidy-Welch 2001, 59).

The sculpture of the 'prior's door' itself complements the adjoining bosses that show the life of Christ in the east and north walks. At the apex of the door is Christ in majesty, displaying his five wounds, and flanked by the instruments of his Passion. Additional figures flank the door, contained in alternating triangular and ogeed canopies (Figure 30). The door has been described as one of the finest examples of English carving of its date, and is judged to be contemporary with the east walk bosses, and by the same mason (Sekules 1996, 199). Other thresholds were emphasised through the imagery of the bosses. The temptation of Adam and Eve forms the keystone over the door to the refectory in the south walk (Plate 3A) (Rose 1996, 367). This theme may have been intended as a daily enjoinder against the sin of gluttony, and is paralleled in other monastic contexts, such as the carved serpent over the door to the refectory at the nunnery of Sinningthwaite (N Yorkshire) (Gilchrist 1994, 155).

Although the bosses were positioned to create a narrative sequence that coincided with the clockwise, liturgical use of the cloister, their orientation would not have enabled easy viewing throughout the route. The height of the vaults allows the iconography to be discerned clearly enough, and the individual bosses face in a single direction in each cloister walk, so that they can be read in sequence. However, the bosses are not all arranged so that they can be viewed during the clockwise procession of the cloister. Those in the east walk are arranged in this manner, placed in relation to the 'prior's door', but those in the north walk are aligned for viewing from the door into the nave (in the west cloister walk). This door also serves as the starting point for viewing the Apocalypse cycle, in an anticlockwise perambulation of the west and south cloister walks.

While the bosses were ordered in a sequence that coincided with biblical chronology and the liturgical use of the cloister, they were orientated to permit careful viewing during daily use of the cloister. The bosses were intended to stimulate memory and spiritual meditation, and they were aligned for convenient study during routine use of the cloister. Those in the east walk were seen by the monks on their daily route from the church to the chapter house and dormitory stairs. Those in the north walk were studied from the monks' carrels, or during the periods that they were permitted to walk and talk in the cloister. Those in the west and south walks are arranged to be read beginning from the north-west corner of the cloister, which contains the door from the outer parlour (see p. 132) and from the nave. Any secular visitors to the cloister would have entered through one of these doors, and the orientation of the bosses suggests that they were positioned to enable

FIGURE 30. Fourteenth-century ceremonial door in the north-east corner of the cloister (the 'prior's door'), with Christ in majesty. Photograph © Roberta Gilchrist.

secular visitors to appreciate their narrative message. The Apocalypse cycle began in the bay containing the door to the dark entry, and was completed in the bay that contains both the door to the outer parlour and the nave. The Apocalypse cycle may have been commissioned partly for the visiting laity: the prestigious visitors and benefactors who were welcomed in the outer parlour and received in the chapter house, and the relatives of ailing monks who visited them in the infirmary, exiting the cloister at the dark entry.

Book cupboards
Cupboards for storing books (*armaria*) are still visible in the east and south cloister walks, contained within the thickness of the outer wall. These occur singly or in

groups of two, three or four per bay. Two in the east walk retain wooden doors, and one in the south walk was reopened in 2002; a further seventeen blocked openings are visible. The cupboard in the south walk was reopened as part of a conservation programme to the cloisters, located in the third bay from the east. The cupboard provides an aperture 1.2m high, 0.6m wide and 0.6m deep, formed of rendered brick with a timber ceiling, and with slots for shelves (Thomas 2002) (Figure 31). The profile of the arch is consistent with a fourteenth-century date, and the accounts of the pitancer record work to the cloister cupboards in 1329–30 (DCN 1/12/18). This particular cupboard was made as part of the rebuilding of the cloister, but others were simply refaced. An example in the western end of the south walk was unblocked in 1993, and still possessed a Romanesque arch (*Medieval Archaeol* 39 (1993), 275).

0   Metre   1

FIGURE 31. Book cupboard in the south walk of the cloister. Drawing by Philip Thomas, Cathedral Survey Services. © Chapter of Norwich Cathedral.

The identification of at least twenty book cupboards confirms that the cloister at Norwich was used for reading and study, in common with those of other monasteries. The *Rites of Durham* recorded that the cloisters there contained 'great almeries or cupboards of waynscott all full of bookes' (Fowler 1902, 83). The specific functions of the north walk at Norwich are not clear, although this would have been the warmest of the cloister walks, receiving the most sunlight. For this reason it may have been used for the talking permitted on weekdays (Tolhurst 1948), or as a study space provided with carrels. Evidence for carrels constructed in wainscot or stone survives at Durham, Chester and Gloucester. The north walk at Durham retains peg marks indicating the locations of either former carrels or the wainscot book cupboards described in the *Rites of Durham* (Williamson 1983, 201). At Gloucester, the south walk is likely to have been shut off by screens. There were ten windows provided towards the cloister garth, but below the transom the lights were replaced by twenty little recesses or carrels. Each carrel was lit by a small, two-light window and was set beneath a segmental arch with a richly decorated cornice above (Verey and Brooks 2002, 428).

The lavatorium

The two southern bays of the west cloister walk at Norwich contained the *laver* or *lavatorium*, the ritual washing-place that was located outside the monks' door to the refectory. The monks washed their hands here before and after every meal, in reference to Christ's washing of the disciples' feet before the Last Supper. An additional rite was carried out weekly at the *lavatorium*, the *mandatum fratrum*, the ritual washing of the feet. This was interpreted as a spiritual cleansing of the soul, a re-enactment of the *Vita apostolica* that transformed the cloister into a biblical space (Fergusson 1986, 178; Cassidy-Welch 2001, 63). In Cistercian and Benedictine monasteries, foot washing on Saturdays and Maundy Thursday remained a solemn ritual throughout the Middle Ages (Harvey 1993, 129). In English monasteries, the *lavatorium* most often took the form of a recessed trough in the wall of the cloister, supplied by water tapped from a central supply (Godfrey 1952, 91). Occasionally, they were freestanding structures placed in the centre of the cloister garth.[8]

The *lavatorium* at Norwich is a recessed trough set into arched niches in the west wall of the cloister (Figure 32), made by the masons James and John Woderofe in 1443–4 (Woodman 1996, 174). Each of the two bays has three vaulted niches, which are now occupied by statues of recent monarchs.[9] This feature was constructed after the main work on the cloisters was completed, and replaced an earlier *lavatorium* in the same location. The rolls of the pitancer provide further insight into the use of this area, recording that in 1420–1, work was carried out 'from where

---

[8] This arrangement was more common in Cistercian houses in Spain and Portugal, and in Britain was more closely associated with the Cluniacs (for example at Much Wenlock, Shropshire, but occurring also at the monastic cathedral of Durham).

[9] Sculptures by Gilbert Ledward of King George VI and Queen Elizabeth and of King George V and Queen Mary were added as part of the conservation and refurbishment of the cloisters in 1935.

FIGURE 32. The fifteenth-century *lavatorium*, located in the two southern bays of the west walk of the cloister, adjacent to the refectory door. Photograph © Roberta Gilchrist.

the towels hang, with the door of the refectory, and the lavatories, and the door of the guest-hall' (Fernie and Whittingham 1972, 41). The three bays to the east of the refectory door were not provided with book cupboards, but instead were used to hang towels (*manutergia*) for the monks to dry their hands after washing at the *lavatorium*. This daily ritual is elaborated in the *Rites of Durham*. The monks were called to meals by a bell hung next to the *laver*, which was rung 'to geve warning, and at leave of ye clock, for ye mouncks to come wash and dyne, having ther closetts or almeries on either syde of ye frater house dour keapt alwaies with swete and clene towels . . . to drie ther hands' (Fowler 1902, 82).

The *lavatorium* was a ritual space bound up with monastic ideas of purity and spiritual cleansing. Its symbolic significance necessitated the supply of the cleanest possible water. A remarkable plan survives from Christ Church, Canterbury, showing the water supply during the priorate of Wibert (1153–67) (Willis 1868). The plan reveals that the water travelled first to the *lavatoria* of the infirmary cloister and main cloister, supplying them with the purest water, before servicing the remaining buildings. Excavations on the site of the refectory at Norwich recovered evidence for the nature of the water supply to the *lavatorium*. A section of lead pipe with a diameter of 90mm was excavated from a linear feature at the west end of refectory. This was a stratified artefact from a medieval deposit (Wallis 2002a, 19), and represents the only evidence at Norwich cathedral of a piped medieval water supply. The location of the pipe suggests that it may have been an offshoot from the culverted supply to the infirmary (p. 37). The pipe is likely to have fed a lead tank beneath the *lavatorium*, with water supplied to the basin by taps or spigots, comparable to the *lavatorium* at Gloucester.[10]

THE MONASTIC AND LAY CEMETERIES

In common with many monasteries, Norwich cathedral-priory was provided with separate cemeteries for the monks and the laity. While most monasteries located their main cemetery to the north of the church, opposite the monastic cloister, at Norwich this situation was occupied by the bishop's palace (Figure 7). Its position neatly segregated the two cemeteries, but severely restricted the area available for burial. The lay cemetery was located to the north-west of the cathedral church, adjacent to the main western door, while the monastic cemetery occupied space directly to the east and south-east of the cathedral church. Both cemeteries hosted the cells of anchorites, and the lay cemetery became the location of a chantry college and charnel chapel. The monks' cemetery contained the office of the sacrist, revealing his close connection with rites of burial. Both the cemeteries of the monks and laity were further reduced by later medieval developments, creating greater pressure on burial space. The monks' cemetery was encroached upon from the mid thirteenth century by the buildings associated with the prior's lodging. Additional chapels were added projecting from the ambulatory of the presbytery, and the Lady chapel was extended from the eastern end in the mid thirteenth century.

The size of the lay cemetery was halved with the creation of the college of St John the Evangelist in 1316, located to the north-west of the cathedral church. This choice for the location of the chantry college may indicate that burial space was not in great demand. Servants of the priory are likely to have been buried in the churchyard of St Mary in the Marsh, while the wealthiest lay people would have sought burial inside the cathedral church. This impression is supported by Norman Tanner's study of over 1500 wills from Norwich, dating 1370–1532. Only six lay people (0.5%) requested burial in the cathedral church or its cemetery. In contrast, almost five per cent of the total number of clerical will-makers, including secular priests, requested burial here (Tanner 1996, 278). This evidence suggests that the sympathies of the townspeople were directed more towards the city's large number of parish churches, and in particular towards the church of St Peter Mancroft, which served, in effect, as the merchants' cathedral. The cathedral was a late addition to the network of parochial churches in the city, and lost further ground to the friaries. The mendicants were highly successful in attracting lay burials in Norwich, and were able to procure papal indulgences on behalf of every person interred within specified cloisters. The Norwich Franciscans' cloister was known as the Pardon cloister,

---

[10] An elaborate fan-vaulted structure survives in the north walk at Gloucester, and projecting into the garth. It is a broad stone ledge with a trough, and originally was provided with a lead tank of water tapped by spigots, at which the monks washed. It also retains associated features, such as a trefoil-headed opening for the summoning bell, and a two-bay recess (opposite the *laver*) where the towels were hung.

and that of the Augustinian friars was termed the *scala caeli* (the ladder to heaven). Competition between the cathedral and friaries was fierce, and in 1379 the cathedral demanded one quarter of all the friars' burial payments (Simpkins 1906, 237).

In contrast, most citizens of Winchester were buried in the cemetery of the cathedral church until the sixteenth century, despite the existence of fifty parish churches in the medieval city (Greatrex 1993, 156). Several cathedrals or abbeys in the west of England served as the sole or major burial ground for their city's dead, notably Exeter, Hereford, Gloucester and Worcester (Orme 1991, 162; Barrow 1992, 81–8). This monopoly over the burial of the dead is demonstrated tangibly by the great density of plague burials recovered from excavations near the west front at Hereford cathedral (Stone and Appleton-Fox 1996). Similarly, investigation of an area only 30m square within Worcester's lay cemetery yielded a mass of skeletal remains representing between 85 and 200 individuals (Guy 1994, 2).

Burial of high-ranking clergy and laity would also have taken place beneath the floor of the cathedral church, and perhaps also in the chapter house, as occurred at other monasteries. Excavations in the chapter house at Durham revealed a series of bishops' burials (Fowler 1880), while at Norwich episcopal burials were concentrated in the church (p. 146). The chapter house was sometimes used for the burial of children associated with a monastery (Gilchrist and Sloane 2005), for example at Oxford Blackfriars (Lambrick 1985). At Norwich, this practice is suggested by the twelfth-century *Life of St William*. For a time, William was buried in the chapter house, where a light was fixed on his tomb. The description of digging his grave in the chapter house suggests that by the mid twelfth century the space had already been well used:

> A grave was dug in the cemetery just under the wall of the chapter-house where the body might be entombed in a wooden coffin. But while they were digging, strange to tell, a sarcophagus was actually found there resting upon another; and both one and the other was clean and pure within, because evidently never had any dead man's corpse been laid therein (Jessopp and James 1896, 53).

The hierarchy of burial spaces at Norwich is clearly indicated in the *Life of St William*, which describes how the twelve-year-old boy's corpse was moved on four occasions during the ten years after his death (Shinners 1988). After discovery of his remains in Thorpe Wood in 1144, they were transferred rapidly to the monks' cemetery, 'the sepulchre having been decently prepared at the entrance of the cemetery on the cloister side' (Jessopp and James 1896, 54). By 1150, a cult had begun to develop around this doubtful saint, and his body was translated to the position under the chapter house, evidently a space of greater sanctity. In 1151, a tomb was created to the south of the high altar, where pilgrims could visit William's remains in a progress of the ambulatory. By 1154, these pious visitors were disrupting the offices of the monks in the presbytery, and William's tomb was relocated to the chapel of St Stephen and the Holy Martyrs, to the north of the ambulatory (now the Jesus chapel). Finally, in the fifteenth century, it was moved to a position near the *pulpitum*, and is likely to have been the focus of a series of episcopal and clerical burials that were excavated on this site in 1899 (St John Hope 1899; St John Hope and Bensly 1901, 113).

The monks' cemetery

The position of the monks' cemetery is confirmed in the cathedral's *Customary*, which describes the route of the procession on Palm Sunday as moving from the bishop's chapel to the cloister, through the cemetery (Tolhurst 1948, 77). Such processions connected the monks' cemetery with the liturgical spaces of the monastery, and integrated the living and dead monks as a single monastic community. This rite is described in a passage of the late twelfth-century *Life of St William*, in which the monks' cemetery is described as the 'inner cemetery' (*cimiterio interiori*).

> As is usual with the service of the dead, having been finished, the glorious martyr was taken into the inner cemetery to be laid in his tomb, the whole convent of the brethren going before him in a procession with psalms and praises (Jessopp and James 1896, 54).

Monastic cemeteries commonly occupied a space to the east and north/south of the presbytery (depending on the location of the cloister), such as the 'centorie garth' at Durham cathedral-priory (Fowler 1902, 87). In some cases, the monks' cemetery was divided from the lay cemetery by a wall: at the cathedral-priory of Christ Church, Canterbury, this arrangement was depicted on Prior Wibert's plan of the water supply (c.1165), and the footings of the wall have been excavated (Driver et al. 1990, 95–7). Burial arrangements at secular cathedrals introduced measures for the segregation of religious personnel of different ranks, in addition to the distinction drawn with the laity. At Salisbury, the canons are likely to have been buried in a small walled area called 'Paradise', to the east and south of the church, while the priests of the vicars choral were buried in a graveyard to the north and west of the cathedral (Cocke and Kidson 1993, 8). At Wells cathedral, an act of chapter dating from 1243 carefully delineated zones of burial: canons were to be interred in the cloister to the south of the church, priests in the cemetery to the east of the Lady chapel (which projected eastward from the east cloister walk), and laity in the western cemetery; dignitaries could be buried in the cathedral nave (St John Hope 1910, 233–4).

Archaeological evidence for burial in the monks' cemetery at Norwich is limited to the recording of disarticulated human remains to the north-east of the cathedral church, observed during the excavation of service trenches in this area. The date of the associated inhumations is unknown, but the only burial to have been excavated *in situ* was post-medieval (Warsop and Boghi 2002). Burials excavated to the west of the north transept have been interpreted as pre-dating the cathedral, and are thought to have been associated with the Saxon parish church of Holy Trinity (Bown 1997).

The monastic cloister alleys were also employed for occasional burials of patrons: for example, Walter de Berney, a patron of the rebuilding of the cloister, was buried here in 1379 (Blomefield 1745 [1806], 38). It seems unlikely that the cloister garth was used for burial in the Middle Ages. By the fifteenth century, it was a tended lawn rather than a formal paradise garden, a form documented at some monasteries (Noble 1997, 14; Noble 2000). At Norwich, the position of the garden that was reserved for spiritual meditation is more likely to have been adjacent to the Lady chapel (ibid.), and therefore within the monks' cemetery. In the late eighteenth century, a great number of burials of unknown date were cleared from the cloister garth, most likely associated with its use for post-medieval burial by the parish of St Mary in the Marsh. In 1782, Dean Lloyd used the material from the cloister graveyard to level the green in the Lower Close, earning this space the grim sobriquet 'Skeleton Square' (Bolingbroke 1922, 34).

Management of the cemeteries is likely to have fallen to the sacrist, although the Norwich obediential rolls are silent on this matter. The customary from the abbey of St Augustine's, Canterbury (c.1330–40), records that the sacristan held the responsibility of determining who should be buried in the monks' cemetery, and ensuring that no earlier graves were disturbed by new inhumations (Sherlock and Woods 1988, 4 n. 2). Graves are likely to have been dug by servants of the priory, although the *Life of St William* states that William's grave in the chapter house was 'made ready by stone masons and plasterers' (Jessopp and James 1896, 123). These specialist labourers may have been required specifically for an interior grave that employed a stone coffin. It was customary for the infirmarer to prepare monastic corpses before their burial, and in 1347, the Norwich infirmarer purchased a hair cloth (*cilicio*) for the wrapping of a dead brother (Saunders 1930, 132). The use of hides as shrouds was relatively common among monastics from the eleventh to the thirteenth centuries, but the Norwich example is relatively late. This practice may have carried the connotations of religious penitence (in the manner of a hair-shirt), or it may have been intended to help in preserving the body (Gilchrist and Sloane 2005).

Anchorites' cells

In the fifteenth century, new chapels were created in the angle between the south transept and the eastern arm of the cathedral church, within the area of the monks' cemetery. There is evidence to suggest that this space contained an anchorite's cell, although no medieval documents survive to corroborate this proposal. Robert Willis reported that an anchorage was uncovered in this position in 1847, with an opening into the church protected by a grate, enabling the occupant to see the high altar (Stewart 1875, 183–4).[11] The grate was described some years later as an old oak window frame, measuring two feet square, with iron bars (Clay 1914, 79, n. 3). The cell was lost in 1957, when the architect Bernard Feilden established the new vestry

---

[11] Stewart (1875, 184) recorded that the grate was given to the Norwich Museum.

and chapter room on this site. He recorded that a small circular feature in the south aisle wall was destroyed (Feilden 1996, 738). Although he identified it as a prison cell, the feature corresponds with that interpreted by Willis as an anchorhold.

The siting of the circular cell, and the provision of a squint protected by a grate, support its identification as an anchorhold. A second anchorite's cell at Norwich cathedral is documented in the refectorer's rolls for 1305, which refer to 5d rent from the 'house of the Anchoress'. In the same year, 2d was spent on carting timber from her house and carting the walls of her house 'outside the churchyard' (Saunders 1930, 142–3). Although the precise location of the anchoress's cell is unknown, the description suggests a freestanding structure adjacent to the lay cemetery. It may be suggested therefore, that two cells existed in the cemeteries of the cathedral-priory, one attached to the south of the presbytery, and the other at the west end of the church. A third anchorhold existed in the parish churchyard of St Helen (on Holme Street, p. 32), which was within the precinct until c.1270 (Rawcliffe 1999, 49).

Anchorites were religious men or women who took vows to remain permanently enclosed and solitary. Their cells were attached to monastic or parish churches, usually positioned to the north or south of the chancel, with a hatch or squint through which to view the elevation of the Host at the high altar (Gilchrist 1995, 185). Anchorites' cells are known to have existed at the cathedral churches of Worcester, Durham and Chichester, all in different spatial locations in relation to the church. According to the *Rites of Durham*, there was an anchorite's cell at the east end of the north alley of the choir, and at Chichester a cell communicated with the Lady chapel at the east end. Worcester's cell was placed to the north-west of the church and was located in the cemetery, referred to in the fifteenth century as the 'anckras house by ye charnel howse' (Clay 1914, 80–81).

From the fourteenth to the sixteenth centuries, anchorites were most popularly supported in the eastern counties of England (Warren 1985, 36), and Norwich demonstrated a particular regard for the anchoritic vocation, supporting at least forty-seven anchorites at parish churches and religious houses between 1370 and 1549 (Tanner 1984, 58).[12] Siting of the anchorhold in the cemetery, as at Norwich and Worcester cathedral-priories, signalled the withdrawal of its occupant from the living world to that of the desert of the early Christian hermits. Anchorites inhabited a liminal plane between the living and the dead: to be immured in a cell represented a symbolic death and entombment with Christ. The vocation of the anchorite was highly esteemed, and the presence of a holy man or woman brought great prestige to any church. Norwich Blackfriars sponsored a cell for female anchorites from the late fifteenth century up to the 1530s, and evidence of the cell can still be seen to the north of the friars' chancel (Gilchrist 1995, 184). Competition

---

[12] More recent research has identified thirty-nine documented anchoresses supported at monastic and parish churches in Norwich from the eleventh century to the Reformation (Gilchrist and Oliva 1993, 97–9); the example from Norwich cathedral brings the total to forty.

with the Dominicans had prompted the cathedral to erect a preaching cross in the lay cemetery by the fifteenth century (discussed below). This rivalry, in addition to the broad local support for anchorites (Gilchrist and Oliva 1993, 75), may have stimulated the desire to sponsor anchorites' cells within the monks' cemetery and near the lay cemetery.

The sacrist's office (the sextry)

In addition to the management of the cemeteries, the sacrist had responsibility for the overall maintenance of the cathedral church, and the sacristy or sextry was positioned to facilitate both of these major roles. The sacrist funded repair and replacement of church fabric, regular cleaning, the care of sacred vessels and vestments, and the provision of candles and mats. An average of £50 was spent each year on consumables for the cathedral church, including £30 in wax for candles (10–12 hundredweight), incense and herbs, oil for lamps, wine and rushes to be strewn in the church for the feasts of Easter, Pentecost and the Nativity (Saunders 1930, 105–6).

The sextry was located to the east of the cathedral church, and controlled a minor gate into the precinct from Bishopgate (DCN 1/4/59). The gate became known as the sextry gate, and the monks' cemetery as the sextry yard. An inventory compiled by the sacrist in 1436 suggests that his office comprised a hall, cellar and upper and lower chamber, in addition to separate small rooms over the cloister, in which armour was stored (DCN 1/4/76). This accommodation was comparable to the sacrist's dwelling at Worcester cathedral-priory, which was attached to the north side of the choir. This included a kitchen and dining hall, but also accommodation for guests and employees (Greatrex 1998, 14). At Ely, the sacrist also controlled a main gate into the precinct (Holton-Krayenbuhl et al. 1989), where a commercial zone developed. The Norwich sacrist developed a more commercial zone of shops at the Erpingham gate, in the upper inner court (see p. 189).

The remains of the medieval sextry survive in Numbers 59–60 (Figure 33). The north–south running range of this L-shaped building was the medieval sextry, against which an east–west range was built, possibly in the sixteenth century. This complex was connected to the sextry gate between the precinct and St Giles' hospital. This is described in a lease of 1570 between the chapter and Isabel Gardiner, as 'the gate leading to the hospital . . . with the two towers' (DCN 47/1). A number of service buildings and workshops were located in the sextry yard, including: a specialised bakehouse for the baking of communion wafers, two waxhouses for candles, a leadhouse and glasshouse for the making and repair of windows, and a carpenters' house and lodge (DCN 1/4/76). Floor surfaces possibly associated with the sextry or its workshops were recorded during an archaeological watching brief to the west of Numbers 59–60. These comprised two successive mortar floors, the upper of which extended for at least 7.3 metres north–south, and contained small tile fragments (Warsop and Boghi 2002, 4). From the same approximate area, three offcuts of ivory waste were recovered (ibid., 5), perhaps indicating production or repair of church artefacts. The monastic leadhouse, or plumbery, was the location

FIGURE 33. The remains of the sacrist's office (the sextry), located to the east of the cathedral church and surviving in Numbers 59–60. Photograph © Roberta Gilchrist.

for storing and working lead for the roofs of the monastic buildings, and cames for forming their stained glass windows. This structure survived until c.1640; its approximate location is therefore well established on the basis of post-medieval leases (DCN 47/1–2), coinciding with that of the Victorian house at Number 57. Further workshops may have been located to the north of the church: substantial quantities of limestone waste were excavated to the west of the north transept, and were interpreted as a masons' yard (Bown 1998).

The lay cemetery and the Carnary college
There is no archaeological evidence at Norwich from which to estimate the density of burial in the lay cemetery. The use of this space for interments is confirmed by Bishop Salmon's foundation of the Carnary college in 1316, 'in the west part of the cathedral cemetery' (Calendar of Patent Rolls 1313–17, 525; Saunders 1932a).[13] The lay cemetery was also used for a number of purposes other than burial, including occasional markets and fairs (p. 189), and from the fifteenth century, for the delivery of out-door sermons. The area between the Carnary college and the bishop's palace became known as green yard, a preaching space developed in an attempt to

[13] We also have the oral testimony of former boys of the Norwich School, some of whom recall inhumations being disturbed in 1939, when air-raid shelters were dug on the site of the present play ground of the school (*Old Norvicensian News,* March 2002, 21–2).

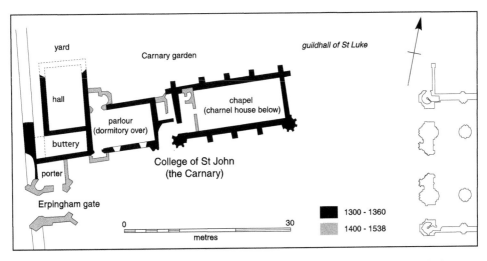

FIGURE 34. Plan of the Carnary college, founded 1316 by Bishop Salmon (including approximate location of the guildhall of St Luke). Drawing by Margaret Mathews.

counter the growing influence of the city's friaries (Dodwell 1996b, 247). Green yard became a preaching area with a permanently constructed pulpit and seats for civic dignitaries, from as early as 1469. The intensity of commercial and evangelical activity in this place would not have precluded its continued use for burial.

To the north of the Erpingham gate into the precinct are the buildings of the college of St John the Evangelist, the chantry foundation established by Bishop Salmon in 1316, and known colloquially as 'Le Charnel' only decades after its foundation (Cattermole in prep.) (Figure 34). Facilities for the storage of charnel[14] developed from the thirteenth century, and were provided in the cemeteries of several English cathedrals: to the north of the church at Worcester, Durham and St Paul's, and to the west of the church at Norwich, Exeter and Winchester. In common with Norwich, the charnel chapels at Exeter and Worcester were episcopal foundations (Orme 1991). In contrast with these cathedrals, however, Norwich was never the major burial ground for the city's dead. The intensity of use at Exeter was revealed when the three metre crypt was excavated, uncovering a dense mass of bones approximately one metre deep, sorted into groups of arms, legs and skulls (Henderson and Bidwell 1982).

Chantry colleges such as the Carnary were established after c.1300, staffed by secular priests who offered masses for the souls of their patrons, and lived communally, sharing a hall, parlour and dormitory. The Carnary's close proximity to the cemetery was confirmed when Salmon increased the chantry to six priests in 1322, describing the priests as 'dwelling within the boundary of the cathedral cemetery'

---

[14] Nicholas Orme has suggested that the term charnel derives from the Latin *carnarium*, from *caro*, meaning flesh. It originally referred to a flesh-hook or larder, but in medieval usage meant a mass grave. The adjectival form 'carnary' was in use from the fourteenth century (Orme 1991, 169, n. 2).

(Saunders 1932a, 50–61). The college was contained in a separate enclosure within the corner of the cemetery, as indicated by the sacrist's account for 1471–2. A mason was paid for repairing the northern wall of the Carnary garden, and for 'cresting the same wall and the other wall between the green yard and the same garden' (DCN 1/4/93). The charnel vault beneath the chapel was administered directly by the sacrist, and he received a large share of the offerings made in the upper chapel.

The college of St John developed very distinct educational and professional associations. By the early fifteenth century, the chantry chaplains were teaching boys of the cathedral school (DCN 1/4/78). From 1389, there are records of the brotherhood or guild of barber-surgeons meeting in the chapel (Toulmin Smith 1870, 27). At Exeter and St Paul's cathedrals, the charnel chapels were adopted by the skinners' guilds for their religious celebrations. Nicholas Orme has suggested that the link possessed 'a certain grim aptness' since the skinners worked with carcasses and bones (1991, 166). Given their familiarity with human subjects, the Norwich barber-surgeons shared a more gruesome affinity with the charnel chapel.[15] By the late fifteenth century the college had become a lodging house for court officials. The Carnary college became an inn of court, providing accommodation near the consistory court, likely to have been held in the bishop's chapel.[16] A chained law library was established, after Bishop Goldwell bequeathed books in his will dated 1498 'for the use of those who are working on precedents, pleas and other things to study at will' (Blomefield 1745 [1805], 541).

By the fifteenth century, the area between the Carnary college and the bishop's palace was used for preaching. Pulpits were established near the charnel chapels at St Paul's and Exeter cathedrals, and at Worcester the charnel chapel was used for a library and theology lectures (Orme 1991, 168–9). The closest parallel to Norwich is the charnel chapel at the Augustinian hospital-priory of St Mary Spital, London, where an adjacent open-air pulpit was provided alongside an elaborate two-storey gallery. These associations confirm that medieval cemeteries were highly public places, appropriate for large assemblies. The Norwich green yard also accommodated the guild hall of St Luke, referred to in post-medieval leases as St Luke's House. From a lease of ground to John Baret in 1544, it can be suggested that this structure was located just to the north of Number 69. In 1552, a lease of St Luke's house to Thomas Thurleby suggested that 'a grammar school was lately kept' there (DCN 47/1), thus locating the school of the Carnary college.

The remains of the college are well preserved, and include the Carnary chapel, raised over an undercroft, and a domestic range linked to the west. Later medieval chantry colleges were generally arranged around one or more quadrangles

---

[15] The Norwich skinners had a particularly close association with the cathedral, founded in 1376 and dedicated to the Trinity, the Virgin and 'seynt William ye holy Innocent and digne marter' (Shinners 1988, 136). William, the reputed boy-saint, had been an apprentice skinner and was buried in the cathedral, but there is no evidence connecting the guild of skinners to the Carnary chapel.

[16] Following destruction of the bishop's chapel, the consistory court was moved to the Bauchon chapel of the cathedral church (Bensly 1908).

(Cook 1959), but the domestic accommodation of the Carnary college formed an L-shaped plan. It is distinctive also from the more usual linear plan of small colleges, such as Thompson (Norfolk) where a hall with attached parlour and services was located approximately 400m away from the parish church to which the college was attached (Whittingham 1980e). Observations have been made by Paul Cattermole during alterations to the Carnary complex over the last thirty years, during its use by the Norwich School.

The two-storey domestic range of the college is contained in Number 70, and indicates two major phases of medieval construction. The original range was a ground-floor hall, aligned north–south and built into the precinct wall. This was later remodelled as a partially two-storey building, with a first-floor chamber placed over the buttery and pantry at the south end, the east and west windows enlarged, and a gallery inserted over the upper (north) end of the hall. The hall was open to the roof, and fragmentary remains survive of the tracery from the window on its east side (Figure 35). This range is likely to have served as a refectory. The gallery

FIGURE 35. Remains of a traceried window in Number 70, formerly an open hall within the domestic range of the Carnary college. Photograph © Roberta Gilchrist.

over the hall led to the upper floor of new domestic quarters in a projecting wing, added eastwards to abut the chapel. The lower floor of the new wing was a parlour. This remodelled building produced the L-shaped plan, with a passage between the two wings. The hall was located on the west side of the passage, with the service rooms and a porter's lodge to the south, against the front (south) wall of the building. The communicating doorways associated with the screens passage and service rooms still survive as blocked features. The parlour was situated to the east of the cross-passage and extended to the west wall of the chapel. Surviving inventories of the college suggest that major refurbishment took place in the last decades of the fifteenth century (Cattermole in prep.). The college had its own gateway through the precinct wall, which was reorganised to connect with the Erpingham gate (c. 1420), with direct communication in its north wall.

Excavations on the site of the Carnary in 1975 uncovered the northern end of the hall, dating from the first phase of the college buildings, together with yard surfaces and rubbish pits. There was also evidence of a possible eleventh- or twelfth-century hall, suggested by post-holes and pits, indicating that earlier structures had existed in this corner of the cemetery (Norfolk SMR No. 280; *Medieval Archaeol* 20 (1976), 167, 191; Atkin and Evans 2002, 45–50).

The Carnary chapel was at first freestanding, but has been encroached upon to the east and west (Figure 36). The chapel itself is a lofty and well-lit structure raised over a basement, an undercroft lit by circular windows, and had a bell turret at the

FIGURE 36. The Carnary chapel, shown in relation to Number 70 (left) and the Erpingham gate. The circular windows to the undercroft enabled visitors to view the charnel remains in the crypt, and give the visual impression of a reliquary. Photograph © Roberta Gilchrist.

north-west angle. The crypt of the chapel was used principally for storage of charnel, but from 1421–76 was also the location of the Wodehous chantry, established
by Henry v at the request of the Agincourt veteran, John Wodehous (Cattermole in
prep.; Sims 1996, 455). Scars in the fabric indicate that the west wall of the crypt also
possessed a window, sited at what is now the internal door to the undercroft. This
window was blocked and a door inserted into the upper chapel, with access via stairs
covered by a pentice roof, the straight scar of which is still visible in the west wall. A
new stair turret was constructed against the west wall, reusing two piers from the
previous phase. A porch was added to the chapel, and a new domestic range was added
to the west c. 1480, causing the west window of the chapel to be blocked. The chapel
retains the oldest roof in the close, a trussed rafter construction likely to be original
to the foundation of 1316. It possesses fine windows and mouldings, attributed by
Whittingham to the masons John Ramsey and William Ramsey Snr (Whittingham
1980b, 361–2). The porch retains an early fourteenth-century door, and is known
as the Lyhart porch, displaying the rebus of Bishop Walter Lyhart in the central boss.

Eric Fernie has suggested that the form of the Carnary chapel places it firmly
within the tradition of palatial architecture (1993, 182). He proposes that its lineage stems from two-storey chapels including Charlemagne's palace chapel at Aachen
(c. 800), the late eleventh-century bishop's palace at Hereford, and thirteenth-
century chapels at Sainte-Chapelle, Paris (1240s), and St Stephen's in the palace of
Westminster (1292).[17] It is proposed here that the Carnary chapel at Norwich was
influenced instead by the visual culture of medieval death, and that its architecture
possessed an additional iconographic meaning connected with its purpose as a repository for charnel. It is significant that the circular windows to the undercroft of
the Carnary chapel allowed visitors to the precinct to peer into the crypt, in order
to view the charnel remains. This arrangement was in keeping with contemporary
traditions for shrines and reliquaries, in which the physical remains of saints could
be glimpsed (see pp. 250–51).

Not only did the form of Salmon's chapel draw from imperial imagery, it in-
voked the cult of saints' relics, and promoted dialogues between the living and the
dead. Salmon may have intended its design to strengthen the cathedral's position in
attracting intercessory prayers, since it lacked a prominent saint's shrine and failed
to win the burials of prosperous townspeople. By collecting the displaced bones
from the city's parish churchyards, Bishop Salmon was forcing the citizens of Norwich to visit the cathedral regularly in order to commemorate their ancestors. The
establishment of the charnel chapel, together with the preaching yard, the anchorites' cells and the cloister rich with Apocalyptic meaning, was part of a considered
strategy to combat the cathedral's mendicant competitors, and to regain the loyalty
of the local laity.

---

[17] M. W. Thompson has noted the frequency with which two-storey chapels occur in association
with bishops' palaces, suggesting that the lower level may have been intended for housing relics (Thompson 1998, 65), instead of the charnel stored at Norwich.

5

The Conventual Ranges: Community, Hierarchy and Hospitality

THE ranges flanking the cloister to the east, south and west, provided domestic accommodation for the monks and their visitors. Beyond their utilitarian purposes, these buildings possessed symbolic meanings that were articulated through their architecture. The dormitory reflected the communal aspirations of the Benedictine Rule, and the forms of the refectory and chapter house expressed their corporate, quasi-liturgical functions. The primary purpose of the west range was hospitality, and this objective was best served by adopting the secular hall as model. Although Benedictine monasteries followed a common and predictable plan, each house had its unique modifications of the typical layout, and idiosyncrasies evolved as buildings were replaced through the lifecycle of the monastery. This chapter considers the use of space in the conventual buildings: multi-disciplinary and comparative evidence is harnessed to provide new interpretations of Norwich cathedral-priory (Plate 9).

From the St Gall plan and modifications to it introduced at Cluny, we know that monastic buildings were arranged in a very specific order in relation to the church and cloister, according to the function that they served (Figure 37). We can expect the dormitory of the monks (*dorter*) to be in close proximity to the church, allowing easy access for night services. The dormitory was housed on the upper floor of the east range of the cloister, over the chapter house and the warming room. The chapter house, where the community met daily to read a chapter from the Rule of St Benedict, and to discuss the business of the monastery, is absent from the St Gall plan, but was a feature added by Cluny (Horn and Born 1979, vol. 2, 343). The south range would have accommodated the refectory (*frater*), distancing the noise and smells of its kitchen from the church. At St Gall, the west range was reserved for cellarage, space that was used for the storage of food and wine, but in later Benedictine monasteries this range was adopted regularly as a guest hall. At St Gall, separate facilities were envisaged for the novices, the young monks who undertook a training period between their ceremonies of clothing and profession. St Gall's *novitiate* is shown together with the infirmary, to the north-east of the church; each had a separate cloister but a chapel was shared between them (Horn and Born 1979, vol. 1, 311). Over time, Cluny moved the *novitiate* to a space within the monks' dormitory, a practice that is believed to have been observed at English monasteries.

Norwich cathedral-priory was a new foundation, constructed on land that had

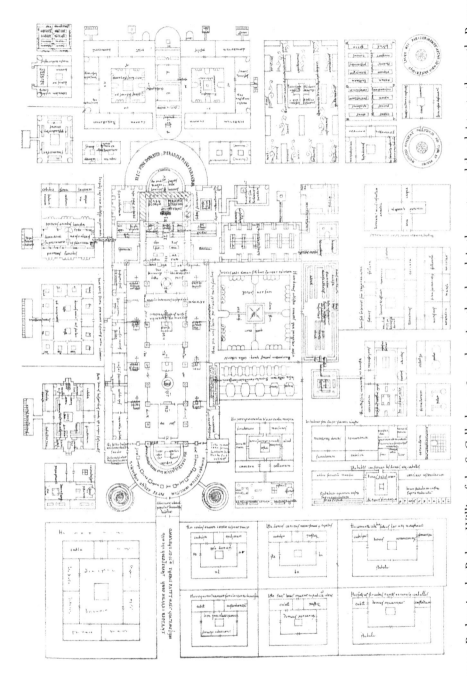

FIGURE 37. Redrawing by Robert Willis of the St Gall plan, c. 820, showing the church in the centre and the cloister to the south. Reproduced from *Archaeol J* 5 (1848).

been occupied formerly by parish churches and timber houses of the late Saxon town (see pp. 21–4). When work began, c.1096, it was possible to sweep away the Saxon structures, and to alter the site's levels in order to build the cloister. The ground was lowered on the site of the west range, and raised for the east and south ranges, with the finished level of the cloister constructed at least 800mm lower than the monastic ranges (see p. 80). This clean slate allowed the ideal disposition of monastic space to be achieved, so that the claustral ranges at Norwich closely follow the St Gall schematic. This was not always feasible at Benedictine abbeys that had been refounded on the sites of earlier monasteries. At the cathedral-priory of Worcester, for example, which was established on the site of a minster of the 690s, the dormitory was placed on the west side of the cloister rather than the customary east, and aligned east–west rather than the usual north–south. Adjustments in the alignment of dormitories were required also at Winchester (Greatrex 1998, 14), Coventry (Rylatt and Mason 2003), Gloucester and Chester (Atherton Bowen 1992, 18), perhaps resulting from the orientation of earlier buildings that were still standing, or due to the topographical restrictions of densely settled sites. At Gloucester, the Benedictine abbey of the late eleventh century reused the site of a Saxon minster founded in 678–9, and part of the walled Roman town (Heighway 1999). The existing cemetery and topography required siting of the cloister to the north of the church, in common with the refounded monasteries at Christ Church and St Augustine's, Canterbury (Kent), Malmesbury (Wiltshire), Chester (Cheshire) and Repton (Derbyshire). Such cloisters were deprived of heat and warmth from the sun, which were maximised by positioning to the south of the church. Similar topographical restrictions at Rochester (Kent) required the cloister to be placed adjoining the chancel, rather than to the nave of the cathedral church.

The East Range

The east range is the only conventual block at Norwich to have disappeared completely, but the arrangement of buildings can be discerned from features surviving in the east cloister walk and in the prior's residence (surviving as the deanery), elements of which formerly abutted the east range. This range projected from the south transept of the cathedral church, and was separated from it by a slype that linked the cloister and the monks' cemetery. It was not uncommon to have a slype or passage in each of the claustral ranges; for example at Gloucester, three slypes survive. At ground level the east range contained the chapter house and the warming room, and above these was the dormitory of the monks. The dormitory and chapter house were strongly symbolic of the communal life of the monastery, a factor that may have motivated their early removal following the Dissolution (see p. 209).

The treasaunce

The slype to the south of the transept survived until reordering of this area by the architect Anthony Salvin in the 1830s. The *treasaunce*, as it was known in medieval documents, was a vaulted space that provided access between the cemetery and the infirmary, and it was sometimes incorporated into liturgical processions. If weather permitted, it was part of a route taken on principal feast days, when the monks exited the church by the north transept, processed around the Lady chapel and through the monastic cemetery, and entered the cloister via the slype (Tolhurst 1948, xxxv).

The sixth bay of the east cloister (from the north) contains the blocked west door of the slype, c.1320 (Woodman 1996, 164), with complex cusping and a crocketed, ogeed hood. The slype was shown extant in John Adey Repton's plan of the cathedral church and cloisters dated 1794 (Pierce 1965, 14). A chamber above the *treasaunce* was used to store muniments, the documents of the priory, which were held in chests (Dodwell 1996c, 330); similarly at Durham, the space over the slype was used as a library.

The chapter house

The chapter house was the most sacred and formalised space of the conventual buildings. It was closely connected to the liturgy of the church and to the commemorative practices of the cemetery, associations that were strengthened by physical proximity. The monks would have processed to the chapter house after morning mass, in the same order of hierarchy that they followed for the liturgy.

The chapter house was also an administrative space that reinforced the corporate identity and efficient working of the monastic community. Each day would have seen a reading of the necrology (the list of deceased monks and noteworthy benefactors of the priory), followed by the reading of a chapter from the Rule of St Benedict, and the discussion of routine administrative matters; occasionally, important visitors were also received here (Cassidy-Welch 2001, 106).

The chapter house was the preferred site of burial for monastic superiors from the eleventh century up to the thirteenth or fourteenth centuries (Gilchrist and Sloane 2005). At Norwich, the use of the interior of the chapter house for interments is confirmed by the late twelfth-century *Life of St William*. It was the first intramural site chosen for the grave of the alleged boy-martyr, and a lamp was kept burning at his sepulchre during the night (Jessopp and James 1896, 53, 188). The chapter house was the focus for commemorative practices which linked the living and dead members of the monastic community. In common with the cloister itself, the chapter house represented continuity: through daily remembrance of dead brothers and patrons, the monastery maintained a connection with the past (Stratford 1978, 54).

The authority of the monastic prior was emphasised by his burial within the chapter house, but his position was also reinforced by social and spatial practices. Part of the administrative routine revolved around a regime of discipline: monks were accused of breaches of monastic order or confessed to them voluntarily, and the prior meted out appropriate punishments. Such penances would generally have comprised fasting or exclusion from the refectory for a short period, but might also include corporal punishment in the chapter house or incarceration in the monastic prison (Cassidy-Welch 2001, 116–25). The disciplinary function of the chapter house is confirmed by the location of the prison adjacent. At Norwich, the monastic prison was sited beneath the south transept, and it was in the east range at Durham cathedral-priory and at Cistercian Waverley (Surrey).

The accepted form of the Norwich chapter house is based on John Britton's early-nineteenth-century plan, which showed a polygonal apse with two windows on each of seven bays (Britton 1817, plate 1; Fernie and Whittingham 1972, 29). William Bensly reported that the site of the chapter house at Norwich had been excavated in 1889, revealing the original Norman, semicircular apse just inside the later polygonal east end (Bensly 1908, 44). Arthur Whittingham observed the north wall of the chapter house in 1932, during excavations for telephone lines to the south of the transept (MC 186/48 648x3 (3)). A watching brief in this area in 2003 also observed the north wall, surviving 0.2m below modern ground surface (Wallis in press). Today, only the entry bays to the chapter house from the east cloister walk survive intact (Figure 38); until c.1850, these openings were blocked with stone (Stewart 1875, 163), added when the chapter house was demolished in the 1560s. A number of fragments of worked stone recovered from the refectory excavations may represent parts of the demolished chapter house, including a pair of engaged shafts with a bold wave moulding (Heywood, in Wallis in press).

On the basis of antiquarian accounts, it can be suggested that the chapter house at Norwich was built in the early twelfth century. It was approximately 85ft

FIGURE 38. The chapter-house screen, dating to the 1320s. Drawing by Philip Thomas, Cathedral Survey Services. Copyright Chapter of Norwich Cathedral.

by 45ft externally (25.9 × 13.7m), projecting from the east range and terminating
in a semicircular eastern apse. The floor area at Norwich was fairly typical at 355
square metres, and slightly more generous than that at Winchester cathedral-priory
(28.9 × 11.5m) or Benedictine Peterborough abbey (27.6 × 10.8m). The apsidal
chapter house projecting from the eastern range was the generic English type, with
the plan at Norwich resembling the chapter houses at Battle (Sussex; before 1080),
Gloucester (1085), Bury St Edmunds (c.1105), Reading (Berkshire; 1120s) and
Durham (1130s) (Fergusson and Harrison 1999, 243 n. 10). Peter Fergusson and
Stuart Harrison have proposed that the chapter house at Monte Cassino in Italy was
the archetype for the apsidal termination (ibid., 94). Monte Cassino was the monastery where St Benedict composed his monastic rule, the heart of Benedictine monasticism. Its chapter house was rebuilt with an apse before 1087, and subsequent
buildings recalled the essential significance of Monte Cassino through emulation of
the apsidal form.

   The location and ground-plan of the chapter house at Norwich are well at-
tested, but the question remains as to whether the building occupied one storey or
two. Several pieces of evidence suggest the possibility of a two-storey chapter house,
which would have interrupted the space of the dormitory over the east range. In
order to accommodate the vaulting of the chapter house within a single storey, some
monasteries created subterranean chambers, with the chapter house floor placed
below the level of the cloister (for example, at the Yorkshire Cistercian monasteries
of Jervaulx and Byland). The sunken cloister at Norwich (see p. 80) would have pre-
vented such an arrangement. The placement of the dormitory stairs to the south of
the chapter house confirms that direct access was not possible from the dormitory
to the church. The extended length of the dormitory may have resulted from the
need for additional accommodation, to compensate for the space that would have
been lost by a full height chapter house.

   Further evidence for a two-storey building survives in the vestibule of the
chapter house as it was rebuilt in the last two decades of the thirteenth century.
The rebuilding retained the same dimensions, but the apse was reconstructed in
polygonal form. The reordering created an internal division with a vestibule at the
western end. The vestibule in the western bay of the chapter house carried a gallery
with doors to reach the *treasaunce* directly from the dormitory stairs. This arrangement is suggested by the communar's rolls (Fernie and Whittingham 1972, 30),
and by the surviving flat ceiling over the east face of the entry. This passage would
have provided an alternative route to the church to be used for night offices, with
the monks passing through the chapter house vestibule and slype at first-floor level,
and descending into the south transept via night stairs. The need for such a passage
implies that the main body of the chapter house was full height. It mirrors the arrangement in two-storey chapter houses at the cathedral-priory of Rochester and at
Cistercian Rievaulx (N Yorkshire), where the western bay served as a vestibule with
a passageway over, leading from the monks' dormitory to the church (Fergusson and
Harrison 1999, 92).

The rebuilding of the chapter house after the riot of 1272 was funded by Richard Uphall of Tasburgh, and a foundation inscription survives to the north of the chapter house entrance. This recently conserved inscription is partly legible, and formerly read 'Ricardus Uphalle hujus operis inceptor me posuit'. The reconstruction of the chapter house was recorded fully in the communar's rolls: the tracery ironwork was purchased in 1288, it was roofed in 1291, and glazing began in 1292 (Fernie and Whittingham 1972, 29–30). The surviving entrance consists of three uniform arches with ogeed tracery infill, dating to the 1320s (Woodman 1996, 164). In common with chapter-house entries at Benedictine Chester, Durham, Gloucester and Westminster, only the central arch functioned as an entrance, with the flanking arches glazed to provide light. The spatial layout of the chapter house at Norwich placed the seat of the prior in the most sacred space, in the eastern apse, with the monks seated on tiered benching around the perimeter of the main rectangle. In addition to benches for the monks there were seats provided for the boys of Norwich cathedral, an association that was significant in the twelfth century for the placing of the tomb of William. 'As for the place which he has chosen for himself that he may abide in, it is the chapter-house, and his tomb is to be placed among the boys' seats' (Jessopp and James 1896, 120).

The siting of the prior's seat and pulpit in the eastern apse created the ideal stage for the main performances of the chapter house: the reading of the Rule, the necrology and the meting out of discipline (Stratford 1978, 55). The quasi-liturgical character of the chapter house was reinforced by its shared orientation with the cathedral church, and the prominence of its eastern apse. The rebuilding of the chapter house at Norwich in the 1290s did not involve substantial reordering of the spaces of the east range. A conservative layout was retained, in contrast with the centrally planned chapter houses that were favoured in contemporary rebuildings. For example, a polygonal chapter house was finished at Westminster abbey by 1253 (RCHME 1924, 12), and polygonal chapter houses were built in the thirteenth and fourteenth centuries at the secular cathedrals of Lincoln and Wells (Somerset) (following the precedent of Worcester in the first quarter of the twelfth century) (Stratford 1978). The addition of the vestibule to subdivide the chapter house created a more private, enclosed space. This contrasted with the more open form of the twelfth-century building that would have been fully visible from the east cloister walk (as suggested by the surviving chapter house arcade at Winchester cathedral-priory).

The warming room

The bay directly to the south of the chapter house contains the surviving early fourteenth-century doorway that led to the dormitory stairs. Two bays further to the south is a blocked doorway that led to a ground-floor room (Figure 39). On the basis of comparison with other sites, this is likely to have been the location of the warming room or house, which would have been equipped with a substantial fireplace. At Chester, for example, the surviving warming room contains two fireplaces and the day stairs to the dormitory (Pevsner and Hubbard 1971, 146). This

FIGURE 39. The east walk of the cloister, with the blocked door to the former warming room (right). Photograph © Roberta Gilchrist.

chamber was provided as a place for the monks to warm themselves in the intervals between the divine services, and to meet occasionally for conversation (Horn and Born 1979, vol. 1, 258). Monastic customaries suggest that the warming house was sometimes used for the periodic tonsure, blood-letting and for the preparation of manuscripts (Fergusson 1986, 171). The heated environment was also an ideal place to hang the monastic laundry to dry (Fergusson and Harrison 1999, 140), a practice that may explain the depiction of the monastic laundress on a boss located in the eastern cloister alley at Norwich (Plate 2A).

Whittingham identified a chamber referred to in the Norwich obediential rolls, 'le camboly', as the warming room or house, which was provided with a new fireplace in the mid 1290s. He suggested that this term could have derived from *caminolium*, meaning a little fireplace (Fernie and Whittingham 1972, 31). At Norwich the warming room was the responsibility of the refectorer, who served special dishes there on feast days. The refectorers' rolls record that a screen was made for the '*cambole*' in 1441. In 1423 a distinction was made between a knife purchased for the presiding table in the refectory, and one for the *cambole* (DCN 1/8/71).

The subdorter: the novitiate and school?
The east range at Norwich projected a considerable distance beyond the southern limit of the cloister. In 2003, the foundations were observed of the wall continuing beyond the cloister, 1.9m wide and just below the modern ground surface (Wallis

in press). The vaulting of the undercroft of the former range can still be discerned as scars in the fabric of the west walls of the modern deanery.[1] Reference to its repair in the 1440s confirms that the southern end of the dormitory was near the infirmary garden (Stewart 1875, 177). The function of the ground floor of the southern extension to the dormitory is unknown, but it could feasibly have housed the novices, as Whittingham's plan implied (1949). Evidence of internal divisions was observed in a watching brief in 2003, perhaps consistent with the provision of cells for the novices (Wallis in press). The Rule of St Benedict indicated that a separate *novitiate* should be kept 'where the novices work, eat, and sleep' (McCann 1952, Chapter 58). The subdorter in the east range was the location of the novitiate at Clairvaux in the mid twelfth century, and also at Cîteaux and Jervaulx (Jansen 1998, 66). In such cases, the east cloister walk is likely to have been adopted for the work and recreation of the novices.

At the cathedral-priory of Durham, the novices' chambers were located in the south end of the dormitory, on the first floor (Fowler 1902, 85). At Benedictine Westminster, they slept in an enclosure within the dormitory, and the traditional place for the novices to study with their master was the west cloister walk (Harvey 2002, 60–61). The Plan of St Gall shows the *novitiate* sited with the infirmary, and sharing a chapel (Horn and Born 1979, vol. 1, 311). The close proximity of the infirmary and subdorter at Norwich may be pertinent in this respect. If the novices were housed beneath the south end of the dormitory, they were immediately adjacent to the infirmary chapel of St Nicholas, and may have shared the chapel with the infirm monks (see p. 174). The east cloister walk is likely to have been used for their study carrels.

This may also have been the original location of the monastic school, sited to make best use of the instruction offered by the iconographic capitals of the Romanesque cloister (see p. 80). The benches of the east cloister walk retain graffiti of the medieval game of 'three men's morris', perhaps suggesting its recreational use by schoolboys or novices. Similar evidence can be found in the cloisters of Canterbury, Westminster, Gloucester and Salisbury. A school for young boys would have been essential when the priory was first founded, when 'oblates' entered the monastery as children to be trained for their profession as monks on reaching maturity. After 1215, the practice of receiving infant oblates was prohibited by Canon Law, and a monastic school in the cloisters was no longer required (Harries et al. 1991, 5–6). However, two levels of instruction were essential within the priory: elementary training for novices, and more advanced theological and legal education for the monks (Greatrex 1991, 555). It seems likely that both levels would have been imparted in the east range, located in the warming room and perhaps the chapter house. The chapter house was used for divinity lectures shortly after the Refor-

---

[1] These scars were visible when Willis examined the fabric in the 1840s (Stewart 1875); the vaulting profiles outlined in tile on the east face of the east cloister were an addition made by Whittingham in the twentieth century.

mation (Houlbrooke 1996, 535), and may have served this purpose earlier. The presence of young boys in this area is indicated in the late twelfth-century *Life of St William*. After William's corpse had been exhumed from the monks' cemetery and brought to the cloister, the author of the *vita* recorded that he witnessed a vision of William and Bishop Herbert de Losinga. According to Thomas of Monmouth, William selected the site of his own tomb to be among the boys in the chapter house.

> Then the most blessed boy and martyr raised himself up and calling upon the Bishop, said, 'Give order, lord and father, that a little resting-place be made ready for me in the chapter-house, because there for a little while, as a boy among boys, I desire to rest' (Jessopp and James 1896, 121).

The dark entry and the prior's chamber

Between the east range and the refectory was a second slype, giving access to the infirmary court to the south, and communicating directly with the infirmary cloister (see p. 173). This passage survives today as 'the dark entry', a ground-storey, barrel-vaulted chamber of twelfth-century date (Figure 40).[2] In contrast with the slype in the east range, the dark entry had a residential chamber over it. The use of this space for a prestigious function is indicated by the quality of the wall paintings that once embellished it. These were recorded in 1873 (Figure 41), and consisted of a mid-thirteenth-century scheme of roundels, one of which retained the lower half of a lion, in imitation of a textile hanging (Park and Howard 1996, 387–8). Two features in the south elevation of the dark entry give an indication of its former use.

During repair to the fabric in 2003, the remains of a blocked Romanesque window were observed. This aperture was at the same level as the windows on the south wall of the refectory, and would have lit the twelfth-century chamber. Another feature was observed in the south-east corner of the upper storey of the dark entry. A fragment of thirteenth-century tracery was projecting from the external corner at an angle of forty-five degrees. The tracery was certainly *in situ*, and may indicate the former existence of a stair in this position, or perhaps a garderobe tower. The chamber was also provided with a stair down into the refectory, which still survives, and gave direct access to the refectory's upper end. It is suggested here that the chamber over the dark entry is likely to have served as the prior's private chamber, before construction of his lodging to the east of the cloister in the late thirteenth century (below, p. 156). Before the rebuilding of the cloister (and the creation of an upper storey over the cloister walks), the chamber over the dark entry would have been a self-contained space. This arrangement would have been ideal for the accommodation of the prior, sited close to the monks' dormitory but retaining privacy, and allowing direct communication with the high table in the dais end of the refectory. If there was no direct communication between the dormitory and the dark entry, a stair would have been required in the south-east corner to provide access

---

[2] It was reopened in 2004 to facilitate disabled access to the cloister, having served as the Song School during the twentieth century.

FIGURE 40. The dark entry: a twelfth-century, barrel-vaulted chamber that provided access between the cloister and the infirmary court. To the left of the door is a squint, and to the right is a lamp locker. The door on the right provided access to the passage beneath the dormitory that led to the prior's lodging. Photograph © Roberta Gilchrist.

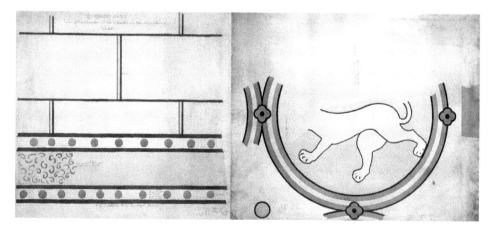

FIGURE 41. Former wall paintings in a chamber over the dark entry, recorded by J. H. Brown in 1873. Photograph by Terence J. Burchell. Reproduced with permission of the Norfolk Record Office and the Chapter of Norwich Cathedral, NRO DCN 131/121/1–2.

to the chamber. A garderobe would also have been needed, since the prior would have had no direct link to the monks' latrine block. There was also symbolic value to siting the prior's chamber over this access point to the cloister. From the late Saxon period onwards, apartments located over gateways were associated with lordship.

It is clear that ingress to the dark entry was carefully managed. Next to the door leading from the south cloister walk into the dark entry there is a squint (Figure 58). This aperture opens out into the cloister, indicating that a porter controlled access from the cloister into the dark entry, and to the prior's hall and infirmary beyond (p. 158). Before construction of the prior's lodging in the late thirteenth century, the porter would have been able to control access to the prior's chamber, especially if it was gained exclusively by a stair from within the dark entry. The dark entry was also provided with two lamp lockers, one adjacent to the door leading into the cloister, and one by the door leading to the infirmary. The careful control of access to the cloister was emphasised also at Durham cathedral-priory. A former monk writing in the late sixteenth century recalled that 'there were no strangers nor other persons suffered to molest or trouble any of the said Novices or Monkes in their Carrells, they being studying on their bookes within the Cloyster, for there was a Porter appointed to keep the Cloyster door' (Fowler 1902, 85).

The main doorway in the south elevation of the dark entry was inserted in the later Middle Ages, replacing an earlier Norman door. On the basis of the similarity of its mouldings with the porch at the parish church of St Laurence, Norwich, a date for this door has been suggested of the last quarter of the fourteenth century (Fawcett 1996, 221–2).

The dormitory and the library

The upper floor of the east range was occupied by the monks' dormitory. Monastic dormitories were designed initially as massive, undivided spaces: their openness represented the unity of the monastery and its aspiration to the communal vocation (Jansen 1998, 70). The Rule of St Benedict gave clear guidance on how the space should be used.

> Let them sleep each one in a separate bed. Let their beds be assigned to them in accordance with the date of their conversion . . . There shall be a light burning in the dormitory throughout the night. Let them sleep clothed and girt with girdles or cords . . . Being clothed they will thus always be ready, and rising at the signal without any delay may hasten to forestall one another to the Work of God . . .
>
> . . . For bedding, let this suffice: a mattress, a blanket, a coverlet, and a pillow. The beds should be examined frequently by the abbot, lest any private property be concealed in them (McCann 1952, 71, 127).

At Norwich, the chamberlain provided mattresses and quilts of striped cloth for the monks, in addition to fur coverlets for winter use (Saunders 1930, 117).

Fully extant monastic dormitories are rare survivals, but the example from

Cistercian Cleeve (Somerset) suggests that the monks' beds were aligned east–west, and placed on either side of a small lancet window. This arrangement allowed the central space to be kept clear for movement through the dormitory, and ensured that each bed space was well lit. A stone staircase led from the east cloister alley up into the dormitory, to be used during the day, and a night-stair was provided at the northern end of the dormitory for direct access to the church for night services. At Durham cathedral-priory, the dormitory was moved to the west range when the prior took over the east range for his private accommodation. The earlier dormitory survives over an undercroft with a row of central piers, and retains the day stairs from the cloister (Markuson 1980). The dormitory in the west range at Durham was rebuilt in 1398–1404, and the contract for the rebuilding survives, specifying that 'every two bedchambers of the monks will have one good window appropriate for their studies' (Shelby 1976, 93–4). This dormitory is still standing at Durham and reveals an arrangement of two rows of windows: the upper row of larger (two-light) windows provided general lighting and ventilation, and the lower row provided double the number of smaller, straight-headed windows to light individual beds (Jansen 1998, 67; Pevsner 1983, 204). When the dormitory at Winchester cathedral-priory was rebuilt in the 1370s, glass was purchased for a main window on the west front and for 'private windows', presumably those around which the beds of the monks were arranged (Greatrex 1998, 14). Such windows would have been covered with curtains to provide warmth, such as the blue buckram curtains recorded at Westminster (Harvey 2002, 61).

There is evidence to suggest that monastic dormitories were partitioned in the later Middle Ages: for example, the later dormitory at Durham retains slots showing its division into cubicles. Evidence for this practice survives in the extant west wall of the dormitory at Cistercian Jervaulx (N Yorkshire). Socket holes between the windows have been interpreted as the fixings for timber partitions that were used to form individual cells or cubicles when the wall was built at the beginning of the thirteenth century (Coppack 1990, 73). At Rievaulx, the dormitory was shortened to half its length in the later Middle Ages, and partitioned into cells, some lit by windows and provided with window seats (Coppack 2002, 202).

The dormitory at Norwich was apparently rebuilt or reordered by the early fifteenth century: the sacrist's account for 1427 refers to 'the new dormitory' (DCN 1/4/63). It appears that the space of the common dormitory had been subdivided into cells by the later Middle Ages, and that its southern end had been converted into a library with studies. The communar's rolls record a payment of 4d in 1474 for the cleaning of the library and the outer part of the cells in the dormitory against the coming of the king (DCN 1/12/70e). In 1479, a sum of 12d was spent for repairing windows in the dormitory over the step leading to the studies (DCN 1/12/71). Barbara Dodwell concluded that a specially designed book room was in use at Norwich by 1386–7, earlier than at Durham, Westminster and Canterbury (Dodwell 1996c, 337). She calculated that the cathedral's library grew to include four to five hundred volumes, including service books (psalters, missals, bibles), homiletic (devotional) literature, biblical commentaries, philosophy, law and history. The elevated position of the library in the south end of the dormitory provided the view of a cherry orchard to the south-west (Noble 1997, 9).

The monks' latrine

The Rule of St Benedict specifically allocated time for 'the necessities of nature', between Matins and Lauds (McCann 1952, 48–9). The monks' latrine at Norwich was linked to the dormitory at right angles, providing direct access at first-floor level. Flushed sewers were the typical standard for medieval monasteries, and the main latrine block was usually located to the south of the dormitory. Internally, the space of the latrine would have been partitioned to allow privacy, as suggested by the *Rites of Durham*: every seat 'was of wainscott close of either syde verie decent so that one of them could not see one another' (Fowler 1902, 86). It has been be suggested that straw and pitchers of water would have been provided for sanitation (Horn and Born 1979, vol. 1, 261). Although monastic archaeology often employs the term '*reredorter*' for the latrine, this was a polite term coined by nineteenth-century antiquaries, meaning behind or beside the dormitory. The account rolls of the priory refer to the latrines as *necessaria*, while they are known as *privvies* in the *Rites of Durham*.

Monastic latrines can be studied from surviving and excavated examples, and from the Canterbury waterworks plan of c.1165 (Tatton-Brown and Sparks 1989). The plan shows the extensive *necessarium* as a block measuring 30ft by 172ft (9.2m × 52.5m), constructed over an undercroft, at right angles to the dormitory. The upper level was partitioned into cubicles, and a massive drain ran below to flush the latrines. The ruins at Cistercian Rievaulx retain the sockets that held partitions for the cubicles, each containing a wooden seat placed over the drain (Coppack 1990, 98). From the waterworks plan it has been suggested that fifty-five cubicles were provided at Christ Church, Canterbury, while a figure of twenty-three has been suggested for Worcester cathedral-priory and thirty at Cluniac Lewes priory (Sussex) (ibid.).

Part of the north wall of the monks' latrine at Norwich survives as the south wall of the deanery (Figure 42). This would have been an internal elevation of the medieval latrine, but is now external. The remains of six blocked windows survive in the upper part of this wall. From their spacing, it can be proposed that originally twelve windows would have existed. It may be suggested that twelve windows were provided on both the north and south walls of the latrine block, each lighting a cubicle. On this basis, a figure of twenty-four cubicles can be estimated for Norwich, assuming that twelve cubicles were provided on each side of the latrine block, with a corridor between them leading from the dormitory. The block would have measured approximately 9.8m by 27.5m.

The east wall of the deanery corresponds with the east wall of the former latrine (Figure 43), and still retains a pair of arches (1.8m × 0.9m wide), with triple order square mouldings. The southern arch has been relocated and now contains a door. The chamfered mouldings of these arches are the same on both sides, with no

FIGURE 42. The north wall of the former monks' latrine (the deanery south elevation), showing blocked medieval windows and crowstepped gables dating to the 1660s. Photograph © Roberta Gilchrist.

evidence of rebates for medieval doors (Whittingham 1938). It is therefore unlikely that the arches were entrances, but rather that they spanned two drainage channels beneath the latrine. The survival of the monks' latrine adds further evidence for the management of water supply and drainage at Norwich, and in particular the siting of the great drain which ran to the south of the refectory. The monks' latrine was flushed by this culvert, but it was also provided with cleaning doors to periodically cleanse the latrines. These are evidenced by four blocked arches in the lower part of the south deanery wall.

By the fifteenth century, the library at Norwich was positioned in the southern end of the dormitory. Entrance to the latrine would therefore have been via the library. The library's malodorous situation may have contributed to the supposed deficit of scholarship in the cathedral-priory![3] This location is confirmed by the communar's accounts for 1419, which record a payment of 2s 1d to a glazier for

---

[3] According to Blomefield (1745), Jessopp (1888, xvi) and Saunders (1930, 179–80); but see reappraisals by Dodwell (1996c) and Greatrex (1991).

0   Metres   10

FIGURE 43. The east wall of the former monks' latrine (the deanery east elevation), showing medieval arches that spanned a drainage channel. The southern arch now contains doors, and the adjacent arch to the right has a small window inserted in the blocking. Drawing by Philip Thomas, Cathedral Survey Services. © Chapter of Norwich Cathedral.

mending the great window at the entrance of the latrine building and in the library (DCN 1/12/47).

THE SOUTH RANGE

The refectory

> At the meals of the brethren there should not fail to be reading . . . And let there be the greatest silence, so that no whisper and no voice but the reader's may be heard there (McCann 1952, 93).

In common with the dormitory, the open space of the refectory represented the communal vocation of the monastery. A bell summoned the monks at Norwich to the refectory for meals once or twice a day, depending on the season, and a bell was kept at the prior's high table (Saunders 1930, 144). Excavations on the site of the refectory recovered a small bell that may be an example of one from the prior's table (Wallis 2002a, 17). Seating in the refectory was based on seniority within the monastery, just as it determined the order of the monks' beds in the dormitory and their position in the choir, chapter house and in liturgical processions. Throughout the meal, silence was maintained, and a brother read from an elevated pulpit placed along a side wall.

From a combination of historical and architectural evidence, it can be estimated that the refectory at Norwich was built c. 1125–1145. It may therefore have been planned by Herbert de Losinga, but was completed by his successor, Bishop Eborard. It is situated on the south side of the cloister, and today much of its north, east and south walls remain standing (Figure 44). For much of its post-medieval history, the shell of the monastic refectory contained a prebendary house and garden (see p. 215). It was restored in the 1870s to the appearance of a Romanesque ruin, purging it of later domestic accretions. In 2001–4, the site was developed as a new refectory for the cathedral, providing the opportunity for archaeological investigation.

The form for the monastic refectory had been established by the ninth century, when the St Gall plan was drawn. From this date, the monastic refectory was organised with an upper and lower end. The upper end was the more prestigious space reserved for the prior's table, and the lower end communicated with the kitchen to simplify the serving of food. The main entrance from the cloister was at the lower end, while the upper end remained a more private space. At Norwich, the upper end communicated directly with the prior's chamber over the dark entry (see p. 115), anticipating the arrangement of secular halls, with the lord's solar at the upper end. The typical bipolarity of the later medieval hall appears to have origi-

FIGURE 44. The shell of the twelfth-century refectory in 2002, showing the approximate medieval ground level. The changes in the thickness of the wall face beneath the windows represent the former wall-passage and the band of interlaced blind arcading that formerly lined the open hall. Photograph © Roberta Gilchrist.

nated in the spatial practices of monastic refectories such as Norwich (Thompson 1995, 57). Within the monastic context, however, the upper end achieved a more sacred resonance through its location in the eastern end of the building.

The refectory at Norwich was constructed on a gigantic scale: at 51.8m by 13.7m (170ft × 45ft) it must have dwarfed the sixty monks for whom it was intended. Its vastness is demonstrated by comparison with contemporary refectories at the Norfolk Cluniac monasteries of Thetford and Castle Acre, which measure approximately 28m by 8m, and with the largest Cistercian refectories, which reached only 35–8m in length (Fergusson 1986). For comparison with a cathedral-priory, Worcester's refectory measures 36.6m × 11.6m. Norwich rivals the capacious refectory at Benedictine Westminster, which measured 50 by 11.3m internally (164 × 37ft) (RCHME 1924, 84). From the early twelfth century, it was usual to place monastic refectories over an undercroft. Two-storey refectories were constructed at the cathedral-priories of Durham, Worcester, Canterbury and Carlisle, and employed in houses of canons and nuns from the 1170s and '80s. The two-storey form is considered to have possessed iconographic significance, based on the archetype of the *cenaculum*, the upper room in a building in Jerusalem where the Last Supper took place (Fergusson 1986). Norwich was one of a small group of monasteries to have employed an open, ground-floor hall for the refectory (Figure 45), in common with the refectories at Benedictine Westminster and Chester abbeys.

The evidence for the ground-floor refectory at Norwich is based on five pieces of archaeological evidence (and the absence of documentary references to a refectory undercroft). First, the refectory was provided with the highly unusual feature of a gallery or wall-passage around its four walls, to allow circulation at the clerestory level of the windows. Evidence for the gallery survives across the eastern end of the building, where it is 0.8m wide; adjacent to the south-eastern stair turret it can be seen that the gallery also extended across the south wall, where it is 1.2m wide. Secondly, there was a decorative band of interlaced, blind arcading below the windows. The blind arcades were divided into bays by pilasters that rose to form the supports of the wall-passage. Sections of the original arcade survive on the east and north walls, confirming that it was used to enhance the appearance of the entire building (and not just the dais end). The placement of the main decorative element of the blind arcading *below* the windows indicates that the principal space was at ground level, and confirms that the refectory was not placed over an undercroft. Third, there is no evidence for access to an upper floor over the south range. The siting of the *lavatorium* and the iconography of the bosses confirm that the entrance to the refectory was in the south-west corner of the cloister (see pp. 92, 89). The stair turret adjacent to this spot, in the north-west corner of the refectory, is almost entirely outside the west wall, and was positioned to facilitate *external* access from an upper chamber of the hostry in the west range. Fourth, excavations have confirmed that the eastern end of the refectory was raised, thus locating the dais on the ground floor. Make-up deposits at the eastern end of the refectory sealed Late Saxon features and the foundation trenches of the refectory. These seem to have been dumped deliberately to raise the ground level (which naturally slopes down towards the east) (Wallis in press). Finally, there was archaeological evidence for a decorative floor, comprising a few areas of tile impressions representing a later medieval floor that had destroyed earlier levels (ibid.). The refectory at Norwich retained the

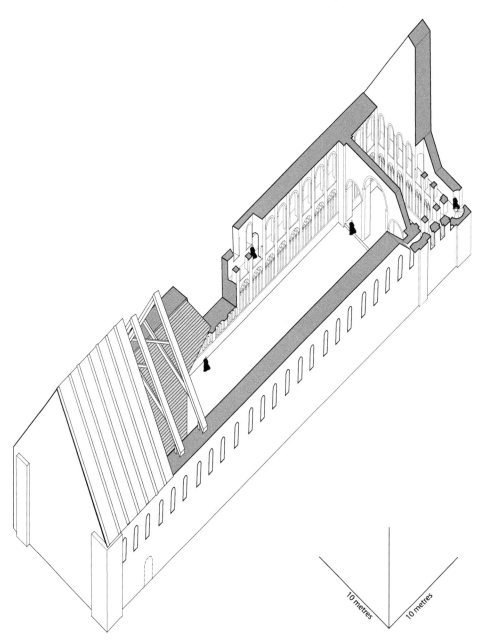

FIGURE 45. Axonometric drawing of the refectory, showing the wall-passage, blind arcading and the proposed screen marking the dais end. Drawing by Margaret Mathews.

ground-floor arrangement, even after the refurbishment that was required by the riot and resulting fire of 1272.

Peter Fergusson (1986) has argued that the usual location of the refectory in an 'upper room' conveyed the apostolic significance of the monastic dining space, in imitation of the Last Supper. At Norwich, this metaphor may have been achieved through the provision of steps leading up into the refectory from the lower level of the south cloister walk, steps that were necessitated by the sunken cloister (see p. 80). The placement of the refectory over an undercroft was particularly important to the Cistercians, who minimised social distinctions in the community by arranging the dining tables along the walls. At Cistercian Fountains, for example, the stone legs survive *in situ* that would have supported wooden tabletops. This allows a reconstruction of one table across the eastern end, and others flanking the side walls (Goodall 2001). Although the Cistercians removed or minimised the emphasis on the dais, some Benedictine houses continued to use the space of the refectory to reinforce relationships of hierarchy. The prior and senior offices would have been seated on the dais, and the rest of the community would have been positioned along the side tables according to their seniority. The dais was in some cases distinguished by a raised floor or by special architectural embellishment. Excavations in the refectory at Durham revealed evidence for two steps leading up to the dais, which was a platform 4m (13ft) wide which ran across the whole width of the refectory (Gee 1966, 71–2). At Christ Church, Canterbury, the refectory was distinguished by arcading at the dais end, which was raised above a passage (Newman 1969, 212). It has been suggested that the dais at Norwich was further articulated by the provision of a stone screen (Heywood 1996).

Towards the eastern end of the north wall of the refectory at Norwich there is a shallow depression in the wall face above the level of the gallery, which is lined with ashlar. At the corresponding position on the north (exterior) face of this wall there is a flat buttress, dating to the twelfth century. It is likely that this feature marked the extent of the dais, or upper end of the refectory. Arthur Whittingham conjectured that the dais was marked simply by the positions of two buttresses extending slightly into the refectory, from the north and south walls (Whittingham 1943). However, the presence of a buttress on what was the *external* side of this wall has given rise to the proposal that an arcade of two or three bays projected from the scar on the north wall (Heywood 1996, 106). Certainly, a buttress would have been needed to counteract the thrust of a major structural feature projecting from the north wall. Recent excavations on the site have located the corresponding buttress projecting from the south wall, but any intermediate foundations that may have supported an arcade had been robbed from the centre of the building (Wallis 2002a). Heywood suggests that the buttress supported a two or three-bay arcade which defined the dais of the refectory; he argues that the shallow depression in the upper level of the north wall allowed passage around the screen at clerestory level. If a screen was located in this position, it would have placed unprecedented emphasis on the maintenance of hierarchical relations within the community.

Monastic refectories were sometimes divided longitudinally by arcades that bisected them into two aisles of equal dimensions, perhaps to facilitate the provision of vaulted ceilings. At Cistercian Fountains, for example, the springing of an arch survives in the centre of the end wall, suggesting the position of the former arcade (Goodall 2001, 60). Excavations by William St John Hope at Benedictine Gloucester suggested a similar arrangement, with the first refectory divided down the middle by a row of square Norman piers (St John Hope 1897, 110). The use of an arcade to screen the eastern end would have been highly unusual, and prefigures the marking of the upper end in later secular halls. Screens divided the solar at the upper end from the main body of a secular hall, against which the high table was placed. The north–south orientation of the arcade at Norwich prompts comparison with the *pulpitum* and rood screens of the cathedral church. It may be suggested that the hierarchical arrangement of space within the refectory was reinforced by constructing an arcade to segregate the eastern end, a spatial pattern that borrowed from the traditional regulation of sacred space in the church.

The refectory at Norwich is of flint-rubble construction with ashlar dressings of fine-grained Caen and coarser, oolitic limestones (such as Ancaster or Ketton). Parts of the twelfth-century design of the internal walls can be seen on the north wall, which survives to a height of some 7.6m (Plate 4B), and on the southern end of the east wall. These remains reveal that the refectory consisted of an open hall with a gallery around the four walls, providing passage around the building at an upper level. In the north wall there is a fifteenth-century doorway leading down into the south-west angle bay of the cloister. Recent excavations have located the floor-level of the monastic refectory, confirming that it was elevated approximately 0.8m above the adjacent cloister walk, and suggesting a height of approximately 7m between the medieval floor and ceiling.

Evidence for the construction of the refectory was recorded during excavations on the site in 2001–3, by the Norfolk Archaeological Unit. Late Saxon features were sealed by a distinct soil horizon that is interpreted as the clearing of the site in preparation for the monastic buildings. There was evidence of small-scale activity before or during the refectory's construction, including pits, post-holes and two hearths. The footings of the three surviving walls were recorded, with a width 0.5m greater than the walls of the superstructure. The foundation was made up of horizontal bands of flint alternating with a chalky clay and sand mix, similar to the banded foundations recorded beneath the former Lady chapel (Cranage 1932). Substantial post-holes were excavated running parallel with the south wall of the refectory, likely to represent scaffolding used during its construction (Wallis 2002a, 8).

It is possible that all four corners of the medieval refectory were provided with a stair turret. The exception may be the north-eastern corner: although excavations located a stair in this position, its date could be post-medieval. The stair turret in the south-eastern corner stands relatively complete, as a result of its restoration in 1873. It was entered from within the refectory and gave access to the gallery, and also to the prior's chamber above the dark entry. The turret in the north-western corner is very fragmentary, but a straight joint in its north wall suggests that there was a doorway through to the west range. Within the turret there are the remains of two cupboards. This north-western stair is almost entirely outside the west wall, in contrast with the south-eastern stair, which is contained wholly within the thickness of the wall. The blocked door opening on the north side of the turret may have led to a first floor chamber at the south end of the hostry (occupying the west range). Open access to the monastic refectory strongly indicates that the southern, upper chamber of the hostry was at some time reserved for guests of monastic status. A former stair has been proposed for the south-western corner (Whittingham 1949), although no evidence of this is remaining.

Extending across the length of the north wall is an arcade of twenty-four window openings, with semicircular arches, which originally lit the refectory from above the height of the twelfth-century cloister roof. In fact, only four of these windows were extant in 1873, when a plan to restore the cloisters was brought to the chapter by John Henry Brown, surveyor to the fabric (DCN 127/64). This restoration involved the demolition of prebendary houses built into the medieval cloister, located respectively over the dark entry and on the eastern end of the refectory, and at the south-western angle of the cloister. Brown's submission included elevation drawings in water-colour of the buildings as they existed in 1873, together with details of the proposed restoration (Plate 4A).

The north wall of the refectory was shown by Brown to have faced onto a garden in 1873, as it did until 2002. He recorded only four Romanesque windows *in situ* and the fragmentary remains of at least two others, as opposed to the twenty-four windows that exist today. Five square windows of indeterminate, postmedieval date were depicted, together with a central, crowstepped gable, likely to be seventeenth-century in date (see p. 232), and a chimney associated with domestic accommodation in the upper west cloister. A single pitch roof was shown over the door leading from the refectory down into the cloister. The refectory north wall incorporated substantial amounts of brick and tile, which have since been removed, including a parapet and capping for the lower section of the wall that previously supported the medieval wall-passage.

Brown's proposed restoration included reinstating the twenty-four Romanesque windows in the north wall of the refectory, and he had planned to replicate a band of interlaced blind arcading below the windows. There are fragmentary remains of the arcading at the western end of the north wall and on the interior of the east wall, which were to serve as his model. The scheme for the arcading was rejected due to costs, but the windows were all unblocked and/or restored. Only the three most western arches escaped restoration or refacing, although there is consistent evidence across the wall that there was an arch between each window spanning across the gallery.

Surviving evidence allows reconstruction of the appearance of the refectory as it would have appeared in the thirteenth century (Plate 5), before refurbishment prompted by the fire of 1272. In this reconstruction, the blind arcading has been extended around the full extent of the refectory, and it has been used as the basis for the conjectured screen marking the dais end. The south wall has been reconstructed using the north wall as a model, and a pulpit is shown, although the precise position of this feature at Norwich is unknown. At Benedictine Chester, the ground-floor refectory of the thirteenth-century retains the pulpit on the south wall, which was reached by stairs placed in the thickness of the wall. The refectory at Worcester cathedral-priory was remodelled in the 1320s–30s over a Norman undercroft: it retains part of a stone canopy that was located over the pulpit, set in the second window recess from the east on the north side (Morris 1978, 126). The wall-passage at Norwich would have facilitated access to the pulpit, and it seems unlikely that it would have been provided with its own stairs.

The wall painting shown below the arcading in the reconstruction is suggested by a scheme from the chamber above the dark entry, recorded by Brown in 1873 (DCN 131/121/1–2), and dated stylistically to c.1250 (Park and Howard 1996, 387–8). This comprises a masonry pattern and a dado band of marbling with dotted borders. Colour would have been used also to highlight architectural detail, and is suggested at Norwich by pigments surviving on the capitals of the Romanesque cloister (red, green and yellow), and recorded on the capitals of the infirmary by John Adey Repton (Pierce 1965, 37: red, black and gilded). Excavations in the refectory recovered an oyster shell that contained a small amount of green pigment, possibly a palette used during painting of the buildings (Wallis 2002a, 35). The scheme was more vivid than the Cistercian style evidenced at Fountains, where the refectory walls were painted with discrete white on white, but less startling than the interior of Rievaulx's refectory, where the shocking pink walls were relieved with false jointing and rosettes (Fergusson and Harrison 1999, 142). The space above the arcade would have contained a crucifix or pertinent image. For example, the east wall of the refectory at Worcester retains a wall painting of Christ in Majesty, dating to the early thirteenth century. The nature of the Norman roof structure at Norwich is unknown: it could have been an open timber roof, a timber barrel vault, or a painted ceiling. The reconstruction shows a ceiled roof space as one possibility that would have been in keeping with the grand scale and finish of the refectory. The form of the ceiling shown on the reconstruction is conjectural, and is based on a simplified version of the surviving painted ceiling at the church of St Michael at Hildesheim, Lower Saxony. There is evidence to suggest that the cathedral church had an open timber roof; for example, the eastern face of the crossing tower is painted and must have been visible through a roof structure.

Excavations on the site revealed two unusual features projecting from the south wall of the refectory (Wallis in press). Stone-lined pits or tanks were inserted against the south wall, requiring partial removal of the footings. The eastern pit was modified for use in the post-medieval period, but the western pit was well preserved. The feature was 3.1m long and c.2.6m deep, and approximately 1.9m wide. It was constructed of masonry walls and a central pier, with a mortared floor and rendered walls. The pier was made up partly of worked stone, with a moulding suggesting a date of the mid thirteenth to fourteenth century, although these blocks could have been reused. A date later than the mid thirteenth century is indicated, and supported by an artefact contained in the primary fill of the feature, a fifteenth-century Venetian glass vessel (Wallis 2002a, 9). Although the construction is reminiscent of a tank, there was no evidence of a pipe or drain connected with a water supply, and the feature was kept clean or closed until the end of monastic occupation. Similar features have been excavated in the chapter house at the cathedral-priory of Worcester. Two small chambers dating to the fourteenth century were built into the Norman buttresses of the chapter house. One was constructed of unmortared ashlar blocks (1.3m × 0.9m), and covered with a monolithic stone to serve as a roof (Crawford 1997, 4); the other had vertical sides but no evidence of a floor or roof (Crawford and Guy 2000, 4). In common with the Norwich examples, the features at Worcester showed no evidence of either a water supply or tidemarks to indicate use as a sump or soakaway. This can be contrasted with a sunken feature excavated adjacent to the refectory at the Benedictine nunnery of Polsloe, near Exeter. This was lined with ashlar and had water fed to it through earthenware pipes, confirming its use as a cistern (*Medieval Archaeol* 23 (1979), 250).

It may be more appropriate to compare the chambers at Norwich to a secure store, such as the example excavated at the Templar preceptory of South Witham (Lincolnshire) (Mayes 2002). Footings that projected from the north wall of the chapel at South Witham may have supported a wall-safe for protecting the *confraria*, the funds collected by the military orders to assist in the crusades (Gilchrist 1995, 84). The Norwich refectorer's rolls record that the building stored 'precious objects', and in 1471 a carpenter was paid for binding the precious objects of the refectory with ironwork (DCN 1/8/95). Comparison with practice at the cathedral-priory of Durham is revealing, where the most important objects were stored in a concealed cupboard in the refectory. The *Rites of Durham* record that 'all the cheif plate did lie only in that Ambry [cupboard], that served the whole Convent in the said Frater house . . . a fine work of carved wainscott before it, which had a fine strong lock on the said Ambry, that none could perceive that ther was any Ambry at all' (Fowler 1902, 81). The construction of the subterranean chambers at Norwich may have been prompted by the devastating fire of 1272, in which the books, vessels and plate of the refectory must have perished. These features may be interpreted tentatively as concealed, fireproof safes, built into the Norman foundations sometime after the fire of 1272.

The excavations in the refectory recorded the contents of post-medieval pits that were dug into the site. These produced copious evidence of worked stone and glass, including moulded stones with red and black pigment, and medieval coloured glass, including flashed ruby, flashed blue, green, yellow and pink. Both the architectural fragments and glass suggested a date of the later thirteenth century, and these fragments are likely to represent the post-medieval disposal of demolition debris from other monastic buildings, such as the infirmary, chapter house and Lady chapel (Wallis in press).

Dining and diet in the monastic refectory
The rolls of the refectorer and other obedientiaries supply further information on the appearance of the building and the food that was consumed within it. The dais was noted in 1299, and the presiding table in 1319; a cover for the pulpit or lectern was purchased in 1306, and the refectory was lit by a central candelabrum in 1451. Its windows were frequently repaired, and its walls were plastered and painted in 1289, 1314 and 1422. Four servants staffed the refectory, and a stipend was paid by the cellarer for a specialist sauce maker (*salsamentarius*) (Saunders 1930, 44, 99). The diet of the monks at Norwich appears to have been typical of later medieval monastic fare. Barbara Harvey has argued that the monks at Westminster consumed a diet rich in protein, largely comprising meat, fish, cheese and eggs. Their average daily consumption was 2lbs of meat and 2.5lbs of bread per day, with any leftovers passed to the almonry for distribution to the poor (Harvey 1993, 58–9). The Norwich monks were served with pork, mutton and beef on the days that they were allowed to eat meat (Sundays, Mondays, Tuesdays and Thursdays), and fish was served on the remaining days (herring, whiting, cod, roach and eels) (Dodwell 1996, 238). Great quantities of eggs were consumed throughout the year, with the exception of Lent (Saunders 1930, 96). The bread allowance at Norwich was a 2lb loaf a day, to be divided between dinner and supper. Small amounts of cooked vegetables and stewed fruits were consumed, representing the produce of the monastic gardens and orchards. Archaeological excavations on the refectory recovered animal bones indicating beef, mutton and pork, in addition to domestic bird bones and possibly wild species. Fragments of seal and porpoise may represent the consumption of marine mammals during periods of abstaining from meat (Curl, in Wallis in press).

The kitchen
There is no doubt that a number of different kitchens were in existence in the medieval cathedral-priory at Norwich, with the obediential rolls referring variously to two cookhouses under the charge of the cellarer, the prior's cookhouse, the almoner's cookhouse and the sacrist's cookhouse. The development of specialist chambers for the consumption of meat also required dedicated kitchens. It was customary within monastic houses to provide a specialist meat kitchen near the infirmary.

The main kitchen was located adjacent to the lower (western) end of the refectory, and it is likely that food would have been served through a hatch linking the two buildings. At Carlisle, for example, the surviving refectory contains a hatch in its west wall that communicated with the kitchen. The location of the kitchen at Norwich was proposed by Whittingham. He investigated the sites of the refectory kitchen and the infirmary meat kitchen in 1965, although the detail of his excavations cannot be deciphered from the records he left (MC186/50 648x4 (21)).

It seems likely that Whittingham identified the locations of the refectory kitchen and meat kitchen on the basis of standing remains that can be traced today. In 1995, the facing collapsed from a section of wall that extends southward from the south wall of the refectory. This wall is currently the west wall of the car park, and beneath its facing is a blocked doorway or passage, 2.6m high and 0.9m wide. It is suggested here that this was the west wall of the refectory kitchen, with a door leading westward to the guest hall of the hostry. Food would have been conveyed to the refectory through a hatch or door in its south wall, subsequently masked by modern openings. Remains of the supposed meat kitchen lie to the west of the current car park wall, in the garden of Number 67. This amorphous ruin of mortared flint was rediscovered in 1994, when the garden was cleared.

Whittingham's plan of the priory shows the positions of the hearths in the refectory kitchen and meat kitchen, suggesting that his excavations had located them. The plans of the kitchens were not recovered, but it is quite possible that these were substantial structures. They would have been freestanding buildings constructed in flint rubble to guard against the danger of fire. Imposing monastic kitchens survive at Durham and Glastonbury, respectively octagonal and square in plan, with lateral fireplaces (Wood 1965, 249–50). The monastic kitchen at Norwich survived until 1569, when an indenture agreed that William Clerk should have covenants for 'the pulling down of the old kitchen' (Williams and Cozens-Hardy 1953, 27).

The West Range

The fourth range enclosing the monastic cloister was the most flexibly deployed, with functions varying according to monastic order. The Cistercians used the west range initially for the accommodation of lay brothers, while others employed this space principally for the accommodation of guests. Consistent with monastic hierarchies of sacred space, the west range was reserved largely for non-religious, or less overtly religious uses. By the twelfth century, many Benedictine and Augustinian monasteries used the west range at least partly for the private accommodation of the prior (Thompson 2001, 66). The Benedictines vowed to provide hospitality, and cathedral-priories extended their hospitality to a wide social range of visitors and pilgrims.

> Let all guests that come be received like Christ, for he will say: *I was a stranger and ye took me in.* And let fitting honour be shown to all, but especially to churchmen and pilgrims (McCann 1952, 119).

The west range at Norwich was used for the reception of visitors and to provide meals for both lesser guests and for the servants of more distinguished travellers (Saunders 1930). Although the west range was integral to the monastic cloister, its main entrance was through a porch from the upper inner court. Monastic guests were accommodated in the chambers of the west range, particularly the southern chamber adjoining the refectory. Ecclesiastical visitors took their meals with the monks in the refectory, while high-ranking secular guests were entertained and accommodated in the prior's lodging. The best model to meet the purpose of hospitality was the secular hall, and the west ranges of many monasteries are directly comparable to their secular counterparts. At Norwich, the west range consists of the fragmentary remains of the hostry, or guest hall, with the outer parlour located to the north. The hostry was staffed by a pantryman, butler, servant and door-keeper (Saunders 1930, 129). Regular visitors were able to converse with the monks in the outer parlour, above which was a chapel for the use of guests staying in the hall. In the location of the guest hall, outer parlour and upper chapel, Norwich displays the classic features of the monastic west range and its core requirements for hospitality (Brakspear 1933, 139).

The locutory, or outer parlour

The chamber between the hostry and the cathedral church functioned as an outer parlour, or *locutory*, facilitating communication between the monks and their secular guests. The almoner's roll for 1354 confirms that a 'keeper of the *locutory*' was employed to maintain this important social interface (Saunders 1930, 69). Here, monks would meet secular visitors or relatives, or perhaps local merchants, with permission for brief conversation.

It is likely that the outer parlour was also the site of a daily ritual described in the Norwich *Customary*: the ceremonial washing of the feet of three poor men, performed daily before dinner (Tolhurst 1948, xxxvii). The *mandatum hospitum* was given greater prominence by St Benedict than the *mandatum fratrum*, performed by the monks at the *lavatorium* (see p. 92). The monks washed the feet of the poor as an act of humility and charity, demonstrating 'that Christ is most truly welcomed' (McCann 1952, 88–9). The ritual is described in the eleventh-century *Customs of Farfa*, where the brothers assembled after dinner to wash the feet of paupers, using a cauldron of heated water and three towels of linen. It has been suggested that the monastic parlour would be the only possible location for this ritual (Horn and Born 1979, vol. 1, 309). The site of the outer parlour at Norwich would certainly be ideal to serve this purpose. The paupers would have been brought from the almonry at the Ethelbert gate (see p. 182) to the outer parlour. After the ceremony the monks would have moved directly into the west walk and proceeded to the *lavatorium* outside the refectory, where they would have washed in an act of ritual purification before entering to dine.

The *locutory* or outer parlour at Norwich is a four-bay structure with a wide barrel vault on moulded transverse arches. The three eastern bays make up the primary twelfth-century building. The fourth (western) bay is an extension dating to the late thirteenth century, dated by the plate tracery of its window (Figure 46). The main entrance is in the western elevation, and a second door in the eastern wall provided access to the cloister. In the south-facing elevation, the second bay from the west contains the remains of a chimney for a medieval wall fireplace. This fireplace still survives in the interior of the outer parlour, consisting of an unblocked opening with single roll moulding. Externally, the third bay of the south elevation retains a flat buttress and the fourth is taken up by a twelfth-century stair turret, leading to a chamber above the outer parlour. A *piscina* survives in the east wall of the outer

FIGURE 46. The outer parlour or *locutory*, located between the cathedral church and the former hostry. Photograph © Roberta Gilchrist.

parlour, now external to the building, above the level of the existing flat roof (Figure 47). This consists of two twelfth-century basins flanked by shafts that have been cut off. The presence of this feature confirms that the former chamber above the outer parlour functioned as a chapel. It seems to have been reserved for visiting priors and monastic guests who were accommodated in the hostry, and it was referred to in medieval documents as the chapel of St Edmund.

The outer parlour at Norwich can be compared with that at Battle abbey (Sussex), which is a vaulted structure of three bays which retains the *piscina* in the chapel above, comprising two basins within a pair of pointed arches. Two fireplaces were added to the outer parlour at Battle in the sixteenth century (Brakspear 1933, 146–8), showing a similar development to the outer parlour at Norwich.

FIGURE 47. The basins of the *piscina* located in the former chapel over the *locutory*. Photograph courtesy of Philip Thomas.

The hostry

It has been proposed previously that the hostry at Norwich was a vaulted structure with an upper hall above (Whittingham 1949; Heywood 1996, 108). It is suggested here that it was instead an open hall with two-storeyed chambers at either end. It is certainly the case that the preferred arrangement of the monastic guest hall was over an undercroft, as indicated at Chester, Battle, Castle Acre (Norfolk) and Bardney (Lincolnshire), among others (Brakspear 1933). However, in contrast with the prevailing monastic taste, Norwich cathedral-priory seems to have retained the use of ground-floor halls for both the refectory in the south range and the guest accommodation in the west range.

The standing remains of the former hostry comprise the porch and east wall, now the west wall of the cloister (see p. 78), both constructed in flint rubble with ashlar dressings (Figure 48). The materials of the hostry would have created a strong visual contrast with the ashlar facing of the cathedral church and outer parlour, and it is possible that the external elevations would have been plastered and painted. The porch led through the west wall of the range, where a thirteenth-century doorway survives. The height of surviving masonry above the entrance suggests that the porch had a chamber over it. The internal elevation retains a lamp locker next to the door. The porch was an essential element of the visitors' buildings, and acted as a welcoming signal, guiding new arrivals to the precinct towards the guest accommodation. It was regularly positioned midway along the length of the west range, as

FIGURE 48. The remains of the hostry, showing the east wall of c.1100 and the ruins of the thirteenth-century porch. Photograph © Roberta Gilchrist.

at Norwich and Castle Acre (Norfolk), and may have indicated the location of the lower end of the hall or the screens passage (Rowell 2000, 83).

The former east wall of the hostry stands to an average height of 7.5m above its foundations (Figure 24). Excavations have shown that this wall stands directly on naturally derived gravels (at 5.3–5.4 OD). The medieval floor level in the hostry can therefore be estimated at c.5.4 OD, approximately 0.8m above the level of the adjacent west cloister walk (4.6 OD). This difference in levels precisely mirrors the arrangement of the refectory in relation to the south cloister walk. The west façade of the wall is faced with large broken flints, and substantial areas have been refaced. There are five circular, double-splayed windows, and the partial remains of a sixth. If these openings formerly extended across the entire length of the wall, it can be suggested that originally there would have been nine circular windows.

There are indications that the guest hall did not occupy the full length of the range. Evidence remains of the quoins that bonded two partition walls into the former east wall of the hostry, creating separate chambers at either end of the range. The east wall itself is thicker where the former chambers existed, indicating a different wall treatment or structural requirement. The northern section of the range was partitioned by an east-to-west orientated wall, indicated by the survival of a vertical line of stones. These stones represent the inside corner of a room. To the south of the door leading into the cloister, there is evidence for a former wall that would have partitioned the southern part of the range. The evidence here is much more fragmentary than that which is associated with the removed wall to the north, although the basic structural evidence with internal quoins is the same. Immediately to the south of the removed southern lateral wall there is a recess with a shallow, stone arch. The left-hand jamb is made up of random stone quoins, and the right-hand side is severely eroded. Access to the west walk of the cloister was through a surviving fifteenth-century doorway, with a moulded, outer arch. The doorway reflects the difference in levels between the later medieval hostry and cloister.[4] Three steps down into the cloister were provided, and the bases of the arch of the doorway rest on the bench that lines the west wall of the cloister.

The suggestion that the west range was a vaulted structure with an upper hall is based principally on analogy with other monastic west ranges. There is also some physical evidence to suggest a change in the wall face from coursed to uncoursed flintwork. This, seen in conjunction with the sections of thicker wall at both ends of the range, has been taken to represent the scar from former vaulting that has been stripped away (Heywood 1996, 108). Further evidence to support this hypothesis was the apparent outline of the vault profile, seen at the end of a surviving string-course, marked out in patches of rubble and tile. These patches were added in the twentieth century (most likely by Whittingham); when the wall was conserved in 2004, no stratigraphic evidence for vaulting was detected behind the patches of rubble and tile. If the interpretation of a vaulted structure is accepted, the length of the vaulting bays can be suggested by the distance between it and the end of the hall, as indicated by the vertical line of quoins. An attempted reconstruction of the vaulting, based on a typical square-plan, vaulting module, revealed that vaulting modules would not fit the known length of the hall (Smith 1996). In addition, vaulting would have created a cramped and unusable upper storey, with the circular windows located at knee height.

The west range is more likely to have consisted of an open hall with two-storeyed chambers at either end (Figure 49). This interpretation is supported by the description of upper and lower chambers and a great hall in the hostiliar's inventory of 1534–5, and by the mention in the hostiliars' rolls for 1440, of poles required to open the high windows of the great hall. In addition, there are references in 1470–1 to the purchase of a pulley with a rope, required to shut the hatch of the guest hall to exclude doves, and payment for scaffolding in 1473–4, needed for painting the hostry hall (DCN 1/7/ 105; 107). Together, these references convey the impression of a lofty hall open to its roof. How can the change in the wall face be explained, if not by the former existence of vaulting? It seems likely that there was a purely decorative arcade extending along the length of the open, ground-floor hall, perhaps comparable to that which survives in fragmentary form in the refectory. The wall thickens out beyond each end of the open hall of the hostry, presumably in order to give additional bearing for floor joists. The existence of upper chambers in these

---

[4] The threshold of the door is at 5.2 OD, with the adjacent cloister pavement at 4.6 OD.

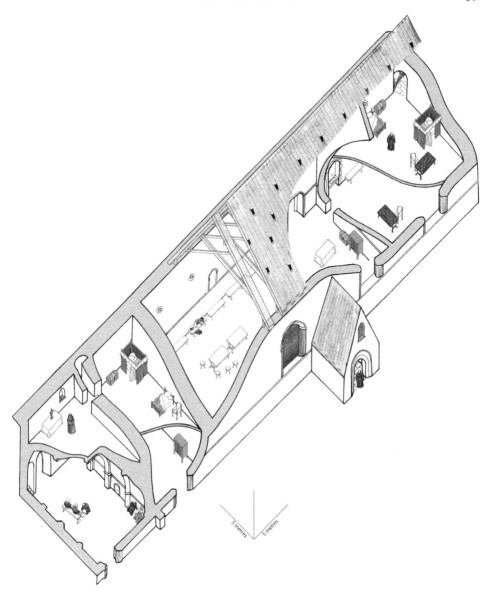

FIGURE 49. Axonometric drawing of the hostry, showing room use and furnishings according to an inventory dated 1534–5. Drawing by Margaret Mathews.

positions is also suggested by the surviving stair turret at the south-east corner. It
was suggested above that the evidence for a blocked door in this position implies
that direct access was possible between the southern chamber of the hostry and the
wall-passage of the refectory.

The southern chamber would have contained the shallow recess to the south
of the doorway through to the cloister. The recess is parallel with the *lavatorium*, on

the other side of the wall, in the west cloister alley. Compared with the *lavatorium,* however, the recess is crudely constructed and formed on a different alignment. It is possible that the recess contained a secondary *laver,* provided for the guests' participation in the monastic cleansing ritual. The hostiliar's inventory of 1534–5 notes that ground-floor chambers in this range were reserved for visiting religious, in particular the priors of Yarmouth and Aldeby, which were cells of the cathedral-priory (DCN 1/7/148). Also, the hostiliars' rolls of 1358–9 confirm that a conduit made of brass was located in the hall chamber (DCN 1/7/18), and in 1530 there were repairs to the 'conduit pertaining to the basins' (DCN 1/7/147). It seems likely that water was piped to the guest hall directly from the *lavatorium* in the west cloister walk. If the southern chamber of the hostry was reserved for monastic guests, it may have been considered appropriate to provide a secondary *laver* for their use. The religious status of the guests would also explain the requirement for direct access from the south chamber to the refectory, via the stair turret at the south end of the wall.

Three excavations were conducted by Arthur Whittingham on parts of the west range, in 1934, 1937 and 1969. These excavations remain unpublished but his notes survive, together with the script of an unpublished lecture to the Norfolk and Norwich Archaeological Society (Whittingham 1935). The excavations of the 1930s took place when alterations were made to the Choir School, formerly sited to the south-west of the cathedral. Whittingham took this opportunity to investigate re-mains adjacent to the extant east wall of the west range, which he took to be Saxon, and therefore believed to be the earliest fabric on the cathedral site. Whittingham reported that the foundations of the west wall of the range had been entirely robbed away. He suggested that the range had been widened in the thirteenth century by approximately 9ft (2.7m), from the evidence of the extant outer parlour. In 2003, the Norfolk Archaeological Unit excavated three trial pits in the hostry as part of an evaluation in advance of new development for an educational facility (Wallis 2003). They confirmed that the foundations of the extant east wall of the hostry sit directly on naturally derived sands, indicating that the Norman builders levelled the site comprehensively before construction began.

Whittingham excavated the chamber that was situated between the outer parlour and the guest hall. His plans show that the chamber had a door to the clois-ters and another on the west, but that there was no door communicating with the guest hall. He suggested that the structure comprised an undercroft with a chamber above. A lime floor was excavated, which had been replaced after subsidence, sealing deposits of animal bones and burnt refuse. Large quantities of painted plaster, lime plaster and mortar were noted, together with stained glass, some still in its lead came. Whittingham surmised that this material had fallen from the upper chamber, which he identified as the 'Great Chamber' or 'St Edmund's Chamber', on the basis of the surviving sixteenth-century inventory of the hostry.

Next to the outer door of the undercroft was the base of a fifteenth-century buttress and a single wall, suggesting that a small room had been built against the range. The room was partially excavated, revealing a lime floor with a border of bricks. Whittingham suggested that this room had been destroyed by fire, evidenced by moulten lead and wood ash from the roof; he later proposed that the structure had functioned as a garderobe. A passage was identified from the court outside the outer parlour, which also had a lime floor. Whittingham's primary interest seems to have been the stained glass, which he had conserved at Bonn University. He dated the glass to c.1300 and described trees, flowers, foliage and two figures, one of which he proposed was St Peter (MC 186/47 648x4 (7)).

In 1937, excavations took place at the western end of the refectory and the south end of the hostry hall (MC 186/50 648x4 (26)). Whittingham reported locating a privy pit under an arch next to the guest hall door from the cloister, presumably referring to the recess or *laver* discussed above. This pit was not fully excavated, but its fill was post-medieval, including eighteenth-century pottery, earthenware and bottles. Cellars of unknown date were also disturbed. Excavations in 1969 located further evidence of eighteenth and nineteenth-century cellars, pits and ceramics, including Delft, earthenware and transfer-printed wares (MC 186/50 648x4 (24) and (32)). It is likely that these remains related to a prebendary house that was established on the site of the communar's office to the west of the hostry site, c.1620, and demolished in the nineteenth century.

Whittingham proposed that the west range had been widened in the late thirteenth century, as part of the rebuilding that followed the fire of 1272. He assumed that the first building had corresponded in width with the twelfth-century phase of the outer parlour, in other words the three eastern bays. He conjectured that when the outer parlour was extended by a single bay to its present dimensions, the hall and its ancillary rooms were extended by the same amount. Unfortunately, his excavations in 1934, in the northern end of the former range, revealed no evidence to corroborate the postulated earlier narrow width of the hall. Archaeological evidence confirms only that the west wall of the hostry hall was in line with the extended outer parlour. The surviving remains of the porch doorway correspond with the extension to the outer parlour. Excavations by the Norfolk Archaeological Unit revealed that the wall adjoining the porch survives substantially, with buried remains extant to a height of c.0.6m above the footings (Wallis 2003). The maximum thickness of the wall is 1.3m, and to the south of the porch a recess survives (c.1.4m × 0.7m) with a possible base for a window colonnette, perhaps a bay window to the hall. A resistivity survey on the site revealed no evidence for foundations or demolition debris on an alignment consistent with the postulated early phase, but high resistance anomalies suggested a wall in line with the extant porch (Stratascan 1995). Ground penetrating radar has suggested that much of the thirteenth-century west wall may survive *in situ* as buried deposits (Stratascan 2003).

The provision of hospitality
The guest rooms at Norwich were provided with tapestry cushions, feather mattresses and pillows, embroidered quilts and linen tablecloths. Like the guest hall described in

the *Rites of Durham*, 'the chambers and lodginges . . . weare most sweetly keapt, and so richly furnyshed' (Fowler 1902, 90). Little archaeological evidence has survived to indicate the quality of furnishings in the hostry, with the exception of the fragmentary remains of a drinking vessel, a green-glazed aquamanile in the shape of a horse (Wallis 2003, 7). However, an inventory in the hostiliars' rolls of 1534–5 details the contents of seven rooms in the hostry (DCN 1/7/148). The rooms included the chapel of St Edmund, the great chamber of St Edmund, the lower chamber or the chamber of the Prior of Yarmouth, the chamber of the Prior of Aldeby, the lower accounting-house, the upper accounting-house and the great hall. All of these rooms can be located in the west range of the cloister.

Further information can be gleaned from the 148 obediential rolls of the hostiliar (DCN 1/7, 1319–1535). Mention of a lead roof to the chapel of St Edmund (1485) suggests that it occupied the upper floor of the range, and confirms that it was the chapel located over the surviving outer parlour. The hostry solar, or 'plancherloft', was first referred to in 1319, and until 1486. Its name implies an upper storey room with planchering or floor-boarding; the provision of beds to the plancherloft confirms that it was a sleeping space. A screen was added in 1339 and a fireplace in 1450. Repairs and plastering of the walls and porch were recorded in 1481. Beneath the 'plancherloft' a new chamber was made in 1421. A latrine, probably an en-suite garderobe, was mentioned from 1451 until 1473. This may coincide with the structure excavated by Whittingham; it is not clear whether he identified its function from the hostiliars' rolls, or from excavated evidence. While the location of a garderobe tower adjacent to the cathedral's west front may seem incongruous, it was mirrored in arrangements at the cathedral-priory of Coventry (Rylatt and Mason 2003). The hostiliar regularly purchased lime to cleanse the latrines, and was unique among the obedientiaries in this housekeeping measure (Saunders 1930, 129).

The great hall or guest hall was mentioned in the first surviving roll of 1319. It was lit by a 'chill', a hanging oil-burning lamp, until a candelabrum was suspended from the middle of the hall in 1439. The hall was heated by a 'cage' in 1331, and by a 'cresset' in 1422, which was an iron frame used to contain a fire. There was fencing at the door (1339) and a latrine (1343). There was a servants' chamber (1343), in which a screen was erected in 1348. As noted above, there was piped water to the hall, which gained its supply from the cloister *lavatorium* (1390). A door led from the hall to the upper inner court (1421), and there is a reference to a bell door (1404). The hall was plastered in 1422 and painted in 1473. It had a lead roof and guttering, and as noted above, poles were required to open its high windows (1440).

The hall step, which may refer to the surviving porch, was lit by a lantern (1442), and glass windows were made for it in 1457. There was fencing on either side of the crossing in the hostry entrance (1473). The northern part of the hall was plastered in 1473 and a fireplace was added in 1491. A cookhouse, connecting with the hall, was noted from 1380 until 1518. Upper and lower accounting houses are referred to from 1416 until 1534. Chambers allocated to the prior of Yarmouth

(1445–1491), the prior of Aldeby (1492–1522) and the prior of Lynn (1456–1526) possessed plastered and painted walls with fireplaces and paved floors.

The hostry had a garden described as a 'herber' containing stone pots, perhaps a private garden provided for guests to withdraw from the bustle of the inner court (Noble 1997, 10, 13). This had low chalk walls (1377) that were thatched (1464). Box appears to have been grown in the garden (1470), suggesting low, enclosing hedges. Flagstones were provided in 1471 and a pentice (single-pitch, lean-to roof) was made in 1498. The pentice enclosed an area to the north (?west) of the range, which also contained a well (1326), which was described as next to the guest hall (1443). The hostry gate was made in 1431 and it was provided with a fetterlock (1438). A wall outside the hostry gate was positioned against the green (1521).

This wealth of historical and archaeological evidence permits a vivid picture of the west range and upper inner court as it would have appeared in the later Middle Ages. But certain questions concerning the provision of hospitality at Norwich cathedral-priory remain unresolved. It is clear that the chambers at the north and south ends of the west range were reserved for monastic guests, as seems apparent from both the historical records and the direct access that was provided from the southern chamber to the refectory. The central space of the range was taken up by a ground-floor hall that was used principally for dining and reception. High-ranking guests were accommodated in the priors' lodgings from the later thirteenth century, but where did ordinary secular visitors sleep? The sustained demand for guest accommodation prompted the expansion of west ranges at other monasteries. This sometimes took the form of new blocks adjoining the west range, as at Bardney, Castle Acre, and Battle (Brakspear 1933). At the Benedictine abbey of Gloucester, a new ground-floor hall and two-storey chamber were built to the west in the fourteenth century, separated from the west range of the cloister by a small yard (Heighway 1999).

The emphasis on hospitality in cathedral-priories resulted in the development of detached guest halls in the later Middle Ages. At Winchester, for example, the 'Pilgrims' Hall' is likely to represent such expanded guest accommodation. This massive, ground-floor hall was detached from the cloister and located in the southern quarter of the precinct (Crook 1991). Similar accommodation was developed at St Augustine's, Canterbury, where a surviving range is located by the great gate, comprising a first floor hall of three bays over an undercroft kitchen (Tatton-Brown 1991, 73). At Worcester, a building known as the 'Guesten Hall' survived until 1862; this was a detached hall located to the east of the chapter house, near the priory gate and the almonry. Internally, it had elaborate figural and heraldic wall paintings, and externally, there were half-length sculpted figures mounted on a parapet (Park 1998). These life-like figures would have peered over the parapet as if watching the people below. This extraordinary device would have distinguished the guest hall, further marking it out as a beacon for visitors to the precinct.

Based on these comparisons, we must anticipate that Norwich cathedral-priory would have developed additional guest accommodation in the later Middle

Ages. The almoner's account for 1484 suggests that expansion was achieved by extending the hostry to the south, towards the almonry. The almoner, Thomas Fulmerston, paid expenses for a new building 'partly in the hostry and partly in the almonry' totalling £39 2s 2¼d (DCN 1/6/99).[5] The extended building was created in the space between the cellarer's range to the west and the kitchens and infirmary to the east. A distinction between the hostry hall and this guest hall is implied in the records for the distribution of daily rations of bread: there were routinely twenty guests in the hostry hall and another fifty transient visitors, workmen and servants from the monastic manors, accommodated in the common hall (Saunders 1930, 162). This 'great common hall' had its own storeroom, which was rebuilt in 1534 at a cost of £6 8s (DCN 1/1/107). The archaeological implication is clear: one or more major medieval buildings remain to be mapped in the area of the upper inner court at Norwich. To fulfil its obligations of hospitality, the cathedral-priory at Norwich remodelled and expanded the west range of the cloister in the later Middle Ages, and its final extent remains unknown.

[5] Dr Paul Cattermole generously provided the details of this entry in the almoner's rolls, comprising thirty-two lines of expenses. An old building is stripped of its roof, old windows are taken out and preserved, new windows are purchased, and several loads of brick and lime are used. The carpenter was Andrew Couper and masons included John Antell and Robert Everard.

6
Landscapes of Power:
the Bishop's Palace
and the Prior's Lodging

To the north of the church and cloister of Norwich cathedral-priory was the bishop's palace, a complex that signalled his supremacy through the strategic use of landscape design and architectural form. Herbert de Losinga modelled an episcopal landscape that would dominate the precinct of Norwich cathedral, and convey imperial imagery to signal the 'near royal' status of the bishop (Faulkner 1970, 130). There was no tangible focus of competing power within the monastery until the thirteenth century, when the prior's lodging was developed to the east of the cloister, sited audaciously to align the prior's private chambers with the high altars of the cathedral church and the bishop's chapel.

THE BISHOP'S PALACE

The site of the bishop's palace was established early in the precinct's development: the primary wing was completed by founder-bishop Herbert de Losinga (1091–1119), and formerly projected directly from the cathedral's nave. There was no standard position for bishop's palaces in relation to cathedrals, but in general a western site in the outer court was preferred, as at Canterbury, Worcester, Rochester and Ely (Thompson 1998, 35). Old Sarum and Lichfield, like Norwich, had their bishop's palaces to the north of the cathedral church. The siting at Norwich follows the St Gall plan, which shows the abbot's house to the north of the church in line with the transept (Horn and Born 1979, vol. 1, 321). Within a cathedral-priory, the bishop was the titular abbot, although all practical aspects of this role were performed by the prior.

Herbert claimed that the siting of his palace was determined by his consideration for the priory, so that his residence 'should not cause disturbance to the peace of the monks' (*First Register*, quoted in Fernie 1993, 89). It is evident in the physical remains of the palace, however, that de Losinga sought to create an elite landscape, using natural topography and earthwork construction to create the best vantage point. Feudal institutions such as castles, palaces and cathedrals were frequently placed in commanding topographical positions. Further, it has been suggested that by the mid twelfth century, Norman magnates were developing designed landscapes, 'areas adjacent to residential sites that had undergone conscious manipulation in order to produce a specific effect, aesthetic or otherwise' (Liddiard 1999, 170). The bishop created an earthwork platform or *motte* on which a fortified tower was erected, establishing a site from which he could view the construction and development of his cathedral-priory. For two decades the bishop's tower would have visually dominated the marshy grounds of the precinct, before completion of the cathedral's crossing tower to the height of the roof ridge of the church. The bishop's intentions can be compared with the later builder of Castle Rising, Norfolk (c. 1140), sited by William d'Albini II on a false crest to promote visibility, with the keep exercising 'a commanding *visual* presence over the surrounding countryside' (Liddiard 1999, 176). Rising was sited on an earlier seigneurial settlement, perhaps indicating 'that the *social* advantages of a specific location were exploited by Norman castle builders' (ibid.; emphasis original). The bishop's palace reused the site of the former parish church of Holy Trinity, verified by Saxon burials that have been observed beneath the primary wing of the palace (see p. 23). De Losinga may have intended to promote a sense of ecclesiastical continuity, through the adoption of the precise site of the earlier church and cemetery. It may be suggested that the vocabulary of the Norman 'designed landscape' pre-dated the construction of private castles, and can be discerned in earlier episcopal residences such as Norwich. It has been observed by John Blair that bishops were architectural innovators in other respects, such as the early adoption of the courtyard plan (Blair 1993), and their experimentation with landscaping may have developed in parallel with these new architectural forms.

The architecture of the cathedral church was also ordered so as to convey the bishop's commanding presence. The plainness of the interior is interrupted by the special embellishment that was given to the north transept, signalling its close association with the bishop (Fernie 1993, 81–3; Franklin 1996, 117–20; Gilchrist 1999, 128). The door leading from the bishop's palace to the north transept was decorated with triangular arches and carved beasts' heads, while the exterior was surmounted by a relief carving of a bishop offering a blessing with his right hand and holding a crozier in his left.[1] Eric Fernie has argued that the carving represents the seventh-century saint Felix, the first bishop of East Anglia (Fernie 1993, 83–7). The treatment of the door's interior is also nostalgic, with the use of triangular-headed arches and gabled billet more in keeping with late Saxon construction. Just as the placement and treatment of the bishop's throne were intended to create a sense of antiquity (see p. 74), the bishop's entrance to the cathedral was adorned with the trappings of the past. De Losinga transmitted dual messages through the landscaping of his palace and the careful treatment of episcopal areas of the cathedral church. By stressing both ecclesiastical continuity and Norman authority, the site of his new see would be given greater legitimacy.

Later bishops were resident only intermittently at the see palace, and moved

[1] The original sculpture is now displayed in the south ambulatory, and a copy is in place over the north transept door.

regularly between episcopal manors of the diocese: for example, in 1354 Bishop William Bateman spent only one week at the palace during a six-month itinerary (Thompson 1998, 12). Two particular bishops, Suffield and Salmon, invested substantial time and resources in the palace and its vicinity, enhancing the episcopal enclave that de Losinga had envisaged. In 1249, Bishop Walter Suffield (1244–57) established St Giles' hospital on the cathedral's lands to the north of the precinct. Although the hospital was outside the palace and precinct, the higher ground of the bishop's palace overlooked St Giles, providing the bishop with an enduring view of his foundation. Bishop John Salmon (1299–1325) expanded the size of the palace grounds considerably in the early fourteenth century, taking in land to the north of the original wing (see p. 28). The western boundary of the palace abutted the cathedral's lay cemetery, and by 1316, the south-western part of this area had been dedicated to the college of St John the Evangelist.

The college was established by Bishop Salmon (1299–1325) to serve as his own chantry foundation, and to provide a charnel facility for the storage of the bones of people buried in the city's parochial cemeteries (see p. 34). As noted previously, the form of the Carnary chapel can be compared to a shrine or reliquary. The charnel fragments in its crypt could be viewed through ocular windows, reminiscent of the holes provided in the *foramina* shrine, through which the bones of saints were visible. The Carnary chapel can also be considered within the palatial tradition of two-storey chapels, including Charlemagne's palace chapel at Aachen (c.800) (Fernie 1993, 182). In common with his predecessor Bishop de Losinga, Salmon drew on architectural symbolism to enhance the grandeur of the palace and cathedral at Norwich. It may be no coincidence that Charlemagne's palace at Aachen seems to have provided the archetype for both the two-storey chapel, and for the gallery-level passage that linked the cathedral church with the accommodation of the palace. The two-storey chapel recalled imperial imagery, and situated the Carnary college within Salmon's visionary scheme for the bishop's palace.

Salmon also ambitiously expanded the palace buildings, on a scale comparable to that of Bishop Burnell's remodelling at Wells (1274–92) (Wood 1965, 34). Salmon's rebuilding coincided with the major reconstruction of many of the priory's buildings after the riot of 1272, but it may have been intended more to mark his personal success as chancellor to Edward III (1319–23). He extended and heightened the earthwork platform or terrace on which the palace was constructed, emphasising three distinct vistas: south towards the bishop's entrance to the north transept, and east and west towards the episcopal chantry foundations of St Giles' hospital and the Carnary college.

Salmon's work completed the landscape of power that was forged principally by three of the bishops of Norwich. Others demonstrated their prominence through funding the rebuilding of elements of the church (see p. 76), and by establishing their own elaborate tombs within the presbytery, of which those of Bishop Wakering (d. 1425) and Bishop Goldwell (d. 1499) survive (Finch 1996, 470–2). Notably, the tomb-shrines of Suffield and Salmon received pilgrims' offerings well into the fourteenth century (Shinners 1988, 135), reflecting the popularity of these bishops throughout the period of tension between the monks and the citizens of Norwich. From the foundation up to 1550, there were twenty-four bishops buried in the cathedral church, from a possible total of twenty-nine. Episcopal burials were carefully sited: there were nine bishops buried in the presbytery, five in the Lady chapel, two in the choir, four in the nave, and four in unknown locations in the church (St John Hope 1899; St John Hope and Bensly 1901, 113).

In 1899, a group of burials was investigated in the eastern bays of the nave, to the west of the *pulpitum* and near the altar and shrine of St William (Figure 50). This group of burials provides our only insight to date into the funerary practices of the cathedral. The skeletons were interred within wooden coffins in brick vaults, the largest of which was over 2.4m long, 1m wide and 1m deep (8ft × 3ft × 3ft); the vaults were plastered internally and covered with slabs which rested on a brick lip, beneath the floor pavement. The survival of associated organic material was exceptional. The grave believed to have been that of Bishop Thomas Brown (1436–45) contained a skeleton interred in a single, woven garment, with a thin layer of what was presumed to be hay covering the body. The body identified as that of Bishop Walter Lyhart (1446–72) was fully clothed in mass vestments, mitre, gloves and accompanied by a bishop's crozier, with a bundle of what was reputed to be heather placed over his feet (St John Hope and Bensly 1901, 116–21). An uncoffined burial in grave clothes was accompanied by a gilt bronze signet ring showing the small device of a bird; this heraldry has been identified subsequently as possibly that of Prior William Spynk (Sims 1996, 461). These graves are comparable with ecclesiastical interments excavated at other cathedrals, for example, at York minster and the chapter houses at Durham and Lincoln (Ramm 1971; Fowler 1880; Bruce-Mitford 1976). They are consistent with the tradition for ecclesiastics to be buried clothed, and in particular adorned in the vestments worn at their consecration. The lavish dressing of episcopal burials suggests that the corpses were prepared for a period of lying in state. The garments themselves held particular significance: the vestments worn at an individual's consecration symbolised their death and rebirth through religious orders. It was fitting that they should be worn at a monastic's second death, and their subsequent rebirth through the Resurrection (Gilchrist and Sloane 2005).

Four main phases of development can be proposed for the medieval bishop's palace, and a distinctive symbolic scheme can be detected in its architecture (Figure 50). In contrast with the bishop's palaces at Durham, Winchester and Wells, the buildings at Norwich were not placed around a courtyard, but rather developed in a linear fashion. The primary construction was completed by de Losinga, comprising a single residential wing projecting at a near right angle from the north side of the cathedral's nave. To the east of this was a free-standing, apsidal chapel, traced archaeologically in 1859 (Harrod 1864). Slightly later in the twelfth century, perhaps under Bishop William Turbe (1146–73), a hall was added to the north-east corner of the residential wing. This addition created an L-shaped arrangement, comparable to the T-shaped complexes dating to the thirteenth century at the archbishop's pal-

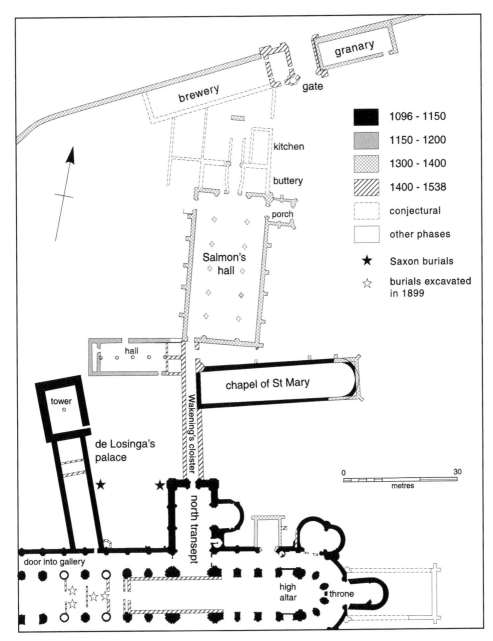

FIGURE 50. Plan of the bishop's palace. See Plate 9 for full phased plan. Drawing by Margaret Mathews.

ace at Canterbury (Rady et al. 1991), and the bishop's palace at Worcester (Emery 2000, 464), and common in manorial architecture of the thirteenth and fourteenth centuries (Grenville 1997, 98). In the fourteenth century, Salmon added a magnificent aisled hall to the north-east, unsurpassed in scale by any episcopal hall.

He inserted stone vaults into the Norman tower and adjacent hall, and rebuilt the bishop's chapel with a rectangular eastern end. In common with developments at other see palaces, the earlier hall became the bishop's chamber block. In the fifteenth century, a gatehouse was added in the northern precinct wall, and a cloister was constructed to link the great hall, smaller hall and chapel to the north transept, attributed to Bishop Wakering (1415–25) (Browne [1680] 1954, 126).

In some respects the development of the medieval bishop's palace at Norwich was typical of English see palaces, which seem to have begun with two-storeyed blocks in the continental style, later developing secondary halls (Thompson 1998, 32). However, the Norman phases at Norwich were unusual in two significant respects. First, the primary feature of the palace was a three-storey fortified tower, to which hall accommodation was added subsequently. Secondly, a direct physical connection existed between the bishop's palace and the cathedral church, comprising an early twelfth-century link to the nave at gallery level. The provision of a tower at one end of the original block can be compared with early Italian episcopal palaces, which were two-storey ranges with accommodation over a vaulted undercroft, sometimes provided with a tower at one end (Miller 1995). This arrangement, in common with the provision of communicating access at first-floor level, drew from the precedent of Carolingian imperial palaces.

The significance of episcopal access to the gallery of cathedral churches can be traced at Lincoln and Canterbury in the late eleventh century. Richard Gem proposed that the west end of Lincoln minster appears to have been constructed as a defensible tower or block, rather than as a conventional westwork (Gem 1986). David Stocker and Alan Vince have developed this theory, working from topographical and architectural evidence, to suggest that the minster's west end was built as a free-standing great tower, which served as the bishop's hall block within the first castle at Lincoln (Stocker and Vince 1997). They propose that there were two entirely different castles built at Lincoln: the first, founded 1068, was an emergency measure focused on the reoccupation of the Upper Roman city. Part of this work would have been the great tower in stone built by Remigius adjacent to, or part of, his new cathedral (Stocker 1994). Just as at Norwich, the completion of the cathedral church at Lincoln, consecrated in 1092, seems to have been secondary to the bishop's tower. The proximity of the bishop's hall in the west tower would have facilitated a gallery-level entrance to a possible tribune gallery. A similar juxtaposition occurred at Christ Church, Canterbury, where Lanfranc constructed a palace adjacent to the cathedral's west front, which would have allowed direct access to a tribune gallery from the archbishop's private accommodation (Rady et al. 1991, 4).

Episcopal access at Norwich consisted of a vaulted passage that led from the bishop's tower to the gallery of the north aisle of the nave. The passage was secondary to the tower, with the former constructed c.1096, and the passage added approximately two decades later, before 1119. The resulting pattern of access to the cathedral was paralleled at Notre Dame in Paris (Thompson 1998, 31), and in the later Middle Ages at cathedrals including Ely, Trondheim (Norway) and Roskilde

PLATE 1

Drawing by Richard Wright, c. 1630–50, showing the cathedral from the north. Reproduced with permission of the Norfolk Record Office, NRO ACC 1997/215.

PLATE 2

A. Carved boss showing a laundress protecting the washing from a thief, in the east cloister (fourth bay from the north). Photograph © Roberta Gilchrist.

B. Carved boss depicting a green man, in the east cloister (second bay from the south). Photograph © Roberta Gilchrist.

C. Carved boss from the life of Christ series, showing Christ Carrying the Cross, in the east cloister (fourth bay from the north). Photograph © Roberta Gilchrist.

PLATE 3

A. Carved boss above the refectory door in the south cloister walk, showing the temptation of Adam and Eve by the serpent. Photograph © Roberta Gilchrist.

B. Carved boss of the Three Marys at the Sepulchre, in the north cloister (second bay from the east). Photograph © Roberta Gilchrist.

C. Carved boss from the Apocalypse series, in the south cloister (sixth bay from the east). Photograph © Roberta Gilchrist.

'And when he had opened the fourth seal, I heard the voice of the fourth beast say, Come and see. And I looked, and behold a pale horse: and his name that sat on him was Death, and Hell followed with him' (Revelation 6: 7–8).

PLATE 4

A. J. H. Brown's elevation of the north wall of the monastic refectory as it existed in 1873. Only six of the medieval windows remained *in situ*, and a crowstepped gable matched those of the deanery. The prebendary house is shown on the eastern end, before its demolition. Photographed by Terence J. Burchell. Reproduced with permission of the Norfolk Record Office and the Chapter of Norwich Cathedral, NRO DCN 127/64.

B. Refectory north wall before construction of new restaurant (2001–4): digitally rectified photograph by Roland Harris. Copyright Chapter of Norwich Cathedral.

PLATE 5

Reconstruction of the monastic refectory before the fire of 1272. Drawing by Margaret Mathews.

PLATE 6

Water-colour from Mrs Stanley's sketchbook (c.1837–49), showing wing of the bishop's palace before the remodelling of 1859 severed the connection to the nave. Reproduced with permission of Norwich Castle Museum and Art Gallery: 1916.151.3.

PLATE 7

Water-colour of the south transept by David Hodgson, c. 1832, before remodelling by Anthony Salvin removed the house incorporating the slype, and the medieval passage between the dark entry and the prior's lodging (deanery). Reproduced with permission of the Norfolk Record Office and the Chapter of Norwich Cathedral, NRO DCN 128/1.

Plate 8

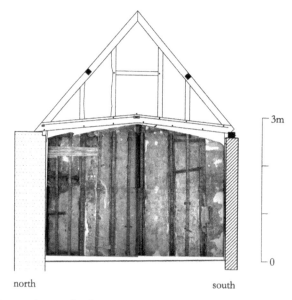

north   south

A. First-floor gable inserted into the former infirmary chambers (Number 65), as part of the re-modelling to create a prebendary house. Gable drawn by Robert Smith, photographs by Terence J. Burchell, publication drawing by Philip Thomas.

B. Detail of wall painting on the first-floor gable in Number 65, showing a candelabra scheme in black and white on a background of red, dating to the mid sixteenth century. Photograph by Terence J. Burchell.

(Denmark). The arrangement may be compared with the exclusive access of the king from palace to royal chapel, and the likely model is Charlemagne's palace at Aachen, in which a first-floor connection provided direct passage for the emperor from the great throne room or hall, southwards towards the church. It seems that de Losinga's architectural model for the bishop's palace evoked the grandest imperial imagery, a message that would be repeated in the architectural schemes of Bishop Salmon.

The cathedral's *First Register* records that the bishop's residence was completed during de Losinga's episcopate (1096–1119), with the exception of the great hall. Architectural dating of the surviving fabric is difficult, since its face is obscured by flint rubble (Figure 51), and the interior has been modified substantially to accommodate the Norwich School since 1958. Eric Fernie has observed that the simple rectangular profiles and tooling of the transverse arches in the undercroft, similar to those in the aisles of the cathedral, confirm a date contemporaneous with de Losinga (Fernie 1993, 55). The cathedral's *Customary* describes 'the chapel of St Mary in the bishop's court' (ibid., 55). This chapel was identified by Henry Harrod's excavations in 1859, which focused on the complex of buildings associated with Bishop Salmon. Harrod discovered that Salmon's chapel was not the first bishop's chapel on the site: beneath the foundation of his chapel, was 'the massive apse of one of Bishop Herbert's time' (Harrod 1864, 36). The axis of the bishop's chapel varies slightly from

FIGURE 51. The eastern elevation of De Losinga's palace (now the Norwich School). Photograph © Roberta Gilchrist.

that of the cathedral, but its siting must have deliberately aligned the sanctuaries of both buildings.

Several pieces of evidence point to there having been two Norman phases of construction to complete de Losinga's wing. In particular, it may be proposed that the fortified tower at the north end was the primary building, since it differs from the passage to the south in its wall thickness. The wing of the bishop's palace joins the cathedral church at an oblique and uncomfortable angle, perhaps indicating that the tower was constructed before the alignment of the church had been established. This may suggest that the passage was added subsequently, when the first phase of building the cathedral had been completed. It is also instructive to consider the relationship of the bishop's tower to his private chapel, located directly to the east. Both buildings share their alignment, but neither was planned in relation to the cathedral church. This suggests either that the tower and chapel were contemporary, and pre-dated the setting out of the cathedral, or that the chapel was earlier, and formed the focus for the location of the bishop's tower. Harrod's excavations on the site of the bishop's chapel revealed an apsidal building (Harrod 1864, 36), but provided no concrete evidence to enable us to distinguish between a late Saxon and an early Norman structure. The distinctive alignment of the tower and chapel may suggest that de Losinga sited his hall block to the west of an existing Anglo-Saxon church, the same pattern evidenced at Lincoln (Stocker 2004), and at de Losinga's native Fécamp. Both the shared alignment of the bishop's tower and chapel, and their close proximity to excavated Saxon burials, suggest that the chapel of St Mary is a strong candidate for the location of the Saxon parish church of Holy Trinity.

Pictorial evidence provides further insight to the bishop's palace before its remodelling in 1859. A water-colour from Mrs Stanley's sketchbook, dated to Edward Stanley's episcopate (1837–49) (Plate 6), shows the complete north–south wing, before the remodelling of 1859 severed the connection to the nave of the cathedral, and altered the building joining the tower to the north (*Norwich Mercury*, 5 May, 1858). This drawing depicts three separate structures making up the wing, all with different roofs, room depths and external treatments. The water-colour depicts three discrete structures, confirming plan evidence of the same date (DN/ADR 10/4/3). In summary, a date for the tower is proposed of c.1096, built immediately to provide a secure base from which the bishop could oversee construction of the cathedral and priory. Approximately twenty years later, once the first phase of the church had been completed, the vaulted passage was added to create a wing of two-storey accommodation and a direct connection with the church. Documentary and archaeological evidence combines to confirm that before de Losinga's death in 1119, the cathedral had been completed to the point where the passage from the bishop's palace joined it (see p. 69).

By 1120, the palace was a wing of private rooms linked directly with the nave of the cathedral at its fourth and fifth bays, allowing the bishop to enter at gallery level, where a blocked doorway can still be seen. This door provided him with an

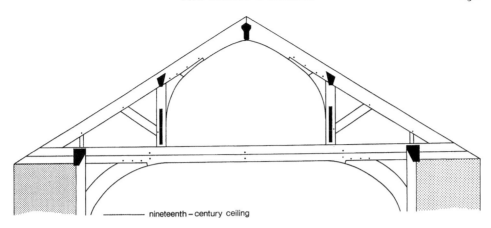

nineteenth – century ceiling

FIGURE 52. A queen-post roof was inserted into the tower of De Losinga's palace in the fifteenth century (now hidden by a nineteenth-century ceiling). Drawing by Robert Smith. Reproduced with permission of Robert Smith.

alternative to the ground-level entrance in the north transept, and a gallery-level route that would still bring him through the strategically decorated spaces of the transept. The residential accommodation was placed over a barrel vault, and terminated to the north with the original tower, which has been described as a miniature keep (Whittingham 1949; Heywood 1996, 109). Its external dimensions are approximately 15.6m by 11.9m, and its walls vary in thickness from 1.8m to 1.9m. It retains an inner door on its south-east corner (hidden in cupboards), chimney flues on the north wall, a garderobe chute in the west wall, and a wall-passage over the outer door, which retains some of its timber centring. A keep was constructed in the bishop's palace at Wolvesey (Winchester) (Biddle 1986), but the structure at Norwich had a wall thickness of only 1.8m, and is likely to have been a fortified great tower, containing a hall. Into this Norman tower, Bishop Salmon inserted a rib-vaulted undercroft of four bays, with a central octagonal pier and hollow chamfered arches (Pevsner and Wilson 1997, 220). The wide fireplaces in the north wall suggest that this structure served as the kitchen, with a prison documented below, c. 1400 (Whittingham 1980a, 365–6). A plan made in 1858 before remodelling of the palace, shows a later building joining the tower on the north side (DN/ADR 10/4/3). In a redrawing of this plan, Whittingham described this feature as a forebuilding to a keep (1980a, 365), implying a Norman date. Pictorial evidence suggests instead that the building linked to the north of the keep was considerably later, perhaps seventeenth century.[2] The nineteenth-century remodelling of the tower included a groin vault that hides a fifteenth-century queen-post roof (Figure 52). On the eastern face of the original wing of the palace, two blocked Romanesque windows can still be

[2] An engraving by John Kirkpatrick, dated c. 1686–1728, shows a long building with a Dutch gable in this position, and two small structures abutting its northern end (Norwich Castle Museum, Fitch Collection 1698.76.94; shown on p. 561 of Atherton et al. 1996).

FIGURE 53. The eastern elevation of De Losinga's palace, showing blocked Romanesque arches and stringcourse. Photograph © Roberta Gilchrist.

seen, together with a mutilated stringcourse and two large blind arches, suggesting that a further structure projected from the east (Figure 53).

In the latter part of the twelfth century, an east–west range was added to the east of the primary wing (Figure 54). It can be dated by a blocked doorway at the eastern end of the south wall, with horizontal chevron ornament (Figure 55). Surviving evidence confirms that Bishop Salmon inserted stone vaults in this structure in the fourteenth century to create a two-storey hall, with private chambers at the upper level. There is an inserted undercroft of four double bays supported on a double row of columns, with quadripartite vaulting and ribs springing from a central pier. The unanswered vault springings at its eastern end indicate that the undercroft originally continued further east, as indicated on Whittingham's plan of 1949. Harrod observed a staircase arrangement suggesting that this range served as private chambers, communicating directly with the later great hall and rebuilt chapel to the east (Harrod 1864). The provision of a ground-floor aisled hall and two-storey chamber block was common in higher status settlement from the twelfth century (Blair 1993), and is found, for example, at the bishop's palace at Lincoln (Thompson 1998, 38).

Of Bishop's Salmon's new hall (1318–25), only the two-bay porch survives (Figure 56). The excavated plan shows that the scale of the hall was exceptional,

FIGURE 54. The small hall in the bishop's palace, added in the twelfth century, with vaulting inserted in the fourteenth century. Photograph © Roberta Gilchrist.

at 36.6m long by 18.3m wide (120ft × 60ft). Harrod (1864) uncovered the foundations of this massive, aisled hall of six bays, with kitchen, pantry and buttery indicated at the north end. The size of Salmon's hall was exceeded only by the early thirteenth-century archbishop's hall at Canterbury, known from the Parliamentary Survey to have been 168ft long and 64ft wide (Rady et al. 1991, 6). It compared with later fourteenth-century halls of the highest status, such as the royal palace of Westminster (Grenville 1997, 109). Salmon's social aspirations were reflected in the dimensions of his hall and in the lavishness of its decoration, with this little-known structure representing the apogee of the great aisled halls (Wood 1965, 40).

Today, the detail of the porch is difficult to discern fully, but it was recorded by John Adey Repton, c.1798 (Pierce 1965). The two-storey porch opened out of the hall, and comprises two open bays rather than the more usual single bay. It retains shafts with lively foliage capitals, supporting tierceron vaults. The vaulting of the porch is completed by carved bosses, including foliage and three morality scenes, interpreted as Covetousness (a rich man in a net, tussling with a workman for a church), Absolution (a penitent woman being blessed by a priest) (Fernie and Whittingham 1972, 33,) and Lust (the devil perched behind a man and woman holding hands). The arcading of the hall survives against the west wall of the porch,

FIGURE 55. The blocked doorway of the small twelfth-century hall in the bishop's palace. The raised ground level dates from the reconstruction of the bishop's chapel in the late seventeenth century. Photograph © Roberta Gilchrist.

where there are ogee-headed niches on either side of the door. Harrod suggested that the services were located to the north of the hall. The evidence for his attribution is likely to have come from a survey made of the bishop's palace in 1646. This describes chambers to the north of Bishop Salmon's porch: 'An old building conteyning 54 foote in length, and 20 in breadth, the lower roomes were formerly the butteries to the greate old hall burnt downe' (Stewart 1875, 185). The location of the services at the north end would place the upper end of the hall to the south, allowing private access for the bishop to his chambers above the old (east–west) hall, and providing excellent views of vistas to the north transept, Carnary college and St Giles' hospital.

Additional service buildings were located to the north and north-east of the fourteenth-century great hall. On either side of the bishop's gate (see p. 54–5) were the granary and brewery, indicated by the survey of 1646:

> There is a longe row, a range of buildings at the entrance of the outward court yard conteyning in length 289 foote and in breadth about 20 foote. In this range of buildings there is a gatehouse Tower, strong and in good repair; and two other old towers, one in decay. A middle part of this range conteyning 58 foote in length is imployed for stables. At the west end of this rowe of build-

FIGURE 56. The extant porch that led into Bishop Salmon's hall. The hall was constructed 1318–25, demolished c.1550 and excavated in 1864. Photograph © Roberta Gilchrist.

ings is about 100 foote in length imployed for a brewhouse, by the gatehouse Tower is a Porters lodge of one roome, and under is a Dungeon called the Bishops prison (Stewart 1875, 185).

To the east of the gate the former granary survives, a refaced fifteenth-century building, with three lancet windows on the north elevation. The south elevation is made up of the same finely-knapped flint bricks that survive in the lower courses of the current bishop's chapel, representing the southern bay of Salmon's hall (see p. 231). These outbuildings are tucked within the defensive wall of the precinct, constructed of flint rubble, which at this point shows signs of arches that carried a wall-walk.

'Wakering's cloister' was added c.1420, a single-storey walkway that provided covered access from the bishop's palace complex to the door in the cathedral's north transept. Evidence of its penticed roof structure survives in the external north wall of the north transept (Gilchrist 1999, 114, 120, 126), and the walls of the cloister passage were drawn in 1816 before their subsequent demolition (Britton 1817). Foundations believed to be associated with Wakering's cloister were observed during a watching brief in 1989 (Norfolk SMR No. 26387).

The Prior's Lodging

The heads of monastic houses resided initially in the common dormitory, but separate residences developed from as early as the twelfth century. The architectural form taken by these lodgings was closely modelled on the secular hall, embodying the status and obligations of the prior as a feudal lord. M. W. Thompson has observed that these residences reveal the contradictions evident in the roles of a monastic superior – the tension between the asceticism of religious life and the luxury due to a high-ranking lord (Thompson 2001, 65). Their accommodation mirrored that of a self-contained manor house, providing hall and chamber, chapel and outbuildings. The prior's lodging sometimes became a semi-autonomous household employing a substantial staff, as at Canterbury, Durham, Ely and Westminster (Emery 2000, 39). At Norwich, the expenses of the prior's household were accounted primarily by the master of the cellar, including most repairs to buildings and the stipends of staff, such as the prior's cook in 1335 (DCN 1/1/33). The size of the prior's household can be estimated from the purchase of cloth made in 1256 to clothe fifty people in the prior's household: six clerks, fifteen *homines de ministerio*, nine squires, nine *garciones* and eleven unclassified individuals (Saunders 1930, 87).

The superiors at Benedictine and Augustinian monasteries developed the west range of the cloister for their private accommodation, with well preserved examples surviving at Castle Acre (Norfolk) and Battle (Sussex) (Brakspear 1933; Wood 1965, 23–8). The exceptional status of the abbot at Bury St Edmunds encouraged him to relocate his residence on three occasions. He moved from the dormitory to the west range, and from there to a site near the cellarer's gate, and finally by the late thirteenth century to a riverside location away from the cloister (Whittingham 1951). From the thirteenth century, Cistercian abbots developed lodgings detached from the cloister, as the west range was often taken up by the accommodation of the lay brothers. The west range of a cathedral-priory was devoted to its duty of hospitality, so that residences for their priors were developed adjacent to the cloister, for example to the south at Ely, Winchester and Durham, and to the east at Norwich. The prior's lodging extended hospitality to visitors of the highest status: in 1343, the master of the cellar at Norwich complained of the financial strain of the previous eight years, which had seen four visits from the king and three from the queen (Saunders 1930, 80). High-ranking laity were given gifts of rings and brooches by the prior, and his table was stocked with expensive freshwater fish (sturgeon, pike, lampreys, eel tarts), sugars, reserved wine and porpoises (for consumption as fish during Lent). Players and minstrels were paid for entertaining guests during meals in the prior's hall.

A date of c.1284 is generally given for the building of the prior's hall at Norwich, based on a reference in the accounts of the master of the cellar for 1284, referring to payment for the windows in the prior's chamber and cellar (Saunders 1930, 87). It is likely that before the construction of this separate lodging, the prior resided in a self-contained chamber over the dark entry (see p. 115). A late thirteenth-century date is consistent with evidence for the first phase of the prior's lodging, comprising a ground-floor hall with a private chamber contained in an end solar (Figure 57). The hall was entered by a deep porch that connected with a vault beneath the monks' dormitory, entered via the dark entry. A second phase saw the

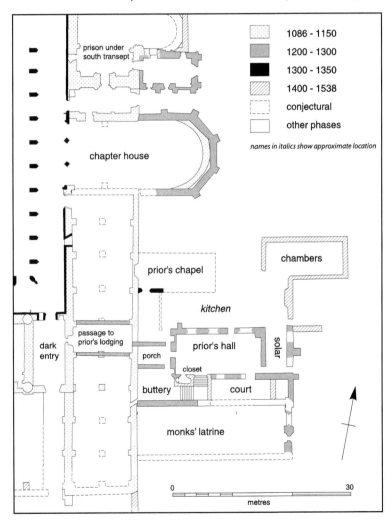

FIGURE 57. Plan of the prior's lodging. See Plate 9 for full phased plan. Drawing by Margaret Mathews.

addition to the north of a detached private chapel for the prior, c.1330. In the early sixteenth century a major refurbishment took place, involving the insertion of a floor into the open hall, expansion into a courtyard to the south, the creation of a gallery access to the chapel, and the building of a new residential wing to the north. Appurtenances noted in the obediential rolls include a private garden and orchard next to the prior's carting stable (Noble 1997, 4), features likely to have been sited directly to the east towards the outer court. Although none of these outbuildings survive, at Winchester a medieval stable range still exists to the south of the prior's lodging, a timber-framed building with a clasped-purlin roof (Munby and Fletcher 1983, 108). By the late fifteenth century the prior at Norwich had his own kitchen, evidently placed between his hall and chapel. In 1471, the refectorer paid a carpenter 15d for repairing the door below the vault next to the chapel and cookhouse of the prior (DCN 1/8/95), clearly referring to the vault beneath the monks' dormitory. This vault was entered from the dark entry, the slype leading from the cloister to the infirmary. The survival of a squint next to the door to the dark entry confirms that a porter was positioned here to regulate the monks' access to both the infirmary and the prior's lodging (Figure 58).

The prior's hall is aligned east–west and constructed in flint rubble with stone dressings. It was built to the north of the monks' latrine and parallel with it, with the enclosed space between the two buildings forming a narrow courtyard approximately 3.4m by 0.6m (11ft × 2ft) (Whittingham 1938). The hall itself measures 14.3m long by 6.7m wide (47ft by 22ft) and was lit by three windows in each side wall. Two of these remain in the north wall, and the splay of a third was discovered in 1928, during renovations by Dean Cranage. The surviving Geometric tracery confirms a late thirteenth-century date: each window has two lights and a pointed arch with an inverted foil (Figure 59). The painted beams of the original ceiling of the hall were discovered in 1889, above the later panelled ceiling (Fox 1892). They show no damage from smoke blackening, indicating that the prior's hall had a wall fireplace. The traditional open hall was comparatively rare in medieval towns, even amongst the wealthier classes (Pearson 2005; contra Pantin 1962). The choice of this form for the prior's hall, and the guest hall in the west range, may indicate the deliberate cultivation of a connection with the rural manor house, and its traditional connotations of feudal lordship.

The sides of the rafters of the thirteenth-century roof were decorated with chevrons, alternating white and red, and outlined with black (Fox 1892). There were also heraldic devices such as lions and eagles, and quatrefoils containing male busts. It has been suggested that these busts may have belonged to a series representing the five senses, since one of the surviving two gestures towards his eyes, while the other drinks from a cup (Park and Howard 1996, 403). With its overtones of sensory indulgence and luxurious consumption, this scheme would have been particularly appropriate to the newly constructed prior's lodging. Stylistically the paintings are consistent with a late thirteenth-century date, and are therefore a very rare survival of early domestic decoration.

FIGURE 58. Dark entry and squint from the cloister, controlling access between the infirmary, prior's lodging and cloister. Photograph © Roberta Gilchrist.

The hall was entered from the lower end by the porch, through a doorway reached from the passage under the dormitory (Figure 60); the passage survived until the 1830s (Plate 7). The blocked door survives in the fabric of the deanery, and in 2003, a watching brief recorded the foundations of the two walls that formed the passage, with a tiled surface between them (Wallis in press). In the north wall of the porch there are the remains of a moulded jamb that may have formed a recess for a hand basin or lamp locker. Service rooms were located to the south of the porch and are likely to have served as the pantry and buttery. Blocked doors in the north and south walls of the porch allowed access between these rooms and the kitchen to the north, creating a screens passage. The prior's solar was a small room approximately 14.3m by 3.5m (22ft × 11ft 6in), occupying the space between the

FIGURE 59. Exterior of the prior's hall showing Geometric tracery of the two surviving windows, dating to the later thirteenth century. Photograph © Roberta Gilchrist.

hall and the eastern extent of the building. Thus, the earliest phase of the prior's lodging can be compared directly with the classic tripartite plan of manorial halls, c.1300: a central open hall, with the solar or private apartment of the lord at one end, and the service rooms at the other, separated by a screened cross passage. His solar was directly in line with the high altar of the cathedral church, and with that of the bishop's chapel.

Whittingham suggested that the prior's chapel was constructed sometime between 1310 and 1330 (Whittingham 1967; 1980c). Its presence by 1335 is confirmed by the master of the cellar's purchase of a rope for the veil[3] in the prior's chapel (DCN 1/1/33). Its location is verified by a repair paid by the communar in 1407 for one of the chapter house buttresses next to the prior's chapel (Fernie and Whittingham 1972). From this evidence, the chapel can be identified as part of the surviving fabric of the current deanery. The west wall of the chapel and one jamb of the door in its south wall survive incorporated in later structures that face onto the modern roadway leading to the south transept. The road itself represents the space of the former east range, in which the dormitory of the monks was placed over the warming room. Whittingham recorded that the splay of a thirteenth-century window was revealed when a new window was cut through the former chapel's west

---

[3] This is likely to refer to a veil or cover for the pyx, a container for housing the consecrated host, that was suspended over the altar.

FIGURE 60. The blocked arch represents a former entrance to the prior's hall, via a passage beneath the dormitory that was accessed from the dark entry. Photograph © Roberta Gilchrist.

wall. This was painted with a masonry pattern in red and black, with a rose on each piece of false ashlar jointing. He identified the window as one that would have lit the monks' warming room before the prior's chapel was built abutting it in the early fourteenth century (Whittingham 1967).

A major programme of refurbishment was completed in the first decades of the sixteenth century. It is likely that this remodelling coincided with a visit to the cathedral by Cardinal Wolsey and Queen Catherine in 1520.[4] Within the prior's hall the ceiling was lowered, severing the tracery of the side windows and concealing the painted beams of the earlier roof (Figure 61). The sixteenth-century ceiling has large square panels formed by small battens with a roll and hollow chamfer moulding. A chamber was created above the hall, approached by a stone staircase located in the former courtyard between the prior's hall and the monks' latrine. Access to the stairs was through a four-centred arch with decorated spandrels and Perpendicular mouldings (Figure 62). A hollow shaft in the centre of the stairs provided a new cupboard in the south wall of the prior's hall. Its purpose has never been explained adequately, but two possible functions can be proposed. This small space may have served as the prior's counting room and secure store, a feature known in

---

[4] *Letters and Papers, Foreign and Domestic, of the Reign of Henry VIII*, 21 vols., 1880–91, ii, (I), p. 407. London: Public Record Office.

FIGURE 61. Interior of the prior's hall showing the ceiling inserted in the sixteenth century (blocking the upper lights of the windows). Photograph © Roberta Gilchrist.

contemporary secular halls. Alternatively, it may have been linked specifically with the event of Wolsey's visit. Wolsey had created a silver closet in his dining room at Hampton Court, c.1515–21, in keeping with contemporary Italian treatises that set the style for cardinal's palaces (Foyle 2002, 216). In creating such a feature, the prior of Norwich may have sought to both flatter and impress his eminent guest, revealing a display cabinet that exhibited the priory's finest plate.

In addition to this stylish remodelling of the prior's hall, the guest accommodation was expanded. A wing of new rooms was added to the north-east, extending from the prior's solar. This wing survived until 1829, when it was demolished by Dean Pellew. Whittingham recorded that the door leading to this range of lodgings was uncovered in the corner of the deanery kitchen in 1967 (Whittingham 1967), and it was observed during a watching brief in 2004. Stained glass from the former wing was moved to the east window of the north transept of the cathedral, comprising four panels showing angels supporting shields. The heraldry of three of the shields suggests that the construction and embellishment of the range was again connected with Wolsey's visit. One panel shows the royal arms surmounted by a crown, one shows the arms of Wolsey with his cardinal's hat, and another shows those of Bishop Nykke with his mitre (King 1996, 418). The addition of the new wing created a courtyard space to the north of the prior's hall, increasing the resemblance of this complex to a self-contained, manorial residence. A final modification introduced another fashionable element: a two-storey timber passage was created

FIGURE 62. Interior of the prior's hall showing stairs inserted in the sixteenth century. Photograph © Roberta Gilchrist.

to provide private access from the prior's hall to the chapel. Such two-storey corridors were created in manorial and monastic contexts by the fifteenth century, with a stone example surviving in the prior's house at the abbey of Much Wenlock (Shropshire) and a timber 'long gallery' at Abingdon abbey (Oxfordshire) (Wood 1965, 337). Although altered by Dean Pellew in the 1820s, the gallery at Norwich survives within the modern deanery. The need for such access suggests that a western gallery had been created in the prior's chapel, an arrangement common in later medieval palaces and manor houses (Grenville 1997, 118).

The prior's lodging at Norwich was modest in comparison with the complexes that developed at the cathedral-priories of Durham and Ely. At Durham, the original accommodation was expanded in the fourteenth century, adding a new hall to the existing complex. In order to create this hall, the prior took over the monks' dormitory, requiring a new dormitory to be built by Bishop Skirlaw (1398–1405). The former dormitory became the prior's hall, arranged at right angles to a two-storey prior's chamber, forming an L-shaped lodging with an earlier chapel to the south. The principal apartments were at first-floor level over an undercroft, opening from the upper end of the hall (Emery 1996, 82–3). A new roof was inserted in the prior's hall in the fifteenth century, a period which also saw the insertion of floors and a new roof into the prior's hall at Winchester (Munby and Fletcher 1983, 108). The most impressive accommodation developed at Ely between the twelfth and fourteenth centuries. A group of halls developed gradually around a small court, eventually expanding to four ranges and a chapel, all with their principal chambers located over undercrofts (Holton-Krayenbuhl 1999). These apartments had their own self-contained, first-floor circulation, separating distinguished guests from the undercrofts below, which would have provided both storage space and accommoda-tion of lower status. The prior's household at Ely included knights, secular chaplains and approximately twenty-one domestic staff (ibid., 337), but the sophisticated lodgings were not developed to serve the prior alone. Their plan and pattern of ac-cess repeated those of royal palaces, reflecting the regular hospitality that the priory provided for royal and high-ranking guests.

Just as secular lords exercised the right to discipline on their manors, the heads of monastic houses commanded a monastic prison, which could be used to punish both tenants of the Prior's Fee and recalcitrant monks. The prison at West-minster, for example, was located over the abbey gatehouse (Harvey 1993, 74), and at Peterborough abbey it connected with the outer gate. The Benedictine Rule ad-vised the head to 'adapt himself to circumstances, now using severity and now per-suasion, displaying the rigour of a master or the loving kindness of a father' (McCann 1952, 21). The site of monastic discipline was the chapter house, the customary location of confessions and accusations of breaches of order. Punishment of the monks could range from a period of prostration on the presbytery steps, to beating, and incarceration in chains (Cassidy-Welch 2001, 123–6). At Norwich, the bishop kept a prison beneath the porter's lodge at the gate to his palace, and the prior kept a prison in the precinct. Its maintenance right up to the Dissolution is recorded in the accounts of the communar: in 1533, he paid 13d for cleaning and repairing a latrine in the prison and for making one new bedstead in the same place (DCN 1/12/108). Post-medieval sources suggest that the prison was located close to the chapter house and the prior's lodging, actually below the south transept of the ca-thedral church. John Adey Repton's plan of the cathedral in 1798 shows the prison beneath the south end of the transept, labelled 'the dungeon to the gaol' (Pierce 1965). A house for the gaoler was sited nearby, and by 1615 had been absorbed into a prebendary house (Whittingham 1985, 108). The close proximity of the monastic chapter house and prison completed the aura of authority that surrounded the prior's complex.

7

Charity and Commerce:
the Infirmary and the Inner Court

S PECIALISED areas developed within the precinct to meet the needs of the monastic community and the obedientiaries of the priory. The relatively self-contained infirmary was established immediately to the south of the cloister by the late twelfth century. Beyond this were the charitable and practical institutions of the inner court, neatly segregated to fulfil the functions of philanthropy and self-sufficiency. This chapter considers evidence for the infirmary and inner court areas, where charitable and commercial concerns jostled cheek by jowl.

THE INFIRMARY

> Before all things and above all things care must be taken of the sick, so that they may be served in very deed as Christ himself; for he said: *I was sick and ye visited me* . . . For these sick brethren let there be assigned a special room and an attendant . . . Let the use of baths be afforded to the sick as often as may be expedient; but to the healthy, and especially to the young, let them be granted seldom. Moreover, let the use of fleshmeat be granted to the sick who are very weak, for the restoration of their strength (McCann 1952, 91).

Compassion for the sick and elderly was central to the Benedictine way of life. Their training for care of the sick was both spiritual and medical, including an understanding of humoral theory. According to the Galenic theory of the four humours (based on the writings of the Greek Galen, c.129–200 AD), the human body was made up of four basic elements, which also made up the universe: fire, water, earth and air. Health and temperament were determined by the balance between the four humours, which corresponded with the bodily substances of phlegm, blood, yellow bile and black bile. Fire, which was hot and dry, produced yellow bile in the body, and led to a choleric complexion. Water, which was cold and wet, produced phlegm, and the phlegmatic disposition. Earth, thought of as cold and dry, was black bile in the body, and associated with the melancholic. Air, hot and wet, made blood, and the sanguine temperament. It was believed that the humoral balance could be altered by food and drink, and for this reason St Benedict allowed the sick to consume meat.

By the later Middle Ages it was common practice for monks to be phlebotomised regularly, in order to maintain the appropriate humoral balance (Harvey 1993, 96–7). At Norwich, in common with other Benedictine monasteries, a knowledge of astrology was needed to determine the auspicious days for bleeding the monks (Greatrex 2002). On average, each monk was bled once every six to seven weeks, followed by three days' sojourn in the infirmary, where the rules governing diet and liturgical routines were relaxed. Carole Rawcliffe has estimated that thirty per cent of the community at Norwich may have passed through the infirmary in any year (2002, 63), with treatment of day-patients alongside acute, chronic and injured cases. These patients would have benefited from bed-rest, away from the intense demands of the monastic offices, and the warmer and cleaner environment that characterised medieval hospital care. The Norwich infirmary was staffed by four to five attendants, including a keeper of the sick, a servant of those who had been bled, a laundress, a boy and a clerk of the chapel (Saunders 1930, 132). In contrast with medieval hospitals, the patients of the monastic infirmary could expect specialised medical care. The infirmarer himself would have had some medical training, but from the thirteenth century could not perform surgery, due to prohibitions on the clergy shedding blood. At Norwich, the communar paid barbers to let blood and cut hair from the thirteenth century, but in the fourteenth century a full-time servant (*clericus minutorum*) bled the monks (Rawcliffe 2002, 46). Local surgeons were occasionally bought in by the infirmarer, in addition to physicians trained in the Galenic tradition to diagnose through the examination of urine (ibid., 47); similar practices were recorded at Westminster (Harvey 1993) and Ely (Holton-Krayenbuhl 1997, 168).

Today, a visitor to Norwich cathedral would find the remains of only four columns of the former infirmary, stranded forlornly in a car park. Fortunately, multidisciplinary evidence can be mustered to recreate the entire infirmary complex for the first time (Figure 63). It was an area located to the south of the refectory, approached from the cloisters through the dark entry and via the infirmary cloister. There were enclosing walls to the west and south of the complex, a recreational garden separating it from the refectory, and a working medicinal garden to the south. Bounded on all four sides, this complex contained the infirmary hall and chapel, its own latrine block, and specialised chambers to the south. These later medieval chambers survive encompassed within the modern houses of Numbers 64 and 65.

This complex has been identified as the infirmary on the basis of the fragmentary remains of the arcade of an aisled hall. The capitals and bases of the piers of the arcade can be dated stylistically to the last quarter of the twelfth century, a date coincident with that given in the cathedral's *First Register* for the construction of a new infirmary by Bishop John of Oxford (c.1183) (Fernie 1993, 159). It has been suggested that this was the second infirmary, built after the original structure was consumed in a fire of 1171 (Buston 1945, 128). The arcade confirms that the building was an aisled, ground-floor hall, corresponding with the layout typical of monastic and hospital infirmaries, where patients occupied beds in the screened side aisles and the central space was kept clear for the movement of staff (Gilchrist

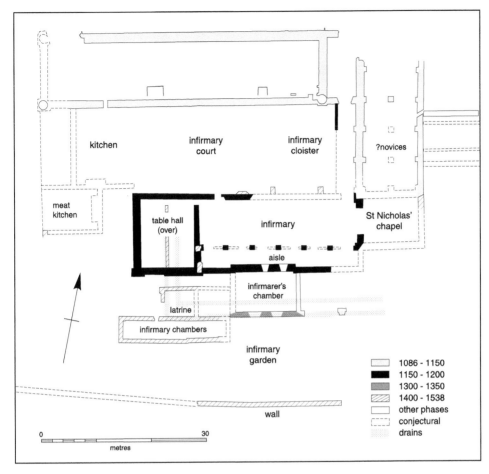

FIGURE 63. Plan of infirmary. See Plate 9 for full phased plan. Drawing by Margaret Mathews.

1995, 17). Its location in relation to the cloister is less typical, however, since direct communication between the infirmary and cemetery was usually provided. This arrangement is shown in the plan of St Gall, with the infirmary to the east of the church, together with the chambers of the physician and for blood-letting (Horn and Born 1979, vol. 2, 211). After construction of the prior's lodging at Norwich, the route to the cemetery from the infirmary would have been indirect, requiring passage through the infirmary cloister, the dark entry, the east cloister alley and the slype to the north of the chapter house.

At English Benedictine monasteries the position of the infirmary is usually to the east or north-east of the cloister, adjacent to the monastic cemetery and the presbytery of the church. For example, the cathedral-priory of Ely located its infirmary to the south-east of the church, and that at Canterbury was to the north-east. Cistercian infirmaries were more frequently sited to the east, and it has been argued that this location was the general rule for English monasteries of any order. David Bell has identified the small number of exceptions to this rule, noting the infirmary to the south of the cloister at Cistercian Furness (Lancashire), to the west of the cloister at the cathedral-priory of Durham, to the south at Augustinian Haughmond (Shropshire), and to the north at the Premonstratensian abbey of Easby (N Yorkshire). He proposes that this strong preference for eastern siting results from practical, medical and spiritual concerns, but was determined primarily by the need for clean water (Bell 1998, 211–13). It was usual for the watercourse to pass first through the infirmary, in order to provide the purest water to this area (see p. 38). Water was connected with healing through the sacrament of baptism, bringing together the connotations of physical and spiritual cleansing, and recalling Christ's baptism by John the Baptist in the River Jordan (Mark 1:4–5). English Benedictines reserved regular bathing for the sick, alongside blood-letting, as a medical treatment to balance the correct humours (Harvey 1993, 134). Monastic libraries such as Norwich contained classical and Arabic medical treatises (Rawcliffe 2002, 58; Noble 1997, 7), and it was understood that clean water and the removal of waste were essential in checking the transmission of disease.

According to medieval notions of contagion, infections were transported by mists and noxious smells caused by stagnant water or sewage, and absorbed into the body through the pores. Bell has argued that the consistency in siting infirmaries to the east of the cloister stems also from this understanding of contagion, citing the Hippocratic notion that the healthiest location was in the east (Bell 1998, 220). How then, do we account for the location of the infirmary at Norwich, to the south of the cloister? There were no substantial buildings to the east of the cloister until c.1285, when the prior's lodging was constructed, ruling out the factor of building congestion. The water supply at Norwich would have facilitated either a southern or eastern position, as the position of the latrine of the monks indicates. However, if the water source to the precinct was directed from the west, a southern location would have provided the infirmary with the purest water. A more localised understanding of contagion may be an additional factor. Carole Rawcliffe has noted that Norwich had leper hospitals sited at gates located to the north, south and west of the city. She explains the absence of one on the eastern perimeter thus: 'Because the prevailing wind came from the east, especially in summer, and it was believed that contagion spread on the air, no leper hospitals were built on that side of the city' (Rawcliffe 1995, 48). One of these leper hospitals, St Mary Magdalene in Sprowston, was established by Herbert de Losinga to the north of Norwich. The rationale for siting in relation to prevailing winds is likely to have been understood by the monks of his cathedral-priory, so that an alternative location for the infirmary was found to the south of the cloister.

The infirmary hall

The hall survived roofed and largely intact until the summer of 1804, when it was demolished to improve the view of the deanery. Its former use was uncertain to the antiquaries that recorded its destruction, since it had been conflated with the 'dorter' in leases and descriptions dating from the seventeenth century. It was described variously as the dormitory (Sayers 1806), the refectory (Gibson 1806), and the prior's hall (Harrod 1857), but was not identified in print as the infirmary until 1945 (Buston 1945). By fortunate coincidence, John Adey Repton was in Norwich shortly after the building had been destroyed. He recorded details of the piers of the arcade, a ground-plan of the infirmary hall, and attempted a reconstruction of a section through the south elevation (Repton 1806) (Figure 64). A number of local artists depicted the building before and during its demolition, with sketches by R. Ladbrooke, John Crome, the Rev. Andrew Gooch and David Hodgson, the last of which was executed some years later on the basis of drawings completed by his father (Buston 1945).

The surviving architectural remains of the infirmary hall represent an arcade of six bays in length, and a section of the south wall (now incorporated in Number 64). Four piers of the arcade survive fully and a further fifth partially, together with part of the western respond of the arcade. Two types of pier were used in an alternating sequence: one is a central drum with four small detached shafts; the other is square with rounded corners (Fernie 1993, 161). The use of alternating piers took its architectural cue from the nave of the cathedral church. The fourth pier retains evidence of the springing of the former arches. The fourth and fifth piers and respond were incorporated in a prebendary house of c.1600, which was destroyed by bombing in 1942 (the original Number 63: Figure 82). Before its destruction, Whittingham noted evidence for a medieval door opening in this former house, leading from the north-western corner of the infirmary hall towards the proposed site of the meat kitchen (MC 186/47). The south wall of the infirmary was shared with structures abutting the hall to the south, and three blocked openings are still visible in what was originally the internal elevation of the south wall. One of these openings would have served as a door communicating between the infirmary hall and associated chambers (discussed below).

From Repton's plan made in 1804, it can be seen that the infirmary hall was a central vessel with a single aisle to the south, with an external length of 100ft

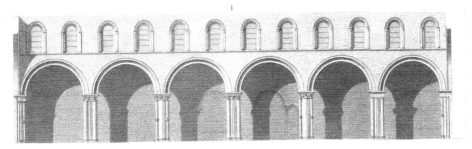

FIGURE 64. Reconstructed section of the infirmary by John Adey Repton, 1804. Reproduced from *Archaeologia* 15 (1806), with permission of the Society of Antiquaries of London.

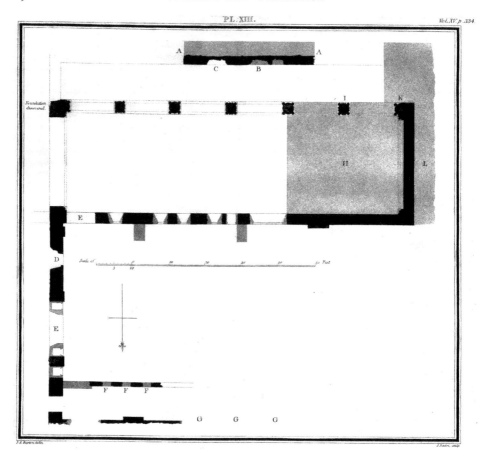

FIGURE 65. Plan of the infirmary by John Adey Repton, 1804. Reproduced from *Archaeologia* 15 (1806), with permission of the Society of Antiquaries of London.

(c. 30.5m; Figure 65). He noted that its walls were constructed of flint and rubble, with flat buttresses in masonry (Repton 1806, 335). There was no corresponding arcade to suggest a northern aisle, and the surviving north wall to the hall was constructed with two external buttresses. Repton showed a substantial wall projecting northwards from the eastern end of the hall, directly aligned on the dark entry. He marked the position of a surviving Norman arch (D), and a row of three bases (F), which he considered to have been relocated to this position (ibid.). From the roof structure and ornament he concluded that the hall had originally been open to the roof, with a floor later inserted between the arcade and the windows above. Although today the piers are severely eroded, Repton recorded them in a pristine state. The capitals were 'highly enriched and ornamented by painting and gilding, and the arches are painted only' (ibid., 334) (Figure 66).

The local artists who were Repton's contemporaries were more concerned to capture the overall scale and setting of an ancient building that had been sentenced

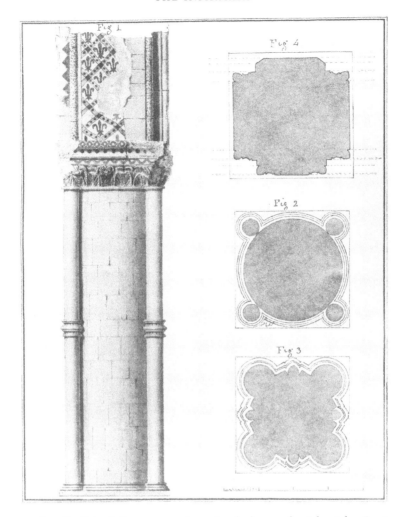

FIGURE 66. Detail of the infirmary arcade and polychromy, by John Adey Repton, 1804. Reproduced from *Archaeologia* 15 (1806), with permission of the Society of Antiquaries of London.

to demolition. Although less accurate than Repton's measured record, their drawings were completed largely before demolition had begun, in contrast with his. The sketches depicted the infirmary from the south-east, and those by Ladbrooke and Gooch convey useful information on the south and east elevations. In the eastern elevation, both show a massive blocked arch. Ladbrooke shows a window with tracery above the arch, (Figure 67), a feature confirmed by Crome and Gooch (see Buston 1945). The south elevation is shown with coping above the arches of the arcade, where the roof of the former aisle would have joined the main vessel of the hall. Above this are pairs of round-headed windows, also shown in the drawing by Hodgson (see Buston 1945). These windows are very similar in form and spacing to

FIGURE 67. The infirmary from the north-east, by R. Ladbrooke, 1804. Reproduced with permission of the Society of Antiquaries of London, from *Norfolk Red Portfolio*, f. 27.

those that survive on the north wall of the refectory, and it can be suggested that in both buildings a pair of windows occupied each bay. Two large windows were later inserted into the south wall, and gables formed in the roof, perhaps coinciding with the insertion of a floor into the hall. There are indications that at least part of the hall had an upper storey by the fourteenth century. In 1330, payments were made to the servant of the infirmary solar (DCN 1/2/101a), and the pitancer paid for a new window in the infirmary solar in 1336 (DCN 1/12/20).

These pictorial sources all indicate that there was once a large transverse arch in the east end of the hall. This is the only evidence to confirm the former existence of a chapel in the eastern end of the hall, which would have been separated by the arch in the manner of the nave and chancel of a parish church. This arrangement was standard in monastic and hospital infirmaries (Gilchrist 1995, 17), although it has been suggested that some Benedictine examples had a stone screen separating the chapel from the hall and aisles (Byard 2000; Holton-Krayenbuhl 1997, 131). The infirmary chapel at Norwich seems to have been dedicated to St Nicholas (Fernie and Whittingham 1972, 31), and the *Customary* confirms that the feast of St Nicholas was given particular attention by the priory (Tolhurst 1948, xvi). Whittingham's plan of the priory showed the chapel projecting to the outer wall of the east range. Its form and dimensions remain conjectural, and it could have projected further east beyond the line of the east range.

The plan of the infirmary at Norwich was unusual in possessing only a single aisle, in common with the twelfth-century infirmary at St Augustine's, Canterbury, located to the north-east of the church (Tatton-Brown 1991). The Norwich infirmary was six bays in length, larger than Westminster's five-bay infirmary hall, but a modest size in comparison with the contemporary nine-bay hall at Ely, and seven-bay halls at Canterbury and Peterborough. These large, aisled halls provided lofty spaces that allowed air to circulate, aiming to minimise the risk of contagion (Rawcliffe 2002, 60; Bell 1998, 221). Infirmaries at both Ely and Norwich were distinguished by alternating piers in the arcade, with the better surviving example at Ely showing that these were matched pairs across the hall, and continuing into the chapel (Holton-Krayenbuhl 1997, 133). In their plan, elevation and decorative details these infirmaries were modelled on their cathedral churches, a parallel that would have held particular resonance for medieval patients. The monastic infirmary was in effect a church, where the healing of Christ was more efficacious medicine than any that could be offered by the infimarer (Bell 1998, 226).

A number of architectural fragments were retained when the infirmary hall at Norwich was demolished in 1804,[1] and an exceptional pair of medieval doors was also salvaged, now housed in the Castle Museum, Norwich. The doors are decorated with five horizontal rows of scrolls, and the semicircular top is filled with two affronted dragons (Geddes 1996, 431–2). Jane Geddes has compared the doors to those of the York minster chapter house (c. 1280s) and has suggested a date for their construction of the late thirteenth century. The precise location occupied by the doors is unknown, but a possible position is the large opening that was shown by Repton in the north wall of the refectory. This would have led from the court or garden that separated the infirmary and refectory.

The infirmary cloister
The quality of the surviving doors, together with Repton's record and description of the polychromy, indicates that the infirmary hall was a richly embellished structure. It seems likely that a formal entrance from the cloisters would have been provided, and certainly a covered way would have been required to convey corpses from the infirmary hall for burial in the cemetery. The former existence of an infirmary cloister can be suggested from occasional references in the obediential rolls. In 1333–4, the master of the cellar funded work around the cloister door against the infirmary (DCN 1/1/38a), and between 1423 and 1426, the communar paid for repairing the infirmary cloister (DCN 1/12/50–1). This structure was evidently still standing in the mid-eighteenth century, when Blomefield described it as 'the long gallery or walk, well enclosed where the sick monks used to walk, still remaining whole' (Blomefield 1745 [1806], 46). Foundations likely to represent the infirmary cloister were recorded in 2004, when paving was laid outside the dark entry.

The location of the infirmary cloister can be clarified with reference to post-medieval leases and to the Parliamentary Survey of 1649. It was incorporated into

[1] Many were reused to construct outbuildings in the curtilage of Number 64, but a small number were labelled and retained in the cathedral's stone collection in the gallery of the church. These additional fragments support a late-twelfth-century date for the hall, and include a voussoir with dog-tooth mouldings, a cushion capital with angle tucks, two fragments of capitals with fluted and acanthus volutes, and a section of a spandrel for the springing of an arch (Norwich Cathedral Worked Stone Inventory M0086/90/95/96/199).

a later house known as Newells' Tenement, which was a 'corner house' on the cloister over 'two vaults' (DCN 47/2). The abuttals from leases of this property can be mapped to show that it lay between the dark entry and the infirmary. Whittingham's interpretation of the 1649 survey was that the dark entry and the infirmary cloister had once been contiguous. He suggested that the southern section, the infirmary cloister, was blocked off in about 1707 (1985, 109, 114). This suggestion is supported by Repton's plan of 1804, which shows a north–south aligned wall projecting from the infirmary, and in line with the dark entry. The infirmary cloister seems to have been a single passage or pentice projecting from the west wall of the east range, and leading to the dark entry. It provided a sheltered approach from the cloister, and created an enclosed space between the infirmary and the refectory. This space was used as part of the infirmarer's garden, which was further separated from the kitchen to the west in 1429, when the infirmarer paid for making a wall in the infirmary garden next to the door of the cookhouse (DCN 1/10/17). Based on the infirmarer's accounts, Claire Noble has concluded that the infirmarer also had a larger, working garden to the south of the infirmary complex, containing beehives for honey-production and flowering plants for the distillation of remedies. It may have taken the form of raised beds in a grid-design, laid out with paths separating them (Noble 1997, 8, 6). Large amounts of saffron were grown in the garden and sometimes sold; saffron was used popularly as a prophylactic against plague, tuberculosis and sweating sickness (ibid.).

The infirmary cloister at Norwich was a covered passage, in contrast with the formal infirmary cloisters provided, for example, at the cathedral-priory of Canterbury, the Cluniac monastery at Thetford, and the Cisterican abbey at Rievaulx. Similar passages from the south cloister walk were provided at the Cistercian houses of Kirkstall and Fountains, and a comparable construction is evidenced at Ely. By c.1220, access between the infirmary and cemetery at Ely was by a vaulted passage known as the 'dark cloister' (Holton-Krayenbuhl 1997, 127). The Norwich infirmary cloister was connected with the southern end of the east range and the east cloister walk, the areas proposed to have been associated with the novices. This juxtaposition mirrors the close association between the infirmary and novitiate at St Gall (Horn and Born 1979, vol. 1, 311), and may explain fifteenth-century references to the Norwich infirmarer purchasing mattresses for the boys (Rawcliffe 2002, 50).

The chamber of the infirmarer
The survival of medieval fabric in Numbers 64–65, together with their proximity to the infirmary hall, has led to their identification as chambers integral to the functions of the infirmary (Whittingham 1949). This development of ranges to the south of the infirmary hall is directly paralleled at Ely, where two blocks abutted the infirmary from the late twelfth and late thirteenth centuries (Canonry House and the Black Hostelry, respectively) (Holton-Krayenbuhl 1997, 138). Recent refurbishment and development of these buildings at Norwich provided the opportunity for

closer scrutiny of standing fabric, and excavations that uncovered three phases of development, together with details of the priory's system of water supply (Percival 2001). The core of Number 64 is a medieval chamber that abutted the south aisle of the infirmary hall, and shared the south wall of the aisle to form its north wall. A blocked door can be seen on the north (external) elevation of the north wall: a two-centred pointed arch with keeled bowtell mouldings (Figure 68). Two further blocked openings of semicircular stone arches survive to the east of this door. The door led from the south aisle of the infirmary to the medieval chamber that survives within Number 64. Inside this chamber, Whittingham recorded two medieval windows during alterations in 1933. He dated these to c.1175, and recorded a rebate

FIGURE 68. The remains of the infirmary, including one of the extant piers (right) and the blocked openings that led from the infirmary aisle to the infirmarer's chamber. Photograph © Roberta Gilchrist.

for shutters in one window (MC186/47 648x4). These features correspond with the semicircular arches still visible on the external face of the wall, and functioned as external windows until the chamber was built abutting the infirmary aisle.

The south wall of the medieval chamber also survives within Number 64. It retains the remains of two blocked windows. Both have just one side of the window jamb surviving, and both have the same keeled bowtell moulding seen in the arches in the external elevation of the north wall. The surviving mouldings in the north and south wall of the chamber date its construction to the fourteenth century. Whittingham was confident in assigning a date of 1309, and in describing this structure as 'the infirmarer's chamber' (1949). He based this assertion on a reference in the communar's rolls for 1308, noting that the mason John Ramsey was paid £5 16s 3d for the construction of the infirmarer's new camera (Fernie and Whittingham 1972, 32). The 'camera' is likely to have been the obediential office of the infirmarer.

Beneath Number 64 is a vaulted brick cellar of three compartments, the eastern and central of which are separated by a brick arch. Whittingham suggested that this cellar originally belonged to the adjacent building to the west (Number 65), that he had identified as 'the infirmary chambers'. When he recorded the cellar in 1933, he could see the respond of another cross arch in the western part of the undercroft.[2] He observed that the western arch had been removed when the cellar was partitioned at an unknown date (MC 186/48 648x3). The medieval undercroft beneath Number 64 does not correspond with the alignment of the chamber above, and it is possible that it originally related to buildings to the west of the infirmarer's camera. The form and construction of the cellar beneath Numbers 64–65 is consistent with a type of medieval undercroft known to have been common in Norwich, and which survives also beneath the cellarer's range (discussed below).

Excavations and watching briefs conducted at Number 64 by the Norfolk Archaeological Unit uncovered archaeological evidence for the earlier form of the infirmarer's camera, before its rebuilding of c.1308. The excavation of a robber trench to the east of the medieval chamber was interpreted as the original east wall of the infirmarer's camera. This trench is likely to have resulted from the methodical demolition of the wall down to the base of its foundations, followed by the removal of the stone for reuse. The wall would have abutted the infirmary hall in line with the east wall of the aisle, making the original chamber twice as large as its fourteenth-century replacement. The remains of two large walls were recorded *in situ*, one of which was the south wall of the infirmary hall. The second was a north–south aligned wall that formed the eastern wall of the second phase of the infirmarer's camera (Percival 2001, 14). A third wall was found to have some fabric surviving above ground, incorporated in the curtilage wall of Number 64. This contained the sill and jamb of a medieval window from the east wall of the original infirmary chamber.

---

[2] The features that he recorded were destroyed by the insertion of a concrete slab in 1975, to strengthen the floor above.

The infirmary chambers

Number 65, proposed by Whittingham to have been the infirmary chambers, abuts Number 64 to the west. It is a two-storey block of flint rubble construction, with a timber-frame jetty to the south facade. Its main build is likely to be later medieval, but the earliest visible fabric derives from its subdivision and redecoration in the mid sixteenth century, shortly after the Reformation (see pp. 213–14). The south elevation retains evidence of three brick openings at low level, which could conceivably relate to a former cellar.

The infirmary latrine

Excavations to the north of Number 65 revealed the infirmary's latrine, a building positioned in the angle between the infirmarer's camera (Number 64) and the infirmary chambers (Number 65). Parts of the north and west walls of a small medieval building were excavated, together with a series of mortar floors. Its function was determined without doubt when a massive medieval drain was discovered intact. The drain has walls of flint and mortar 0.9m thick, which were constructed in a trench that must have been 3.0m wide and at least 2.5m deep. The interior was back-filled with sand and gravel capped with clay, to produce a slope to assist the flow of water. Arches were constructed at the major junctions of the drain, and it was vaulted in flint and Caen stone (Figure 69). After the erection of the arches a flint and rubble barrel vault was constructed (1.2m wide and 2m high). Excavations within Number 65 uncovered another section of the drain, indicating that beneath the latrine it had changed direction, turning from a north–south alignment to run west–east (Percival 2001, 18–19). Here, it was possible to observe the profile of two surviving arches of the drain, which appeared to be twelfth-century, with later infill between the arches in brick. In total, a section of approximately 5m of the medieval drain was observed.

Stripping of plaster within Number 65 uncovered two twelfth-century arches (Figure 70). It seems likely that these were windows in the south wall of the latrine building (Percival 2001, 22), and they show that the infirmary latrine was a single-storey building, in contrast with the two-storey latrine of the monks (see p. 119). The windows would have been blocked when the infirmary chambers were constructed against the infirmary latrine. The drain and associated latrine are therefore earlier than either the extant infirmarer's camera or the infirmary chambers (Numbers 64 and 65), the former of which was rebuilt in the early fourteenth century. By the fifteenth century, the infirmary latrine was evidently in dire need of repair. After an uncomfortable stay in the infirmary, the monk John de Elingham contributed money towards the improvement of the adjacent *domus necessarium*. This included repair of the latrines, pavement and 'great gutter', and the construction of new seats and windows in 1454 (Rawcliffe 2002, 51).

The Norfolk Archaeological Unit also excavated a section of the medieval boundary wall belonging to the infirmary complex. Approximately 10m to the

FIGURE 69. The medieval drain that served the infirmary latrine (section to the north of Number 65). Photograph © Norfolk Archaeological Unit; photographer John Percival. Reproduced with permission of NAU.

south of the infirmary chambers was a fragment of a medieval flint rubble and lime mortar wall (Percival 2001, 16). This was in line with a section of later medieval wall recorded by Whittingham, which extended some 15m (Whittingham 1949), providing evidence of an internal boundary wall that enclosed the infirmary complex. The excavations in the infirmary area produced very few medieval artefacts, with the exception of one sherd of Grimston-type ware with applied, incised decoration likely to have originated from a face jug (Percival 2001, 23). In 1956, a late medieval tripod-pitcher with internal, yellow glaze was reported from the infirmary area (Norfolk SMR No. 225).

East   West

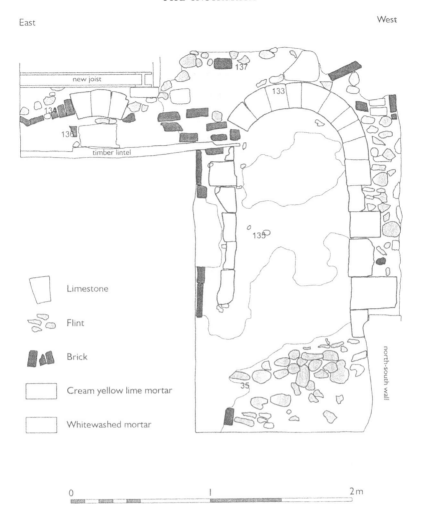

FIGURE 70. The remains of two twelfth-century windows in the former infirmary latrine (Number 65). Drawing © Norfolk Archaeological Unit; illustrator David Dobson. Reproduced with permission of NAU.

The development and use of the infirmary complex

While the physical outline of the infirmary complex has been largely established, questions remain concerning its later medieval development, and the division of functions between the infirmary hall and its chambers. Two major trends can be observed in later monastic infirmary halls: the development of separate dining chambers and the subdivision of common space into private chambers or lodgings. Special dining rooms developed within infirmaries to accommodate the eating of meat that was allowed to the sick and recently phlebotomised. At Westminster, for example, the *misericord* developed in approximately the mid-thirteenth century (Harvey 1993, 41). At Canterbury cathedral-priory, a 'table hall' was constructed abutting the north side of the infirmary hall from c.1260; the remains of the table hall built by Prior Hathbrand (1342–3) survive as a rectangular flint building adjoining the east end of the former infirmary's north aisle (Newman 1969, 216). Peterborough abbey's table hall survives in the same position in relation to the infirmary, consisting of a fifteenth-century building containing a large fireplace (Pevsner 1961, 369).

A similar dining chamber existed at Norwich by c.1330, created after the infirmary hall had been divided by the insertion of a floor. An addendum to the *Customary* in 1379 confirms that monks eating in the 'lower infirmary' should have sufficient materials for heating (Tolhurst 1948, 243). The infirmarer regularly purchased turves and faggots for heating, candles, covers for the 'great table', vessels, spoons, fresh rushes and matting for the floor (Rawcliffe 2002, 67). Whittingham's plan of the priory suggests that this dining chamber was in the west end of the infirmary hall. Certainly, this position would have afforded easy access to the kitchens, as indicated by the door opening in the house on this site that was destroyed in 1942. The confirmation that the dining chamber was heated suggests that the space may also have been used for bleeding the monks. At Norwich a *camera minutorum* was documented (DCN 1/8/48), in contrast with the separate hall constructed at Ely in the early fifteenth century (Holton-Krayenbuhl 1997, 126). The proposed situation of the blood-letting chamber at Norwich is significant in another respect: its location in the west end of the infirmary hall would have been directly over the great drain.

A warm, easily cleaned space was essential for the blood-letting operation, and would have served equally well for bathing (Harvey 1993, 96 n. 122). Like most English monasteries, Norwich seems to have had no self-contained bathing house, in contrast with the cathedral-priories of Canterbury and Ely, where the bathhouses were sited to the south of the infirmaries. Indeed, the monks of Norwich complained about the lack of tubs and other facilities for bathing and shaving. In response, the prior ruled in 1379 that the brethren could bathe whenever they wished, with the modest expenses of the *balneatione fratrum* met by the cellarer (Rawcliffe 2002, 60). An additional specialist space is indicated at Norwich: an apothecary's area for the infirmarer to prepare medications. While the infirmarer at Westminster used local apothecaries, the Norwich infirmarer prepared his own *materia medica*. Honey and sugar were bought for the preparation of electuaries; other substances purchased for possible medical application include ginger, cinnamon, peony, liquorice, fennel, rice, cloves, mace, cassia, aniseed, zedoary, poppy seeds, prunes, turpeth, agaric, nutmeg, stomatic, frankincense and dragon's blood (Rawcliffe 2002, 63). Ginger was apparently the most frequently employed ingredient at Norwich (Saunders 1930, 133). In common with spice lists from other major Benedictine abbeys, it is not always possible to identify securely the exotic ingredients that were purchased (Bond 2001a, 72). The most expensive spice was certainly saffron, and Norwich was most unusual in being self-sufficient in this commodity; other monasteries purchased imported saffron from Spain, France and Italy (ibid.).

PLATE 9

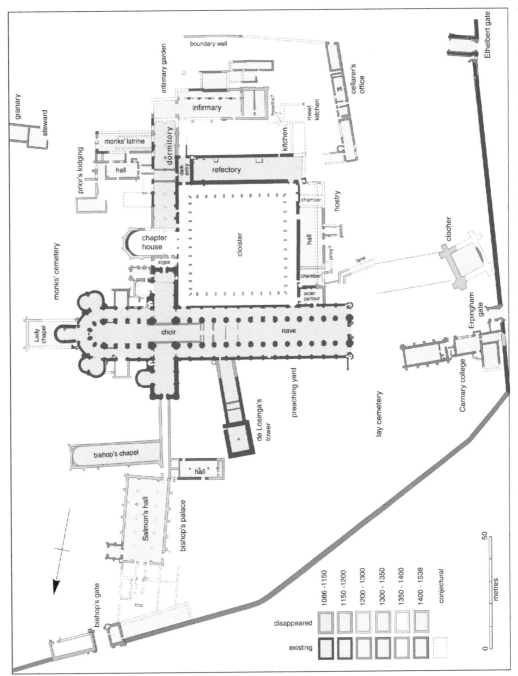

Plan of the monastic buildings, using a measured survey by Roland Harris and Philip Thomas as the base plan, and including some conjectural elements from Whittingham's plan of 1975. Drawing by Margaret Mathew.

PLATE 10

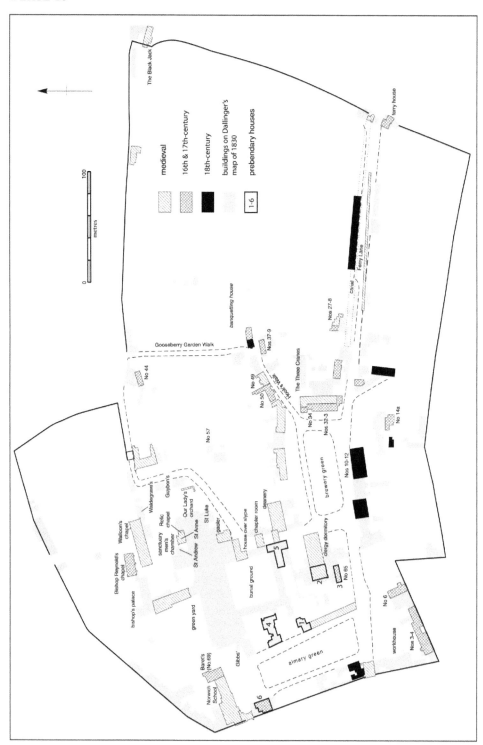

Post-medieval plan of the close, c.1550–1800. Dallinger's map of 1830 has been used at the base plan, to show locations of buildings that no longer exist. Features noted in sixteenth-century leases have been added, and the six prebendary houses are numbered in order of their construction. Drawing by Margaret Mathews.

During the fifteenth century, the infirmarer purchased distilling equipment including glass phials, pots and flasks, and an alembic weighting 25lbs. A clay-built furnace to be fuelled by peat was constructed in a stillhouse, to allow the distillation of fortified waters, oils and tinctures (Rawcliffe 2002, 61; Noble 1997, 9). The purchase of glass vessels for monastic infirmaries was relatively well recorded, although the survival of the material in the ground is very rare. Both English and imported glass was used for medical purposes, with 'phials' and 'jordans' (urinals) the most common forms; glass was also used for preparing pigments such as vermilion, and for alchemical use (Moorhouse 1993, 137–40).

It was common in the later Middle Ages to subdivide monastic infirmaries into chambers that would afford greater privacy to the inmates, a trend that pre-dated the subdivision of the halls of medieval hospitals into cubicles, as excavations have shown at St John, Cirencester (Leech and McWhirr 1982). At the abbey of Bury St Edmunds, the western end of the infirmary hall was partitioned to accommodate long-stay patients (Rawcliffe 2002, 49). It seems to have been more common, however, to subdivide the aisles of the hall into private chambers, as indicated at Peterborough by the later fourteenth century (VCH Northants 2 (1906), 450–2). Infirmary aisles were also adopted for the construction of private residences for officers of the priory, with a chamber for the sub-prior created in the south aisle at Canterbury, and an impressive lodging created in the north aisle at Ely for the sacrist Alan of Walsingham. At Westminster abbey, the infirmary hall was demolished following a fire in 1298, and the existing cloister was erected with its four ranges of chambers and 'lodgings' (RCHME 1924, 92). This trend for senior monks to withdraw to private chambers in the infirmary was also witnessed at Cistercian monasteries. At Fountains, the infirmary was partitioned by the thirteenth century into a series of ten or twelve 'bed-sitting rooms', each with a hearth and latrine; while at the Cistercian houses of Byland, Kirkstall (Yorkshire), Waverley (Surrey) and Tintern (Monmouthshire), a series of apartments replaced the space of the common infirmary (Coppack 2002, 201).

The development of the infirmary buildings at Ely demonstrates this process to its full extent, adopting the common space of both aisles for lodgings and chambers, and inverting the central space of the infirmary hall to serve as an open passageway between these apartments. The north arcade of the infirmary hall at Ely was blocked in the fourteenth century, and the north aisle was replaced by three buildings, the easternmost being the first-floor hall of Alan of Walsingham. The south aisle was partitioned to form a separate compartment, into which the aisle of the chapel was later absorbed. By the sixteenth century, the entire south aisle had been incorporated into other structures, and the roof of the central vessel of the infirmary hall had been removed to form a passage (Firmary Lane). This open passage gave access to the lodgings that had been formed out of the north and south aisles (Holton-Krayenbuhl 1997).

There are references in the Norwich obediential rolls to the creation and occupation of chambers, but it is not clear whether these were located in the aisle of the infirmary hall or in the separate buildings located to the south. It is evident that a solar had been provided in the hall by the mid-fourteenth century, located over the table hall. Between 1346 and 1348, the infirmarer purchased substantial quantities of building materials that may have related to the construction of the free-standing block of chambers (Number 65). This included 2 fothers of lead, 500 corner-stones, 48 wooden posts, 500lbs of Spanish iron, 61 ells of canvas and 600 pieces of wain-scot (Rawcliffe 2002, 56; DCN 1/10/5, 6, 29). Private chambers were referred to, for example that occupied by Henry Prior in 1479–80 (ibid.), and an early chamber housed William the sacrist, referred to in the late-twelfth-century *Life of St William* (Jessopp and James 1896, 145). There is also mention of a parlour in the infirmary, where relatives could visit monks who were confined (Rawcliffe 2002, 69). It seems likely that this room would have been in the infirmary chambers, furthest from the monks' cloister. The frequency of secular visitors to the infirmary may have prompted the construction of the later medieval wall enclosing it to the south. There was evident concern that seculars strayed beyond the parlour, and in 1514 Bishop Nykke complained that women were gaining access to the infirmary itself (Jessopp 1888). Norwich was not unique in this regard: the hall constructed in the infirmary complex at Ely for Alan of Walsingham was to be used for the entertainment of female relatives of the monks, if no suitable alternative was available (Holton-Krayenbuhl 1997, 169).

The Upper Inner Court: Commerce and Philanthropy

Education and charity: the monastic almonry

The position of the almonry complex can be located from references in leases dating from the late sixteenth century, placing it within the south-west corner of the precinct.[3] The almonry's position next to the Ethelbert gate, the main entrance to the medieval priory, can also be predicted from the functions it served (Figure 71). Almonries were located next to the main gates of monasteries including Christ Church and St Augustine's, Canterbury, and the remains of almonry halls survive at Ely and Evesham (Worcestershire) (Rushton 2002, 66–7). A monastic almonry dispensed food to the poor, and provided hospitality and accommodation for pilgrims. The accounts of the Norwich almoner reveal that lepers were also amongst the recipients of gifts distributed at the gates. These donations included cloth, shoes, peat turves for fuel, ale, meat, fish and eggs (Saunders 1930, 170). In the early fourteenth century, the Norwich almoner distributed 240–75 loaves per day to the poor, but financial pressure reduced this to just 78 loaves per day by the 1400s (Rawcliffe 1995, 83–4). By the end of the twelfth century, pilgrims and travellers were greeted at the almonry as they entered the precinct, while it was common

---

[3] In 1649, the almonry was being used as a storehouse, and was described as 'a long ruinous thatched building'; the almoner's office and granary could also still be discerned along the south precinct wall (Whittingham 1985, 107, 110, 112).

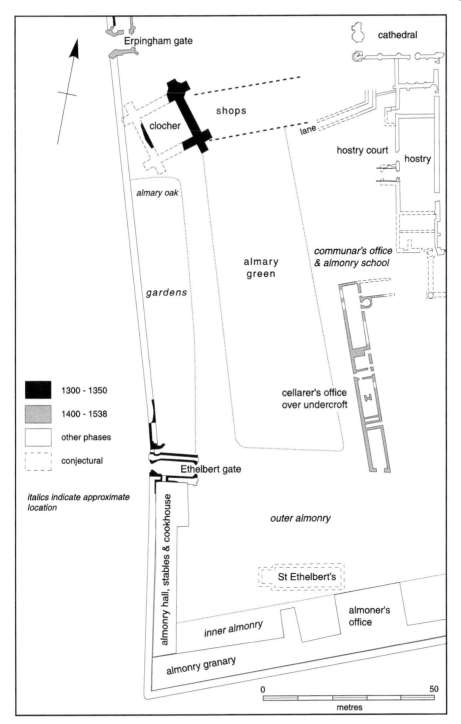

FIGURE 71. Plan of the upper inner court, to the west of the cathedral church. See Plate 9 for full phased plan. Drawing by Margaret Mathews.

for higher-ranking and monastic guests and their servants to be accommodated in the hostry (Harvey 1993, 16). Those of the highest status received hospitality in the prior's lodging.

The monastic almonry at Norwich gave special assistance to the sick poor, and consequently, the almoner received more gifts from local laity than any other obedientiary (Rawcliffe 1995, 27). There is no indication of paupers residing in the almonry, as they did at the abbeys of Reading and Westminster (Harvey 1993, 18), although the priory maintained hospitals elsewhere in Norwich, at Sprowston and St Paul's. The almonry was also the site of the monastic school by the fourteenth century (Harries et al. 1991). It has been suggested that an earlier school for child oblates had been located in the east range of the cloister, but by the late twelfth century Benedictine monasteries had abandoned the practice of receiving oblates. Instead, a school for poor scholars was established outside the cloister. In 1535, the monks of Norwich reported that 'there are thirteen boys dwelling within the monastery and receiving free instruction in the *scola grammaticalis* or "almery scole". They are also given food and clothing, which costs us 26s 8d per head per annum' (Greatrex 1994, 169).

The almonry school at Norwich was in existence during the priorate of William de Kirby (1272–88/9), making it the earliest school of its kind, pre-dating the next foundation, that at Ely in 1314 (ibid., 171). Norwich was unusual also in its early link with music, appointing a master to teach the boys singing and grammar. In addition to the master, there was also a servant of the almonry school, who collected leftover food from the monastic refectory for the boys' alms; this was supplemented by bread provided by the almoner (ibid., 172). The boys were paid to perform useful tasks in the priory, such as sweeping the cloisters in the 1430s (Harries et al. 1991, 8). By the late fourteenth century, fee-paying boarders were also accepted, children drawn from the ranks of the landed and burgess classes of Norwich (ibid., 7). At Westminster and Durham, novices were sometimes recruited from schools attached to the monastic almonry (Harvey 1993, 74). At Norwich, the connection was explicitly musical: the boys sang in the church of St Mary in the Marsh on Sundays and feast days, and in the fifteenth century participated in the singing of the daily Lady Mass in the Lady chapel (Greatrex 1994, 173, 179).

The physical form taken by a monastic almonry is illustrated by the hospice for pilgrims and paupers that is shown on the plan of St Gall. This complex was also located to the west of the cloister, and near the monastic cellarage. The hospice itself was a large rectangular hall, with benches that ran around its circumference (Horn and Born 1979, vol. 2, 144). Its counterpart in the later medieval monastery is best represented by the excavated example at the Augustinian priory of Thornholme (Lincolnshire). In the late fourteenth century, the almonry at Thornholme was built outside the gatehouse, comprising an almonry hall, with hearth, oven and wall-benches. A cross-passage divided the hall from two chambers, one of which had a latrine (Coppack 1989, 200). The changing layout of the almonry complex at Westminster abbey has been reconstructed on the basis of expenditure recorded in the obediential rolls. By c.1300, the complex included an almonry courtyard, around which was placed a chapel, hall, *hospicia*, granaries and lay brothers' hall, and an outer area which included meadows, gardens, stables and barns, and a vineyard. The entire complex was bounded by a bank and ditch (Rushton 2002, 70–71). By 1450, the frontage of the almonry at Westminster had been built up to include thirty-two shops, and the interior space subsequently became commercialised with the creation of 'rents' or tenements, some of which were converted from stables in the meadow (ibid., 75, 77).

Some of these physical features can be traced through the almoner's rolls at Norwich. References to building work and repairs in the almoner's accounts make a clear distinction between the interior almonry and the exterior almonry. The outer, or exterior, almonry was bounded by thatched walls by the fifteenth century (DCN 1/6/87), and contained the almoner's stables (DCN 1/6/94). This area may also have held accommodation for pilgrims, and a granary and cookhouse were required for feeding guests and preparing loaves of bread for the poor. There are references to the stipend of the page for the almoner's cookhouse (DCN 1/6/59), and the costs incurred for making an oven, and emptying latrines (DCN 1/6/51; 55). In 1474–5, there was major building work in the outer almonry, with the purchase of 1.5 tons of freestone and labour for making walls and windows in stone; the following year 5,200 bricks were purchased (DCN 1/6/89). A former range against the west wall of the precinct has left an outline suggesting that there was a shallow vault in this position, typical of a medieval brick undercroft (Number 2).

The inner, or interior, almonry was approached by a great gate (DCN 1/6/87), and had a door that was kept locked (DCN 1/6/94). This space contained the almoner's office, and in 1476, two fireplaces were made here; the next year, a small accounting-house or exchequer was erected (DCN 1/6/94–5). This glimpse afforded by the obediential rolls suggests that there was an inner court occupied by the almoner's administrative office, perhaps located against the south precinct wall. There was an outer court for housing pilgrims and their horses, the combined presence of which required regular payments for carting away muck from the almonry gates. The imprint of a vault in the precinct wall indicates that a two-storey structure was placed against it. In contrast with the almonry at Westminster, this space at Norwich was never intensively commercialised. At both Norwich and Westminster, however, the almonries were bounded spaces designed to contain the poor and limit their access to the precinct.

It is not clear whether the boys of the school were housed in the inner or outer almonry: in 1419, thatch was purchased for the 'chamber of the boys', and in 1476, clay was used to plaster the 'building where the boys lie' (DCN 1/6/46; 94). It seems that their schoolroom was located in the nearby cellarer's range (see below). In the 1530s, repairs were made to the almoner's stables to convert one into an inhabitable tenement and building (DCN 1/6/34). The use of the almonry for residences of the laity is suggested by the example of Master Conrad, a Cambridge physician who was paid to examine the urine of sick monks. He was permitted in 1471 to rent a chamber and garden in the almonry complex, for use during his extended visits (Rawcliffe 2002, 48). The close proximity of the infirmary and almonry reflect the medieval connection between charity to the poor and care of the sick, both of which were among the corporal acts of mercy.

Monastic warehouse: the master of the cellar's range

A long, narrow range of medieval buildings on the east side of the upper court is the best candidate for the master of the cellar's range (Figure 72). This attribution is made on the basis of both the location and form of the buildings. In Benedictine and Cistercian monasteries, the cellarer's range was sited in or near the west range of the cloister (France 1998, 4). The main purpose of the range was storage, since the cellarer was responsible for provisioning the monastic community, encouraged by St Benedict to 'look upon the utensils of the monastery and its whole property as upon the sacred vessels of the altar' (McCann 1952, 83). At Norwich this role was held by the master of the cellar, the most powerful of the obedientiaries. The likely location of his office is the site of Numbers 66–68, houses that incorporate the remains of a row of two-storey buildings that were provided with cellars for additional storage. This range was located facing the Ethelbert gate, where merchants would have entered the precinct and crossed the almary green to the master of the cellar's office. It is proposed that at this site, he had his administrative centre, and storage space for precious goods reaching the precinct from the city. The value of commodities stored

FIGURE 72. Exterior of Numbers 66–68, the medieval cellarer's office. Photograph © Roberta Gilchrist.

here is confirmed by the need to appoint a keeper of the cellar gate, who was paid a stipend (DCN 1/1/31). In the lower and outer courts, the master of the cellar maintained storage for provisions arriving by water.

The northern block (Number 68) has largely been refaced, but two bays of the medieval roof survive in the north end of the building (Figure 73). The arched brace roof is constructed with a relatively shallow pitch and has curved wall braces, a ridge piece and one purlin on each side. Its decoration suggests a fifteenth-century date: all the elements have a small hollow chamfer, and the cornice beam has two additional deep chamfers, plus a small roll moulding. The block to the south (Numbers 66–67) retains a medieval roof at the south end of the building. This roof of six bays is also arched brace with a single purlin on each side, plus a ridge piece. The cornice beams are decorated with a combination of ogee and hollow chamfers, plus brattishing and a single roll, again suggesting a fifteenth-century date. Alterations to the interior and exterior were made following bomb damage in 1942, but a medieval door survives in the east elevation, which provided access to the upper chambers. A vaulted brick cellar survives beneath the central section of the block (Figure 74). This contains four side chambers, each approximately 2–3m deep, and each with a lamp locker in the rear wall.

It has been suggested that originally there were at least eighty domestic examples of brick undercrofts built in Norwich during the fifteenth century (or certainly before 1550) to provide level, fire-proof foundations for timber-framed houses.

FIGURE 73. Arched brace roof in Number 68, suggesting a fifteenth-century date. Photograph © Roberta Gilchrist.

FIGURE 74. Vaulted brick cellar beneath Number 67, showing two of the four side chambers, each with a lamp locker in the rear wall. Photograph © Roberta Gilchrist.

Given the lack of lighting to these undercrofts, it has been proposed that they were employed primarily for storage (Smith and Carter 1983). Some fifty-four extant domestic examples have been identified, but subterranean provision for the city's medieval monastic buildings has not been identified previously. In contrast with the secular examples, those of the priory were constructed beneath stone buildings, and the example beneath this range included niches for lights. There were brick cellars constructed beneath the offices of several monastic obedientiaries: the master of the cellar (Number 66), the infirmarer (Number 64), the almoner (Number 2), and beneath the brewhouse (Number 33). This group of brick undercrofts suggests that in the fifteenth century, the offices of the obedientiaries were adopting forms of construction typical of the mercantile buildings of the city of Norwich.

On his plan of the priory, Whittingham suggested that the cellarer's range continued further north beyond Number 68, where it contained the office of the communar. References in the rolls confirm that this office was in the master of the cellar's range, and that it housed the almonry school by 1387. In this year, the communar paid for repairs to the school door, describing it as next to the entrance to the great hall (DCN 1/12/33), referring to the hostry. This can be compared to the contemporary situation at Westminster, where the east side of Dean's Yard was shared by the cellarer's building to the north, and the grammar school to the south (RCHME 1924, 89). By 1532, the Norwich almoner was paying a fee of 12d to the communar, for leasing his vault in which the grammar school was kept

(DCN 1/6/137). In 1525, the priory's barber was living in the communar's accounting house, and for this reason was given an annual stipend of only 20s (DCN 1/12/101).

Commerce at the threshold: the clocher and the west-front shops

The area bordering the upper inner court was teeming with merchants and craftworkers. Tombland, directly to the west of the precinct, was used for a weekly market and for the prior's fair, held for nine days at Whitsun; from the thirteenth century it was also home to alehouses, butchers and ironmongers (Campbell 1975, 13–14). The Prior's Fee, to the north of the precinct, was occupied by stonemasons and bell-founders (Harries, et al. 1991, 13), and the Guild of St Luke, associated with bell-founders, pewterers and glaziers, was located in the green yard, in the cathedral's lay cemetery. Other guilds were associated with the cathedral church, including those of the skinners and pelterers, carpenters, and those devoted to St George, the Holy Trinity, and the Holy Trinity and St Mary, five of the nineteen guilds that were recorded as being active in Norwich in 1388 (Tanner 1996, 276). At Pentecost, a fair was held in the cemetery and the green yard, from which the sacrist collected the rents from stalls (DCN 1/4/32).

Just inside the Erpingham gate was a detached bell-tower or campanile, referred to as the *berefridus* (belfry) or *clocher*. This tower contained five large bells that complemented the set of five contained in the cathedral's crossing tower (LeStrange 1883, 151). Paul Cattermole has observed that the cathedral's *Customary* (c.1260) refers to the 'bells in the choir' to be used for daily services, and the 'greater bells' to be employed for major festivals and feasts. He suggests that this distinguished the bells in the crossing tower from the heavier bells of the *clocher*, with the latter reserved for special use (Cattermole 1996, 495–501). Bartholomew Cotton very clearly indicated that the *clocher* was in existence before the riot of 1272, and was a target singled out by the enraged townspeople (Luard 1859). The sacrist was responsible for the cathedral's bells, and his accounts confirm that the *clocher* was rebuilt with Barnack and Caen stone, c.1300–07, and surmounted by a leaded spire with a weather vane (Cattermole 1996). The upper parts of the tower and spire were shown in Cunningham's perspective of Norwich in 1558, and Joris Hoefnagel's view of 1581 (Chubb and Stephen 1928, plates xviii–xix), although it had been partly demolished by c.1569.

The location of the *clocher* was first suggested by L'Estrange (1883), on the basis of lease abuttals from the late sixteenth-century Ledger Books. Actually, before this publication, parts of the tower's foundations had been uncovered by J. H. Brown, surveyor to the cathedral. His plan of 1881 shows the east wall of the *clocher*, and two corners with angle buttresses, with a thickened north-east corner for a newel stair (MC186/51 648x4). The foundations suggest a substantial tower, 45ft (14m) square externally, and internally 36½ft (11.12m) square. This evidence was confirmed in 1956, when excavations for a water main in the roadway in front of Number 71 exposed massive masonry foundations, together with sherds of later medieval and post-medieval pottery (Norfolk SMR No. 43). A fragment of the north-west corner of the *clocher* still survives in the cellar of Number 71.

The Norwich *clocher* is part of a wider tradition of detached bell-towers at cathedral and monastic churches in southern England, with surviving examples at Chichester (Sussex), Evesham abbey (Worcestershire) and the Benedictine nunnery of Elstow (Bedfordshire) (Cobb 1980, 19). J. P. McAleer has shown that from the thirteenth century onwards, seven cathedrals and eight monastic churches had such towers, together with a number of parish churches. He contrasts the variety in their form with the greater uniformity of the Italian *campanili*, and notes the general absence of detached bell-towers from France and Germany (McAleer 2002, 77). The Norwich *clocher* did not compare in size with the huge bell-towers of Salisbury and Westminster, but was perhaps comparable to that at St Paul's (ibid., 73). McAleer was unable to identify any functional reason for the construction of detached bell-towers at churches that also possessed crossing towers containing bells. However, it is suggested here that the topographical siting of the bell-towers indicates their broader social purpose. They were located at public access points to monastic and cathedral precincts, often in the cemetery, on the side of the church away from the cloister. At Christ Church and St Augustine's, both in Canterbury, the towers were on the south, and at Worcester, Lichfield, Chichester and Tewkesbury, they were to the north of the church. Salisbury, like Norwich, had a detached bell-tower in the north-west corner of the precinct (ibid., 59–66). It may be recalled that the Norwich *Customary* reveals that the heavier bells of the *clocher* were reserved for special feasts and festivals (Cattermole 1996). It seems likely, therefore, that the detached bell-towers were erected so that their special peals could be heard by townspeople bordering the precinct, sited at lay entrances to announce these festivals and beckon the faithful. The siting of the detached bell-towers near lay cemeteries suggests a more specific purpose: they are likely to have tolled the traditional death-knells for members of the monastic community or laity buried in the cathedral cemetery. The *clocher* was sited in close proximity to the entrance to the lay cemetery to the north-west of the cathedral church, and immediately adjacent to the charnel house beneath the Carnary chapel. The detached bell-tower was integral to the mortuary landscape that was established to enhance the activities of burial and commemoration of the laity within the precinct.

There is no doubt that the Norwich *clocher* was located in a public, secular part of the precinct. From the fifteenth century, the area of the inner court within the Erpingham gate became the focus of commercial activity. The path between the gate and the west door to the cathedral church became a commercial lane, flanked on one side by the buildings of the Carnary college, and on the other by shops and tenements that joined the east wall of the *clocher*. These shops were developed as a commercial concern by the sacrist, who collected annual rents from the 'shops below the gate' and the 'garden next to the clocher' (DCN 1/4/56–67). The occupants of these shops included goldsmiths, embroiderers, carpenters, masons, glaziers and a saddler (Bolingbroke 1922; Noble 1997); trades drawn from local occupations, and of utility to both the priory and travellers stopping in the precinct. The relative locations of these features can be reconstructed with reference to the leases of the early Ledger books (DCN 47/1–2). In 1542, the west wall of the precinct from the Ethelbert gate to the Erpingham gate was occupied entirely by gardens. A lease of 1564 indicates that joining to the south of the *clocher* were a garden, a carpenter's house and a mason's house, with the row totalling forty-one yards in length. According to a lease of 1558, the 'almary oak' stood just to the south of the *clocher*, between the green and the precinct wall. This big oak was a tree under which the Courts of the Manor of Amners were held on St Luke's day (Bolingbroke 1922, 2), the manor that Herbert de Losinga took over when he established the cathedral (Metters 1985, 20).

This commercial sector compares closely with contemporary developments at Chichester and Ely. At Chichester, the first stage of the surviving detached bell-tower is plain on its north and east sides, suggesting that it was surrounded by shops and tenements when it was constructed, c.1400 (Tatton-Brown 1994, 245). The evolution of the north range at Ely demonstrates the commercial speculation of another cathedral sacrist. This medieval range is sited on the north boundary of the cathedral precincts, at a gate that was controlled by the sacrist. Excavations and study of standing buildings have shown that a two-storey range was developed in the fourteenth century, between the sacrist's gate and Goldsmith's tower, a chamber over an undercroft (Holton-Krayenbuhl et al. 1989). The *Chronicle of Ely* reveals that in the late fourteenth century, the entrepreneurial sacrist, Alan of Walsingham, purchased four shops that were next to the cemetery. He absorbed these within his department, enclosing them with a stone wall. One shop was used for a goldsmith's, and another was a wine cellar (ibid., 64). The Norwich sacrist had ample space to develop his own row of shops, which he leased to craftworkers who were eager to catch the passing trade of pilgrims, guild members and fair-goers.

THE LOWER INNER COURT: PROVISIONING THE PRIORY

Two complexes of medieval buildings survive along the north and east sides of the lower green (Figure 75). These can be identified as service buildings that were under the control of the master of the cellar. The layout of the lower court or brewery green had been established by approximately the mid fourteenth century; earlier there were timber buildings and gravelled roads in the central space of the green (see p. 56). The group of buildings lining the north side of the green is thought to have been connected with the monastic granary, Numbers 51–56. Those forming the eastern boundary of the green were the monastic brewhouse and bakehouse, today incorporated within Numbers 32–34. The functions originally served by these buildings are suggested by obediential accounts and post-medieval leases. An inventory compiled by the sacrist in 1436 distinguishes between a malt granary and a wheat granary (DCN 1/4/76), which were distinct from the granary and hay grange 'at the water', in the outer court. The granary can be located by a lease of

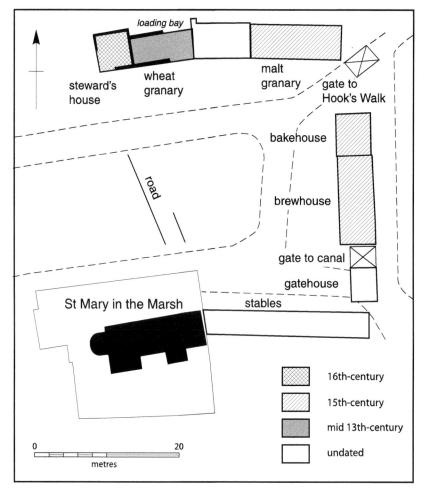

FIGURE 75. Plan of the lower inner court, to the south-east of the cloister. Drawing by Margaret Mathews.

1550 to Mr Tedman, of 'all those houses being under the great Granary . . . from the entry next the stairs going upp into the said granary unto the gable wall at the East end' (DCN 47/1). The bakehouse and brewhouse were closely connected, indicated when the lead vessels and furnace in the brewhouse and bakehouse were mended in 1337 (DCN 1/1/34). The monastic brewhouse was leased at the Reformation complete with its 'bruing and baking houses'. In 1569, it was leased to Ambrose Nutting, 'berebruer', including 'the brewhouse and horsemyll, myllhouse and going gere, also the copper fatts and other necessary vessels and one plot before the said brewhouse to be taken from the Comon Grene' (DCN 47/2).

Whittingham proposed that the granary ran at first floor level along the full length of a long range represented by Numbers 51–6, with the granarian's house at the east end, and the steward of the manor's house at the west end (1985, 114).

Surviving architectural evidence suggests instead that there were a number of separate, possibly self-contained structures, corroborated by a change of alignment that can be observed between Numbers 53 and 54. All the buildings are constructed in flint rubble. Starting at the eastern end, the ground floor of Number 51 has a low ceiling, while the first and second floors are higher, the latter with a single butt-purlin roof, with arch braces on haunched wall-posts, set into the flint rubble wall. The east gable retains two mullioned windows, possibly of early sixteenth-century date. The west gable end seems to be an original partition between Numbers 51 and 52: there is a substantial wall on the ground floor containing two fragments of an entry arch. One feature confirms that the eastern compartment of the range was used for more than storage: the east gable retains a large fireplace with stone jambs. This would suggest that the ground-floor chamber was used to house a servant of the priory, perhaps connected with the granary.

Number 52, joining to the west, was constructed with the first-floor level open to the apex of the roof. Such an arrangement would have allowed maximum space for storage of goods, and parallels later medieval merchants' houses. The internal arrangements of this building are all post-medieval, but the roof itself probably dates from the fifteenth century. It has curved braces extending down from the principal rafters to the wall-posts, with one butt-purlin in each pitch. This is the same construction as the roofs over Numbers 54–55, although the two blocks are on a different alignment, and the roof ridges are at different heights. The evidence of the roof confirms that Numbers 51 and 52 were constructed as discrete buildings. Unfortunately, any evidence for the relationship of this structure to those at the western end of the range was lost with the collapse of Number 53 (the Dial House) in 1903, while it was undergoing restoration (DCN 24, 1904). However, the different alignment of Number 52, and its higher roof ridge, suggests that it was also constructed independently of Numbers 54–55.

There is convincing evidence to suggest that Numbers 54 and 55 were built and functioned as a single entity (Figure 76). Moreover, the remains of an open arcade at the rear of the building confirm that it possessed a loading-bay to receive goods entering the precinct by cart or canal (Figure 77; see also p. 56). In total, there were six open arches supporting the first floor, which are now blocked. The arcade was composed of double order arches springing from a circular abacus, which has deep under-cut mouldings and is supported by elongated brackets. This feature dates the building to the mid thirteenth century, although the roof is more likely to be fifteenth century. Two and a half bays of the roof are contained within Number 55, and are identical to the four bays which can be seen in Number 54, with curved braces extending down from the principal rafters to the wall posts, and with one butt-purlin in each pitch. Within Number 54, there are substantial ceiling beams throughout the building, the presence of which supports the theory that it was used for storage. It is also clear that when constructed, the roof was open to the second floor.

The structure visible within Number 56 the Close dates no earlier than the

FIGURE 76. Exterior of Number 55, part of the medieval granary fronting onto the brewery green. Photograph © Roberta Gilchrist.

seventeenth century (Figure 78), although a medieval wall painting survives on the first floor, depicting the Crown of Thorns and IHS alternating with the monogram 'Maria'. It appears that this structure was built against the existing gable wall of Number 55, and was not integral to the structures that join it to the east. A lease of 1561 confirms that the building was in existence by the sixteenth century, and that it contained the 'stywards chamber'. This chamber was leased to John Debney, 'situate and being at the end of the granary between the Deans Garden on the north and brewers green on the south' (DCN 47/1).

The surviving buildings suggest that there were at least three separate medieval structures: Number 51, Number 52, and Numbers 54–55. Number 56 seems to be a later addition, perhaps dating to the early sixteenth century, while the relationship of the former Number 53 cannot be established with any certainty. The arcade surviving at Number 54–55 confirms its original purpose as a major warehouse, and it is likely to have coincided with the documented wheat granary. The sacrist's inventory of 1436 listed in the wheat granary, 'three great cables, two pulleys with four sheaves of malt, two pulleys with two sheaves', along with blankets, sheets, coverlets and mattresses, confirming that the space was also used for accommodation (DCN 1/4/75). The malt granary did not contain lifting equipment, and may have been a smaller building located closer to the brewhouse. Numbers 51 and 52 are likely to have stored various provisions including malted barley, and to have housed monastic servants in the heated ground-floor chamber of Number 51.

FIGURE 77. Thirteenth-century arcade at the rear of Number 55, indicating a loading bay behind the monastic granary. Photograph © Roberta Gilchrist.

The monastic granary (Numbers 54–55) was used for the storage of threshed grain. Bread remained the mainstay of the monastic diet at Norwich and elsewhere, with a daily allowance of a 2lb loaf (0.9kg) of the best bread for each monk (Saunders 1930, 91). Two lower grades of bread were also produced, for feeding servants and distributing at the almonry. Monastic barns, for the storage of unthreshed grain, are relatively common survivals at monastic granges, and occasionally at home granges adjacent to abbeys, such as those at Glastonbury (Somerset) and Abbotsbury (Dorset). Architectural evidence suggests that there was a widespread programme of monastic barn construction from c. 1200, continuing into the fifteenth century. In contrast, evidence for granaries is extremely rare. There are only two other surviving examples: the granary adjoining the great barn of the Shaftesbury abbey grange

FIGURE 78. Exterior of Number 56, the steward's house, likely to date to the sixteenth century. Photograph © Roberta Gilchrist.

at Bradford-on-Avon (Wiltshire), and a ruined granary at Neath abbey's grange at Monknash (Glamorgan), which is over 60m long. Granaries have been excavated in the outer courts of Thornholme (Lincolnshire) and Mount Grace (N Yorkshire) priories, and at the preceptory of South Witham (Lincolnshire) (Bond 2001a, 60). The demand for grain storage near the cloister is reflected at the Cistercian abbey of Rievaulx (N Yorkshire), where the former lay brothers' dormitory had been converted to a granary by the time of the Dissolution (Coppack 1999).

The fabric of the bakehouse and brewhouse range reveals a complex history (Figure 79), with major alterations in the seventeenth century and later (see p. 232), resulting in a symmetrical, double-pile plan. The medieval range was constructed in flint rubble and was one room deep, with a brick cellar beneath the middle of the block. The brewhouse is considered to have been located at the southern end (Numbers 31–32), where some evidence of medieval fabric survives. The rear wall of Number 32 contains two blocked arches: internally, they have been plastered over, but externally two orders of chamfered brick survive. The colour and texture of the bricks suggest an early-fifteenth-century date, and the feature may suggest a loading-bay, comparable to the earlier example at Numbers 54–55. Within the cellar of Number 33, there is a chamfered corner formed in ashlar, which could be medieval in origin. The roof above the front of the building has hipped ends, which extend the roof to the rear of the building; the roof structure has butt-purlins, with two purlins in each pitch. To the north, the bakehouse block reveals its medieval

FIGURE 79. Exterior of Numbers 32–34, the medieval bakehouse and brewhouse, fronting onto the brewery green. The front of the brewhouse was extended in the seventeenth century to create a double-pile plan. A datestone survives for this work: 'RJA 1682'.

origins on its west and east façades, with a buttress visible on the west, and stone quoins on the east.

Monasteries consumed prodigious amounts of ale, which was generally safer than water to drink. Barbara Harvey has suggested that the monks of Westminster would have had a basic allowance of about one gallon of ale each day. Although weak by modern standards, this was the monastery's best, or first ale, drawn off every quantity of malt entering their brewery (Harvey 1993, 58). The pairing of the bakehouse and brewhouse appears to have been standard in monastic planning. They are shown as a linked unit on the plan of St Gall, and on the plan of the waterworks for Canterbury cathedral-priory (c.1165), the latter located in a large inner court to the north of the cloister, next to a small granary (Horn and Born 1979, vol. 2, 252). These features have rarely been examined archaeologically. Monastic brewhouses have been excavated at Thornholme and Nuneaton (Warwickshire), the latter containing a small vat in a circular projection at the corner of the building, possibly for steeping barley before spreading it out to germinate (Andrews et al. 1981, 64–5). Only three monastic bakehouses have been excavated, at Bradwell abbey (Essex), Grove priory (Bedfordshire) and Thornholme, the last of which was converted in the thirteenth century from an earlier building, and the principal feature of which was a large, sub-circular bread oven against one wall (Coppack 1990, 108). Unfortunately, the internal arrangements of the bakehouse and brewhouse at

Norwich do not survive. The missing fittings are illustrated by the surviving bake-house and brewhouse at the nunnery of Lacock (Wiltshire), which was made into a country house by Sir William Sharington in 1539. Part of the sixteenth-century inner court retains a bakehouse, which also has a fireplace that was used for heating the malt, hops and water for beer; the attached brewhouse retains the mashtun for heating the mixture, and a huge cooling trough with a vat beneath it that was used for fermenting.

Although absorbed within the later houses of the close, Norwich cathedral retains a remarkable number of the medieval service buildings of the inner court, including the infirmary chambers, the master of the cellar's office, the bakehouse and brewhouse, and the granary, with its attached storage and offices of the steward and granarian.

8

The New Order:
the Post-medieval Cathedral Close,
1538–c.1700

THE cathedral-priories present unique potential to study continuity and change through the period of the Reformation and into the later sixteenth and seventeenth centuries. And yet, the study of cathedrals has neglected this crucial period. Although recent historical research has addressed this lacuna (Lehmberg 1988; 1996), archaeological and architectural study of post-medieval cathedrals has focused almost exclusively on the church (e.g. Tatton-Brown and Munby 1996). This chapter explores the impact of the massive social, political and religious changes of the later sixteenth and seventeenth centuries on the cathedral close at Norwich. The reshaping of the buildings and landscape of the close are followed up to c.1700, allowing consideration of important new trends that followed the Civil War and the restoration of cathedral chapters in 1660 (Plate 10).

THE NEW CATHEDRAL COMMUNITY

The impetus to suppress the monastic houses had gathered momentum during the 1530s, although precedents had been set in Germany and Scandinavia in the 1520s. In 1534, the Act of Supremacy required all clergy to declare an oath acknowledging royal supremacy over the church, and renouncing the jurisdiction of the pope. This challenge to spiritual authority was followed by an economic attack: in 1535, all the monasteries were ordered to reveal the value of their possessions and holdings. They were visited by the king's commissioners, who compiled the *Valor Ecclesiasticus*, a survey that facilitated the eventual sale of monastic properties (Caley and Hunter 1810–34). Commissioners also evaluated the moral and disciplinary condition of religious houses, frequently producing blatantly biased accounts that embellished lapses in sexual behaviour: in the case of the cathedral-priories, Norwich and Carlisle were charged with such improprieties (Lehmberg 1988, 81). Shrines and images were scourged from cathedral churches, following injunctions in 1536 and 1538. But the monastic cathedrals were to undergo a more fundamental change, when the priories that served them were suppressed (1539–42).

Norwich cathedral was never formally dissolved, but was instead converted by Henry VIII in 1538 to a new secular establishment under a dean and chapter. It has been suggested that this special treatment was occasioned by the poor management, or great malleability, of Bishop Repps (Lehmberg 1988, 81). However, this assessment may be inconsistent with the exceptional terms that were negotiated for the new foundation (Houlbrooke 1996, 507). When Norwich cathedral was converted on 2 May 1538, the royal charter was unusual in stipulating its staffing by both canons and prebendaries, allowing the continuity of personnel. The canons were in fact the senior monks of the cathedral-priory, who were given an office for life in the new foundation, but not replaced when they died. The last prior and twenty-one monks[1] became the dean, sixteen canons and six prebendaries, with all members of the chapter receiving salaries. Other new foundations were unable to absorb the majority of their former monks. At Durham, for example, only twenty-seven of the sixty-six monks were given office in the new cathedral in 1541. These generous terms were only transitional arrangements. In 1547, the Norwich chapter was required to surrender their church to royal commissioners, and new letters patent of foundation stipulated staffing by only the dean and six prebendaries (Houlbrooke 1996, 509). The prebendaries were to be priests, 'not only learned and erudite, but also adorned with a title of learning'; the minor, or 'petty' canons, were to be chosen by the dean 'for the purpose of singing the praises of God and reading the appointed lessons in the temple of the Church' (Williams and Cozens-Hardy 1953, 8–9). Norwich was also authorised to draw up its own statutes, in contrast with arrangements for all other cathedrals. In fact, the chapter failed to do so, and statutes were issued eventually by James 1 in 1620, which remained in force until 1941.

By 1547, arrangements at Norwich had come into line with cathedrals that had had statutes imposed upon them in the early 1540s. These specified the staffing of cathedrals by canons or prebendaries, who would reside in separate houses in the precinct. The lesser staff of the cathedral, the minor canons, singing men, choristers and masters of the grammar schools, were expected to dine communally in a common hall (Lehmberg 1988, 93). These living arrangements were modelled on the medieval secular cathedrals, with their separate communities of canons and vicars choral. Distinctions among the cathedral community were reflected also in arrangements for their burial. The minor canons and their families were to be buried in the south transept at Norwich, while the lay clerks and other officers were to be interred in the north transept (Finch 1996, 469). For the former monastic cathedrals, such changes introduced new distinctions and hierarchies that were in direct opposition to the communal life exalted by the Rule of St Benedict.

Deans replaced priors in the former monastic communities, and generally continued to live in the priors' lodgings. They maintained hospitality within their households, but not to the generous level expected of medieval priors. Stanford Lehmberg has suggested that deans lived 'as if they were members of the lower

---

[1] Baskerville (1933) notes that three junior monks were retained as subdeacons, and that others held livings at St Mary at Plea (Norwich), Earlham, Felthorpe, Stoke-by-Clare college and Woodbastwick, perhaps in addition to their stipends at the cathedral. In 1555, Thomas Jolly, a former monk of the priory, held no living and was returned as a crown pensioner.

aristocracy or upper gentry', a lesser standing than that enjoyed by their monastic predecessors but still a position of considerable means. Continuing the comparison with secular society, he likens the standards of living of the canons and prebendaries to privileged 'lesser country gentlemen' and minor canons to 'middling merchants'. He suggests that the singing men lived closer to subsistence level, more akin to the lifestyle of artisans or agricultural labourers (1996, 155).

Norwich was a relatively small and poorly endowed cathedral, having lost its wealthy properties at the refoundation. Consequently, prebends at Norwich may not have been attractive economically, and many of the appointed prebendaries were not resident or even regular visitors to the close (Houlbrooke 1996, 515). Absenteeism and pluralism were rife in the new foundations, as prebendaries held numerous positions and visited their cathedrals infrequently. At Norwich, they were required to be resident four months each year, and to attend the services once a day, four times a week during their residence. In 1674, they asked for this requirement to be relaxed to just two months of residence a year, but with the requirement to attend services more regularly during that time (Lehmberg 1996, 74). Ralph Houlbrooke has observed that only half of the Norwich prebendaries were resident in 1567, and only one kept house in the close in 1613 (1996, 516–7). Despite these absences, in 1566 it was prohibited to sublet properties that had been allocated to the dean, prebendaries or petty canons (Williams and Cozens-Hardy 1953, 23), increasing the likelihood that the houses of the close would fall into disrepair. With the prolonged absences of the prebendaries, it was clearly the minor canons and singing men who maintained the spiritual and liturgical roles of the mother church of the diocese. Their lives represent some degree of continuity with the medieval monastic community.

At Norwich, the first generation of the new foundation enjoyed a remarkable social continuity: the prior, most of the monks, and the servants of the monastery found positions in the reformed establishment. There were to be around one hundred lay officers in the new foundation, including: eight lay clerks, six bedesmen, subsacrists, two vergers, a beadle, a sexton and under-sextons, a high steward and under-steward, a chapter clerk, two cooks, a porter, a butler and a caterer, the keeper of the ferry, the auditor and the coroner (Williams and Cozens-Hardy 1953). At first, there was resistance to the presence of women, or married clergy, in prominent spaces of the close. In 1549, a new house was built abutting the east end of the Carnary chapel and adjacent to the west front of the cathedral. Land for the building was leased to Dr John Baret, a former *lector* at the priory, who was contracted after the Dissolution to lecture on Holy Scripture twice a week (Dodwell 1996b, 247); Baret was also rector of Hethersett and St Michael at Plea, Norwich (d. 1563). He was granted this prime site 'provided that no person or persons shall dwell in any house which should be built upon any part of the said parcel of ground but only a prist or prists or other man or men being sole and not married' (DNC 47/1).

Social life in the cathedral close gradually became more diverse, as buildings

of the former monastic corporation were leased to secular tenants of varied occupations. Greater numbers of women and young children frequented the close,
in part resulting from the acceptance of clerical marriage between 1549 and 1553,
and again from 1558 to 1561. Women were also appointed to important positions
when the priory's domestic structure was replaced. The brewhouse continued in
operation under secular management, and in 1550 was leased to Johanna Vanstall,
widow of Norwich, 'the said Vanstall covenanted to serve and deliver to the dean
and chapter so moche of the best beer' (DNC 47/1). When the Catholic Queen
Mary ruled between 1553 and 1558, clerical marriage was again forbidden. Her
position recalled the earlier medieval controversies over clerical marriage. Male
clergy had been distinct from laymen, resulting from their ordination as priests and
their vow of celibacy (Elliott 1999). The acceptance of clerical marriage removed
a barrier that had previously set the clergy apart from laymen. In 1554, the dean
and two of the prebendaries of Norwich cathedral were deprived of their benefices
because they were married (Houlbrooke 1996, 518). When Elizabeth took the
throne, she maintained the ban on clerical marriage, and in 1561 ordered that the
wives and children of cathedral clergy should be ejected from their precincts. Elizabeth maintained that their presence was a violation of the intentions of founders and
a hindrance to study and learning (Lehmberg 1988, 143). Despite this, from the
1560s onwards, the Norwich chapter always included married men (Houlbrooke
1996, 518).

The newly available premises in the close soon attracted the full range of
urban recreations. In 1569, Dean Gardiner noted that the brewhouse had become
an unlicensed tippling house for 'all evil and naughty persons'. A visitation by Bishop
William Redman in 1596 required that 'the many Alehowses now used in the lib-
ertie' should 'be putt downe' (Williams and Cozens-Hardy 1953, 38). Despite this
admonition, an alehouse was set up illegally in 1604 by Symon Mosse, one of the
singing men (ibid., 41–2). Drinking within the close could lead to public disorder,
and in 1616, Dean Suckling had Ellis Goodwyn 'set in stocks' for 'extraordinary
drinking' (ibid., 52). A tavern known as The Three Cranes was established in the
former bakehouse before the end of the seventeenth century (DCN 24/4), one of
several inns of the close that were well known in the eighteenth century.[2] From the
early seventeenth century, the relative order and regulation of the monastic precinct
had been replaced by the disorder typical of any urban community, with the inhabitants grumbling of illegal alehouses, blocked drains and festering rubbish (Atherton
1996, 637–8).

The dean and chapter managed the close in a similar vein to that which the
corporation of Norwich exercised in the city. Both authorities feared disorder, and

---

[2] Later alehouses were established at Number 14a (The Garden House), at Number 70, Bishopgate
(The Black Jack), near the water gate (The Ferryhouse), and above the Ethelbert gate (The Gatehouse).
The last of these was an early-eighteenth-century music club, popular with minor canons and lay clerks,
which sang bawdy songs but later became the Norwich Glee Club (Bolingbroke 1922, 5). These alehouses
had all disappeared by the first half of the nineteenth century, including The Three Cranes in 1805.

attempted to control popular social recreations such as alehouses (Pound 1988, 119). There were repeated attempts to manage the social composition of the close through the exclusion of nonconformists, Catholics and the poor, but these efforts were never fully successful. A workhouse was set up in the former almonry, near the Ethelbert gate, until it was demolished in 1703 for the construction of Number 2, by Thornagh Gurdon (Bolingbroke 1922, 4–5).[3] The census of 1676 showed that the close accommodated the greatest concentration of Catholics in Norwich (Atherton 1996, 641), despite the chapter's lease clause barring papists and recusants from living in the close (DCN 24/4). These sentiments contradict the actions of Bishop John Parkhurst in 1565. Whether motivated by tolerance or desperation, he leased the bishop's chapel to the nonconformist Walloon congregation for use as their church.

The Walloons occupied the chapel until 1637, when the high church establishment of Charles I considered it unacceptable for a nonconformist congregation to be camped in the grounds of the bishop's see. Bishop Corbett made repeated attempts to eject the Walloons, writing to them in 1634, 'Your discipline care not much for a consecratated place, and anye other roome in Norwich . . . may serve your turne as well as the chappel: wherefore I say unto you . . . depart, and hire some other place for your irregular meetings' (Britton 1836, 70). The presence of the Walloon congregation in the close may account for an unusual grave excavated just to the north of the Jesus chapel, between the cathedral church and the former bishop's chapel. Contrary to Christian tradition, this burial of a middle-aged male (35–50 years) was orientated north–south. Its relatively shallow depth, and the coffin nails associated with it, suggest a post-medieval date. The excavators conjectured that the unorthodox orientation could be indicative of nonconformist practice (Warsop and Boghi 2002, after Bashford and Pollard 1998). The spatial location and unusual orientation of the grave suggest the possibility of a Walloon burial, or perhaps one associated with the Civil War use of the bishop's chapel as a meeting-house for sectaries (Atherton and Morgan 1996).

THE CATHEDRAL CHURCH

Throughout this period of tremendous upheaval, the services of the cathedral churches provided some sense of continuity, remaining largely unreformed until Henry's death. Major shrines were dismantled, and at Norwich a mason was paid to take down St William's tomb, and install in its place eleven altars that had been removed from the dissolved church of the Blackfriars (Lehmberg 1988, 75). Henry's son, Edward VI, enforced a stronger wind of Protestant change in 1547, requiring the destruction of all shrines, altar tables, images and stained glass, the regular

---

[3] Later workhouses were established in the former infirmary (1744–56) and on the site of Number 57. The latter was The Magdalene, a female penitentiary, from 1827 until 1861 (Atherton 1996, 650–51).

preaching of sermons, and the performance of masses in English rather than Latin (ibid., 101). This year also saw the dissolution of the chantries, affecting private chapels in cathedrals and parish churches, as well as chantry colleges such as the Carnary college at Norwich. Destruction associated with the Edwardian reforms seems to have included the medieval funerary monuments and brasses of Norwich cathedral. Although their loss has been attributed previously to the Civil War period, Jonathon Finch has shown that most of the damage had been done before the beginning of the seventeenth century (Finch 1996, 474–5).

Within cathedral churches, spatial iconoclasts challenged traditional beliefs concerning the sanctity of space. The liturgy was pared down to its bare bones, as the clergy retreated into the contained spaces of the choir and presbytery. Mary's reign (1553–8) provided brief but expensive respite, as traditional worship was restored, requiring the reinstatement of books, plate, vestments, processions and roods (Lehmberg 1988, 128). Subsequently, services became more stationary, as processions disappeared and seating was introduced to allow relative comfort during interminable services. In 1637, Charles I ordered that the whole corporation of Norwich should attend the cathedral every Sunday for the entire service, not just the sermon, demanding their presence for up to three or four hours (Atherton and Morgan 1996, 549).

The new social order came to be reflected by the seats provided in the choir, with hierarchies articulated through distinctions in vertical and horizontal space. Galleries were set up in the choir at Norwich, as they were at Wells, Chichester and Winchester, in order to accommodate large numbers in a restricted area. Galleries served this purpose in parish churches also; for example, they become a more common feature in London parish churches in the 1620s and '30s (Schofield 2003). Ian Atherton and Victor Morgan have written that 'the position, style and type of seat, the route to that seat, even the size, quality and binding of the prayer books in those seats, reflected this hierarchy and the dignity of persons sitting there' (1996, 546). Dignity was sorely tested by the cold and draughty seats and by the abominable behaviour of those sitting above. The corporation of Norwich complained that 'some made water in the gallery on the aldermen's heads and it dropped down onto their wives' seats . . . somebody most beastly did conspurcate and shit upon an alderman's gown . . . and some from the galleries let fall a shoe which narrowly missed the mayor's head' (Lehmberg 1996, 208). Just as the close had taken on the characteristics of any urban space, the cathedral church resembled a public theatre or assembly place, where political tensions were played out.

Archbishop Laud (1633–45) reasserted the importance of traditional ceremony, including the reverence due to holy spaces such as the choir. He opposed the cluttering of cathedral interiors with fixed seating, since this was at odds with medieval practice. He ordered the removal of seats from the choir at Durham, York and Salisbury, and from the nave at Worcester and Gloucester (Lehmberg 1996, 14–15). The galleries on the south side of the choir at Norwich are shown in a drawing of c.1630, which depicts two-tier 'closets' and the position of fixed seating for

FIGURE 80. The earliest drawing of the cathedral's interior, c.1630. The south side of the choir, showing two-tier 'closets' designated for seats of the mayor and corporation. Reproduced with permission of Norwich Castle Museum and Art Gallery: Bolingbroke Col. 1922.135.860.

the corporation and the choir (Figure 80). Double galleries were also placed across the transepts, which were remodelled in 1767 as boxes with ornamental cresting. Those in the south transept were removed in Anthony Salvin's restorations of the 1830s, but the galleries in the north transept were retained until 1851 (Gilchrist 1999, 111).

The provision of hierarchical seating was repeated in the green yard to the north of the nave. This space remained an important location for sermons, stemming from its use as a preaching yard from the fifteenth century, and the cathedral was one of the few places in Norwich that maintained regular weekly sermons (Atherton and Morgan 1996, 547). Writing in the late seventeenth century, Sir Thomas Browne provided a detailed account and plan of the green yard as it may have appeared before the Civil War (Figure 81). This shows the entrance to the green yard through the north aisle of the cathedral nave, leading to two ranks of galleries facing a central pulpit. The galleries against the nave of the cathedral were those of the dean and chapter, while those alongside the bishop's palace were reserved for the mayor and corporation. Unallocated seats were also available on benches on the grass. Browne's plan is supported by archaeological evidence in the elevation of the north wall of the nave, where putlog holes survive as scars left by the two-storey

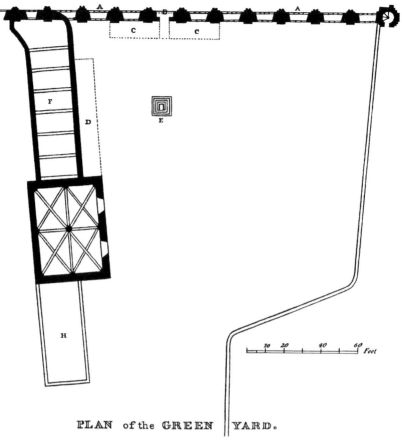

PLAN of the GREEN ‖ YARD。

FIGURE 81. Plan of the green yard, the preaching yard that was located to the north of the cathedral nave, showing the gallery of the mayor and corporation (D; abutting the bishop's palace), the dean and chapter gallery (C), and the pulpit (E). Plan from Sir Thomas Browne's *Repertorium* (1680).

galleries. Similar preaching yards were set up at St Paul's (Lehmberg 1996, 207), and at Chichester and Exeter cathedrals (Orme 1991, 168).

The long naves of cathedral churches became redundant spaces, often serving as open thoroughfares, as at Winchester, Salisbury, Exeter, Worcester and St Paul's (Cobb 1980, 124; Lehmberg 1988, 289). The nave at Norwich was a bustling thoroughfare and public way into Bishopgate until the early nineteenth century (Gilchrist 1999, 111–2). The cathedral maintained spatial emphasis on the main east–west axis, until a new door was created in the north ambulatory in the eighteenth century, and buildings adjoining the south transept were swept away in the nineteenth century. The statutes of 1620 stated that the doors to the cathedral were to be opened at seven o'clock each morning and closed following evening player in the winter; during the summer months they were to be open from sunrise to sunset (DCN 28/1). In 1595, the chancellor of Norwich commanded 'that in tyme of devine service the officers attendant . . . should see that the noyse made and used in the church . . . maye be herafter appeased and wherby the service may be the more quietly performed' (Williams and Cozens-Hardy 1953, 38). Archaeological excavations at Chester cathedral have shown that the nave remained an unpaved space used only for burial of the poorer inhabitants of the precinct (Ward 2003). At the cathedral of Coventry, suppressed by Henry VIII, the nave quickly lost its holy resonance: excavations have revealed that it became a dumping ground for the city's butchers, and home to herds of pigs and packs of dogs (Soden 2003). Such hazards extended to the naves of cathedrals still in use. At Ely, Chichester, Durham and Wells, 'dog-whippers' were paid to keep dogs out of the church (Lehmberg 1996, 214). Some cathedrals used the nave for sermons, for example at Gloucester, where fixed pews had been established by the early seventeenth century, and at Ely, where the congregation assembled in the nave and promenaded until the prayers were over, when they took their seats for the sermon (Evans 1961, 9).

Superfluous chapels were reassigned to new uses. Parts of several cathedrals were given over to parish churches, including the Lady chapel at Ely, the north transept at Chichester, the south transept at Chester, and St Luke's chapel at Norwich (Cobb 1980, 20). The Lady chapel at Norwich may have succumbed to neglect rather than to wilful iconoclasm. In 1569, the 'decayed chapel called our Ladies Orchard with one orchard to the north of the chapel' was leased to Isabel Gardiner (DCN 24/2). Chapels to the north of the presbytery were leased to secular tenants and developed as domestic housing. In 1551, Alexander Chapman, gent, was residing in the 'Sanctuary Men's Chamber', by the north transept. He leased the old chapels adjacent to this chamber, St Andrew's and St Anne's, and was given permission 'to alter and transpose the same two chapels to make them mete and convenient for his purpose' (DCN 24/1). His modifications were evidenced in the chamber above St Andrew's chapel, which formerly contained a Tudor fireplace (L'Estrange 1864, 184). A domestic dwelling was also made in the room over the Jesus chapel, which was held in 1586 by Robert Cooper, in addition to 'an old decayed chapel called Our Ladys Chapel' (DCN 24/2). By the time of the Parliamentary Survey in 1649, these chapels were incorporated into a house occupied by two singing men of the cathedral, who had tenants including two men and a widow (Metters 1985, 33). The chapels had been demolished by the mid eighteenth century (Blomefield 1745 [1806], vol. 4, 7), but their roof-lines were still visible a century later (L'Estrange, 1864; Goulbourn 1884). The foundations of the former chapels of St Anne and the Relic chapel were surveyed by C. J. Brown in 1896 (MC 186/347), when the chapel of St Andrew was restored to ecclesiastical use, after having housed the hot water system (Gilchrist 1999, 112).[4]

---

[4] The location of these chapels has been the subject of considerable debate. Based on the *Customary* (Tolhurst 1948), Whittingham determined that the apsidal chapel in the north transept was dedicated to St Andrew, while the fourteenth-century chapel extending from the north ambulatory was dedicated to St Anne; L'Estrange (1864) had argued precisely the reverse. The Sanctuary Men's chamber is mentioned

The chapel of the Carnary college was purchased in 1550 by the Great Hospital (which had been St Giles' hospital before the dissolution of the chantries), with the intention of establishing a poor house at the western edge of the cathedral close. Instead, the corporation moved the Norwich Grammar School to the former college buildings by 1554, having previously established it in the buildings of the dissolved Blackfriars (Harries et al. 1991, 25, 52). The crypt of the Carnary chapel was not used for teaching, but was let instead to the corporation, and to grocers and wine merchants. The medieval charnel remains that it had contained must have been dispersed soon after the Reformation. Charnel practices seem to have ended promptly with the Reformation, with charnel houses closed including those at St Paul's cathedral and the parish churches of London (Harding 2003).

A rare visit to the cathedral church by the monarch was an occasion to be commemorated. Elizabeth visited Canterbury and Rochester in 1573, and Lichfield and Worcester in 1575, but after her visit to Norwich in 1578, confined her sojourns to the more comfortable hospitality of country houses (Lehmberg 1988, 279). Her visit to Worcester prompted the painting of her royal arms to the south of the high altar, requiring plastering over of the mutilated statues of a chantry chapel in this position (ibid., 111). She visited Norwich in August 1578, and attended a service at the cathedral, where a *Te Deum* was sung, before withdrawing to the bishop's palace where she was accommodated. A new organ was installed for her visit (Saunders 1932b, 15), and a special payment was recorded to the composer and singing man Osbert Parsley (Colthorpe 1989, 320), whose painted funerary monument of 1585 survives in the nave. Thomas Browne recorded that Elizabeth had been seated 'on the north side of the Quire between the two arches', in other words directly parallel with the high altar, and comparable to the position of her seat when visiting Worcester. Browne described a series of heraldic paintings that were made in the north walk of the cloister shortly after Elizabeth's visit, which had disappeared by the time he was writing, 'the rayne falling upon the wall washed them away' (Browne 1680 [1954], 137–8). The cloister was 'handsomely beautified' with the arms of those who had attended the Privy Council: Howard Duke of Norfolk, Clinton, Russell, Cheney, the Queen's Achievement, Hastings, Dudley, Cecil, Carey and Hatton. He suggested that previously the cloister tracery had been glazed with painted glass showing the arms of Morley, Shelton, Scales, Erpingham, Gournay, Mowbray, Savage, and Thorpe, presumably destroyed during the Civil War. In the 1930s, new arms were painted in the north cloister walk, representing the arms of the descendants or contemporary holders of office of those who had attended the meeting of the Privy Council at Norwich in 1578.[5]

in the sacrist's rolls from 1404. L'Estrange placed this chamber adjacent to the Jesus chapel, whereas Whittingham believed it to have been located over the chapel in the north transept. Whittingham suggested that the Relic chapel was sited over the reliquary arch to the north of the high altar, and in the chamber projecting to the north, a position also proposed by Goulbourn (1884) and followed here.

[5] From east to west, these twentieth-century arms represent the Earl of Leicester, Bacon, the Duke of Newcastle, Lord Hastings, Queen Mary, Queen Elizabeth I, Queen Elizabeth II, the Queen

The Transformation of the Monastic Buildings

It has been suggested that perhaps half of the religious houses dissolved between 1535–40 were put to new uses, many of them as domestic conversions to serve as the city residences or country seats of Henry VIII's courtiers. In recent years, the transitional phases of monasteries have received considerable attention from archaeologists and architectural historians (e.g. Doggett 2001). Maurice Howard has emphasised that such studies should not dwell negatively on the destruction of the former monasteries, but might instead highlight the processes of renewal and imaginative adaptation that these conversions engendered (Howard 2003). Certain general tendencies can be observed in the adaptation of monastic buildings to private residences, and these form a useful comparison with the processes of change that accompanied the refoundation of the former monastic cathedrals. A crucial difference, of course, is that the cathedrals enjoyed a considerable continuity of purpose and personnel. To what extent did the reshaping of the monastic buildings contribute to the establishment of a new way of life within the cathedrals?

The reuse of monastic buildings usually involved the selective *retention* of structures that would serve well for domestic accommodation, and the deliberate *destruction* of the overtly sacred and corporate spaces of the monastery. The church, chapter house and cloister were the architectural spaces specifically eliminated.[6] These elements were the strongest symbols of the collective identity of the monastery, and their demolition can also be perceived as a form of iconoclasm, with their removal integral to the long process of conversion. Additionally, monastic dormitories were targets of early destruction, and it has been argued that this act was intended to prevent monastic reoccupation (Greene 1992, 183). The east range of the cloister was the location of the chapter house and the dormitory, and its destruction would have dealt a decisive blow to the communal aspirations of any monastery. The former lodgings of the monastic prior or prioress were the most likely to be retained: their self-contained chambers and facilities for hospitality suited conversion to new courtier houses, particularly in London. Christopher Phillpots has suggested that such adaptations turned the conventual buildings 'inside out', removing the central, sacred buildings and focusing on those that had previously been peripheral (Phillpots 2003). Monastic gatehouses were also frequently selected for retention. Often their upper chambers had accommodated porters, with the consequence that domestic features such as fireplaces and garderobes had already been provided. At Norwich, the chambers over the Erpingham and Ethelbert gates were leased out

Mother, Salisbury, the Duke of Norfolk and Hobart (Colthorpe 1989, 318). The wall paintings represent benefactors of the programme of conservation to the cloisters in 1935. The arms of patrons were also displayed in stained glass set into each bay of the restored cloister, designed by E. W. Tristram and made by J. A. Knowles of York (Paine & Stewart 2004, 1).

[6] Within the general pattern exceptions can be cited, such as the retention of the church at Netley and Mottisfont (Hampshire) and the cloister at Lacock (Wiltshire), or the development of the outer court as the new house at Battle (Sussex) (Howard 2003).

for domestic use, but also those over minor gates such as the sextry gate and the gatehouse leading to the ferry.

The process of converting the monastic buildings of the former cathedral-priories took place gradually, over an extended period stretching from their dissolution to their restoration following the Civil War. Immediate work was undertaken to accommodate the newly defined groups of clergy that served the cathedral, followed by the conversion, demolition and reuse of the spaces of the precinct by secular tenants and property speculators. Cloisters were generally retained, suggesting that the monastic tradition that they represented continued to be valued by the new foundations. In contrast, the core ranges were demolished or abandoned, just as secular conversions tended to turn the former monastic buildings 'inside out'. More radical change occurred in some circumstances, as at Winchester, where the puritan Bishop Horne (1560–80) demolished the cloisters and chapter house (Cobb 1980, 124). At Rochester, most of the monastic buildings were taken over by Henry VIII for use as a residence between London and Dover. They were altered substantially in the 1540s and '50s and returned to the chapter in 1558; today, the chapter house and dormitory undercroft survive (St John Hope 1900, 203–12).

The processes of demolition and the salvage of materials may also have been distinctive at cathedrals. Monasteries that were converted to secular houses were sometimes cleared by drastic measures, including the use of gunpowder and undermining (Morris 2003), but the continuity of use at cathedrals required a more careful and systematic approach. Significant evidence comes from the refectory at Norwich, where recent excavations have recorded evidence of holes for scaffolding along the south refectory wall. Pottery from the primary fill of the post holes indicates that the scaffolding was erected when the site was cleared after the suppression of the priory. The site remained empty until the construction of a prebendary house in the east end of the refectory, c.1620, and the interior was used for digging large pits in which to dispose of demolition debris from the chapter house and Lady chapel (Wallis in press). Although much of the shell of the refectory was retained, scaffolding would have been required to remove the roof trusses, once the roof and its lead covering had been removed. The interior floor surfaces of the monastic ranges were comprehensively scoured away before any new building commenced: excavations in the refectory and hostry have identified the level of the medieval floors, but any evidence for occupation had been removed entirely (Wallis 2002a; Wallis 2003).

At Norwich, the accounts for 1538 show large payments incurred 'by reason of the alteration and mutation' of the cathedral (Houlbrooke 1996, 508). The specific remodelling that was undertaken can be pieced together through later sources, notably leases, chapter books, and the Parliamentary Survey of 1649 (Plate 10). These documents sometimes record the destruction of a former monastic space, comment on its dilapidation, or permit its transfer to a new tenant. The silences in these sources can be equally articulate, indicating the early demise of a major monastic feature. More positive evidence derives from the buildings that survive to the present day, or plans or photographs recording those that were retained into the nineteenth century. Where possible, monastic structures were remodelled for their new purpose, and the erection of wholly new buildings was not common until the seventeenth century. This process can be discerned in the treatment of monastic buildings such as the hostry and infirmary. The skeletons of the hostry porch and infirmary arcade were revealed when prebendary houses on these spots were de-molished in the early nineteenth and twentieth centuries, respectively.

In common with other monastic conversions, the prior's lodging at Norwich enjoyed the smoothest transition. This became the deanery, a pattern mirrored at the former cathedral-priories of Canterbury, Winchester, Durham, and Worcester. There was greater pressure on accommodation for a new cathedral such as Chester, which had been transformed from the Benedictine abbey of St Werburgh. At Ches-ter, the bishop took the former prior's lodging in the upper part of the west range, and the dean was consigned to a former chapel in the outer court (Ward 2003).

The bishop's palace at Norwich was neglected in the early post-medieval pe-riod, partly through lack of funds, after episcopal lands had been reduced at the Reformation, but also through lack of interest, since bishops were seldom resident permanently in the palace until the nineteenth century (Atherton 1996, 659–60).[7] There was a century of depletion following the Reformation, culminating in the Civil War. In 1535, Bishop Nykke leased Salmon's great hall to the corporation of Norwich to hold its guild-day feasts. The city transferred the event to Blackfriars Hall in 1548, causing Bishop Thomas Thirlby (1550–54) to pull down the hall. With the elimination of the great hall and chapel (the latter leased to the Walloon con-gregation), the remainder of the palace was reasonably well cared for, and a survey taken in 1594 records a large house with forty rooms (ibid.).

There were three other groups of cathedral personnel who required domestic accommodation: the prebendaries (or canons), the minor, or 'petty' canons, and the singing men. In contrast with the expectations of medieval monks, the prebendaries were to be housed in private residences, demanding self-contained accommodation with independent kitchens. There were few ready-made dwellings in monastic pre-cincts that met this specification, and it was necessary to establish houses within the shells of the monastic buildings. At some other cathedrals it is possible to precisely identify the prebendary housing from the cathedral's statutes, which set out the location of the houses entitled to the holders of each prebendary stall. The absence of formal statutes at Norwich led to the more organic development of housing for the clergy.

Prebendary housing was seldom developed from the core monastic ranges, but rather from the adjacent buildings of the inner court. This was the pattern at Canterbury, where the refectory and dormitory were demolished in the 1540s, and

---

[7] Bishop John Pelham (1857–93) employed Ewan Christian to remodel the palace in 1858–9. He severed the palace from the cathedral by removing the passage which had linked de Losinga's wing to the nave, and rebuilt the north-west corner. The new palace required demolition of the later range north of the keep, and absorbed the later twelfth-century east–west wing.

houses for eleven prebendaries were established in the remaining buildings; unusually, the twelfth prebendary house was newly built in 1547 (Tatton-Brown 1989, 193). Lodgings at Westminster were created from the infirmary and the cellarer's range (RCHME 1924, 76). At Worcester, the existing houses of the sub-prior and master of the guest hall were developed as prebendary housing (Lehmberg 1988, 84). Typically, the monastic buildings were subdivided both horizontally and vertically to make smaller chambers, and large stacks were inserted to heat the new rooms. Such conversions can be compared with the earlier work of adapting the nunnery of St Radegund, Cambridge, which was suppressed in 1496 to establish Jesus College. The former dormitory of the nuns was subdivided and stacks were inserted to create heated studies (Evans et al. 1997). Similarities can also be seen with the conversion of guild hospitals after the dissolution of the chantries in 1547. For example, York's Trinity and St Anthony's hospitals saw the insertion of longitudinal and transverse partitions in their undercrofts, and the provision of chimney stacks for heated chambers (Giles 2003). Less effort was required to convert the domestic accommodation of the secular cathedrals, in which canons and vicars lived in individual dwellings. At Salisbury, for example, the updating of the canons' houses included the removal of domestic chapels, and the addition of features such as studies and nurseries (RCHME 1993, 24–5).

The cathedrals' communal buildings were retained only where an alternative purpose required a large space: the monastic refectories at Worcester and Chester owe their survival to the King's Schools that were established within them in the sixteenth century, and that at Carlisle housed the library after the Civil War. The dormitory at Westminster was employed for Westminster School, and from 1620, the Chapter Library was established in its northern part (RCHME 1924, 82). At Durham, twelve houses for the prebendaries were carved from the monastic buildings, leading to the unusual survival of the monastic dormitory in the west range of the cloister.

Similar processes of adaptation can be seen at Norwich. The infirmary chambers were subdivided (below), and central stacks were inserted in the gardener's chequer (Number 49) and in a medieval range sited next to the canal, in the former monastic outer court (Number 27).[8] At Ely, two buildings of the inner court were remodelled to create self-sufficient accommodation, each with its own kitchen in the undercroft (Holton-Kraybenbuhl 1999, 329). At Norwich, medieval fireplaces in the *locutory* and infirmarer's chamber were reused in the creation of independent kitchens, and some new houses were provided with basement kitchens (Numbers 2, 7 and 71). Halls generally fell out of use (such as those associated with the former hostry, infirmary and refectory), while their subsidiary chambers were developed for private lodgings.

---

[8] Whittingham suggested that Numbers 27–28 were built in 1646 by Edmund Spendlove, Bailiff of the Liberty of the Precinct (Whittingham 1985, 110), but the evidence of the building suggests that this was a medieval range modified in the seventeenth century.

The monastic refectory, dormitory and hostry hall at Norwich were stripped of their lead roofs by the 1560s. The fate of the dormitory is the most difficult to trace. It disappeared from records immediately after the Dissolution, and is easily confused with 'the dorter', a term used misleadingly after the Reformation to refer to the former infirmary. The southern part of the dormitory was at first retained, accommodating the 'great kitchen of the Petty Canons' in its undercroft (Whittingham 1985, 102). This, together with the 'Old Library' above it, was demolished in 1574 (Williams and Cozens-Hardy 1953, 31). Archaeological evidence suggests that the area was used subsequently as a roadway, with successive accumulations of dumped mortar waste (Voisey 2003). The passage from the cloister through the former dormitory to the deanery was retained as a 'little cloister', demolished only in 1828 (DCN 24/6) (Plate 7).

Prebendary houses
The earliest prebendary houses seem to have included one in the former office of the master of the cellar, one in the western end of the former infirmary, and another in the infirmary chambers. The one located in the cellarage (Number 68) was described in 1649 as 'a tenement being parte of the long leaded house lying on the east side of Almary Greene . . . with an additional building jutting out at the east part therof, containing five romes on the first floore, five chambers in the second floore, and two garetts over parte of them' (Metters 1985, 31). This building had an additional top storey, which was demolished following damage by the air raid on the close in 1942 (Whittingham 1985, 105).

A second prebendary house was established in the western part of the infirmary hall, with the eastern area retained for the use of the minor canons and singing men (see below). The Parliamentary Survey of 1649 described a large property at the western end of the infirmary.

> A faire stone built house lying on the north side of the way betweene the upper and the lower greene within the close . . . containing four stories and four roomes in each story, with a court before it and a garden on the north parte of it (Metters 1985, 46).

This house on the two western bays of the infirmary hall (Numbers 63 and 66) survived until 1942, when it was burnt out by an incendiary bomb (Buston 1945). A photograph taken c.1935–40 shows a substantial three-storey house with attics, and a possible medieval buttress is shown on the north elevation (Figure 82). This house incorporated two piers of the infirmary arcade and the former monastic 'table hall', the dining chamber reserved for the consumption of meat.

Perhaps the best evidence for adaptations done at the Reformation can be found in the former infirmary chambers, which had been converted to a prebendary house by at least 1616 (Plate 8). Number 65 appears to have had a floor inserted in the mid sixteenth century, indicated by the roll and hollow chamfer moulding on the ground-floor ceiling beams. At the first-floor level, refurbishment in 2001

FIGURE 82. Former Numbers 63 and 66, destroyed by an incendiary bomb in 1942. This house incorporated two piers of the infirmary arcade and the two western bays of the infirmary hall (the former monastic 'table hall'). Photograph c.1935–40, © Chapter of Norwich Cathedral.

revealed a sixteenth-century roof structure and east gable wall. The remains of the roof include a tie-beam and the principal rafters of four trusses. At each end of the beam there are carved spandrels with decoration including an armorial shield, a four-lobed rose and entwined foliage. The tie-beam and spandrels have red ochre paint adhering to them. The east gable was revealed to be a timber-framed wall with tie-beam, the latter moulded with hollow chamfers and rolls with a carved spandrel at each end. Between the studs of the gable wall are infill panels of brick, covered by a coat of lime and sand plaster. The north spandrel contains a carved shield and painted monogram, possibly 'W'. The south spandrel contains a carved, stylised rose motif (Smith, in Percival 2001, 10–11). The timbers of the east gable are pegged to the tie-beam of the roof, but are of cruder form and may not be contemporaneous. A *terminus ante quem* for the east gable is provided by a group of wall paintings, c.1550 (see below), that was exposed when a later lath-and-plaster wall was removed. The evidence of the gable wall and its wall paintings combines to suggest that the infirmary chambers were subdivided in the mid sixteenth century through the insertion of a partition wall. The eastern end of the medieval range is contained in the adjacent building, Number 64. The modifications made to the infirmary chambers included its division horizontally, through the insertion of a floor, and vertically, through the erection of the gable wall.

In 1620, it was documented that only three houses had been assigned to the prebendaries of Norwich cathedral, so that a further three still had to be developed (Williams and Cozens-Hardy 1953, 14). One was established in the former communar's office, and extended eastward into the space of the former hostry chamber (Plate 10). A second was formed in the refectory, and a third was built next to the Erpingham gate. In 1649, the prebendary house on the site of the former communar's office was described as 'a house lying on the east side of Almary Greene . . . containing five roomes in the first story, five chambers in the second and three garrets in the third, and two smale plotts of ground adjoyning, and incompassed with a stone wall, conteining in all about half a roode of ground' (Metters 1985, 31). This house was demolished in 1842, revealing the thirteenth-century porch to the hostry hall. In 1937, Whittingham excavated part of the south end of the former hostry hall (MC 186/ 50). He encountered cellars associated with the prebendary house and pits containing post-medieval ceramics. He gave no indication of the date of the cellars; potentially, these may have originated with a medieval undercroft connected with the communar's office.

A prebendary house was established at the eastern end of the former refectory in 1620, extending over the dark entry. The outer walls of the monastic refectory were retained, but excavations have revealed that the interior was comprehensively gutted: this clearance scoured away the medieval floor surfaces and artefacts, leaving little pottery and only a single stratified artefact. Deep pits were dug into the levelled ground surface, into which heaps of broken moulded stone and stained glass were tipped, the latter plucked from its lead came (Wallis 2002a). After this demolition activity, the site was levelled before new building began, with soil either having accumulated or been dumped purposely. The site was divided into two by a cross-wall, with the area to the west used as a garden and orchard, and that on the east developed as the prebendary house. The most substantial remains of the house were those of a cellar (8.6m × 4.2m), and the lower levels of a brick outbuilding and tanks, perhaps the remains of a wash-house documented in 1861 (DCN 24/8 fo. 71ʳ). The 1649 survey described this house as 'over parte of the Darke Entrie, conteyning four roomes on the first floore and a faire celler, 5 smale chambers over them and a garret; also a faire seller under the kitchin. With a yard, garden plott and orchard, inclosed with a stone wall' (Metters 1985, 39).

Much of the shell of the refectory was retained as an open space up to the twenty-first century, with its extant north and south walls containing a garden or orchard. Evidence of cultivation was recovered by archaeological excavations on the site: thirty-two linear features, aligned north–south, were filled with gravely soils and interpreted as well-drained garden beds (Wallis 2002a, 11). These linear beds were superseded by a series of individual planting holes that are likely to represent a former rose garden. This property survived until its demolition in 1873. Its domestic features can be discerned on a water-colour of the south transept by David Hodgson, c.1832, showing a three-storey structure with sash windows (Plate 7); its southern elevation was drawn by J. H. Brown in 1873 (Plate 4A).

The sixth prebendary house was constructed next to the Erpingham gate, on the site of a ruined tenement, and survives as Number 71 (Figure 83). Successive prebendaries John Hassall and Fulk Robartes rebuilt this house, c.1626–8, reusing materials from the close and with funding from the chapter (Whittingham 1985, 105). The house was originally built in flint rubble as a two-storey block with attics, and a cellar that still contains a well. There are substantial later additions in brick, and the interior has been largely gutted. Surviving ground-floor ceiling timbers with end stops suggest that originally a long room ran through the block at the north end. Evidence of the reuse of material from the monastic buildings is indicated by a rear window on the north façade, with trilobe mullions typical of the first half of the sixteenth century. In 1649, the house was described as

> A new house of stone and bricke, built (in parte) upon the wall of the Closse on the west side of the Almary greene, and abutting on Sir Wm Denys Orchard and Stables on the south with in the Close, conteyning three storyes and four romes in each story, with a smale court before the dore and a woodyard and garden to the said house adjoyning. All incompassed and devided with a stone wall and conteyning about halfe a rood of ground (Metters 1985, 30).

Communal spaces

While the prebendaries adopted a more secular style of independent living, the minor canons and singing men retained elements of the communal life of the former monastery. They were expected to continue the tradition of communal dining, and

FIGURE 83. The prebendary house built next to the Erpingham gate, c.1626–8 (Number 71). Photograph © Roberta Gilchrist.

at Norwich the infirmary was converted to 'the canons' hall' or 'the dorture', a common dormitory for the lesser clergy (Sayers 1806, 313). The old monastic kitchen was demolished in 1569 (DCN 24/1), and new facilities were developed to be shared with the deanery. Their kitchen was established in the undercroft beneath the south end of the east range, and a granary was formed in the old monks' latrine. It was necessary to retain the common brewhouse and bakehouse as long as the dining hall continued, and these remained on the sites of their monastic predecessors, retaining the same equipment.

Similar provision was made at other former cathedral-priories: for example, a common brewhouse was established in the monastic guest hall at Winchester (Crooke 1984, 40). Common dining halls were provided for the minor canons and singing men in the monastic refectories at Ely and Gloucester (Evans 1961, 8), and in the monks' latrine at Canterbury (Tatton-Brown 1989, 193). The infirmary at Gloucester was also used to house the minor clergy and singing men, retaining its medieval name of 'Babylon' until it was pulled down in 1630 (Evans 1961, 6). At Chester, the minor canons maintained their communal table and lodgings in the former infirmary (Ward 2003), as at Norwich. The partitioning of monastic infirmaries in the later Middle Ages made them especially well suited for use as small lodgings. This vestige of monastic life ebbed away as it became common for the minor clergy to marry. When statutes were provided for Norwich in 1620, King James urged the restoration of the custom for 'those who meet together and praise God in the choir, should also eat together and praise God at table' (Williams and Cozens-Hardy 1953, 15). In 1627, the Norwich prebendaries claimed that this arrangement had caused such discontent between husbands and wives that the chapter had converted the charges of meals into supplementary stipends (Houlbrooke 1996, 520).

As communal and celibate life waned, the infirmary was developed for self-contained houses; for example, Lawrence Harman, one of the singing men, was assigned 'five chambers in the dorter' in 1645 (DCN 24/2). The Parliamentary Survey of 1649 described two properties on the eastern end of the former infirmary hall, both occupied by singing men (Metters 1985, 46). The rooms over the east cloister were refurbished for domestic use, and the initials of Dean George Gardiner (1573–89) appear on a fireplace in the southern end. Accommodation over the cloister was leased to secular tenants, such as Michael Knot and Elizabeth his wife in 1589 (Williams and Cozens-Hardy 1953, 36), or was used to billet singing men such as John Spendlove in 1621 (DCN 47/2). A house was built over the slype next to the south transept, and extending over the east walk of the cloister, used for the accommodation of minor canons. This was demolished in the 1830s when the architect Anthony Salvin opened up the roadway leading to the south transept. Its gabled roof and domestic chimneys were depicted in illustrations of the south transept (Plate 7).

Chapter houses continued to serve an important function in the new cathedrals, in contrast with their early demolition in wholly domestic conversions of former monasteries. Cathedral chapter houses survive today at Worcester,

Canterbury, Rochester, Exeter, Wells, Bristol, Chester, Oxford, and Gloucester (and the royal peculiar of Westminster), reflecting the significant corporate function that they continued to serve after the Reformation. At Canterbury, the chapter house was converted to the Sermon House (Tatton-Brown 1989, 194), and at Durham, divinity lectures took place in the chapter house from 1559 (Lehmberg 1988, 277). At Norwich, Dr John Baret delivered lectures on the scriptures in the chapter house twice a week from 1542 (Houlbrook 1996, 535). This space retained the disciplinary connotations of the medieval monastic chapter house, with 'purgacyon' taking place here, for example in 1566, in relation to the minor canon John Beldham (Williams and Cozens-Hardy 1953, 24). The Norwich chapter book referred to a chamber 'next to the chapter house' in 1565, but by 1569 William Cantrell was leased 'the parcel of voyd ground late builded called the Chapter House' (DCN 47/2). The functions of the chapter were served on an adjacent site, as a chapter room was developed in the former monastic warming room to the south. This space served as the chapter office until 1828,[9] ensuring the partial survival of the medieval east wall of the warming room (now in a garage of the deanery).

New buildings
A number of new buildings were erected to the west of the cathedral church shortly after the dissolution of the priory. These were developed as properties for leasing, and in 1620, fourteen substantial houses were let by the dean and chapter (Whittingham 1985, 115); in 1649, these properties were occupied by widows, or by the families of gentlemen. The earliest new property to be constructed in the close was built by Dr John Baret in 1549, at the east end of the Carnary chapel. 'School End House' (Number 69) is a timber-framed building on its upper storey, with a ground floor in brick with dressings of flint and reused stone. It has a Dutch gable and the upper floor is partially jettied (Figure 84). When it was first erected, the rear wall of the building did not directly abut the east wall of the chapel. Instead, the house was placed against the east face of the east buttresses of the Carnary chapel. The intervening space between the chapel and the house was probably incorporated during the late eighteenth century, when the present principal stair was inserted, and the timber-framed rear wall removed. In the east wall there is a vertical joint made up of chamfered stone quoins that extend up to the first-floor level. There are two metal pins within the stonework that could be the remains of pintles for a gate fixing. This feature may represent the medieval gate into green yard, later incorporated into Baret's house.

It appears that the chapter deliberately retained space within the close for its own commercial use, or for development by those from within the cathedral community, such as Baret. In 1560 they resisted a petition made by Robert Dudley, Earl of Leicester, on behalf of William Hoggins, for 'the Clocher, the Old Ostrye Hall,

---

[9] Removal of the gaol in 1828 provided the opportunity for construction of new chapter offices and vestries to the east of the south transept (DCN 24/6).

FIGURE 84. School End House (Number 69), the house built by John Baret in 1549, abutting the eastern end of the Carnary chapel. Photograph © Roberta Gilchrist.

the Lybrary, the Granary, be houses of no use to yowe'. They responded that each of these elements retained a purpose:

> the Clocher and bells needed . . . and the decaying thereof should be a blemish not only to the said church but also to the city . . . said Hostry Hall where the commons . . . do Kepe ther comon hospitality . . . the said Lybrary which be so unyted and joyned to the other lodgings that their pulling down would be to the utter destruction of the adjoining lodgings (DCN 47/2).

Their statement was somewhat disingenuous: it is clear that the common hospitality was actually kept in the former infirmary, and the chapter itself was to demolish the *clocher* by 1569, the library in 1574, and the hostry hall just two years after the failed petition.

The hostry hall had been demolished by 1562, when it was leased to the industrious Dr Baret as a 'ground parcel of the late hall called the Ostry Hall', together with 'the late dissolved lodging commonly called the Pryors of Lynne and the Pryors of Yarmouth' (DCN 24/2). Baret was given permission to build a house incorporating the former two-storey chamber that stood between the *locutory* and the former hostry hall. In 1649 this was described as 'a faire house . . . containing six roomes in the first story with six chambers over them and four garrettes: with three smale plottes of ground therto belonging, all inclosed and devided with stone walles and conteyne about halfe a rood (Metters 1985, 46). This house also incorporated the *locutory*, where its kitchen reused the medieval wall fireplace. It was illustrated by J. Storer, 1818 (Figure 85), and J. Newton, c.1849, and was converted to the choir school in 1867. Two houses were also built at the south-west corner of the church. One of these was known as Gibbs' tenement from the 1640s until it was demolished in 1827,[10] when it was 'taken down for the improvement of the west front of the cathedral' (DCN 24/6). The house to the south of Gibbs' was built in 1558 and demolished in 1831 (Whittingham 1985, 114).

New buildings also appeared at the east end of the cathedral church, adjacent to the sextry gate leading to Bishopgate. A long range was located between the medieval sextry and the former Lady chapel. This was known as Guybon's tenement from 1688 onwards (Number 62), and was demolished in 1930 to allow the construction of the war memorial chapel. There were cottages constructed to the north of the sextry (Numbers 59–60), which was known as Waldegrave's from 1650, when it was leased by Sir Henry Waldegrave (Whittingham 1985, 115). It was ordered in 1761 that these cottages were to be demolished (DCN 24/5), but they are shown intact on late nineteenth-century engravings (Purey-Cust 1895, 173) and early photographs.

Clearly, the open spaces at the east and west ends of the cathedral church were highly desirable real estate. New buildings also appeared at the minor entrances to the close. Next to the monastic water gate a ferry house[11] was erected, c.1600, a two-storey block predominantly in brick with some flint, dated by a ceiling timber on the ground floor, with half bracket moulding and knicked end stops. At the eastern end of Hook's Walk, within the outer court, a two-storey block was constructed in brick and flint rubble (Numbers 37–39). This can be dated by a date stone to 1633, and by features including the rear door with its quadrant moulded jambs and moulded bases. The inscription over the door of Number 39 reads 'John Howell and Helen his wife built this house'. In the 1620s, efforts were made to improve housing in the close and increase income for the chapter. Houses were built for leasing purposes, for example by Charles Rawlins, gentleman, who constructed a new house immediately to the south of the deanery and one between the dark entry and the infirmary.[12] These houses were built in brick; the former was three storeys with a kitchen, hall and parlour below (Whittingham 1985, 112).

SEEKING A NEW DOMESTIC STYLE

As the domestic lives of the clergy shed their monastic character, the physical sur-

---

[10] This tenement was named after the organist Richard Gibbs (DCN 47/2). When Gibbs' Tenement was demolished in 1827, its occupant Petty Canon Peter Hansell moved to No. 34, the Close (Whittingham 1985, 111). This property had previously been known as The Three Cranes, but from 1827 was confusingly termed 'Gibbs' Tenement'.

[11] This is still known as Pull's Ferry, after the last ferryman, but previously was known as Sandling's from 1647. John Sandling's initials appear on the south gable of the building (Whittingham 1985, 109).

[12] The first was known as Beeston's from 1701 until its demolition in 1784; the second was known as Newell's from 1703 until its demolition in 1804 (Whittingham 1985, 114).

FIGURE 85. Engraving by J. Storer, 1818, showing a sixteenth-century house at the north-west corner of the cloister, incorporating the monastic outer parlour. The house was demolished c.1863, after which the outer parlour was restored to serve as the Choir School.

roundings of the close took on more secular traits. New buildings incorporated brick in their external façades, in contrast with earlier monastic architecture, which had been of stone construction. Local and urban characteristics appeared in some new buildings, such as the jettied, timber-framed upper storeys of Number 69 and of 54 Bishopgate. Dutch gables, the curved or shaped gables with pediments that were favoured in early modern East Anglia, feature on Numbers 69, 6 and 44, on the ferry house, and formerly on the west wing of the bishop's palace.[13] More rural connections were signalled through the plan types chosen for some remodellings, such as the very early example of a four-square, double-pile plan, selected for the prebendary house that was created next to the Erpingham gate, c.1626–8 (Number 71). This seventeenth-century house type consists of a rectangular block two rooms deep, with the rooms separated by a passage running the full depth. The remodelling of the monastic bakehouse and brewhouse also resulted in this double-pile form (Numbers 31–32; Figures 86–7). Features such as the external staircase at the back of Number 6, and the triple gables of Number 71, place these houses within the architectural context of middle-ranking county gentry. In contrast, the more substan-

---

[13] The north end of the west wing of the palace is shown with a Dutch gable on Kirkpatrick's drawing of c.1720 (Norwich Castle Museum, Kirkpatrick 1735.76.94).

FIGURE 86. Interior of Number 32 (taken c.1995), showing stairs inserted in 1682 as part of an open well plan. Photograph © Roberta Gilchrist.

FIGURE 87. Number 32, showing extension to medieval roof when a front room was added to the medieval block. Photograph © Roberta Gilchrist.

tial houses in the city of Norwich retained the medieval courtyard style, such as the late-sixteenth-century house on Fye Bridge Street known as 'the King of Hearts'. The more remote area of the former great garden in the cathedral's monastic outer court provided a semi-rural context for the aspirations of the gentry. To the north of Hook's Walk there was a property which included a banqueting house,[14] a feature more typical of the country house garden, where fruit, sweets and wine would be served after dinner (Girouard 1978).

The adaptation of the monastic buildings for domestic use integrated some elements of classical ornamentation. There is no evidence of conscious Renaissance design, but rather the adoption of 'anticke', the Tudor fashion for foreign styles of ornament and applied decoration (Howard 1987, 121). The cathedral church was stripped by the Victorians of any classical-style features, but the houses of the close still contain a small number. For example, Number 6 retains at its core a structure of flint rubble that may represent part of the medieval almoner's office. Later renovations created a building with large Dutch gables, housing a moulded plaster ceiling dating to the seventeenth century. Two significant features survive in Number 6 that were moved here from other buildings. An early-sixteenth-century door was transferred here from the deanery when the range of c.1520 was demolished in 1828. The second is a fireplace of c.1600, with moulded jambs and bases; this derived originally from Number 66, part of the prebendary house built on the western end of the monastic infirmary, which was destroyed in 1942.

The reuse of prized decorative features was a common process following the Dissolution. Timber panelling of c.1520 was removed from the dissolved abbey at St Benet Hulme to be reused in the bishop's palace at Norwich (Blomefield 1745 [1806], 4, 47).[15] The panelling can be provenanced by the arms of St Benet's abbey, which appear alongside a scheme that shows heads in roundels, representing the Nine Worthies (Pagan, Jewish and Christian) and twenty-nine famous men and women whose names occur in roundels above. Spolia also featured in the new prebendary houses: the house built on the eastern end of the former refectory incorporated a group of six terracotta fireplace bricks with 'anticke' figurative decoration, dated c.1550–75. These bricks were recovered from the Old Canonry House, which stood on the site until its demolition in 1873. This prebendary house was built c.1620, and therefore the bricks are likely to have been reused from another source.

The bricks represent an unusually large assemblage of terracotta with moulded narrative scenes.[16] David Thomson compared the bricks from Norwich cathedral

---

[14] This feature is indicated in a later probate inventory (Hester Williams, 1729) of the Great-chequer Garden, which refers to the since demolished Banqueting House (DCN Inv 73/4/14).

[15] The survey of the bishop's palace in 1646 refers to old wainscotting in the dining room (Stewart 1875, 185). When the palace was remodelled in 1858–9 these panels were stored in the gallery of the cathedral. Some were reused by Bernard Feilden in the 1950s to decorate the new vestry rooms, and two still remain in the gallery.

[16] A complete brick measured approximately 150 × 100 × 60mm.

with friezes that survive at two buildings in Norfolk: the rectory at Great Snoring (c.1525) and East Barsham (before 1536). He concluded that the stylistic analogy of the friezes, together with the colour and size of the bricks, identifies them as Norfolk products (Thomson 1980, 42–3). Architectural terracotta and decorative brick were used extensively in northern East Anglia (Morris 2000, 195 n. 52), perhaps owing to the absence of good freestone for carving. However, comparison with material from the Netherlands confirms that these bricks were a specialised import to England, used to line fireplaces and hearths. Hearth-bricks were produced in Liège, Antwerp and Utrecht from the mid sixteenth century, depicting stylised 'anticke' patterns in a fine red, unglazed fabric (Gaimster and Nenk 1997, 183). They have a wide archaeological distribution along the east coast of Britain, from Kent to Scotland, and principally in London. It has been suggested that the bricks were adopted by the mercantile population in regions of Britain where close cultural links were established through migration from the Low Countries (ibid.). In East Anglia, they have been recorded also from Cambridge and Wisbeach (David Gaimster pers. com.).

The designs on the Norwich bricks include a scene with two soldiers (Figure 88), two examples of a judgement scene showing a woman with her hands bound (Figure 89), a scene showing a murder in a tent (Figure 90), and two examples of a design exhibiting the profile heads of a man and woman (Figure 91). The fragment of brick showing the soldiers (Figure 88) compares very closely with an intact example found in Thames Street, London, dated to the late sixteenth century (Museum of London, A4626). The close resemblance of the two bricks suggests that they were copied from the same design, perhaps woodwork or a book decoration. This particular scene is taken from the story of Susannah and the Elders, showing the Elders being led way under arrest (Schofield 1994, 152). The judgement scene may be from the same story, depicting Susanna before the Judges;[17] the tent scene is Judith decapitating the Assyrian general Holofernes. All three scenes are biblical, taken from Old Testament Apocrypha. The iconography is noteworthy for its celebration of women who challenged male authority. Such images were popular in sixteenth-century sequences of 'femmes fortes'. This important group of moulded bricks represents the changing lifestyle of the clergy in two respects. First, they demonstrate the increase in standards of living that resulted from the provision of individual lodgings that were heated by fireplaces. Secondly, they indicate the clergy's growing taste for specialised imports, in this case items exhibiting strong feminine iconography that would have been abhorrent to medieval monks.

One example of the new domestic style remains in situ in the prebendary house that was established in the medieval infirmary chambers (Number 65). The wall paintings on the east gable wall are clearly secular in style, and include a grotesque scheme with a head sprouting from a fan motif, and candelabra elements; in other words, symmetrical motifs arranged around a vertical axis (Kirkham 2001). Such

[17] Alternatively, this could be Esther before Ahasuerus.

FIGURE 88. Moulded terracotta brick, dating c.1550–75, depicting two soldiers in a scene from the story of Susannah and the Elders, in which the elders are led away under arrest. Scale 1:1.25. Drawing by Sue White.

FIGURE 89. Moulded terracotta brick, dating c.1550–75, depicting a judgement scene showing a woman with her hands bound; Susanna before the Judges. Scale 1:1.25. Drawing by Sue White.

Figure 90. Moulded terracotta brick, dating c.1550–75, depicting a murder in a tent; Judith decapitating Holophernes. Scale 1:1.25. Drawing by Sue White.

Figure 91. Moulded terracotta brick, dating c.1550–75, depicting two heads in profile; portrait heads of contemporary rulers. Scale 1:1.25. Drawing by Sue White.

decoration may also be considered 'anticke', and has been described as 'an angli-
cized version of Italian motifs', likely to have been copied from the engraved title
pages of books (Pantin and Rouse 1955, 86). The scheme at Norwich was drawn
in black on a background of white or red, with white highlights added (Plate 8).
These motifs, in addition to the use of black and white on a white or red background, can be compared with other schemes of secular wall painting dating to
the mid sixteenth century (David Gaimster, pers. com.). Comparable examples
survive in Suffolk, Essex, Kent, Surrey and Oxfordshire, with the best recorded
example at the Golden Cross, Oxford, dated to c.1550 (Pantin and Rouse 1955,
85). The closest comparison in terms of context is the decoration at Westminster
abbey, also dated to the mid sixteenth century (although over-painted some time
during the twentieth century). A first floor chamber in the former cellarer's range
was decorated with a candelabra scheme in brown on white, including grotesques,
half-figures terminating in foliage and peacocks (RCHME 1924, 89; plate 175). At
Norwich, a frieze ran across the top, and a blank area was left in the middle of the
wall, possibly to incorporate a large piece of furniture (Kirkham 2001, 3). Pigment
samples indicate a palette including vermilion and orpiment on the carved timbers,
red ochre (iron oxide) with yellow particles for the ground, and yellow ochre and
blackened lead on the grotesque scheme. Grey for the frieze was made of a mixture
of charcoal black and calcium carbonate (Kirkham 2001, 4). Based on the dating
of similar schemes of wall painting, the insertion and decoration of the east gable
wall can be placed around 1550, indicating the rapid adoption of secular styles of
domestic decoration within the former monastic buildings.

The standard of living within the new clergy houses can be measured through
assemblages of artefacts and food remains excavated from the former refectory and
infirmary chambers (Number 65). An important group of ceramics was recovered
from the fill of the great drain beneath the infirmary latrine (Figure 92). This included wares contemporary with the adaptation of the monastic building: a bowl
in glazed red earthenware, a medallion from a bartmann in Frechen ware (c.1550–
1700), and a fragment from a Raeren drinking jug from the Rhineland, dated to
the first half of the sixteenth century (Goffin, in Percival 2001, 23). Seventeenth-
century vessels in tin-glazed and glazed red earthenware were recorded, associated
with the production, serving and storage of food and drink. Additional objects recovered included a watering pot and a warming pan in Dutch redware, seventeenth-
century wine bottles of dark green glass, and a phial in olive-green pharmaceutical
glass (Talbot in Percival 2001, 32–3). Tin-glazed earthenware from the refectory
site included a drug jar and a chamber pot; this site also produced imported wares
including Dutch redwares, German stonewares, a fragment of a Martincamp flask
and some fragments of Dutch tin-glazed earthenware (Goffin in Wallis 2002a).
A blue tin-glazed sherd from the refectory site suggests that religious motifs remained attractive to the prebendaries: the base of a dish or charger depicted part
of the Passion of Christ, showing the three figures carrying their crosses before the
crucifixion (Goffin in Wallis 2002b, 14).

FIGURE 92. Post-medieval pottery from the fill of the medieval drain in the infirmary latrine and chamber (Number 65). Photograph © Norfolk Archaeological Unit; photographer John Percival. Reproduced with permission of NAU.

Excavations in the prebendary house on the refectory site recovered a number of artefacts typical of secular or clerical life of the period. Items of dress and furnishings included buckles, pins, buttons and lace-tags, in addition to possible upholstery studs (Lyons in Wallis 2002a). A single book clasp was recovered, comparable to a seventeenth-century example from the city (Margeson 1993, 75). Three cloths seals of possible German origin were recovered, dating to the late sixteenth or seventeenth century, in addition to weights for possible commercial use, knives, a sickle, horseshoes and nine musket balls. A revealing assemblage of post-medieval glass was recovered, representing large numbers of wine bottles, in addition to fragments of wine glasses, goblets and moulded beakers imported from Venice and the Netherlands in the sixteenth and seventeenth centuries. The assemblage of clay pipes dated from the early seventeenth century onwards, with Tudor rose examples from London, and locally-made types including masonic bowls; there was also evidence for the possible manufacture of clay pipes on the site (Ames in Wallis 2002a).

Animal bones from the fill of the great drain beneath the infirmary latrine included sheep, cattle, young pigs, domestic fowl, goose, partridge, hare and fish. Other contexts produced further wild species including rabbit, wood pigeon and crab (Curl in Percival 2001). The prebendary house on the refectory site produced domestic and wild species including fallow deer, bird and rabbit (Curl in Wallis

2002b). The consumption of younger animals and wild species is consistent with a reasonably high standard of living. This evidence, together with that of imported ceramics and glass vessels, perhaps indicates that the prebendary lifestyle was indeed comparable to that of 'lesser country gentlemen' (Lehmberg 1996, 155). The Norwich material can be compared with an assemblage of animal bone from the chapter house of Worcester cathedral, believed to have come from an adjacent prebendary house. This material appears to represent the accumulated waste from several small feasts, all redeposited in a subterranean chamber in the chapter house. The Worcester assemblage can be dated closely by associated clay-pipe fragments to c.1690–1710. Its composition shows an unusually high proportion of domestic fowl (43%) and wild bird and mammals (15%). These particular traits, in addition to the presence of high status indicators such as turkey, fallow deer, partridge and woodcock, suggest the menu of a prebendary's feast (Thomas 1999). Such occasions may have marked the extension of hospitality to visitors in the close, an obligation that was intrinsic to medieval cathedral-priories, and which was upheld in the refounded cathedrals. In contrast with the more inclusive hospitality of medieval centuries, the clergy and their wives would not have offered charitable relief to the poor, but focused instead on the extension of hospitality to their social equals (Heal 1984). Evidence of such practices is reflected in the documented banqueting house in the former monastic garden, serving as an emblem of the gentile aspirations in the close.

THE CIVIL WAR AND ITS IMPACT

The mid seventeenth century saw a violent rupture in the long tradition of English cathedral worship. Between 1649 and 1660, the cathedrals were seized and closed by the Parliamentarians, and the goods and property in cathedral closes were valued and sold. The Civil War had erupted largely due to constitutional conflicts between the King and the Commons (Russell 1990), but it also exercised social tensions that had been brewing since the Reformation. The cathedrals were regarded as bastions of the royalist cause and of traditional forms of Anglican worship. This conflict was sharply defined at Norwich, where two opposing religious factions had existed since the 1570s. The bishop and the cathedral espoused the official, established church, while the city corporation had allied itself with radical religious groups, funding sermons, preachers and lectureships (Atherton and Morgan 1996, 541).

The cathedrals were targeted from late 1642 onwards, when churches and prebendary houses were plundered at Winchester, Exeter, Chichester, Canterbury, Worcester and Rochester (Lehmberg 1996, 28). At Norwich, the service books, organs and vestments were burned in 1643. In this year the House of Commons ruled in favour of the demolition of stone altars, the removal of communion tables from the east end to the nave, the removal of rails, candlesticks, crucifixes, and all superstitious or idolatrous images (ibid., 31). A new wave of iconoclasm swept through the cathedrals, and once again this utilised the dual weapons of material destruction and the rewriting of spatial rules.

The seizure of the bishop's palace at Norwich, on 12 May 1643, is frequently quoted to emphasise the violent destruction that was wrought. Bishop Joseph Hall (1641–56) was ejected after witnessing the symbolic and economic desecration of the palace.

> It is no other than tragical to relate the carriage of that furious sacrilege, whereof our eyes and ears were the sad witnesses, under the presence of Linsey, Toftes the sheriff, and Greenwood. Lord what work was here! what clattering of glass! what beating down of walls! what tearing up of monuments! what pulling down of seats! What wresting out of irons and brass from the windows and graves! what defacing of arms! what demolishing of curious stone-work, that had not any representation in the world, but only of the cost of the founder, and skill of the mason! (Hall 1837, vol. 1, lv).

In 1646, a survey and valuation was made of the palace (Stewart 1875), after which it was leased to James Scambler, and eventually sold to Captain John Blackwell. The lead was stripped from the roof, the great hall turned into a meeting-house for sectaries and the grounds divided into small tenements for poor families.

From 1643, radical religion triumphed in the cathedral, with the corporation nominating Independent ministers to preach on Sundays (Atherton and Morgan 1996, 555). Concepts of sacred space were overturned and politicised: the mayor's seat was relocated at the high altar, with the founder's tomb lowered to improve the mayor's view (Browne 1680 [1954]). On 30 April 1649, the Commonwealth government abolished deans and chapters belonging to any cathedral or collegiate church. The justification was largely financial, with property confiscated to be sold to pay for the war. Thirteen members of the cathedral clergy were deprived at Norwich; like those ejected from other cathedrals, they are likely to have made their livings as chaplains or tutors during the Interregnum (Lehmberg 1996, 52–3).

The treatment of cathedral churches varied: Ely was locked by Cromwell and abandoned (Cobb 1980, 74), and York became a preaching centre for the city. Exeter was shared by the Presbyterians and the Independents, prompting the erection of a massive brick wall to divide the choir from the nave (Lehmberg 1996, 47–9). The worst served were Carlisle and Lichfield, which were the centres of sieges. The west front and six bays of the nave at Carlisle were pulled down by the Scots in 1644–5, and at Durham, the cathedral furnishings were burnt as fuel by 4,000 Scottish prisoners, who had been incarcerated in the cathedral church after the Battle of Dunbar (1650) (Butler and Given-Wilson 1979, 217). The fate of cathedral churches was debated three times by the Rump Parliament, and there were local proposals to demolish both Winchester and Norwich cathedrals. In 1650, the corporation of Yarmouth sought the demolition of 'that vast and altogether useless cathedral' at Norwich, proposing that the materials should be used to strengthen the harbour walls of Yarmouth and to build a workhouse (Atherton and Morgan 1996, 556). Surveys of houses in all cathedral closes were made before their sale in 1649–50; at Norwich, this allowed speculators to erect tenements for letting to the poor at rack rents (Atherton 1996, 639). At best, a decade of deterioration followed, before the restoration of Charles II in 1660, and the reinstatement of cathedral chapters in the same year.

RESTORATION: THE GENTRIFICATION OF THE CLOSE

The chapter returned to Norwich cathedral in July 1660, but the former dean and three of the prebendaries had not lived to see their homecoming (Atherton and Morgan 1996, 558). In common with Salisbury, Norwich had suffered more from neglect than destruction during the Interregnum. Its fabric fared far better than that of Lichfield (Cocke 1993), where buildings were so badly damaged that the 1649 survey valued them only as materials to be sold, or Worcester, where the lead roofs of the cathedral and cloister had been removed to make bullets (Cobb 1980, 162). At Winchester, only the deanery and three prebendary houses survived in good repair, although the remains of others were incorporated in the substantial rebuilding of the close in the 1660s (Crook 1984). At Norwich, the altar was restored and the choir fully furnished within a decade (Atherton and Morgan 1996, 559). By 1670, the chapter claimed to have spent £2800 on repairs and furnishing (ibid., 560), in addition to £300 raised from donations from major families such as the Townshends, and local figures like Sir Thomas Browne (Lehmberg 1996, 68). A new sense of order settled on the cathedral: walking and talking in the church and disorderly behaviour in the precincts during services were punished (Atherton 1996, 642). Physical access to the close was regulated by locking the precinct gates at night, and by employing a resident porter to control access during the day (DCN 24/4; Williams and Cozens-Hardy 1953, 12).

The bishop's palace was repaired by Bishop Edward Reynolds (1660–76), who built a new chapel on the site of the dais end of Salmon's great hall. This was completed in 1672, reusing masonry and tracery from Salmon's destroyed chapel, but also utilising the medieval foundations and lower courses of the southern bay of the hall. This is apparent from the surviving fabric below the stringcourse on the southern side of the chapel, which is constructed of finely-knapped flint bricks, typical of high status fourteenth-century construction in the region. Thomas Browne reported that Reynolds was buried in the chapel that he had rebuilt (Browne 1680 [1954], 134).

Within the close, rebuilding prompted a greater emphasis on the display of the cathedral church, and the enhancement of the quality and appearance of housing. The deanery was substantially remodelled by Dean Croftes (1660–70), who spent £500 adding its distinctive crowstepped brick gables, ornamental gable irons and casements (Figure 42). He removed the ruins of the monks' latrine, reusing its north wall as the external south wall of the deanery. He curtailed the hall, inserting the present fireplace and providing two main rooms upstairs, a drawing room and a dining room of equal size (Whittingham 1967). The ruins of the adjacent refectory were also provided with a central, stepped gable in brick, shown in an elevation drawn in 1873 before its removal (DCN 127/64) (Plate 4A). It may be proposed that the crowstepped gable of the refectory was intended to mirror the character of the deanery, and was built in an effort to create a more cohesive landscape for the deanery.

A small number of new houses were erected, including Number 50, built in 1664 in Hook's Walk (Bolingbroke 1922, 37). This was constructed with a flint rubble ground floor and timber studwork for the first floor (Figure 15). The basic plan was an open stair hall, with one room on two storeys on either side of the hall, and a gallery connecting the two first-floor rooms. The original stair survives, with terminal posts decorated with strapwork, and fretted balusters. The first floor retains seven moulded cross-timbers, most with half bracket mouldings and knicked end stops. Numbers 43–44 were constructed by James and Katherine Hobart of Beeston, who leased property in the close from c.1670 (Whittingham 1985, 115). Their combined initials, JHK, are featured in ironwork on the Dutch gables of this three-storey red-brick block. This sporadic building at Norwich contrasts markedly with the systematic efforts at Winchester, where new prebendary houses were built in brick in the 1660s, focusing on Dome Alley in the south-west corner of the close, formerly the great garden. The first residents provided their own fittings, including wooden panelling documented in the cathedral's 'wainscot book' (Crook 1984). There is a later reference at Norwich to a similar practice: in 1741, £5 was accounted for prebend Prescott to provide wainscotting for his residence (Number 65) (DCN 24/5).

Rather than support new building in the close, the chapter encouraged tenants to rebuild existing houses in a grander style. A good example of this process survives at Numbers 3–4, the granary of the monastic almonry, rebuilt by Jeremy Vinn (d. 1705) and his wife Susan. Their initials appear on the front of the gables of the two houses with the date of 1701, and panelling of this date survives inside. The monastic brewhouse, Numbers 32–33, was remodelled by John Ringall of Easton, gentleman, and his wife Anne in 1682 (DCN 115/1/1/27). The building was refaced with red bricks, and a date stone inscribed 'RJA 1682' was positioned centrally in the front façade, facing onto the lower green. The rebuilding involved the addition of the front range to the medieval block, which previously had been only one room deep. Internal changes involved the insertion of stairs with an open-well plan, creating a pair of houses with mirror-image plans (Figures 79, 86–7).

The modelling of grander residences was accompanied by the new concept of appropriate landscaping, influenced by recent developments at London and Bath (Borsay 1989), but also borrowing from local elite fashions in rural garden design (Taigel 1990). Jeremy and Susan Vinn sought a refined setting for their new residence in the former almonry granary. The chapter refused permission for the erection of coach houses in the upper close in 1701, on the basis that 'soe much hath been layd out to adorn the sayd upper green and the upper walk in the sayd green, at the great expense of Alderman Vinn been made very fine & convenient for the Inhabitants of the Close & of the Citty to walk in' (DCN 24/4). Vinn's contribu-

FIGURE 93. 'Norwich Cathedral, West End' by I. Shaw and R. Groom, 1849. The lithograph shows landscaping of the close near the west front of the cathedral. A formal space for promenading was created through the use of iron railings around the greens, gravel paths and the planting of avenues of limes. Reproduced with permission of Norwich Castle Museum and Art Gallery: Todd 6, Norwich, 202.

tion was part of the chapter's innovative scheme to landscape the close, emphasising the upper and lower greens through planting, and establishing pavements and gravel paths as recreational routes through the close (Figure 93). They purchased lime trees for the upper and lower greens in the 1680s and '90s (DCN 11/3–4–5), paved between the two greens in 1680 (DCN 11/2), and paid subsequently for the maintenance of trees and cleansing of gravel walks (DCN 11/6). In 1698, they recorded that they had 'laid out a great deal of money on the Upper Green, adorning it with rows of lime trees and gravel walks 'for ye Convenience of ye Gentrey

of ye City and Close who usually make ye sayd upper Green their walkeing place
. . . for health and recreation' (DCN 29/4/37). Such features attracted particular
social groups to the upper close, where 'round the Square is pretty Gravell Walks
where the Young Ladyes of ye towne (And at publick times ye County too) makes
the place more Splendid by theyr presence they Generally walk 2 hours from 7 to 9
. . . ' (Bodleian Library, MS Tanner 311, fo. 117[r]).[18] The chapter's concerted efforts
to landscape the close anticipated similar efforts elsewhere by up to a century, for
example at Salisbury, Lichfield and Gloucester, while the provision of recreational
spaces pre-dated the design of pleasure gardens in the city of Norwich by fifty years
(Atherton 1996, 640).

There is some evidence that by the seventeenth century it was considered
desirable to create an appropriate visual setting for a cathedral church. Stanford
Lehmberg has suggested that the removal of domestic and commercial abutments
from cathedrals reflected the novel attitude 'that cathedrals needed to be freestanding, not hemmed in by subordinate structures' (1996, 198). Evidence from Norwich reveals that many of these subordinate structures actually survived until the
early nineteenth century, when those abutting the south transept were swept away
to create a new entrance, and tenements near the west front were removed to improve the vista. Prebendary housing that abutted all three sides of the cloister was
retained until the late nineteenth century, when it was removed for practical rather
than aesthetic reasons, to limit the risk of fire (DCN 24/8). It is clear, however,
that from the late seventeenth century, planting and hard landscaping were used to
enhance the setting of the cathedral church and close. The upper and lower greens
took on the appearance of squares, a form used as the setting for new churches in
contemporary provincial towns (Borsay 1989, 79). Efforts were also made after
1670 to improve the appearance of the cloisters. Robert Taylor, of the precinct,
was employed 'to make cleane cut and keepe hansom the Cloyster yard'; when he
began it was 'all over growne wth weeds netles Docks and all manner of beggery'
(Bodleian Library MS Tanner 133, fo.54).

By c.1700, the cathedral close had cast off the disorder that characterised the
decades following the Reformation, and was once again a tightly regulated, hierarchical space. The upper and lower greens of the monastic inner court had been developed as fashionable gentry housing, with smaller and poorer houses clustering in
the peripheral areas of the former outer court, particularly along the arteries towards the River Wensum, Bishopgate and the Horsefair. The dissolute alehouses of
the late sixteenth century had been replaced by more reputable inns, and traders
took up residence to supply the luxury goods demanded by the gentry and clergy.
The landscape and architecture of the close had been gentrified, but also they had
been effectively secularised. The spiritual life of cathedrals was stagnating, with increasing absenteeism and lack of purpose evident among the clergy. The Act of Tol-

---

[18] I am grateful to Dr Ian Atherton for providing these references to the improvements to the
close in the seventeenth century.

eration of 1689 had deprived them of their primary role in defending Anglicanism against nonconformity. An episcopal visitation of 1692 observed that the dean had been absent from the close at Norwich for the entire year, and that the deanery and prebendary houses had been let to laymen. The chapter's butlers and cooks were paid but were of no use 'where no hospitalitie or house is kept' (Lehmberg 1996, 255).

9

Reading Sacred and Social Space in the English Cathedral Landscape

PERMEABLE SPACES: SACRED, PROFANE AND SOCIAL

THE concept of 'sacred space' has intrigued sociologists, anthropologists and historians for the past one hundred years (since Weber 1905). While there is a modern tendency to perceive a sharp dichotomy between sacred and profane, experienced in relation to both space and time (Durkheim 1912), medieval belief collapsed such distinctions (Eliade 1959). The divine could be encountered in every day life, routine places and mundane objects, and the cult of relics demonstrates that sacredness could be transferred from one to another, like 'holy radioactivity' (Finucane 1977, 26). The monastic cathedral provides unique insight to sacred space. In contrast with other monasteries, a cathedral-priory housed the bishop's see and was the mother church of its diocese. This special role increased the emphasis placed on interaction with the secular world, particularly in relation to hospitality, education and almsgiving. The urban market was at its doorstep, and everyday pilgrims, merchants and secular servants mingled at its thresholds. Yet, at the core of the monastic enclosure remained a self-contained community of contemplative, Benedictine monks. These contradictions characterise the distinctive experience of an English cathedral-priory: its functions were more diverse and hierarchically ranked than other monasteries, but its coenobitic aspirations distinguished it from secular cathedrals in England or on the continent. The survival of cathedrals at the Reformation permits us to study changing perceptions of sacred space through the Protestant transformations of the sixteenth and seventeenth centuries. The Reformation can be appraised as a transition, rather than accepted as a stark cleavage. In this final chapter, the experience of Norwich cathedral is used to chart the changing practices of sacred and social space in the English cathedral landscape, c. 1096–1700.

Sacred space was a powerful structuring principle of medieval life, but it can prove elusive to modern observers. A number of recent studies have examined the medieval origins of the concept of sacred space (Rosenwein 1999; Hayes 2003), and its operation in relation to the physical and aesthetic spaces of monasteries and cathedral churches (Camile 1992; Martindale 1995; Morrison 2000; Cassidy-Welch 2001). The premise that values of sacred space were destroyed at the Reformation has been challenged (Scribner 1990), and its reshaping under Protestantism has been explored in relation to worship and burial (Aston 2003; Harding 2002). In the study of monastic space, different disciplines have generated their own characteristic approaches. Art historians follow a more iconographic method in the study of monastic architecture (Fergusson 1986; Fergusson and Harrison 1999), or give careful study to the proportional ratios that informed the setting out of monastic plans (Fernie 1976). Archaeologists have tended to emphasise more functional and evolutionary approaches to the development of monastic planning (Coppack 1990; Thompson 2001).

Increasingly, scholars of medieval monasticism offer spatial interpretations that are more informed by social theory. For example, Megan Cassidy-Welch (2001) has studied Cistercian monasteries with particular regard to the importance of the changing, historically specific meanings of space, drawing especially on the work of Henri Lefebvre (1974). My own analysis of the impact of gender on female monastic space (Gilchrist 1994) was influenced by Pierre Bourdieu's theory of space as *habitus*, an acquired, common sense knowledge that guides individual agents through social spaces (Bourdieu 1977). These studies emphasise contextual and experiential approaches, highlighting the experience of the body in moving through and inhabiting monastic spaces. Recent studies have challenged the traditional view that medieval sacred space was strictly delineated from profane, secular space. Both Michael Camille and Dawn Hayes have observed that, particularly with regard to cathedrals, this dichotomy is incongruous. The medieval cathedral was a worldly place, where the divine was juxtaposed with secular affairs, including business and legal transactions, games and sport, gossip and sexual intrigue (Camille 1992, 91; Hayes 2003, 53–69). For this reason, the terms sacred and social space are pursued here, in preference to the anachronistic binary of sacred and profane. This chapter will consider the degree to which sacred space was permeable in the cathedral precinct, and the extent to which the religious and secular communities interacted. Such social exchanges were not restricted to living communities; the cathedral landscape also segregated the religious and secular dead, and encouraged their continued engagement with the living.

An archaeological assessment of sacred space considers the construction and use of the built environment, including the sensory experience of moving through and interacting with monastic space. Its study requires attention to the choice of materials, plan and layout, the placement and iconographic content of images, the control of boundaries, and the manipulation of view-sheds to emphasise sight-lines and inter-visibility. A contextual reading is vital to our understanding: close studies of medieval literary and visual sources are more useful here than cross-cultural, theoretical expositions of space. We may also interrogate medieval sources for the contemporary voice. Pertinent in this respect are the observations of the thirteenth-century liturgist, Gulielmus Durandus, Bishop of Mende (Neale and Webb 1843: *Rationale*, 57–8). In discussing consecrated places, Durandus distinguished three levels of place devoted to prayer: sacred, holy and religious. Sacred places were defined as churches that were sanctified and set aside for prayer. Holy places encompassed the

cloisters and lodgings of monks and canons, and churchyards that also possessed immunity or privilege. Religious space referred to any ground in which Christian bodies were interred (Hayes 2003, 117; Ariès 1981, 41). In applying these gradations
to the cathedral-priory of Norwich, we may anticipate relative degrees of sanctity,
and distinctions in spatial practice between the cathedral church, the cloister of the
monks, the cemeteries and the wider precinct (Figure 94). In taking an experiential
perspective, we must also consider movement of the body through these zones, and
the contemporary meanings that certain spaces and buildings held. An emphasis is
placed here on change and the historical contingency of spatial meaning, and equal
consideration is given to both physical space and 'metaphorical' or imagined space
(Cassidy-Welch 2001).

'Metaphorical space' may be understood as the active process of interpreting
spatial orientation and form; in other words, the contemporary iconographic meanings that were read by the medieval viewer as inherent to the structure of monastic
architecture. 'Physical space' encompasses the material character and form of the
monastic precinct, but also the physical movement of people through these spaces.
The study of movement is revealing in several respects: while 'place' may indicate
stability, 'space' is mobile, created by movement of the body from one place to another (de Certeau 1984, 117). Movement through monastic space served as a per-
ceptual mnemonic, with the decoration of certain architectural spaces reinforcing
both social rules and cosmological beliefs (Gilchrist 1994, 159). Access to particular
places, or exclusion from them, was determined by group membership, with divisions drawn along axes of age, gender, social status and religious identity.

Despite the value placed on community and humility, a strict hierarchy prevailed within the common spaces of the monastery. The monastery was structured
according to seniority: order of entry to the priory determined seating in the refectory and chapter house, the placement of beds in the dormitory, and processional
order in the services. The Rule of St Benedict states that

> The brethren shall keep their order in the monastery according to the date of
> the entry, or according to the merit of their lives and as the abbot shall deter-
> mine . . . When a senior passes by, let a junior rise and make room for him to
> seat himself; nor let the junior presume to sit down, unless his senior bid him
> (McCann 1952, 144–5).

Until the early thirteenth century, a school for boys was located in the cloister,
with lessons taught in the chapter house. It seems that the young novices were
trained in the east cloister walk, and that they occupied their own accommodation
at the southern end of the ground floor of the east range (see pp. 113–15). The
elderly monks retired eventually to the infirmary, so that the youngest and oldest
members of the monastery occupied the space beyond the south-east corner of the
cloister, and are likely to have shared the chapel of St Nicholas (see p. 174). Spatial
segregation based on age may have generated tensions in the community. Shortly
before the suppression of the priory, a visitation by Bishop Nykke in 1526 recorded

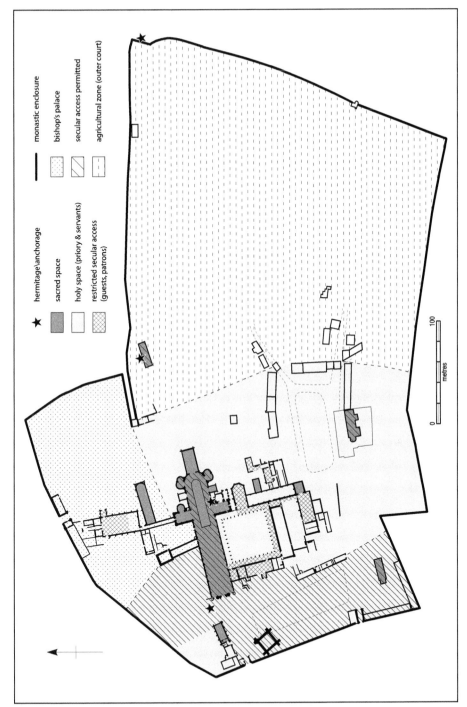

FIGURE 94. Sacred and social space in the medieval cathedral-priory. Drawing by Margaret Mathews.

a convent divided by age and riven by quarrelling factions (Jessopp 1888, xxi). The junior monks were indulging in cards and backgammon, and some younger monks objected to memorising the psalms. The senior monks were accused of abusing their position, and some vainly flouted the common habit, wearing top-boots and gaudy hats with satin rosettes and lappets!

'BOUNDEDNESS'

The quality of boundedness pertained to sacred places such as monastic precincts and cemeteries from the tenth or eleventh centuries. Barbara Rosenwein (1999) has traced the tendency to enclose sacred space back to the early medieval concept of immunity. It originated with the exceptions and prohibitions that allowed kings to control space through royal immunities, and was extended by the papacy to represent the notion of consecrated land. This is demonstrated clearly in relation to the abbey of Cluny in the year 1080. The monks of Cluny had been in dispute with neighbouring parties over physical and spiritual territories. Pope Gregory VII sent his envoy, Peter of Albano, to resolve the matter. Albano chose to arbitrate during the feast of the Purification of the Virgin, a celebration that was central to the monastic liturgy. During the ceremonial observances, 'he declared a completely bounded circle around the monastery into which violators might enter only at peril of eternal damnation' (Rosenwein 1999, 174). The boundaries of a monastery came to represent both its own jurisdiction and the limits of the sacred.

In common with earlier royal immunities, monastic enclosures constructed space, defined boundaries and prohibited ingress. Such prohibitions were intended to guard the purity of the high altar: its sanctity could be polluted by those who were deemed unfit to approach (ibid., 40–41). Women, in particular, were regarded as potential polluters. This view was asserted more strongly following the suppression of clerical marriage in the eleventh century (see p. 3). Theologians reintroduced ancient taboos surrounding the female body: Levitican authority justified the exclusion of women from churches after childbirth or during menstruation (McNamara 1999, 13). The definition of sacred space also demanded the protection of altar vessels and furnishings from the contaminating touch of women, including females that were consecrated as nuns. Previously, women in continental cathedrals had assisted with baptism, maintained lamps and draperies, rung bells and made vestments and linens (ibid., 24 n. 91). Just as sanctity could be transferred, for example through contact with saints' relics, so too could spiritual pollution. This accounts for the Norwich precentor's deliberate choice of a washer*man* to launder the textiles of the church, rather than the washerwomen who were employed by other officers (see p. 16).

The monastic boundaries controlled ingress of secular men and women, and egress of the monks. Symbolically, the cloister created a bounded space within the precinct, giving physical presence to the concept of monastic enclosure. Deriving from the Latin *claustrum*, meaning enclosure, barrier, bolt or gate, the term conveys the inward-looking nature of monastic life. The body of the monk or nun was also a sacred space, defined by their religious profession, their vow of celibacy, and by corporeal practices that set their bodies apart from those of the laity, including distinctive dress, dietary restrictions, regular phlebotomy and higher standards of sanitation. Monastics were regarded as liminal (from the Latin *limen*, threshold) in medieval society. It was perceived that they experienced death twice: first, when monastic vows signalled the death of their former worldly self; and later, when physical death resulted from expiry of the body (Turner 1969). The physical and psychological space that monks inhabited was liminal, a threshold between the secular and the divine, between this world and the next.

Both religious buildings and monastic bodies were consecrated (Hayes 2003), and the monastic emphasis on boundaries stems from a concern to protect the liminal zones of both categories of sacred space. Maintenance of boundaries included the erection of walls and gates, while the entry points through such boundaries were significant in negotiating the interface between secular and religious. This was achieved through the use of sculptural ornament in the elaboration of entrances and access routes (Camille 1992, 56), and the employment of selected materials of construction. The protection of boundaries may account for the distancing of Gothic and Romanesque sculpture at Norwich to the periphery — confined to gates, doors and the upper parts of church (Sekules 1996, 196). The entrances to the cathedral church and cloister were articulated visually according to their specific audience and purpose (see below). Significant boundaries were also emphasised by the siting of the anchorites and hermits of the precinct, religious individuals whose eremitic vocation set them yet further apart from the secular world of the living. Anchorites' cells were established at the gate to the lay cemetery, in the monks' cemetery, and in the churchyard of the parish church of St Helen's, on Holme Street. A hermitage was also sited along Holme Street, near Bishop's Bridge (see pp. 98, 34).

Although protected by physical and symbolic boundaries, the membranes of the precinct were permeable. As discussed in Chapter 1, the permanent population included both religious personnel and their secular servants, in addition to transient lay visitors ranging from kings to paupers. In the later twelfth century, sacred space was compromised in an effort to draw greater numbers of pilgrims to visit the shrine of William (see below). By the later Middle Ages, the monks of the cathedral-priory were forced to compete with the mendicant friars for the spiritual and financial affections of the local laity. They encouraged visitors to the area surrounding the cathedral's west front and lay cemetery, establishing a charnel house in 1316 for the remains of skeletons from the city's churchyards (see p. 34), and a preaching yard for outdoor sermons, from c.1469. In common with cathedral clergy elsewhere (for example, at Chartres: Hayes 2003, 48), the monks of Norwich cathedral resorted to marketing strategies that transgressed medieval spatial taboos.

The visual culture of the precinct also became more accessible to the laity, and notably to women, as secular patronage was actively sought. By the fourteenth century, the cathedral church had three shrines devoted to the Virgin, and one to

St Sitha of Lucca, patron saint of female domestic servants (Shinners 1988). There were two images of Our Lady of Pity at Norwich cathedral by the sixteenth century: the poignant symbolism of the *Pietà* appealed particularly to women, depicting Mary as the grieving mother cradling the wounded body of Christ. These images were located in the nave and in the Bauchon chapel, the latter of which retains a ceiling corbel representing the *Pietà*, and a bracket on the east wall that would have held a *Pietà* statue; from the size of the bracket, it has been estimated that the statue was a massive 2.5m in height (Marks 2004, 129; 140–42). The Erpingham gate, the main portal to the precinct (constructed c.1420–35), prominently displayed sculptures of twelve female saints in the outer order of the arch (Figure 13). Such imagery may indicate the increased accessibility of the precinct to female visitors, and was perhaps intended especially for prosperous widows. Widows were numerous in Norwich, and imagery such as the *Pietà* particularly attracted their bequests (ibid., 139). Women were among the patrons of the furnishings of the cathedral church; their sponsorship can be detected in the armorial shields of the carved stalls of the choir (e.g. Isabella de Beauchamp, d. 1416). In three cases where the misericords were carved with representations of gentry patrons, these showed paired male and female figures, whether husband and wife, or mother and son (Whittingham 1981; Rose 2003).

Within the private spaces of the cathedral, the presence of women still created tensions; this ambivalence is reflected in the iconography of the bosses in the porch to Bishop Salmon's hall (c.1319–25). Of three morality scenes, two concerned women: one depicts the devil perched behind a man and woman holding hands, and the other shows a penitent woman being blessed by a priest. The records of bishops' visitations suggest that it was necessary to remind the monks of Norwich cathedral-priory that women were to be excluded from parts of the precinct. In 1492, Bishop Goldwell was adamant that the presence of women was long ago forbidden and contrary to the Rule. He complained that 'indiscreet gossiping and chattering in the church' took place between the monks and certain women of questionable repute. In 1514, Bishop Nykke repeated that 'women went in and out at pleasure', noting that they strayed beyond the parlour to the infirmary (Jessopp 1888, xvii–xviii).

By the later Middle Ages, women certainly tweaked episcopal anxiety by infiltrating the holy places of the precinct. Following the Reformation, the new cathedral community at first continued to exclude women from certain areas. The clerical celibacy of the eleventh and twelfth centuries had been created alongside constructions of sacred space, and the reassertion of Levitican taboos surrounding the female body. Such beliefs were firmly rooted. The lease in 1549 for building John Baret's house against the Carnary chapel (Number 69) was granted on condition that it was inhabited by 'only a prist or prists or other man being sole and not married' (see p. 201). Sexual propriety within the close continued to be monitored by the chapter. In 1567, the clerk John Toller and the petty canon John Beldam 'made their purgacyons' to the chapter for sexual misconduct with women in the close, the former with a married woman, and the latter with his maidservant (Cozens and

Williams-Hardy 1953, 24, 27). Within a century, the institutions of marriage and the family were reinforced through the material culture of the close, and a new feminine iconography was introduced. The prebendary house built on the former refectory incorporated imported hearth-bricks from the Netherlands, with their bold depictions of 'femmes fortes' (Figures 89–90). Houses were erected jointly by husbands and wives, with joint patronage proudly announced in their façades.[1] After the Civil War, the Chapter actively sought gentile female company, delighted that the landscaping of the close attracted the young ladies of the town for their daily perambulations (see p. 234). Concern with boundaries continued, however, and porters were retained to lock the gates of the close at night. The new foundation was concerned particularly to exclude nonconformists, Catholics and the poor, mirroring the attitudes of the city corporation. This contrasted with the hospitality that had been offered at the fringes of the medieval cathedral-priory, where charity was dispensed to the poor and leprous in the almonry at the Ethelbert gate.

DEGREES OF SANCTITY

Despite the ideological and physical emphasis that was placed on enclosure, it is clear that some parts of the precinct were accessible to the laity; indeed, the priory encouraged secular visitors through a variety of well-chosen strategies. Can distinctions be perceived in the degrees of sacred space that operated with the cathedral-priory (Figure 94)? In the thirteenth century, Durandus would have distinguished between the cathedral church as a 'sacred place', and the cloister, cemeteries and precinct as a 'holy place'. Within the church, the nave was regarded as a more secular space, while the choir and presbytery were intended to be accessible only to the monks. Dawn Hayes (2003) has argued that this delineation was based on the concept of sexual purity, with the nave considered an appropriate space for married, sexually-active people. The connection between sexual purity and sacred space sparked a collective medieval neurosis — a fear surrounding the possibility that sexual intercourse might take place in a church. By the twelfth century, such spaces were protected by apocryphal tales of couples who were miraculously stuck together, as punishment for illicit sex in holy places (Elliott 1999, 61–9). Only celibates could approach the high altar of the cathedral church, a spatial prohibition that was used to promote clerical celibacy. For instance in 1108, Archbishop Anselm attempted to ban English clergy from keeping wives; any who refused to comply were to be separated from their benefices and excluded from the choir (Hayes 2003, 19).

In the later Middle Ages, secular imagery crept into these revered and celibate spaces. The timber choir-stalls of the fifteenth and sixteenth centuries were

---

[1] These include Numbers 37–39, with the inscription 'John Howell and Helene his wife built this house', c.1632; Number 33, with 'JRA 1682' on the gable (John and Anne Ringall); Number 44, with joint initials 'JKH' in metalwork on the gable (James and Katharine Hobart, c.1670); and Numbers 3–4, rebuilt by Jeremy and Susan Vinn, 1701, and exhibiting their initials.

provided with carved seat supports (misericords) and elbow rests, very few of which exhibited religious or biblical symbolism (Whittingham 1981; Rose 2003). The sixty carved misericords that survive at Norwich predominantly represent exotic and mythical beasts, hybrid figures and green men or woodwoses, seasonal and domestic tasks, and classical and medieval stories. Some convey moralistic messages, including allegorical representations of four of the Seven Deadly Sins (Lechery, Gluttony, Avarice, Wrath). A warning against sexual temptation may be read in a carved mermaid suckling a lion (also shown on a misericord at Wells cathedral) (ibid., 49). The mermaid was often depicted in monastic contexts with a mirror and comb, symbolising the dangerous allure of the sensual (for example, in cloister bosses at the nunnery of Lacock, Wiltshire). Although firmly located in the sacred space of the choir, these images beneath the seats of the monks were not readily visible. In common with the comic images in the margins of medieval manuscripts, misericords were a form of marginal visual play. Michael Camille argued that the ambiguity of such images helped to define the sacred, with the divine set in opposition to the travesty and profanity of the marginal (1992, 29). According to such a reading, the numerous animals of the misericords become sexual symbols, a menagerie of human nature and 'sins of the flesh that were, for the soul seeking salvation, expendable' (ibid., 40).

The location of the sacred could be pinpointed at the high altar of the cathedral church: proximity to this sacred epicentre determined access for both the living and the dead (discussed below). This spatial hierarchy extended beyond the church and cemetery to the placement of the monastic buildings, with the most holy and corporate buildings of the convent placed closest to the high altar. The chapter house and dormitory were in the eastern range, moving towards the refectory in the south range and the more secular spaces of the guest hall and outer parlour in the west range. Even the monastic offices of the inner court were ranked according to proximity to the cathedral church. The influential master of the cellar was situated close to the monastic core, while the lower-ranking gardener and chamberlain were pushed to the margins of the outer court.

Power relations within the community danced around the pivotal point of the high altar. The position of the bishop was reflected in the private routes of access that he developed from his palace to the cathedral church: including a first-floor gallery connecting the nave and palace, and a private door in the north transept. His special association with this area was reflected in the rich decoration of the door, the only interruption to the plainness of the interior of the Romanesque church (see p. 144). Most significant in terms of location was the siting of the bishop's private chapel in the palace complex. This was placed parallel with the presbytery, so that the altar of the bishop's chapel was aligned with the high altar and the bishop's throne in the cathedral church. As discussed previously (pp. 23, 150), it is possible that the bishop's chapel was built on the site of the Saxon parish church of Holy Trinity. Both the bishop's tower and chapel depart from the axis of the cathedral church, and it is likely that they were aligned in relation to an earlier feature.

When separate accommodation for the prior was developed from the late thir-teenth century (see p. 156), this was placed to the east of the cloister and directly south of the presbytery, and parallel with it. The earliest phase of the prior's lodging can be compared directly with the classic tripartite plan of manorial halls, c.1300: a central open hall, with the solar or private apartment of the lord at one end, and the service rooms at the other, separated by a screened cross passage. In a secular context this spatial arrangement is perceived to have held symbolic and hierarchical meanings, with the lord's chamber and table located at the raised, upper or high end (Grenville 1997, 89). In the monastic context at Norwich, the orientation of the hall must have held even greater significance, locating the prior's centre of power in the more sacred, eastern space. His solar, or private chamber, was directly in line with the high altar of the cathedral church, and with that of the bishop's chapel. Within the refectory, the prior's table was located on a raised dais at the eastern end. Sur-vival of two buttresses suggests that this reserved area may have been screened from the main space of the refectory (see p. 125). The prior also occupied the most holy space of the chapter house, with his seat and pulpit in the eastern apse.

In the prior's lodging, space was ordered to maintain hierarchical power rela-tions. Here, a more Foucauldian perspective is useful, in which space is regarded as a tool of institutionalised discipline (Foucault 1979). Physical access to the prior's lodging was controlled by a porter, located in the dark entry, a vaulted passage through the south range of the cloister (Figure 40). A squint was used to observe monks approaching the dark entry, indicating that surveillance was used to regulate spatial rules in the cloister, and to limit access to the prior's lodging to the east, and the infirmary to the south. Before the construction of a separate lodging in the late thirteenth century, the prior's chamber was located over the dark entry. Its position over a gateway was symbolic of lordship and authority. The prior's lodging was also sited adjacent to the areas that were concerned with the maintenance of monastic discipline: the prison beneath the south transept, and the chapter house, which was the customary location of confessions and the dispensing of discipline (Cassidy-Welch 2001, 123–6).

Secular visitors arrived at the cathedral with a well-developed sense of medi-eval *habitus*: through regular worship, they had learned which spaces were open to them, and visual clues were in place to guide them in local practice. The Erpingham gate framed the cathedral's west front and the main entrance to the nave, and the large bells of the adjacent *clocher* welcomed the faithful on saints' days. As in all Benedictine monasteries, the nave was reserved for use by the laity, and the eastern arm was the preserve of the cathedral-priory (Figure 18). The monks were guided in their use of space by a more formal knowledge of *performance*: repeated, ritual-ised gestures that were structured by the liturgy. Ceremonial processions through the spaces of the church and cloister reinforced their place within the community, ordered rigidly by the Rule of St Benedict, from the prior and most senior monks down to the junior monks and novices. The choir stalls of the monks occupied the crossing and the first two eastern bays of the nave, separated from the main area of the nave by two screens, the rood screen and the *pulpitum* (see p. 71). The apse contained the sanctuary, with the high altar in the next bay to the west. Behind the altar stood the bishop's throne, in the most prominent position. The laity were prohibited from the presbytery and choir, but could travel through the aisles to the ambulatory, and pass behind the high altar. Here they could view relics, contained in a niche beneath the bishop's throne. At Norwich and elsewhere, it is apparent that even the more sacred, eastern arm of the cathedral church was opened up to seculars on occasion. Pilgrims visited shrines and images in the ambulatory chapels, and the guilds of St Luke and St George met in these spaces (Shinners 1988). In the mid thirteenth century, the bishop preached to the populace from the high altar during Lent and Holy Week (Dodwell 1996b, 239).

Did the laity also venture into the 'holy places' of the precinct? The inner court was split into two areas with functions broadly divided into subsistence and philanthropy; from approximately the mid fourteenth century, these courts were organised around two greens (Figure 7). The philanthropic area of the upper inner court catered especially for the laity, and included the guest hall, cellarage, the almonry and the cathedral school. It was located along the western strip of the precinct, from the boundary wall up to and including the west range of the cloister. Monastic hospitality encompassed the reception of travellers, ecclesiastics, paupers and pilgrims. At the southern end of the upper inner court, adjacent to the Ethelbert gate, the almonry welcomed the poor, although this space was segregated from the main area of the green (see p. 185). More prosperous visitors were drawn to the porch that advertised the hospitality of the hostry, in the west range of the cloister. Its visitors were afforded some privacy by the attached garden, enclosed with box hedging and chalk walls. The public nature of this area, and its occasional squalor, is confirmed in the stinging words of Bishop Salmon. His visitation to the priory in February 1308, stated:

> we lay down and command that the Priory Hall court which is common and seen by many should be properly cleansed from all rubbish, from dung and other filth, as the dignity of the place demands; lest the smell may affect those who pass through the Hall and from such dirtiness the negligence of many may be openly discussed by many (Carter 1935, 30–31).

Adjacent to the hostry was the outer parlour, or *locutory*, where relatives and tradesmen could converse with the monks (see p. 132). This is likely to have been the location of a daily ritual described in the Norwich *Customary,* intended to demonstrate both hospitality and humility. The *mandatum hospitum* was the ceremonial washing of the feet of three poor men, performed daily by the monks before dinner (Tolhurst 1948, xxxvii).

The lower inner court allowed the monastic community to be self-sufficient. Its service buildings were placed to the south-east of the cloister, allowing easy access to the river and to the agricultural resources of the outer court. Today, the remains of the major medieval buildings of the lower inner court survive incorporated in later houses: the brewhouse and bakehouse, and the granary and steward's office. The rear elevation of the granary retains a thirteenth-century arcade, indicating the position of a loading bay on the north side of the building. This feature suggests that goods were transported by cart along a hollow way running behind the brewhouse, after being unloaded on the quay at the top of the canal. The agricultural and industrial features of the precinct were confined to the outer court, located in the water meadows adjacent to the river. This zone contained gardens, fishponds, waterside warehouses, and complexes such as mills and smithies (see pp. 60–65). It was approached directly from the River Wensum, where a water gate to the precinct survives today, and a canal was cut leading to the lower inner court. A series of lanes was developed to allow access through the outer court, without ingress to the inner court (see p. 56). The lane surviving today as Hook's Walk is lined with buildings, including one dated to the thirteenth or fourteenth century (Number 49), which perhaps represents the medieval gardener's office. Hook's Walk may be compared with the terraces of tenements that developed in some of London's monastic precincts, focusing particularly on the cemetery or outer court areas (Sloane 2003).

Holy space was dissipated at the margins of the precinct: the borders of the outer court housed servants and corrodians, obediential offices, and in the later Middle Ages, secular tenants and tenements. The interface between respective zones was made apparent through the positioning of postern gates and lanes. Distinctions were emphasised through the choice of building materials, with the cathedral church, outer parlour and cloister finished with dressed stone, and the ranges of the cloister constructed in flint rubble covered with plaster. The buildings of the inner court were also flint rubble with stone dressings, while those of the outer court were timber (see p. 39). Lead roofing was provided for the cloister and inner court buildings, and glass for their windows; in contrast, thatch covered the roofs of service buildings in the outer court, and shutters protected their windows. Travelling the arterial routes of the precinct, a secular visitor would have recognised the threshold between the outer and inner court on the basis of materials of construction, the placement of gates and lanes, and the use of greens as focal features. Similar visual cues operated at high status secular residences, such as palaces and manor houses.

Turning to the central monastic spaces — the cloister and the infirmary — their scale and visual treatment signalled a more sacred quality. Both the infirmary and the refectory borrowed features from the cathedral church, indicating their ceremonial and religious functions. The arcade of the infirmary followed the alternating piers of the nave, while the refectory repeated the gallery of the church in its wall-passage. If the interpretation is accepted of a screen at the dais end of the refectory (see pp. 125–6), it may have been modelled on the use of screens in the church to create spatial hierarchies in relation to altars. The proportional planning and decorative wall paintings of the church and cloister created a harmonious and unified sacred space.

Was the cloister sacrosanct, protected from secular incursion? By 1492, the bishop complained that laymen were not excluded properly from the refectory, and in 1514, there were allegations that some of the monks danced in the guest hall in the evening (Jessopp 1888, xvii). But some holy places were reserved. The upper floor of the east range was the most remote quarter, regarded as a secure space. The refectorer provided a great chest for the safe storage of jewels in the dormitory (Saunders 1930, 142). By the late fourteenth century, the library was moved to a book room constructed at the southern end of the dormitory (see p. 118), and the muniments were located in a chamber over the slype in the east range (see p. 109). This impression of inaccessibility accords with the results of formal spatial analysis of monastic plans, which has shown that the dormitory, chapter house and sacristy were positioned in the 'deepest' space in relation to secular points of access (Gilchrist 1994, 166). With reference to Cistercian chapter houses, Cassidy-Welch has emphasised the private, intimate nature of the space, interwoven with communal functions of administration, discipline and memory (2001, 108–13). However, she also observes that the chapter house was on occasion a more public space, used to receive secular and ecclesiastical visitors of the highest rank.

The accessibility of the cloister may be reconstructed from the placement of the bosses that were part of the rebuilding that took place from 1297 (discussed below; and pp. 85–90). The bosses were richly carved and painted, and they were placed strategically to take account of patterns of movement through the cloister. Thresholds received particular attention: Christ in majesty was depicted over the monks' ceremonial door from the church to the east cloister, and the temptation of Adam and Eve was placed over the refectory door. As discussed below, the bosses were positioned to create a chronological sequence that coincided with the clockwise, liturgical use of the cloister. However, the most didactic and popular themes were placed so that the carved faces of the bosses could be seen in an anticlockwise movement from the north-western corner of the cloister, accessed from the nave and the outer parlour (Figure 29c). The Apocalypse cycle and the popular legends of St Basil and St Christopher, and the merchant of Constantinople, were told through bosses that were placed with their carved faces to be observed in a route from the north-west corner, via the south walk, to the dark entry. The orientation of the bosses suggests that the imagery of the cloister was commissioned in part for visiting laity: the prestigious visitors who were greeted at the outer parlour and led to the chapter house, and the relatives of the monks, who travelled through the cloister to the infirmary, via the controlled access at the dark entry.

LANDSCAPE OF THE DEAD

Medieval Christians believed that the communities of the living and the dead engaged in an ongoing dialogue. After death of the body, the soul continued to exist in the intermediate state of Purgatory, where it experienced a prolonged and painful purgation of accumulated sin. A reciprocal relationship developed between the living and the dead: the prayers of the living could ease the suffering of the deceased in Purgatory; while the dead joined the 'communion of saints', through which they could intercede on behalf of the living (Gordon and Marshall 2000, 4). It has been suggested that the dead were perceived as an integral part of the community, but as a distinct social group, or even as an 'age class' (Geary 1994, 36). The living and the dead were joined through prayer, but their relationship was also emphasised through the manipulation of the cathedral landscape. The deceased monks remained a part of the monastic community, with their presence reinforced by formal processional routes, such as that followed on Palm Sunday, when the monks processed from the bishop's chapel to the cloister, through the cemetery (Tolhurst 1948, 77). Memory of the dead brethren was structured through daily prayers in the chapter house (p. 109), and encouraged by locating an enclosed garden of contemplation within the monks' cemetery (Noble 1997).

The liminal place of monastics in medieval society was reflected in the layout of the precinct. The cloister of the living monks occupied the transitional space between the urban community (to the west of the precinct) and the dead brethren (to the east). Just as the living members of the secular community were prohibited access to some holy areas, the dead were located according to their religious and social status. The lay cemetery at Norwich was located to the north-west of the church, while the monks' cemetery occupied the more sacred space around the east end. Burial of high-ranking clergy and laity also took place beneath the floor of the nave (see p. 146), and perhaps also in the chapter house, as occurred at other monasteries (Gilchrist and Sloane 2005).

It was usual to exclude seculars from the monastic cemetery. Twelfth-century practice may be gleaned from Thomas of Monmouth, author of the *Life of St William of Norwich*. He remarks specifically on the attendance of 'both sexes' at the burial of the alleged boy-martyr in the monks' cemetery in 1144 (Jessopp and James 1896, 54). He also records the unusual event of the interment of a woman in this cemetery — William's mother, 'for the devotion which we had to the son, we buried the mother with honour in our cemetery' (ibid., 216). Thomas records these events as extraordinary occurrences, bound up with his claims for the boy's status as saint. He also conveys the discomfort of the monastery within a year of the translation of William's remains to the chapter house.

> Already, not only from the neighbouring villages, but from those at a distance so great a crowd began to assemble daily at the tomb of St William, who still lay in the chapter-house, that the brotherhood of monks who abode in the cloister could no longer put up with the daily pressure of so great a multitude. For how could their peace help but being disturbed when every day a large number of men and women passed before them? (ibid., 185–6).

Thomas draws attention to secular men and women visiting the monks' cemetery and chapter house, clearly an unusual circumstance in the twelfth-century cathedral-priory. The tomb was moved to the Jesus chapel in the ambulatory, but three years later these pious visitors were disrupting the offices of the monks in the choir.

In contrast with the exclusive spaces of the monks' cemetery and cloister, the lay cemetery was developed to encourage a high frequency of secular visitors. Medieval cemeteries hosted a colourful range of social activities, including games, dances and commercial events (Gilchrist and Sloane 2005). The lay cemetery at Norwich was the location of regular fairs and markets, and the site of both the guildhall of St Luke and the school run by the Carnary college (see p. 102). By the fifteenth century, it was also the location of the preaching yard, which joined the north side of the cathedral's nave. The space outside the west front of the cathedral was exploited by the sacrist to provide shops for lease to a variety of craftworkers (see p. 189). These shops clustered around the *clocher*, the detached bell-tower; in common with the positioning of such bell-towers at other great churches, the *clocher* was sited in close proximity to the entrance to the lay cemetery.

The location of the *clocher* marked the boundary of a mortuary landscape that was created at the west end of the cathedral. Its bells tolled the traditional death-knells for members of the monastic or lay community who were buried in the cathedral's cemeteries. The *clocher* was immediately adjacent to the charnel house beneath the Carnary chapel, established to store the dry and disarticulated remains of the dead who had been buried in the city's churchyards. It may be suggested that charnel houses were highly public spaces, drawing regular visits from families devoted to intercessory prayer for the souls of departed relatives. At Norwich cathedral, in common with the cathedrals of Exeter and St Paul's, and the hospital-priory of St Mary Spital, London, the charnel house was twinned with the public galleries of the preaching yard (see p. 102), in expectation of a high concentration of lay visitors.

The Carnary chapel was built for Bishop Salmon's chantry college of St John the Evangelist, established in 1316 to the west of the cathedral church and adjacent to the site of the Erpingham gate. The lofty chapel is raised over a basement, an undercroft lit by circular windows (Figure 36). Fernie has suggested that the two-storey form of the chapel places it firmly within the tradition of palatial architecture (1993, 182). However, visitors to the precinct must have been acutely aware of the chapel's links to the visual culture of medieval death, suitably inspired for its purpose of storing charnel. The circular windows enabled visitors to peer into the crypt and view the skeletal remains of their ancestors, just as the shrine or reliquary allowed them to glimpse the relics of saints.

From the thirteenth century, reliquaries contained windows of crystal through which fragments of human bone could be viewed (Bynum 1995, 202). The proportions and form of the Carnary chapel are strongly reminiscent of a reliquary or a saints' shrine, an elevated tomb structure that frequently was shaped like a rectilinear chest, surmounted by a gabled roof (Nilson 1998, 34). The *foramina* shrine was a tomb pierced with large holes to provide access to relics. It was in use from the late twelfth into the thirteenth century, with examples surviving at Whitechurch Canonicorum (Dorset; St Candida) and Salisbury cathedral (St Osmund) (ibid., 44). The ocular windows of the Carnary chapel appear to mimic the round holes of the traditional *foramina* tomb. As Phillipe Ariès observed, the most striking characteristic of the ossuary or charnel is the *visibility* of the bones (1981, 59). The form and siting of the Carnary chapel, placed at the entrance to the lay cemetery and built in the form of a reliquary or tomb, intensified the experience of visiting the lay cemetery. Additionally, the chapel's iconographic association with the cult of relics may have reflected Salmon's personal hope of achieving the status of a saint-bishop.

It is suggested here that the Carnary chapel was intended to serve as a mnemonic of a saint's tomb, encouraging the visibility of the charnel remains through its ocular windows. The iconography of the building reflects the role of the dead as spiritual intercessors for the living, and it was located strategically within the cathedral landscape. The Carnary chapel united the community of the city's dead, integrating the dead buried in the cathedral's lay cemetery with the charnel remains of the dead who had been buried in the parish churches of the city. Further, when viewed from the main entrance to the cathedral through the Erpingham gate, the position of the Carnary chapel emphasised the intercessory role of the dead. The dead were a visible intermediary between the living community, located to the west of the precinct, and the divine, represented by the cathedral church immediately to the east. By pairing the charnel chapel with preaching facilities, the cathedral-priory used the dead as missionaries in their message to the living. More cynically, the dead were appropriated in the cathedral's struggle to wrestle the city's spiritual loyalties away from the friars.

SPATIAL METAPHORS: HISTORY AND COSMOLOGY

Distinctions in sacred space were conveyed through nuances of building location and materials of construction. Buildings also transmitted metaphorical meaning, with the medieval viewer aware of the iconographic content inherent to the structure's form. The most obvious example of such imagery was in the shape of the cathedral church itself, representative of Christ on the cross, with the high altar and presbytery placed at the location of his head and heart. Peter Fergusson has drawn attention to the iconographic meanings of the two-storey refectory and the apsidal chapter house. The former referred to the building in Jerusalem where the Last Supper took place (Fergusson 1986), and the latter was in deference to Benedictine Monte Cassino, where St Benedict composed his rule (Fergusson and Harrison 1999, 94). At Norwich cathedral-priory, specific metaphorical meanings can be discerned in the form of the Carnary chapel (discussed above) and in the embellishment of the later medieval cloister. The Romanesque buildings were influenced by numerous historical themes and imagery, their eclectic sources drawn together to create what might be termed an 'iconography of heritage'.

Creating antiquity in the cathedral landscape
While in many ways Norwich was typical of the development of English monastic cathedrals, in one significant respect it was unique. Norwich alone was established

on a new site, lacking the precedent of a well-established Saxon monastery. There were no ancient saints or relics to enhance the setting of the bishop's see. Consequently, the cathedral's founder chose to mould a holy landscape for his new cathedral-priory, and to imbue this landscape with a sense of Christian antiquity. It was not uncommon in the medieval world to draw on historical antecedents to consolidate a sense of authority (Harvey 2000). In moving the cathedral from Thetford to Norwich, c. 1096 (see pp. 25–6), Herbert de Losinga first cleared the site to provide a blank canvas. He built on a massive scale to create an episcopal foundation that would rival Bury St Edmunds, and the cathedral-priories that had recently been established at Saxon ecclesiastical sites. He selected the most prestigious archetypes to convey his monastery with the authority of heaven and earth, ranging from St Peter's basilica in the Vatican, to Charlemagne's palace at Aachen, and finally to Rufus's palace at Westminster.

In order to provide some sense of religious continuity, de Losinga chose to build his palace on the specific site of the Saxon parish church of Holy Trinity (see p. 23), and he adopted the same dedication for the cathedral church. It is also possible that an earlier religious community was associated with the site, based on its causeway location, and the recovery of Ipswich ware and iron-working debris (p. 21). De Losinga's actions may be compared with Norman castle builders, who built at existing Saxon fortifications to enforce their lordship, for example at Goltho (Lincolnshire) and Portchester (Hampshire) (Creighton 2002, 70). He constructed an earthwork platform and a fortified tower to serve as his base, and set about creating a 'designed landscape' to convey a sense of Norman authority (after Liddiard 1999). The design for the eastern arm of the cathedral church integrated a profusion of turrets, drawing on Carolingian inspiration, and the bishop's palace was provided with a gallery entrance to the church at first-floor level, modelled on Charlemagne's palace at Aachen (see p. 149). A door also led from the bishop's palace to the north transept at ground level, decorated with triangular-headed arches and gabled billet, more in keeping with late Saxon style. The exterior of this door was surmounted by a relief-carving of a bishop, offering a blessing with his right hand and holding a crozier in his left. Eric Fernie has argued that the figure represents the seventh-century saint Felix, the first bishop of East Anglia (Fernie 1993, 83–7).

This deliberately nostalgic treatment continued inside the cathedral church. The *cathedra*, the bishop's throne, appears to have been translated from the previous cathedrals at Thetford and Elmham. Fernie has argued that it was sited in accordance with ancient tradition, placed in the central arch of the apse, directly behind the high altar (see p. 74). It was also elevated, and directly below it there is a deep niche opening in the ambulatory behind the throne. The sunken floor of the ambulatory recalls the use of early medieval ring-crypts to house relics for display to pilgrims. The niche beneath the throne is likely to have held relics, and the throne itself must have been regarded as a relic of the early church in East Anglia. The model chosen for the treatment of the nave altar held the highest spiritual authority. Its position was defined by the placement of four cylindrical piers decorated with spiral grooves. Similar piers were used also at Durham cathedral and in the crypt of Canterbury cathedral, and Fernie argues that they were an iconographic reference to Old St Peter's in Rome (Fernie 1977; 1980; 1993, 129–33). Spiral columns had been reused in the shrine that was built for St Peter by Constantine in the fourth century, to mark the most famous shrine in western Christendom.

It is highly significant that Herbert de Losinga established the cathedral at Norwich shortly after his visit to Rome, to seek absolution from Pope Urban for the simoniacal purchase of his see (Dodwell 1996a). Old St Peter's may also have served as the model for the distinctive sunken cloister at Norwich. The cloister walks were lower than the four surrounding ranges of buildings by a depth of approximately 800mm, creating a subterranean effect. When de Losinga visited the Vatican in 1094, the atrium of Old St Peter's is likely to have been a sunken courtyard to the east of the basilica (Krautheimer et al. 1977, 266; see p. 82), very close in size to the cloister at Norwich. When the bishop began building at Norwich just two years later, he obtained a site with sloping terrain reminiscent of the papal complex, and he chose to reproduce the combination of the spiral columns and sunken cloister that he had seen at St Peter's.

De Losinga did not limit himself to harnessing the past to bring legitimacy to his new foundation. He built on a scale that would rival any contemporary monastery: the cloister at Norwich was unsurpassed in the twelfth century (56.6m × 56.5m), and the monastic refectory was enormous (51.8m × 13.7m), outshining even Westminster's celebrated edifice (50m × 11.3m: RCHME 1924, 84). De Losinga enjoyed close connections with the court,[2] and this may account for a feature of the church and the ground-floor refectory that seems to have emulated the palace of Westminster itself. The clerestory of the church, and the wall-passage of the refectory, may have followed the ground-floor hall at Westminster palace, completed c.1099 by William Rufus (Roland Harris and John Crook, pers. comm.). The twelve-bay hall was the largest in Europe (77m × 24m), with the span of its roof supported by posts or arcades. The wall-passage at Norwich bears some similarity to that at Westminster palace, where the windows were flanked by two minor, round-headed arches that gave access to a barrel-vaulted passage (Wood 1965, 38).

In countering the cathedral's lack of tradition, de Losinga created a landscape that harnessed the Roman and Saxon Christian past, and drew upon iconographic imagery that conveyed the highest spiritual and temporal authority.

The cloister as 'cognitive machine'
The cloister provided access between the monastic buildings, and was a holy space intimately connected with daily monastic life. It served as the focus for monastic memory, with its 'historiated' decoration reinforcing monastic concepts of biblical

---

[2] After succeeding to the throne in 1087, William Rufus summoned de Losinga from Normandy (Wollaston 1996, 23). The bishop lost favour with the king following his trip to Rome, c.1094, but was firmly ensconced in the Westminster court by 1101–2, when he was sent by the king to Rome on royal business (ibid., 26).

time and communal history (Plates 2–3). Its spaces were utilised for contemplation and instruction, and served a mnemonic purpose in meditation and prayer.
This usage explains the capitals from the Romanesque cloister, with their carvings
inspired by classical authors, including Ovid and Virgil (Franklin 1996, 134: see
p. 80), and the bosses of the rebuilt cloister, carved c.1330–1430. Mary Carruthers
has described monastic meditation as a form of craft knowledge, learned through
imitation and practice, and prompted by constant recollection and memory (Carruthers 2000). Following the Roman tradition of rhetoric, monastic meditation
drew upon mental images. Architectural imagery was employed especially, with
particular buildings visualised in order to stimulate memory and composition (ibid.,
16). Monastic memory was 'locational', prompted by specific places and markers,
and architectural space served a cognitive purpose: the cloister was a tool used to
animate recollection and evoke meaning.

The placement of the cloister bosses is significant in relation to both conceptual and physical planes. They represent Christian time in a sequential manner, if
not a consistently linear one, and are located to connect narrative sequences with
physical movement through the cloister (Figure 29B–C). The earliest bosses in the
east walk, outside the chapter house, were carved in foliage patterns, but as work
progressed, 'storied' bosses appeared in the northern bays. These five bays were
decorated with the Passion of Christ (the Flagellation, Carrying the Cross, the
Crucifixion, the Resurrection and the Harrowing of Hell). The south walk continued with the Annunciation, the Visitation of Mary to Elizabeth, and the beheading
of John the Baptist. This walk saw the beginning of an outstanding series of bosses
depicting the Apocalypse, the Revelation of St John the Divine, told through thirty-
eight bosses in the south walk and sixty-four in the west walk. The north walk continued the life of Christ, with thirteen post-Resurrection bosses, followed by the
death, assumption and Coronation of the Virgin, and the lives of favoured saints.

Consistent sequences are ordered according to two entrance points to the
cloister, the door in the north-western corner (discussed above), and the door in the
north-eastern corner, which was the monks' ceremonial entrance from the church.
Processions were made through the cloisters on Sundays, on all principal feasts and
daily during Christmas, Easter and Pentecost. The usual route was clockwise around
the cloister, finally entering the church at the west door in the north walk, making a station in front of the rood at the nave altar, before returning to the choir by
the door in the *pulpitum* (Tolhurst 1948, xxiv–xxv). A clockwise procession of the
cloister would begin with the Passion of Christ, and move through the Apocalypse,
surveying the Judgement and the emergence of heavenly Jerusalem, before re-entering the church through the west door in the north walk. The bosses in the north
walk also read from the door in the north-eastern corner, moving westward, and
continued the story begun in the east walk.

Two major spatial themes emerge from consideration of the cloister bosses.
The first is their relationship to physical movement through the cloister, with the
narrative sequences serving as a *cognitive map* of the liturgy and ritual spaces. Second

is their emphasis on biblical *time*, connecting past, present and future in a linear sweep of movement. The cloister at Norwich served a clear mnemonic purpose; it was a mental map of the life of Christ, the Virgin and the saints. Further, the Apocalypse cycle set the Last Judgement in a locational setting that could be re-visited and contemplated. The cloister was a repository for biblical memory, and processions through its spaces animated the Christian story. The sequence of the bosses prompted monastic memory through the sensory experience of a journey, with movement through space enhancing meditation (after Carruthers 2000, 80). The decoration of the cloister at Norwich with historiated bosses provided a *pilgrim-age space* within the priory: the monks and their visitors could journey through and reflect upon the Last Judgement. Pausing at the door to the nave at the north-west corner of the cloister, they could ponder the judgement of the dead 'according to their works' (Revelation 20: 12), Christ sitting in judgement, and the casting of the damned into hell.

Spatial practice within the cloister at Norwich was determined by the *Custom-ary*, a late thirteenth-century guide to the cathedral's liturgy that was concerned primarily with sequence, and how it should vary according to liturgical and solar seasons (c.1279–88, Tolhurst 1948, vii). In other words, the performance of the liturgy was strictly regulated in terms of both space and time. Shortly after the compilation of the *Customary*, a mechanical clock was constructed at Norwich. This was one of the earliest clocks in Britain, with repairs being recorded to the struc-ture by 1290. The cord was replaced in 1322, indicating that it was a weight-driven machine. The sacrist's rolls referred to it as the *antiquum horologium*, distinguishing this 'old clock' from a new astrological clock that was constructed between 1322 and 1325 (Geddes 1996, 441–2), roughly contemporaneous with the earliest nar-rative bosses.

The emphasis placed on the strict regulation of time was part of the need for consistency of practice and routine in monastic life. The visitation of Bishop Salmon in 1309 instructed the monks to attend services more frequently, and demanded uniform books for the mass, new vestments and 'a reliable and goodly clock by which the brothers may be governed both by day and by night' (Carter 1934, 29). The new astrological clock was not begun until 1322, but this novel device would allow accurate timekeeping to continue throughout the monks' sleeping hours. It was a remarkable construction displaying a gilded sun and moon, and automata in-cluding fifty-nine images and a choir of monks. Master clock makers were brought from London, with gifts, fees and materials bringing the total cost to £59 9s 6d (Geddes 1996, 442). This machine was located in the south transept, adjacent to the chapter house and the 'prior's door', the door from the church that was one of the two fixed points for the biblical chronology of the cloister bosses. The clock's engraved dial was visible on the south gable of the transept, a weighty mechanism of 87lbs (39 kg).[3]

---

[3] The clock is believed to have been destroyed in the seventeenth century (Cattermole 1996,

The *Customary*, the earliest bosses and the clocks all appeared between the late thirteenth and the mid fourteenth century, and were not entirely due to the massive rebuilding that was going on at Norwich. Harald Kleinschmidt has argued that the late thirteenth century was a critical moment in monastic perceptions of time. The earliest astronomical clocks, such as that at Norwich, were developed to facilitate the continuous measurement of long-term astronomical cycles, allowing the calculation of Easter dates and 'providing periodisations of world history as past time' (2000, 26). He also suggests that within monasteries there was a reaction against the new urban, mercantile concept of time, which was concerned with time as an infinite commodity. This seems to have led to a monastic reassertion of finite, biblical measures of past time that ordered chronology from the Creation to the end of the world. The iconography of the Norwich cloister is tangible evidence of this backlash: the bosses represented biblical time and presented the world, and the cathedral-priory, as a divinely created space. The contained and bounded space of the cloister reflected the certainty and finiteness of Christian time.

Liturgical movement through the cloister was a communal performance that forged connections between past, present and future Christian temporality. This integration of movement through physical and cosmological space can be seen elsewhere, in the context of fifteenth-century wall paintings on the north and south walls of the nave of the parish church of SS Peter and Paul, Pickering (N Yorkshire). Kate Giles has observed that when the feasts of the saints and images depicted in the paintings are plotted in relation to the plan of the church, 'it becomes apparent that they are placed in calendrical order, essentially forming a liturgical calendar' (Giles 2000a, 49). She argues that the structure of the church itself became a kind of liturgical calendar, framing medieval time and social practice. The cloister at Norwich represents not just the liturgical calendar, but the entirety of Christian time. In both cases, physical space, movement and cosmological meaning are presented through sequences of visual narrative.

The Norwich bosses suggest not only a concern with the notion of time, but with understanding historical chronology. This attention to history extended to the stained glass of the cloister: in 1437–8, the upper west windows were glazed with 'histories' (Woodman 1996, 174). This apparent interest in history may have resulted from two particular functions served by the cloister, that of the library and of the school. Until the later fourteenth century, the cloister served as the library, providing space for study and the storage of books. Barbara Dodwell suggested that the books owned by the library show a strong interest in historical works, in keeping with the Benedictine tradition (Dodwell 1996c, 336). A school for child oblates was kept in the cathedral from its foundation until at least the late twelfth century (Greatrex 1994, 171). It has been proposed that mention in the commu-

503), and was replaced subsequently with a Jacobean mechanism with two quarter-jacks. An early-nineteenth-century clock remains in the south transept today, so that a clock has been located in this spot for over seven hundred years.

nar's rolls of the upkeep of desks, doors and lockers in the cloister indicates the presence of a school here (Harries et al. 1991, 5). This is further substantiated by the late twelfth-century *Life of St William*, which suggests that boys were taught in the eastern walk of the cloister and had seats in the chapter house (Jessopp and James 1896, 189).

Particularly in the cloister, we can see that monastic daily experience was structured by cosmologies of space and time, and that visual imagery was used to convey metaphorical meaning.

THE RENEGOTIATION OF SPATIAL RULES: ICONOCLASM AND GENTILITY

Studies of monastic life frequently comment on the breakdown of community that can be detected in the later Middle Ages. Cassidy-Welch has critiqued traditional paradigms of monastic space that have presented change as decline, for instance in the introduction of separate abbots' lodgings into Cistercian monasteries (Cassidy-Welch 2001). A more historically sensitive reading places these changes within wider social transformations. The Rule of St Benedict emphasised the achievement of sanctity through the elevation of the community, and the renunciation of the individual self (McCann 1952). By the fourteenth or fifteenth centuries, however, we can see the breakdown of communal spaces at many monasteries, notably in the partitioning of the dormitory, refectory and infirmary into smaller rooms. We can also detect changes in attitudes toward diet and dress, with individual preferences overcoming monastic dictums. From 1384, each Norwich monk had an allowance to purchase his own clothing, although the nature of dress remained regulated.

Can we interpret changes in adherence to communal practice as the *failure* or *decline* of monastic life? Spiritually, the later Middle Ages were characterised by more personal, interior reflection on the divine (Lawrence 1984, 227). The collective practices of monasticism may have been at odds with the more mystical, individually based piety of this period. More generally, it has been proposed that the social use of space was being transformed. If we look at the operation of secular space in contemporary palaces, castles and manor houses, we can detect the rise of private chambers that were used alongside large ceremonial spaces such as the hall (Grenville 1997). This period has been characterised as witnessing the 'retreat from hall to chamber', with the growing significance of private withdrawing chambers and dining rooms (Girouard 1978). The dwindling use of the great hall provides a parallel for the loss of significance of the common dormitory and refectory of monasteries. At some monasteries, the refectory itself was subdivided to house small dining groups. At Norwich, there is no evidence that the massive, ground-floor refectory that was built in the twelfth century was ever partitioned or fell into disuse. Instead, a number of separate dining halls had developed by the fourteenth century, a situation that was paralleled elsewhere. The growing awareness of privacy, and the preference for eating and sleeping in smaller, more companionable groups, represents a great shift in secular medieval mentalities. Monasticism absorbed these new social currents, and reworked traditional living arrangements to accommodate change within the framework of coenobiticism.

Although the Rule of St Benedict had stipulated that the monks should abstain from consuming the flesh of quadrupeds, meat was consumed regularly in monasteries by the later Middle Ages. The Benedictines were no longer concerned with *whether* it was appropriate to feast on meat, but rather *where* such meals should take place (Harvey 1993, 39). The refectory was regarded as a quasi-liturgical space: meals within it possessed a sacred quality, reminiscent of the Last Supper and the communal life of the Apostles that was the prototype for coenobitic monasticism. The symbolism of the refectory prohibited the consumption of meat (flesh) within it, although meals of fish and fowl were acceptable. For this reason, small dining rooms developed in monasteries that were specifically for the consumption of meat. The earliest chambers for eating meat developed in association with infirmaries (see p. 179), but additional facilities soon followed. At Westminster, for example, there were three dining rooms: the refectory, the misericord in the infirmary, and the *cawagium*, the partitioned eastern end of the refectory (Harvey 1993, 41). The two latter spaces were provided for the consumption of meat. At Norwich, a similar situation developed, with the refectory, the table hall in the infirmary (see p. 180), and the *camboly* in the warming room (see p. 113). The eating of meat in separate dining rooms caused some fragmentation of communal dining, and there is evidence from bishops' visitations to suggest that in some monasteries, smaller dining groups or clubs developed. At Durham, it seems that the common refectory was abandoned altogether. The *Rites of Durham* record that the refectory was used only for the feast day of St Cuthbert, and instead 'The monks dyd all dyne together at one table in a place called the lofte which was in the west end of the fratree aboue the seller' (Fowler 1902, 86). Despite the development of three dining chambers, it seems that like its equivalent at Westminster, the refectory at Norwich remained in common use up to the Reformation.

Norwich was the first of the cathedrals to be refounded by Henry VIII as a new secular establishment under a dean and chapter. When it was converted on 2 May 1538, it was unique in being allowed to retain all the monks of the priory as canons or prebendaries (Houlbrooke 1996). There was a great deal of social and liturgical continuity in the early years, but what of sacred space? The notion was cast aside that the entirety of the consecrated building was sacred, and that religious and social standing should determine degrees of access to the most revered spaces of its eastern arm. Margaret Aston (2003) has suggested that the iconoclasm of the Reformation should be regarded as a long process, encompassing first the conversion, and then reinforcement through new devotional practices. The shifting of spatial meanings within the church was as much a part of this iconoclasm as the demolition of cathedral cloisters at Winchester and St Paul's, and the destruction of Lady chapels, such as that at Wells. The greater sanctity of the presbytery and high altar made them the particular focus of the reformers' attentions (see pp. 203–5).

The liturgy was pared down to its bare bones, as the clergy retreated into the contained spaces of the choir and presbytery. The long naves of cathedral churches became redundant, often serving as open thoroughfares, with 'dog-whippers' paid to keep animals out of the church (Lehmberg 1996, 214; see p. 206). The new so-cial order came to be reflected by the seats provided in the choir, with hierarchies articulated through distinctions in vertical and horizontal space. Galleries were set up in the choir at Norwich, in order to accommodate large numbers of men and women in a restricted, and at times undignified, area. These galleries are shown in a drawing of c.1630, which depicts two-tier 'closets' and the position of fixed seating for the corporation and the choir (Figure 80). The most sacred space of the cathedral church resembled the profane and bawdy surroundings of a public theatre or assembly place.

In contrast with monasteries that were converted to private residences, many cathedrals retained the overtly holy and corporate spaces of the chapter house and cloister. The chapter house at Norwich had been lost by 1569, but this feature sur-vived at the great majority of new cathedrals, continuing to serve as places of disci-pline, administration and theological education. The priors' lodgings were retained intact for the new deans, and the monastic ranges were adapted to accommodate the three groups of personnel who staffed all post-Reformation cathedrals: the preb-endaries (or canons), the minor or 'petty' canons, and the singing men. The feudal resonance of the medieval hall was no longer valued, resulting in the demise of the refectory, the guest hall and the magnificent fourteenth-century hall in the bishop's palace. Similar medieval halls were demolished or partitioned at former monastic and archiepiscopal centres as the new order took hold (Rady et al. 1991, 15; Lars-son and Saunders 1997, 95).

In contradistinction to medieval monks, the prebendaries were to be housed in private residences, demanding self-contained accommodation with independ-ent kitchens. From the 1560s onwards, the Norwich chapter included married men, whose homes required new features for specialised use by certain family members, notably studies and nurseries. There were few ready-made dwellings in monastic precincts that met these specifications, and it was necessary to establish houses within the shells of the monastic buildings (Plate 10). Prebendary housing was seldom developed from the core monastic ranges, but rather from the adjacent buildings of the inner court. Typically, these were subdivided both horizontally and vertically to make smaller chambers, and large stacks were inserted to heat the new rooms. Perhaps the best evidence at Norwich for adaptations done at the Reforma-tion can be found in the former infirmary chambers (Number 65), which were converted to a prebendary house. A floor was inserted in the mid sixteenth century, and a gable wall inserted at the first-floor level. A *terminus ante quem* for the inserted gable is provided by a group of secular style wall paintings, dated c.1550 (Plate 8).

While the prebendaries adopted a more secular style of independent living, the minor canons and singing men at first retained elements of the communal life of the former monastery. They were expected to continue the tradition of communal dining, and at Norwich the infirmary was converted to 'the canons' hall', reusing the 'table hall' that had served as the infirmary dining hall by the fourteenth century. The infirmary hall itself was used as a common dormitory for the lesser clergy, known as 'the dorture'. These vestiges of monastic life ebbed away in the early seventeenth century, as it became common for the minor clergy to marry.

With the Civil War there was a new wave of iconoclasm, which included the rewriting of spatial rules within the church. From 1643, radical religion triumphed in the cathedral at Norwich, with the corporation nominating Independent ministers to preach on Sundays (Atherton and Morgan 1996, 555). Concepts of sacred space were overturned: the mayor's seat was relocated at the high altar, with de Losinga's tomb lowered to improve the mayor's view. In 1650, the corporation of Yarmouth sought the demolition of 'that vast and altogether useless cathedral' at Norwich, proposing that the materials should be used to strengthen the harbour walls of Yarmouth and to build a workhouse. The disruption to sacred space during the interregnum can be compared with the treatment of French cathedrals in the late eighteenth century, following the French Revolution. At Chartres, for example, there was a proposal to demolish the cathedral after the removal of its famous relics in 1793. Instead, the building was reinaugurated as a temple dedicated to the goddess of Reason, and later, to the cult of the Supreme Being. The nave was used for lively patriotic dances, and the sacred space of the crypt became a wine cellar for the town's merchants (Hollengreen 2004, 100–101).

The restoration of the Norwich chapter in 1660 brought a renewed sense of order to the close: walking and talking in the church and disorderly behaviour in the precincts during services were punished. Physical access to the close was regulated by locking the precinct gates at night, and by employing a resident porter to control access during the day. Over £3000 was spent in restoring the cathedral and buildings of the close, and this prompted a new emphasis on the display of the cathedral church, and the enhancement of the quality and appearance of housing. The modelling of grander residences was accompanied by the new concept of appropriate landscaping, influenced by recent developments at London and Bath (Borsay 1989), but also following the trends of local elite. In the 1680s and '90s the chapter developed an innovative scheme to landscape the close, emphasising the upper and lower greens through planting avenues of lime trees, and establishing pavements and gravel paths as recreational routes through the close.

The secular cathedral of the seventeenth century retained a concern with sacred space, but this was very different from that of the medieval cathedral-priory from which it had evolved. Protestantism signalled a shift away from the highly sensory experience of medieval worship, and elevated the significance of interior, individual piety (Aston 2003). The sacred was now located in an interior, personal space. This transformed understanding did not result from the single juncture of the Reformation: a sense of individual, personal piety had been developing in monastic communities since at least the fifteenth century. The new spirituality valued intellectual aspiration, evidenced in the adoption of individual lodgings and the proliferation in domestic studies for private reflection. From the Reformation until the Restoration, the concept of consecrated space had retreated to the core area of the choir and presbytery. By c.1700, the cathedral church and its close were once again reserved, holy spaces, and the importance of formal ceremony had been reasserted.

The cathedral's renewed sense of 'boundedness' derived largely from the chapter's concern with social exclusivity. The close established strong connections with the rural gentry, many of whom sought urban retreats within its boundaries. These cultural links are revealed in the local styles that were adopted, including Dutch gables, four-square, double-pile houses (such as Number 71), the ornamental use of brick (including the crowstepped gables of the deanery), and in the addition of country house features (such as the banqueting house in the former outer court). The medieval cathedral-priory had also adopted rural conceits, such as the traditional open halls employed for the prior's hall and the guest hall in the west range. A further distinction was made in facing its central buildings with freestone, in preference to the brick and timber that characterised the surrounding city. In their landscaping of the close in the seventeenth century, the chapter and its tenants were adopting the latest style of elite rural garden, in which walled spaces were replaced by the axial avenue plan. In the late seventeenth and early eighteenth centuries, aristocratic and gentry houses in Norfolk developed avenues of limes, focused on the main façade of the house, with minor avenues and gravel paths laid out on a cross axis (Taigel 1990, 15). A similar setting was created to present the cathedral church as an elite house, and its close as a pleasure garden in which to perform the rituals of gentility. The cosmological meanings of medieval space had been replaced by forms of landscaping and architecture that aimed to construct gentility.

The physical space of the close grew less overtly religious in character, but it remained distinct from the city surrounding it. It has been observed that this period saw cathedral establishments generally become 'increasingly inbred' (Lehmberg 1996, 257), with the chapter of Norwich in particular 'turning in on itself' (Atherton and Morgan 1996, 574). In 1696, prebendary Dr Humphrey Prideaux proudly declared that 'Our Close is as it were a town of itself apart from the city' (DCN 115/1). When Prideaux became dean in 1702, he addressed the cathedral's ailing finances, but remained complacent in the fundamental matter of the cathedral's social and religious purpose. By c.1700, and until their reform in the nineteenth century, cathedrals were esteemed increasingly for their value as tourist attractions, and as polite havens to which the county gentry could withdraw. The close at Norwich had become, according to Dean Prideaux, a place

> where persons of better quality in their widdowhood, declining age or other motives chuse to retire for their more convenient attendance on Gods worship at the Cathedral Church and therefore ought to be protected from anything that may give them vexation or disquiet (DCN 115/1/1/145–6).

With the dissipation of sacred space and religious functions, continuity with the cathedral's medieval monastic tradition was finally severed.

Glossary

almoner: the monastic officer who distributed alms to the poor at the main gate, and maintained the almonry in the precinct.

almonry: a monastic almonry dispensed food to the poor, and provided hospitality and accommodation for pilgrims.

anchorites: religious men or women (anchoresses), who took vows to remain permanently enclosed and solitary. They were accommodated in cells (referred to as anchorages or anchorholds) attached to churches or located within churchyards.

'anticke': the Tudor fashion for foreign styles of ornament and applied decoration.

arcade: a series of arches carried on columns.

bosses: keystones that hold the vaulting ribs in place. At Norwich cathedral, many of the bosses are 'historiated', part of a narrative scheme in which each boss conveyed a story, or was one in sequence of bosses telling a story.

brattishing: ornamental cresting above a parapet or screen.

camera: a private chamber or office.

capital: the decorative top or head of a column set over the shaft.

cathedra: the bishop's throne, and the symbol of the cathedral church of the diocese.

cathedral: the mother church of the diocese, which is the official seat of the diocesan bishop. Medieval English cathedrals were either monastic (served by communities of monks) or secular (served by colleges of priests).

cathedral-priory: an institution unique to medieval England, in which a cathedral had a monastic priory attached to the cathedral church.

cellarage: space that was used for the storage of food and wine, usually located near the west range of the cloister.

cellarer: the monastic officer with responsibility for the purchase of foodstuffs and the upkeep of the kitchen. At Norwich, this role was distinct from the 'master of the cellar', the most influential officer, who was in charge of the prior's chamber, the entertainment of lay visitors and the provision of corn to the entire community, and who oversaw the kitchen, brewhouse and stables.

chamfer: an angle that is shaved off, resembling a splay.

chantry: an endowment to fund the chanting of masses or prayers for the dead.

chapter house: a room in the east range of the cloister where the monks met daily to read a chapter from the Rule of St Benedict, to undertake confession and penance, and to discuss routine administrative matters.

charnel chapel: a chapel combined with facilities for storage of charnel: the dry, disarticulated human bones that were disinterred from cemeteries in the process of digging new graves. From the Latin *carnarium*, from *caro*, meaning flesh.

clerestory: the upper storey of an aisled building that was provided with windows to light the central vessel.

clocher: a term used at Norwich cathedral to refer to the detached bell-tower or campanile; also known as *berefridus* in medieval documents.

coenobitic: a monastic vocation in which religious personnel lived as part of an organised community; from the Greek *koinobion*, meaning community.

communar and pitancer: the monastic officer who dealt with matters relating to all in common, with the exception of the specific tasks of other named officers. At Norwich, this officer was linked with major rebuilding projects.

corrodian: a secular lodger housed in a monastery, funded by a corrody, a form of pension or annuity.

dais: the raised platform at the upper end of a hall, reserved for high-ranking individuals.

dorter: the dormitory of the monks, located over the east range of the cloister.

double-pile plan: a seventeenth-century house type consisting of a rectangular block two rooms deep, with rooms separated by a passage running the full depth.

Dutch gables: curved or shaped gables with pediments.

flushwork: decoration formed of tracery and stonework patterns filled with carefully shaped flints.

foramina: a tomb-shrine that was pierced with large holes to allow pilgrims to touch the relics contained within it.

frankpledge: a system that aimed to preserve the peace by grouping men into compulsory associations of ten, with each member providing surety for the others. The view of frankpledge was the duty of seeing that these associations were observed.

garderobe: euphemism for a privy.

hermitage: a dwelling for a hermit, a religious man who followed an eremitical vocation that required isolation; from the Greek *eremos*, meaning desert.

hostiliar: the monastic officer in charge of hospitality, who maintained the guest hall.

hostry: the guest hall in the west range of the cloister.

jettied: a building with a cantilevered storey or gable.

keeled bowtell: round convex moulding with a sharp profile like the keel of ship.

lavatorium: the ritual washing place at the monks' entrance to the refectory.

locutory: the outer parlour of the monastery, located between the western end of the church and the west range, where the monks could talk with secular visitors.

misericord: a term with two distinct applications, from the Latin *misericordia*, pity or mercy. Generally used to refer to the hinged seats in the monastic choir, provided to support the monks in their long religious offices; these often had rich carvings beneath the seats. It was also a term for the dining chamber attached to the monastic infirmary (the 'table hall'), in which it was permissible to consume meat.

mullion: a vertical member dividing a window into lights.

novices: the young monks who undertook a training period between their ceremonies of clothing and profession.

obedientiary: the monk-officers of the medieval monastery, who received income from specified parts of the priory's estate in order to fund their offices.

oblates: children who entered monasteries for training and education; the practice of receiving child oblates was banned by the later twelfth century.

ogee: an S-shaped double curve (cyma).

peculiar: a church that is exempt from the jurisdiction of the diocese in which it is located. The royal peculiars of Westminster and Windsor retain exemption from civil and ecclesiastical statutory controls.

petty canons: the minor canons of the post-medieval secular cathedral, who were resident permanently in the close, and responsible for the services in the church.

pilaster: a rectangular pier projecting slightly from the face of the wall that it buttresses.

piscina: a ritual basin in which communion vessels were washed and holy water was disposed.

polychromy: decoration with several colours or tints.

prebendary: a canon of the post-medieval secular cathedrals (reformed 1539–42), who were supported financially by individual endowments called prebends. During the sixteenth and seventeenth centuries, many prebendaries were not resident in the close throughout the full year.

precentor: the monastic officer who organised church services and books.

preceptory: a monastery of the Military Orders; used particularly to refer to establishments belonging to the Templars.

Prior's Fee: areas outside the precinct that remained under the prior's jurisdiction.

pulpitum: the screen in a monastic church that divides the choir from the nave.

purlin: a horizontal piece of structural timber supporting the common rafters of a roof; clasped-purlins are held between the rafter and collar on the inner slope of the roof.

putlog hole: a small hole left in a wall resulting from the removal of a cross-piece of timber scaffolding that was used in its construction.

queen-post: two vertical members placed symmetrically on a tie-beam and directly supporting the purlins.

refectorer: the monastic officer charged with overseeing the requirements of dining in the monastic refectory, and the two smaller dining rooms in the warming house and infirmary.

rood: a cross or crucifix. The Rood screen in a monastic church marked the boundary between the ritual nave and the choir; a second screen (*pulpitum*) was located one bay further to the east.

sacrist: the monastic officer who was responsible for the upkeep of the church, including repair and replacement of church fabric, care of vessels and vestments, and the provision of candles and mats.

screens passage: a passageway across the low end of a hall defined by opposing doorways and separated from the main body of the hall by a screen.

sextry: the accommodation for the office of the sacrist (alternatively 'sacristy'), at Norwich located to the east of the cathedral church.

singing men: lesser members of the post-medieval secular cathedral, who were permanently resident in the close and responsible for performing music in church services.

slype: a word used by nineteenth-century antiquaries to refer to a passageway through a range of buildings.

solar: a private apartment.

spolia: plundered or reused materials.

strapwork: decoration resembling leather straps or fretwork, used in the sixteenth and seventeenth centuries.

***terminus ante quem*:** a phrase used to describe an archaeological context which can be deduced to derive from a period earlier than a specific date; Latin meaning 'end before which'.

tie-beam: a horizontal member connecting a pair of principal rafters.

vaulting: an arched structure over a room or space; **barrel**: a vault that springs from opposite parallel walls; **groin**: two barrel vaults intersecting at right angles; **lierne**: a ribbed vault with tiercery ribs; **quadripartite**: divided into four cells by diagonal or transverse ribs; **tierceron**: a rib that springs from the main springing-points to a boss on the ridge-rib.

voussoirs: one of a series of radiating, wedge-shaped stones used to form an arch.

warming room: a room on the ground-floor of the east range of the cloister, which was equipped with a substantial fireplace. This was the only heated space in the communal areas of the cloister.

Bibliography

PRIMARY SOURCES IN THE NORFOLK RECORD OFFICE, NORWICH

DCN 1/1–13	Obedientiary Rolls
DCN 11	Audit Books
DCN 12	Audit Papers
DCN 22	Accounts (including timber, residence repairs and extraordinary accounts)
DCN 24	Chapter Books
DCN 26	Chapter Clerks' Papers
DCN 27	Private Register (leases)
DCN 47	Ledger Books
DCN 51	Estate Rentals and Surveys
DCN 56a	Dilapidations: Houses in the Close
DCN 57	Estate Papers: the Precinct
DCN 113	Dean's Personal Papers: Suckling
DCN 115	Dean's Personal Papers: Prideaux
DCN 118	Dean's Personal Papers: Lloyd
DCN 127	Maps and Plans
DCN 128	Water-colours by David Hodgson
DCN 131	Papers of Cathedral Surveyors
DN ADR 10	Diocesan Records: Norwich Bishop's Palace
MC 186	The Papers of Arthur Bensly Whittingham

PUBLISHED PRIMARY AND SECONDARY SOURCES
AND UNPUBLISHED REPORTS

ALEXANDER, J. 1999, 'The Last Things: Representing the Unrepresentable', in F. Carey (ed.), *The Apocalypse and the Shape of Things to Come*. London: British Museum, 43–98.

ANDRÉN, A. 1999, 'Landscape and Settlement as Utopian Space', in C. Fabech and J. Ringtved (eds.), *Settlement and Landscape*. Jutland Archaeological Society, 383–93.

ANDREWS, D., Cook, A., Quant, V., and Veasey, E. A. 1981, 'The Archaeology and Topography of Nuneaton Priory', *Transactions of the Birmingham and Warwickshire Archaeol Soc* 91, 55–81.

ARIÈS, P. 1981, *The Hour of Our Death*. Harmondsworth: Penguin.

ASTON, M. 2003, 'Public Worship and Iconoclasm', in Gaimster and Gilchrist (eds.), 9–28.

ATHERTON, I. 1996, 'The Close', in Atherton et al. (eds.), 634–64.

ATHERTON, I., FERNIE, E., HARPER-BILL, C., and HASSELL SMITH, A. (eds.) 1996, *Norwich Cathedral: Church, City and Diocese, 1096–1996*. London: Hambledon.

ATHERTON, I., and MORGAN, V. 1996, 'Revolution and Retrenchment: The Cathedral, 1630–1720', in Atherton et al. (eds.), 540–75.

ATHERTON BOWEN, J. 1991, 'The Plan of St Mary's Priory, Worcester', in P. Barker and C. Guy (eds.), *Worcester Cathedral: Report of the First Annual Symposium on the Precinct*. Worcester Cathedral, 7–9.

ATHERTON BOWEN, J. 1992, 'Problems with the Reconstruction of Monastic Topography', in P. Barker and C. Guy (eds.), *Archaeology at Worcester Cathedral: Report of the Second Annual Symposium*. Worcester Cathedral, 18–21.

ATKIN, M., and EVANS, D. H. 2002, 'Excavations in Northern Conesford, in and around the Cathedral Close', in M. Atkins and D. H. Evans, 'Excavations in Norwich 1971–1978, Part III', *East Anglian Archaeology* 100, 7–67.

AYERS, B. S. 1990, 'Building a Fine City: The Provision of Flint, Mortar and Freestone in Medieval Norwich', in D. Parsons (ed.), *Stone Quarrying and Building in England, AD 43–1525*. Chichester: Phillimore, 217–27.

AYERS, B. S. 2003, *Norwich, 'A Fine City'*. Stroud: Tempus (first published 1994).

AYERS, B. S. 1996, 'The Cathedral Site before 1096', in Atherton et al. (eds.), 59–72.

AYERS, B. S., SMITH, R., and TILLYARD, M. 1988, 'The Cow Tower, Norwich: A Detailed Survey and Partial Reinterpretation', *Medieval Archaeol* 32, 184–207.

BARKER, P. 1995, 'The Refectory Undercroft', in P. Barker and C. Guy (eds.), *Archaeology at Worcester Cathedral: Report of the Fifth Annual Symposium*. Worcester Cathedral, 4–11.

BARROW, J. 1992, 'Urban Cemetery Location in the High Middle Ages', in S. Bassett (ed.), *Death in Towns, 100–1600*. Leicester: Leicester University Press, 78–100.

BASHFORD, L., and POLLARD, T. 1998, 'In the Burying Place: The Excavation of a Quaker Burial Ground', in M. Cox (ed.), *Grave Concerns: Death and Burial in England 1700–1900*. London: Council for British Archaeol Res Rep 113, 154–66.

BASKERVILLE, G. R. 1933, 'Married Clergy and Pensioned Religious in Norwich Diocese, 1555', *English Historical Review* 48, 43–64; 199–228.

BELL, D. N. 1998, 'The Siting and Size of Cistercian Infirmaries in England and Wales', in M. P. Lillich (ed.), 211–37.

BENSLY, W. T. 1908, 'The Diocese and Cathedral Church of Norwich', in H. J. Dukinfield Astley (ed.), *Memorials of Old Norfolk*. London: Bemrose & Son, 40–47.

BIDDLE, M. 1986, *Wolvesey Old Bishop's Palace, Winchester*. London: English Heritage.

BINSKI, P. 1995, *Westminster Abbey and the Plantagenets: Kingship and the Representation of Power, 1200–1400*. New Haven: Yale University Press.

BLAIR, J. 1993, 'Hall and Chamber: English Domestic Planning 1000–1250', in G. Meirion-Jones and M. Jones (eds.), *Manorial Domestic Buildings in England and Northern France*. London: Society of Antiquaries Occasional Papers 15, 1–21.

BLOMEFIELD, F. 1745 (1806), *An Essay towards a Topographical History of the County of Norfolk*, vol. 4. London: William Miller.

BLYTH, G. K. 1842, *A History of Norwich*. Norwich: Jarrold.

BOLINGBROKE, L. G. 1922 unpub., 'A Perambulation of Part of the Cathedral Precinct with Notes on its Domestic Buildings and Some of Their Inmates, 24 February 1922'. Lecture manuscript, Dean and Chapter Library, Norwich Cathedral.

BOLINGBROKE, L. G. 1922, Summary of the lecture 'A Perambulation in the Cathedral Precinct', in 'The Proceedings of the Society during the Year 1922', *Norfolk Archaeol* 21, xlvii–li.

BOND, C. J. 1989, 'Water Management in the Rural Monastery', in Gilchrist and Mytum (eds.), 83–112.

BOND, C. J. 1993, 'Water Management in the Urban Monastery', in Gilchrist and Mytum (eds.), 43–78.

BOND, C. J. 2001a, 'Production and Consumption of Food and Drink in the Medieval Monastery', in Keevil et al. (eds.), 54–87.

BOND, C. J. 2001b, 'Monastic Water Management in Great Britain: A Review', in Keevil et al. (eds.), 88–136.

BORSAY, P. 1989, *The English Urban Renaissance: Culture and Society in the Provincial Town, 1660–1770.* Oxford: Clarendon Press.

BOURDIEU, P. 1977, *Outline of a Theory of Practice.* Cambridge: Cambridge University Press.

BOWN, J. 1997, 'Excavations on the North Side of Norwich Cathedral, 1987–8', *Norfolk Archaeol* 42.4, 428–52.

BRAKSPEAR, H. 1933, 'The Abbot's House at Battle', *Archaeologia* 83, 139–66.

BRITTON, J. 1817, *Antiquarian and Architectural Memoranda Relating to Norwich Cathedral Church.* London: Longman.

BRITTON, J. 1836, *Historical and Descriptive Account of the Cathedrals of Salisbury, Norwich and Oxford: The Cathedral Antiquities*, vol. 2. London: M. A. Natalli.

BROOKE, C. 1956, 'Gregorian Reform in Action: Clerical Marriage in England, 1050–1200', *Cambridge Historical Journal* 12.1, 1–22.

BROWN, P. (ed.) 1984, *Domesday Book: Norfolk.* Chichester: Phillimore.

BROWNE, P. 1815, *The History of Norwich from the Earliest Records to the Present Time.* Norwich: Jarrold.

BROWNE, T. 1680 (1954), 'Repertorium, or Some Account of the Tombs and Monuments in the Cathedral Church of Norwich', in G. Keynes (ed.), *The Works of Sir Thomas Browne*, vol. 3. London: Faber, 121–42.

BRUCE-MITFORD, R. L. S. 1976, 'The Chapter House Vestibule Graves at Lincoln', in F. Emmison and R. Stephens (eds.), *Tribute to an Antiquary.* London: Leopard's Head Press, 127–40.

BUSTON W. 1942, 'The Monastic Infirmary, Norwich', *Norfolk Archaeol* 28, 124–32.

BUTLER, L., and GIVEN-WILSON, C. (eds.) 1979, *Medieval Monasteries of Great Britain.* London: Michael Joseph.

BYARD, S. 2000, *English Hospitals from the Conquest to the Dissolution.* Courtauld Institute of Art, University of London: Doctoral Thesis.

BYNUM, C. W. 1995, *The Resurrection of the Body in Western Christianity, 200–1336.* New York: Columbia University Press.

CALEY, J., and HUNTER, J. (eds.) 1810–34, *Valor Ecclesiasticus.* 6 vols.. London: Record Commission.

CAMILLE, M. 1992, *Image on the Edge: The Margins of Medieval Art.* London: Reaktion Books.

CAMPBELL, J. 1975, 'Norwich', in M. D. Lobel (ed.), *The Atlas of Historic Towns*, vol. 2. London: The Scolar Press.

CAMPBELL, J. 1996, 'The East Anglian Sees before the Conquest', in Atherton et al. (eds.), 3–21.

CARRUTHERS, M. 2000, *The Craft of Thought: Meditation, Rhetoric and the Making of Images, 400–1200.* Cambridge: Cambridge University Press.

CARTER, A. 1978, 'The Anglo-Saxon Origins of Norwich: The Problems and Approaches', *Anglo-Saxon England* 7, 175–204.

CARTER, E. H. 1935, *Studies in Norwich Cathedral History*. Norwich: Jarrold.

CASSIDY-WELCH, M. 2001, *Monastic Spaces and their Meanings: Thirteenth-Century English Cistercian Monasteries*. Turnhout, Belgium: Brepols.

CATTERMOLE, P. 1996, 'The Bells', in Atherton et al. (eds.), 494–504.

CATTERMOLE, P. in prep., *The Carnary College, Norwich*.

CHADD, D. 1996, 'The Medieval Customary of the Cathedral Priory', in Atherton et al. (eds.), 314–24.

CHENEY, C. R. 1936, 'Norwich Cathedral Priory in the Fourteenth Century', *Bulletin of the John Rylands Library* 20, 93–120.

CHUBB, T., and STEPHEN, G. A. 1928, *A Descriptive List of the Printed Maps of Norfolk, 1574–1916*. Norwich: Jarrold.

CLARK, J. G. (ed.) 2002, *The Religious Orders in pre-Reformation England*. Woodbridge: Boydell & Brewer.

CLAY, R. M. 1914, *The Hermits and Anchorites of England*. London: Methuen.

COBB, G. 1980, *English Cathedrals: The Forgotten Centuries*. London: Thames & Hudson.

COCKE, T. 1993, 'Ruin and Restoration: Lichfield Cathedral in the Seventeenth Century', *Medieval Art and Architecture at Lichfield Cathedral*. Brit Archaeol Assoc Conference Trans 13, 109–14.

COCKE, T., and KIDSON, P. 1993, *Salisbury Cathedral: Perspectives on the Architectural History*. London: RCHME.

COLTHORPE, M. 1989, 'Queen Elizabeth 1 and Norwich Cathedral', *Norfolk Archaeol* 40, 318–23.

COOK, G. H. 1959, *English Collegiate Churches*. London: Phoenix.

COOPER, I. M. 1937, 'Westminster Hall', *J British Archaeol Assoc* 3rd series 1, 168–228.

COPPACK, G. 1986, 'Some Descriptions of Rievaulx Abbey in 1538–9', *J British Archaeol Assoc* 139, 100–133.

COPPACK, G. 1989, 'Thornholme Priory: The Development of a Monastic Outer Court Landscape', in Gilchrist and Mytum (eds.), 185–222.

COPPACK, G. 1990, *Abbeys and Priories*, London: Batsford/English Heritage.

COPPACK, G. 1999, 'The Suppression', in Fergusson and Harrison, 175–86.

COPPACK, G. 2002, 'The Planning of Cistercian Monasteries in the Later Middle Ages: The Evidence from Fountains, Rievaulx, Sawley and Rushen', in Clark (ed.), 197–209.

CRANAGE, D. H. S. 1932, 'Eastern Chapels in the Cathedral Church of Norwich', *Antiquaries J* 12, 117–36.

CRANAGE, D. H. S. 1941, 'The "Cathedra" of the Bishop of Norwich', *Norfolk Archaeol* 27, 429–36.

CRAWFORD, S. 1997, 'Excavations at Worcester Cathedral Chapter House Lawn, 1996', in P. Barker and C. Guy (eds.), *Archaeology at Worcester: Report of the Seventh Annual Symposium*. Worcester Cathedral, 3–6.

CRAWFORD, S., and GUY, C. 2000, 'Chapter House Lawn Excavations', in C. Guy (ed.), *Archaeology at Worcester: Report of the Tenth Annual Symposium*. Worcester Cathedral, 4.

CREIGHTON, O. 2002, *Castles and Landscapes*. London: Continuum.

CROOK, J. (ed.) 1984, *The Wainscot Book: The Houses of Winchester Cathedral Close and Their Interior Decoration, 1660–1800*. Winchester: Hampshire Record Office.

CROOK, J. 1991, 'The Pilgrims' Hall, Winchester: Hammerbeams, Base Crucks and Aisle-Derivative Roof Structures', *Archaeologia* 109, 129–59.

CROSBY, E. U. 1994, *Bishop and Chapter in Twelfth-century England: A Study of the Mensa Episcopalis*. Cambridge: Cambridge University Press.

CURRIE, C. 1989, 'The Role of Fishponds in the Monastic Economy', in Gilchrist and Mytum (eds.), 147–72.

CURTEIS, T., and PAINE, T. 1992, *The Polychromy of the Norwich Cathedral Cloister Bosses: A Report for the Dean and Chapter*. London: Courtauld Institute of Art.

DE CERTEAU, M. 1984, *The Practice of Everyday Life*, trans S. Randall. Berkeley: University of California Press.

DODWELL, B. 1957, 'The Foundation of Norwich Cathedral', *Trans Royal Historical Soc* 5th series 7, 1–18.

DODWELL, B. 1996a, 'Herbert de Losinga and the Foundation', in Atherton et al. (eds.), 36–44.

DODWELL, B. 1996b, 'The Monastic Community', in Atherton et al. (eds.), 231–54.

DODWELL, B. 1996c, 'The Muniments and the Library', in Atherton et al. (eds.), 325–38.

DOGGETT, N. 2001, 'The Demolition and Conversion of Former Monastic Buildings in Post-Dissolution Herefordshire', in Keevil et al. (eds.), 165–74.

DRIVER, J. C., Rady, J., and Sparks, M. 1990, *Excavations in the Cathedral Precincts*, vol. 2: *Linacre Garden, 'Meister Ormers' and St Gabriel's Chapel*. Canterbury: Archaeology of Canterbury 4.

DUFFY, E. 1992, *The Stripping of the Altars: Traditional Religion in England 1400–1580*. London: Yale University Press.

DURKHEIM, E. 1912 (1995), *The Elementary Forms of Religious Life*, trans. K. E. Fields. New York: Free Press.

EDWARDS, K. 1967, *The English Secular Cathedrals in the Middle Ages*. Manchester: Manchester University Press.

ELIADE, M. 1959, *The Sacred and the Profane: The Nature of Religion*, trans. W. R. Trask. New York: Harcourt, Brace & Co.

ELLIOTT, D. 1999, *Fallen Bodies: Pollution, Sexuality and Demonology in the Middle Ages*. Philadelphia: University of Pennsylvania Press.

EMERY, A. 1996, *Greater Medieval Houses of England and Wales, 1300–1500*, vol. 1: *Northern England*. Cambridge: Cambridge University Press.

EMERY, A. 2000, *Greater Medieval Houses of England and Wales, 1300–1500*, vol. 2: *East Anglia, Central England and Wales*. Cambridge: Cambridge University Press.

EVANS, C., Dickens, A., and Richmond, D. A. H, 1997, 'Cloistered Communities: Archaeological and Architectural Investigations in Jesus College, Cambridge, 1988–97', *Proc Cambridge Antiq Soc* 86, 91–144.

EVANS, H. 1999, 'Report on an Archaeological Evaluation and Subsequent Watching Brief at the Former Gymnasium, Norwich School'. *Norfolk Archaeological Unit, Report no. 445*.

EVANS, S. J. A. 1961, 'Cathedral Life at Gloucester in the Early Seventeenth Century', *Trans Bristol and Gloucesters Archaeol Soc* 80, 5–15.

EWING, W. C. 1849, 'Remarks on the Boundary of the City and Hamlets of Norwich', *Norfolk Archaeol* 2, 1–10.

FAULKNER, P. A. 1970, 'Some Medieval Archiepiscopal Palaces', *Archaeol J* 127, 130–46.

FEILDEN, B. 1996, 'Restorations and Repairs after World War II', in Atherton et al. (eds.), 728–44.

FERGUSSON, P. 1986, 'The Twelfth-Century Refectories at Rievaulx and Byland Abbeys', in C. Norton and D. Park (eds.), *Cistercian Art and Architecture in the British Isles*. Cambridge: Cambridge University Press, 160–80.

FERGUSSON, P., and Harrison, S. 1999, *Rievaulx Abbey: Community, Architecture, Memory*. New Haven: Yale University Press.

FERNIE, E. 1974, 'Excavations on the Façade of Norwich Cathedral', *Norfolk Archaeol* 36.1, 72–5.

FERNIE, E. 1976, 'The Ground Plan of Norwich Cathedral and the Square Root of Two', *J Brit Archaeol Assoc* 129, 77–86.

FERNIE, E. 1977, 'The Romanesque Piers of Norwich Cathedral', *Norfolk Archaeol* 36, 383–6.

FERNIE, E. 1980, 'The Spiral Piers of Durham Cathedral', in N. Coldstream and P. Draper (eds.), *Medieval Art and Architecture at Durham Cathedral*. British Archaeol Assoc Conference Trans 3, 49–58.

FERNIE, E. 1989a, 'Archaeology and Iconography: Recent Developments in the Study of English Medieval Architecture', *Architectural History* 32, 18–29.

FERNIE, E. 1989b, Obituary of Arthur Bensly Whittingham, *Norfolk Archaeol* 40, 131.

FERNIE, E. 1993, *An Architectural History of Norwich Cathedral*. Oxford: Clarendon Press.

FERNIE, E., and Whittingham, A. B. 1972, *The Early Communar and Pitancer Rolls of Norwich Cathedral Priory with an Account of the Building of the Cloister*. Norfolk Record Society 41.

FINCH, J. 1996, 'The Monuments', in Atherton et al. (eds.), 467–93.

FINCH, J. 1996 unpub., 'The Effigy of Sir Thomas Erpingham'. A report submitted to the Norwich Cathedral Fabric Advisory Committee.

FINUCANE, R. C. 1977, *Miracles and Pilgrims: Popular Beliefs in Medieval England*. London: Dent.

FOUCAULT, M. 1979, *Discipline and Punish*. Harmondsworth: Penguin

FOWLER, J. T. 1880, 'An Account of the Excavations Made on the Site of the Chapter House of Durham Cathedral', *Archaeologia* 45, 385–404.

FOWLER, J. T. (ed.) 1902, *Rites of Durham, being a Description or Brief Declaration of All the Ancient Monuments, Rites, and Customs Belonging or Being within the Monastical Church of Durham before the Suppression*, written 1593. Surtees Society 107.

FOX, G. E. 1892, 'A Note on the Discovery of Painted Beams at the Deanery, Norwich', *Norfolk Archaeol* 11, 179–81.

FOYLE, J. 2002, 'An Archaeological Reconstruction of Thomas Wolsey's Hampton Court Palace'. Department of Archaeology, University of Reading: Doctoral Thesis.

FRANCE, J. 1998, 'The Cellarer's Domain: Evidence from Denmark', in M. P. Lillich (ed.), 1–39.

FRANKLIN, J. A. 1996, 'The Romanesque Sculpture', in Atherton et al. (eds.), 116–35.

GAIMSTER, D., and GILCHRIST, R. (eds.), 2003, *The Archaeology of Reformation, 1480–1580*, The Society for Post-Medieval Archaeology Monograph 1. Leeds: Maneys.

GAIMSTER, D., and NENK, B. 1997, 'English Households in Transition, c.1450–1550: The Ceramic Evidence', in D. Gaimster and P. Stamper (eds.), *The Age of Transition: The Archaeology of English Culture, 1400–1600*. Oxford: The Society for Medieval Archaeology Monograph 15, 171–95.

GEARY, P. J. 1994, *Living with the Dead in the Middle Ages*. Ithaca: Cornell University Press.

GEDDES, J. 1996, 'The Medieval Decorative Ironwork', in Atherton et al. (eds.), 431–42.

GEE, E. 1966, 'Discoveries in the Frater at Durham', *Archaeol J* 123, 69–78.

GEM, R. 1986, 'Lincoln Minster: Ecclesia Pulchra, Ecclesia Fortis', *Medieval Art and Architecture at Lincoln Cathedral*, Brit Archaeol Assoc Conference Trans 9, 9–28.

GEM, R. 1996, 'The Care of Cathedrals Measure 1990', in Tatton-Brown and Munby (eds.), 237–9.

GIBSON, W. 1806, 'Observations on the Remains of the Dormitory and Refectory Which Stood on the Southern Side of the Cloisters of the Cathedral Church of Norwich', *Archaeologia* 15, 326–32.

GILCHRIST, R. 1994, *Gender and Material Culture: The Archaeology of Religious Women*. London: Routledge.

GILCHRIST, R. 1994 unpub., 'An Archaeological Desk-based Assessment of Three Areas of Proposed New Development at Norwich Cathedral'. Deposited with Norfolk SMR.

GILCHRIST, R. 1995, *Contemplation and Action: The Other Monasticism*. Leicester: Leicester University Press.

GILCHRIST, R. 1996 unpub., 'A Desk-Based Assessment of the Library and Dark Entry at Norwich Cathedral in Advance of Proposed New Developments'. Deposited with Norfolk SMR.

GILCHRIST, R. 1997 unpub., 'Archaeological Report to Accompany Planning Application for Visitors' Centre at Norwich Cathedral'. Deposited with Norfolk SMR.

GILCHRIST, R. 1998 unpub., 'Norwich Cathedral Close: A Strategic Archaeological Assessment. Report to English Heritage and the Dean and Chapter of Norwich Cathedral'. 3 Vols.. Deposited with Norwich UAD and Norwich Cathedral Archive.

GILCHRIST, R. 1999, 'Norwich Cathedral: A Biography of the North Transept', *J British Archaeol Assoc* 151 (1998): 107–36.

GILCHRIST, R. 1999 unpub., 'Archaeological Assessment of the South Transept, to Accompany Proposal for New Song School'. Deposited with Norfolk SMR.

GILCHRIST, R. 1999 unpub., 'Archaeological Assessment for Number 64, The Close (with Implications for Numbers 63 & 65 The Close)'. Deposited with Norfolk SMR.

GILCHRIST, R. 2002, 'Norwich Cathedral Tower and Spire: Recording and Analysis of a Cathedral's Longue Durée', *Archaeol J* 158 (2001), 291–324.

GILCHRIST, R. 2002 unpub., 'Norwich School Refectory Redevelopment: Archaeological Impact Assessment'. A Report for the Norwich School.

GILCHRIST, R., and MYTUM, H. (eds.) 1989, *The Archaeology of Rural Monasteries*. Oxford: British Archaeol Rep British Series 203.

GILCHRIST, R., and MYTUM, H. (eds.) 1993, *Advances in Monastic Archaeology*. Oxford: British Archaeol Rep British Series 227.

GILCHRIST, R., and OLIVA, M. 1993, *Religious Women in Medieval East Anglia: History and Archaeology, c.1100–1540*. Studies in East Anglian History 1. Norwich: Centre for East Anglian Studies.

GILCHRIST, R., and SLOANE, B. 2005 in press, *Requiem: The Medieval Monastic Cemetery in Britain*. London: Museum of London Archaeology Service Monograph.

GILES, K. 2000a, *An Archaeology of Social Identity: Guildhalls in York, c.1350–1630*. Oxford: British Archaeol Rep British Series 315.

GILES, K. 2000b, 'Marking Time? A 15th-Century Liturgical Calendar in the Wall Paintings of Pickering Parish Church', *Church Archaeology* 4, 42–51.

GILES, K. 2003, 'Reforming Corporate Charity: Guilds and Fraternities in Pre- and Post-Reformation York', in Gaimster and Gilchrist (eds.), 325–40.

GILL, M. 2003, 'The Chapter House Apocalypse Panels', in Rylatt and Mason, 83–9.

GIROUARD, M. 1978, *Life in the English Country House*. London: Yale University Press.

GODFREY, W. H. 1952, 'English Cloister Lavatories as Independent Structures', *Archaeol J* 106, 91–7.

GOODALL, J. 2001, 'How the Monks of Fountains Sat Down to Eat', *Country Life* 29 Nov. 2001, 58–61.

GORDON, B., and MARSHALL, P. (eds.), 2000. *The Place of the Dead: Death and Remembrance in Late Medieval and Early Modern Europe*. Cambridge: Cambridge University Press.

GOULBOURN, E. M. 1884, 'The Confessio or Relic Chapel', *Norfolk Archaeol* 9, 275–81.

GRAVES, C. P. 2000, *The Form and Fabric of Belief: An Archaeology of the Lay Experience of Religion in Medieval Norfolk and Devon*. Oxford: British Archaeol Rep British Series 311.

GREATREX, J. 1991, 'Monk Students from Norwich Cathedral Priory at Oxford and Cambridge, c.1300 to 1530', *English Historical Review* 106, 555–83.

GREATREX, J. 1993, 'St Swithun's Priory in the Later Middle Ages', in J. Crook (ed.), *Winchester Cathedral: Nine Hundred Years, 1093–1993*. Chichester: Phillimore, 139–66.

GREATREX, J. 1994, 'The Almonry School at Norwich Cathedral Priory in the Thirteenth and Fourteenth Centuries', in D. Wood (ed.), *The Church and Childhood*. Oxford: Blackwell, 169–81.

GREATREX, J. 1998, 'The Layout of the Monastic Church, Cloister and Precinct of Worcester: Evidence in the Written Records', in C. Guy (ed.), *Archaeology at Worcester: Report of the Eighth Annual Symposium*. Worcester Cathedral, 12–18.

GREATREX, J. 2002, 'Horoscopes and Healing at Norwich Cathedral Priory in the Later Middle Ages', in C. M. Barron and J. Stratford (eds.), *The Church and Learning in Later Medieval Society: Essays in Honour of R. B. Dobson*, Donnington: Shaun Tyas, 170–77.

GREENE, J. P. 1992, *Medieval Monasteries*. Leicester: Leicester University Press.

GRENVILLE, J. 1997, *Medieval Housing*. London: Continuum.

GUNN, J. 1879, 'Saxon Remains in the Cloisters of Norwich Cathedral', *Norfolk Archaeol* 8, 1–9.

GUY, C. 1994, 'Recent Archaeological Investigations', in P. Barker and C. Guy (eds.), *Archaeology at Worcester Cathedral: Report of the Fourth Annual Symposium*, Worcester Cathedral, 2–5.

HALL, J. 1643 (1837), 'Hard Measure', in P. Hall (ed.), *The Works of Joseph Hall*. 12 vols.. Oxford: Oxford University Press.

HALL, R., and STOCKER, D. (eds.), 2005 in press, *Cantate Domino: Vicars Choral at English Cathedrals*. Oxford: Oxbow.

HALLAM, H. E. 1984, 'The Climate of Eastern England, 1250–1350', *Agricultural History Review* 32, 124–32.

HARDING, V. 2002, *The Dead and the Living in Paris and London, 1500–1670*. Cambridge: Cambridge University Press.

HARDING, V. 2003, 'Choices and Changes: Death, Burial and the English Reformation', in Gaimster and Gilchrist (eds.), 386–98.

HARRIES, R., CATTERMOLE, P., and MACKINTOSH, P. 1991, *A History of the Norwich School*. Norwich: Friends of Norwich School.

HARROD, H. 1857, *Gleanings amongst the Castles and Convents of Norfolk*. Norwich: Jarrold.

HARROD, H. 1864, 'Excavations Made in the Gardens of the Bishop's Palace, Norwich', *Norfolk Archaeol* 6, 27–37.

HARVEY, B. 1993, *Living and Dying in England 1100–1540: The Monastic Experience*. Oxford: Clarendon Press.

HARVEY, B. 2002, 'A Novice's Life at Westminster Abbey in the Century before the Dissolution', in Clark (ed.), 51–73.

HARVEY, D. 2000, 'Continuity, Authority and the Place of Heritage in the Medieval World', *J of Historical Geography* 26.1, 47–59.

HAYES, D. M. 2003, *Body and Sacred Place in Medieval Europe, 1100–1389*. London: Routledge.

HEAL, F. 1984, 'The Idea of Hospitality in Early Modern England', *Past & Present* 102, 66–93.

HEIGHWAY, C. 1999 unpub., 'Gloucester Cathedral and Precinct: An Archaeological Assessment'.

HENDERSON, C. G., and Bidwell, P. T. 1982, 'The Saxon Minster at Exeter', in S. M. Pearce (ed.), *The Early Church in Western Britain and Ireland*, Oxford: British Archaeol Rep British Series 102, 151–69.

HEYWOOD, S. 1996, 'The Romanesque Building', in Atherton et al. (eds.), 73–115.

HISCOCK, N. 1999, 'Making Sense of √2', *AVISTA Forum* 12.1, 20–27.

HISCOCK, N. 2002, 'A Schematic Plan for Norwich Cathedral', in N. Wu (ed.), *Ad Quadratum*. Aldershot: Ashgate, 83–121.

HOLLENGREEN, L. H. 2004, 'From Medieval Sacred Place to Modern Secular Space: Changing Perspectives on the Cathedral and Town of Chartres', in D. Arnold and A. Ballantyne (eds.), *Architecture as Experience: Radical Change in Spatial Practice*. London: Routledge, 81–108.

HOLT, R., and BAKER, N. 1991, 'The Anglo-Saxon and Medieval Precinct', in P. Barker and C. Guy (eds.), *Worcester Cathedral: Report of the First Annual Symposium on the Precinct*. Worcester Cathedral, 13–16.

HOLTON-KRAYENBUHL, A., Cocke, T., and Malim, T. 1989, 'Ely Cathedral Precincts: The North Range', *Proc Cambridge Antiq Soc* 78, 47–69.

HOLTON-KRAYENBUHL, A. 1997, 'The Infirmary Complex at Ely', *Archaeol J* 154, 118–72.

HOLTON-KRAYENBUHL, A. 1999, 'The Prior's Lodging at Ely', *Archaeol J* 156, 294–341.

HORN, W., and Born, E. 1979, *The Plan of St Gall*. 3 vols.. Berkeley: University of California Press.

HOULBROOKE, R. 1996, 'Refoundation and Reformation, 1538–1628', in Atherton et al. (eds.), 507–539.

HOWARD, M. 1987, *The Early Tudor Country House: Architecture and Politics, 1490–1550*. London: George Philip.

HOWARD, M. 2003, 'Recycling the Monastic Fabric: Beyond the Act of Dissolution', in Gaimster and Gilchrist (eds.), 221–34.

JAMES, M. R. 1911, *The Sculptured Bosses in the Cloisters of Norwich Cathedral*. Norwich: Norfolk and Norwich Archaeological Society.

JANSON, V. 1998, 'Architecture and Community in Medieval Monastic Dormitories', in M. P. Lillich (ed.), 59–94.

JESSOPP, A. (ed.) 1888, *Visitations of the Diocese of Norwich, AD 1492–1532*. Camden Society new series 43.

JESSOPP, A., and JAMES, M. R. (eds.) 1896, *The Life and Miracles of St William of Norwich, by Thomas Monmouth*. Cambridge: Cambridge University Press.

JOHNSON, M. 2002, *Behind the Castle Gate: From Medieval to Renaissance*. London: Routledge.

KEEVIL, G., ASTON, M., and HALL, T. (eds.), 2001, *Monastic Archaeology*. Oxford: Oxbow.

KING, D. J. 1996, 'The Panel Paintings and Stained Glass', in Atherton et al. (eds.), 410–30.

KIRKHAM, A. 2001 unpub., 'Condition Report on the Wall Paintings, 63–65 The Close, Norwich, Norfolk'.

KLEINSCHMIDT, H. 2000, *Understanding the Middle Ages: The Transformation of Ideas and Attitudes in the Medieval World*. Woodbridge: Boydell & Brewer.

KLUKAS, A. W. 1984, 'Liturgy and Architecture: Deerhurst Priory as an Expression of the Regularis Concordia', *Viator* 15, 81–106.

KNOWLES, D., and HADCOCK, R. N. 1971, *Medieval Religious Houses in England and Wales*. London: Longman.

KRAUTHEIMER, R., CORBETT, S., and FRAZER, A. F. 1977, *Corpus basilicarum christianarum Romae*, vol. 5: *Vatican City*. Rome: Pontificio Instituto di Archeologia Christiana.

LAMBRICK, G. 1985, 'Further Excavations of the Second Site of the Dominican Priory, Oxford', *Oxoniensia* 50, 131–206.

LARSSON, S., and SAUNDERS. T. 1997, 'Order and Architecture in the Age of Transition: A Social Analysis of the Archbishop's Palace at Trondheim, Norway', *Norwegian Archaeological Review* 30.2, 79–102.

LAWRENCE, C. H. 1984, *Medieval Monasticism*. London: Longman.

LEECH, R., and McWHIRR, A.D. 1982, 'Excavations at St John's Hospital, Cirencester, 1971 and 1976', *Bristol and Gloucesters Archaeol Soc Trans* 100, 191–209.

LEFEBVRE, H. 1974 (1991), *The Production of Space*, trans. D. Nicholson-Smith. Oxford: Blackwell.

LEHMBERG, S. E. 1988, *The Reformation of Cathedrals: Cathedrals in English Society, 1485–1603*. Princeton: Princeton University Press.

LEHMBERG, S. E. 1996, *Cathedrals Under Siege: Cathedrals in English Society, 1600–1700*. Exeter: Exeter University Press.

L'ESTRANGE, J. 1864, 'Description of a Chamber Formerly Adjoining the Jesus Chapel of the Cathedral', *Norfolk Archaeol* 6, 177–85.

L'ESTRANGE, J. 1883, 'The Clocher of Norwich Cathedral', *Norfolk Antiquarian Miscellany*, 1st series 2, 149–58.

LIDDIARD, R 1999, 'Castle Rising, Norfolk: A "Landscape of Lordship"?', *Anglo-Norman Studies* 22, 169–86.

LILLICH, M. P. (ed.) 1998, *Studies in Cistercian Art and Architecture*, vol. 5, (Cistercian Studies 167). Kalamazoo, Michigan: Cistercian Publications.

LUARD, H. R. (ed.) 1859, 'Bartholomew Cotton', *Historia Anglicana*, Rolls Series 16.

McALEER, J. P. 1966, 'The Romanesque Façade of Norwich Cathedral', *Journal of the Society of Architectural Historians* 25, 136–40.

McALEER, J. P. 1993, 'The Façade of Norwich Cathedral: The Nineteenth-Century Restorations', *Norfolk Archaeol* 41.4, 381–409.

McALEER, J. P. 2001, 'The Tradition of Detached Bell Towers at Cathedral and Monastic Churches in Medieval England and Scotland (1066–1539)', *J British Archaeol Assoc* 154, 54–83.

McCann, J. M. 1952, *The Rule of St Benedict*. London: Burns & Oates.

McNamara, J. 1999, 'An Unresolved Syllogism: The Search for a Christian Gender System', in J. Murray (ed.), *Conflicted Identities and Multiple Masculinities: Men in the Medieval West*. London: Garland, 1–24.

Macnaughton-Jones, J. T. 1969, 'Saint Ethelbert's Gate, Norwich', *Norfolk Archaeol* 34, 74–84.

Margeson, S. 1993, *Norwich Households: Medieval and Post-Medieval Finds from Norwich Survey Excavations, 1971–8*. Gressenhall: East Anglian Archaeology 58.

Martindale, A. 1995, 'Patrons and Minders: The Intrusion of the Secular into Sacred Spaces in the Late Middle Ages', in D. Wood (ed.), *The Church and the Arts*, Studies in Church History 28. Oxford: Blackwell, 143–78.

Mayes, P. 2002, *Excavations at the Templar Preceptory at South Witham, Lincolnshire, 1965–67*. Society for Medieval Archaeology Monograph no. 19. Leeds: Maneys.

Marks, R. 2004, *Image and Devotion in Late Medieval England*. Stroud: Sutton.

Markuson, K. W. 1980, 'Recent investigations in the East Range of the Cathedral Monastery, Durham', in *Medieval Art and Architecture at Durham Cathedral*. British Archaeol Assoc Conference Trans 3, 37–48.

Metters, G. A. 1985, *The Parliamentary Survey of Dean and Chapter Properties in and around Norwich in 1649*. Norfolk Record Society 51.

Meyvaert, P. 1973, 'The Medieval Monastic Claustrum', *Gesta* 12, 53–9.

Miller, M. 1995, 'From Episcopal to Communal Palace: Places and Power in Northern Italy (1000–1250)', *Journal of the Society of Architectural Historians* 54.2, 175–85.

Moorhouse, S. 1993, 'Pottery and Glass in the Medieval Monastery', in Gilchrist and Mytum (eds.), 127–48.

Morant, R. W. 1995, *The Monastic Gatehouse and Other Types of Portal of Medieval Religious Houses*. Lewes: Sussex.

Morris, R. 1996, 'The Archaeological Study of Cathedrals in England, 1800–2000: A Review and Speculation', in Tatton-Brown and Munby (eds.), 1–7.

Morris, R. K. 1978, 'Worcester Nave: From Decorated to Perpendicular', *Medieval Art and Architecture at Worcester Cathedral*. British Archaeol Assoc Conference Trans 1, 116–43.

Morris, R. K. 2000, 'Architectural Terracotta Decoration in Tudor England', in P. Lindley and T. Frangenberg (eds.), *Secular Sculpture 1300–1550*. Stamford: Shaun Tyas, 179–210.

Morris, R. K. 2003, 'Monastic Architecture: Destruction and Reconstruction', in Gaimster and Gilchrist (eds.), 235–51.

Morrison, S. S. 2000, *Women Pilgrims in Late Medieval England: Private Piety as Public Performance*. London: Routledge.

Munby, J., and Fletcher, J. 1983, 'Carpentry in the Cathedral Close at Winchester', *Medieval Art and Architecture at Winchester*, British Archaeol Assoc Conference Trans 6, 101–11.

Myers, A. R. (ed.) 1969, *English Historical Documents*, vol. 4: *1327–1485*. London: Eyre & Spottiswoode.

Neale, J. M., and Webb, B. 1843, *The Symbolism of Churches and Church Ornaments: A Translation of the First Book of the 'Rationale Divinorum Officiorum', Written by William Durandus*. Leeds: T. W. Green.

Newman, J. 1976, *The Buildings of England: West Kent and the Weald*. Harmondsworth: Penguin.

NEWMAN, J. 1969, *The Buildings of England: North East and East Kent*. Harmondsworth: Penguin.

NILSON, B. 1998, *Cathedral Shrines of Medieval England*. Woodbridge: Boydell & Brewer.

NOBLE, C. 1997, *Norwich Cathedral Priory Gardeners' Accounts, 1329–1530*. Norfolk Record Society 61, 1–93.

NOBLE, C. 2000, 'Spiritual Practice and the Designed Landscape: Monastic Precinct Gardens', *Studies in the History of Gardens and Designed Landscapes* 20, 197–205.

NOBLE, C. 2001, 'Aspects of Life at Norwich Cathedral Priory in the Later Medieval Period'. Department of History, University of East Anglia: Doctoral Thesis.

NORTHAMPTONSHIRE ARCHAEOLOGY 2002, *Geophysical Survey at Norwich School Playing Fields, Norwich, Norfolk*.

NORTHAMPTONSHIRE ARCHAEOLOGY 2004, *Norwich Lower School Playing Fields: Archaeological Watching Brief*.

NORTON, C. 1994, 'The Buildings of St Mary's York and Their Destruction', *Antiquaries J* 74, 256–88.

ORME, N. 1986, *Exeter Cathedral as It Was, 1050–1550*. Exeter: Devon Books.

ORME, N. 1991, 'The Charnel Chapel at Exeter Cathedral', *Medieval Art and Architecture at Exeter Cathedral*. British Archaeol Assoc Conference Trans 11, 162–71.

PAINE & STEWART, 2004, 'Norwich Cathedral: Examination of the Wall Paintings in the Cloister Walks'. Report for the Dean and Chapter.

PANTIN, W. A. 1962, 'Medieval English Town-House Plans', *Medieval Archaeol* 6–7, 202–39.

PANTIN, W. A., and ROUSE, E. C. 1955, 'The Golden Cross, Oxford', *Oxoniensia* 20, 46–89.

PARK, D. 1987, 'The Wall Paintings of the Holy Sepulchre Chapel', in *Medieval Art and Architecture at Winchester Cathedral*. British Archaeol Assoc Conference Trans 6, 38–62.

PARK, D. 1995, 'The Medieval Polychromy at Worcester Cathedral', in. P. Barker and C. Guy (eds.), *Archaeology at Worcester Cathedral: Report of the Fifth Annual Symposium*. Worcester Cathedral, 6–12.

PARK, D. 1998, 'Rediscovered 14th-Century Sculptures from the Guesten Hall', in C. Guy (ed.), *Archaeology at Worcester Cathedral: Report of the Eighth Annual Symposium*. Worcester Cathedral, 18–21.

PARK, D., and HOWARD, H. 1996, 'The Medieval Polychromy', in Atherton et al. (eds.), 379–409.

PEARSON, S. 2005 in press, 'Rural and Urban Houses, 1100–1500: "Urban Adaptation" Reconsidered', in K. Giles and C. Dyer (eds.), *Town and Country in the Middle Ages: Contrasts and Interconnections, 1100–1500*. Society for Medieval Archaeology Monograph 22.

PENN, K. 1999, 'The Science Block and Former Gymnasium, Norwich School: An Archaeological Impact Assessment'. *Norfolk Archaeological Unit, Report no. 419*.

PERCIVAL, J. W. 2001. 'Archaeological Investigations at Nos 64 and 63/65 The Close, Norwich'. *Norfolk Archaeological Unit, Report no. 631*.

PEVSNER, N. 1961, *The Buildings of England: Northamptonshire*. Harmondsworth: Penguin.

PEVSNER, N., and HUBBARD, E. 1971, *The Buildings of England: Cheshire*. Harmondsworth: Penguin.

PEVSNER, N., rev. E. Williamson 1983, *The Buildings of England: County Durham*. Harmondsworth: Penguin.

PEVSNER, N., and WILSON, W. 1997, *The Buildings of England: Norfolk*, vol. 1: *Norwich and the North-East* (2nd edn). Harmondsworth: Penguin.

PHILLPOTS, C. 2003, 'The Houses of Henry VIII's Courtiers in London', in Gaimster and Gilchrist (eds.), 299–309.

PIERCE, S. R. (ed.) 1965, *John Adey Repton and Norwich Cathedral at the End of the Eighteenth Century*. Farnborough: Gregg Press.

POSTLES, D. 1996, 'Monastic Burial of Non-Patronal Lay Benefactors', *J Ecclesiastical History* 47, 621–37.

POUND, J. 1988, *Tudor and Stuart Norwich*. Chichester: Phillimore.

PUREY-CUST, A. 1895, *Our English Minsters*. London: Isbister & Co. Ltd.

RCHME 1924, *An Inventory of the Historical Monuments in London*, vol. 1: *Westminster Abbey*. London: HMSO.

RCHME 1993, *Salisbury: The Houses of the Close*. London: HMSO.

RADFORD, C. A. R. 1959, 'The Bishop's Throne of Norwich Cathedral', *Archaeol J* 116, 115–32.

RADY, J., TATTON-BROWN, T., and ATHERTON BOWEN, J., 1991, 'The Archbishop's Palace, Canterbury', *J Brit Archaeol Assoc* 144, 1–60.

RAMM, H. G. 1971, 'The Tombs of Archbishops Walter de Gray (1216–55) and Godfrey de Ludham (1258–65) in York Minster, and Their Contents', *Archaeologia* 103, 101–47.

RAWCLIFFE, C. 1995, *The Hospitals of Medieval Norwich*. Studies in East Anglian History 2. Norwich: Centre of East Anglian Studies.

RAWCLIFFE, C. 1999, *Medicine for the Soul: The Life, Death and Resurrection of an English Medieval Hospital*. Stroud: Alan Sutton.

RAWCLIFFE, C. 2002, '"On the Threshold of Eternity": Care for the Sick in East Anglian Monasteries', in C. Harper-Bill, C. Rawcliffe and R. G. Wilson (eds.), *East Anglia's History: Studies in Honour of Norman Scarfe*. Woodbridge: Boydell & Brewer, 41–72.

REPTON, J. A. 1806, 'Description of the Ancient Building at Norwich, which is the Subject of the Preceding Paper', *Archaeologia* 15, 333–7.

REYNAURD, J.-F., and SAPIN, C. 1994, 'La Place du quartier canonial dans la ville', in J.-C. Picard (ed.), *Les Chanoines dans la ville: Recherches sur la topographie des quartiers cononiaux en France; De l'archéologie à l'histoire*. Paris: De Boccard. Cited in Hollengreen 2004, p. 94.

RODWELL, W. 1986, 'Anglo-Saxon Church Building: Aspects of Design and Construction', in L. A. S. Buter and R. Morris (eds.), *The Anglo-Saxon Church*. London: Council for British Archaeol Res Rep, 156–75.

RODWELL, W. 2001, *Wells Cathedral: Excavations and Structural Studies, 1978–93*. London: English Heritage.

ROSE, M. 1996, 'The Vault Bosses', in Atherton et al. (eds.), 363–78.

ROSE, M., and HEDGECOE, J. 1997, *Stories in Stone: The Medieval Roof Carvings of Norwich Cathedral*. London: Thames & Hudson.

ROSE, M. 1999, *The Norwich Apocalypse*. Norwich: Centre of East Anglian Studies.

ROSE, M. 2003, *The Misericords of Norwich Cathedral*. Dereham: The Larks Press.

ROSENWEIN, B. H. 1999, *Negotiating Space: Power, Restraint and Privileges of Immunity in Early Medieval Europe*. Manchester: Manchester University Press.

ROWELL, R. 2000, 'The Archaeology of Late Monastic Hospitality'. Department of Archaeology, University of York: Doctoral Thesis.

RUSHTON, N. S. 2002, 'Spatial Aspects of the Almonry Site and the Changing Priorities of Poor Relief at Westminster Abbey, c.1290–1540', *Architectural History* 45, 66–91.

RUSSELL, C. 1990, *The Causes of the English Civil War*. Oxford: Clarendon Press.

RYE, W. 1883, 'The Riot between the Monks and the Citizens of Norwich in 1272', *Norfolk Antiquarian Miscellany*, 1st series 2, 17–89.

RYE, W. 1904, *Taste and Want of Taste in Norwich: A Lecture by Walter Rye*. Norwich: Gibbs & Waller.

RYE, W. 1906, 'The Precincts of Norwich Cathedral', *Norfolk Antiquarian Miscellany* 2nd series 1, 48–51.

RYLATT, M., and MASON, P. 2003, *The Archaeology of the Medieval Cathedral and Priory of St Mary, Coventry*. Coventry: Coventry City Council.

ST JOHN HOPE, W. H. 1897, 'Notes on the Benedictine Abbey of St Peter at Gloucester', *Records of Gloucester Cathedral* 3 (1885–97), 90–131.

ST JOHN HOPE, W. H. 1899, 'Notes on Recent Discoveries in the Cathedral Church of Norwich', *Antiquaries J* 2nd series 17, 304–10, 353–63.

ST JOHN HOPE, W. H. 1900, *The Architectural History of the Cathedral Church and Monastery of St Andrew at Rochester*. London: Mitchell & Hughes.

ST JOHN HOPE, W. H. 1910, 'The Site of the Saxon Cathedral Church of Wells', *Archaeol J* 67, 223–34.

ST JOHN HOPE, W. H., and Bensly, W. T. 1901, 'Recent Discoveries in the Cathedral Church of Norwich', *Norfolk Archaeol* 14, 105–27.

SAUNDERS, H. W. 1930, *An Introduction to the Obediential and Manor Rolls of Norwich Cathedral Priory*. Norwich: Jarrold.

SAUNDERS, H. W. 1932a, *A History of Norwich Grammar School*, Norwich: Jarrold.

SAUNDERS, H. W. 1932b, 'Gloriana in 1578', *Friends of Norwich Cathedral Third Annual Report*, 12–19.

SAUNDERS, H. W. 1939, *The First Register of Norwich Cathedral Priory*. Norfolk Record Society 11.

SAYERS, F. 1806, 'Notices Concerning the Dormitory of the Cathedral-Monastery of Norwich', *Archaeologia* 15, 311–14.

SCHOFIELD, J. 1994, *Medieval London Houses*. New Haven: Yale University Press.

SCHOFIELD, J. 2003, 'Some Aspects of the Reformation of Religious Space in London, 1540–1660', in Gaimster and Gilchrist (eds.), 310–24.

SCRIBNER, R. W. 1990, 'The Impact of the Reformation on Daily Life', in G. Jaritz (ed.), *Mensch und Objekt im Mittelalter und in der Frühen Neuzeit: Leben – Alltag – Kultur*. Vienna: Österreichische Akademie der Wissenschaften, 315–43.

SEKULES, V. 1980, 'The Ethelbert Gate', *Medieval Sculpture from Norwich Cathedral*, Norwich: Sainsbury Centre for the Visual Arts, 30–35.

SEKULES, V. 1996, 'The Gothic Sculpture', in Atherton et al. (eds.), 197–209.

SEKULES, V. 2001, *Medieval Art*. Oxford: Oxford University Press.

SEKULES, V. 2004 unpub., 'Historiated Cloisters in the Late Middle Ages'. Oxford Conference: The Medieval Cloister in England and Wales.

SHAPIRO, M. 1985, *The Sculpture of Moissac*. New York: Thames & Hudson.

SHELBY, L. 1976, 'Monastic Patrons and Their Architects: A Case Study of the Contract for the Monks' Dormitory at Durham', *Gesta* 15, 91–6.

SHERLOCK, D. A., and WOODS, H. 1988, *St Augustine's Abbey: Report on Excavations, 1960–78*, Kent Archaeol Soc Monograph Series 4.

SHINNERS, J. R. 1988, 'The Veneration of Saints at Norwich Cathedral in the Fourteenth Century', *Norfolk Archaeol* 40, 135–44.

SIMPKINS, M. E. 1906, 'Ecclesiastical History', in W. Page (ed.), *A History of the County of Norfolk*, vol. 2. Victoria History of the Counties of England, 213–314.

SIMS, T. 1996, 'Aspects of Heraldry and Patronage', in Atherton et al. (eds.), 451–66.

SLOANE, B. 2003, 'Tenements in London's Monasteries, c.1450–1540', in Gaimster and Gilchrist (eds.), 290–98.

SMITH, R., and CARTER, A. 1983, 'Function and Site: Aspects of Norwich Buildings before 1700', *Vernacular Architecture* 14, 5–18.

SMITH, R. 1996 unpub., 'Description of Sites of the Former Guest Hall and Refectory, Norwich Cathedral'. Dean and Chapter Archive.

SMITH, R. 1999 unpub., 'The Chamber above the Erpingham Gate, Norwich Cathedral'. Dean and Chapter Archive.

SNAPE, M. G. 1980, 'Documentary Evidence for the Building of Durham Cathedral and Its Monastic Buildings', in *Medieval Art and Architecture at Durham Cathedral*. British Archaeol Assoc Conference Trans 3, 20–36.

SODEN, I. 2003, 'The Conversion of Former Monastic Buildings to Secular Use: The Case of Coventry', in Gaimster and Gilchrist (eds.), 280–89.

SPARKS, M., and TATTON-BROWN, T. 1989, '19 The Precincts', *Canterbury Cathedral Chronicle* 83, 23–8.

STEWART, D. J. 1875, 'Notes on Norwich Cathedral: The Cloisters (from Memoranda by the late Rev. Professor Willis)', *Archaeol J* 32, 16–47.

STOCKER, D. 2004, 'The Two Early Castles of Lincoln', in P. Lindley (ed.), *The Early History of Lincoln Castle*. Lincoln: Occasional Papers in Lincolnshire History and Archaeology 12, 9–22.

STOCKER, D. 2005 in press, 'The Quest for One's Own Front Door: Housing the Vicars Choral at the English Cathedrals', *Vernacular Architecture* 37.

STOCKER, D., and EVERSON, P. 2003, 'The Straight and Narrow Way: Fenland Causeways and the Conversion of the Landscape in the Witham Valley, Lincolnshire', in M. Carver (ed.), *The Cross Goes North: Processes of Conversion in Northern Europe, AD 300–1300*. York: York Medieval Press, 271–88.

STOCKER, D., and VINCE, A. 1997, 'The Early Norman Castle at Lincoln and a Re-evaluation of the Original West Tower of Lincoln Cathedral', *Medieval Archaeol* 41, 223–33.

STONE, R., and APPLETON-FOX, N. 1996, *A View from Hereford's Past: A Report on Archaeological Excavation of Hereford Cathedral Close in 1992*. Hereford: Logaston Press.

STOPFORD, J. 1993, 'The Potential for Studies of Medieval Tiles', in Gilchrist and Mytum (eds.), 87–105.

STRATASCAN 1995, 'A Report on Geophysical Survey carried out at Norwich Cathedral'. Archive of Norwich Cathedral.

STRATASCAN 2003, 'A Report on Ground Probing Radar Survey at Norwich Cathedral'. Archive of Norwich Cathedral.

STRATFORD, N. 1978, 'Notes on the Norman Chapter House at Worcester', *Medieval Art and Architecture at Worcester Cathedral*. British Archaeol Assoc Conference Trans 1, 51–70.

TAIGEL, A. 1990, 'The Early Geometric Garden in Norfolk, c.1550–c.1730', in T. Williamson and A. Taigel (eds.), *Gardens in Norfolk*. Norwich: Centre of East Anglian Studies, 7–18.

TANNER, N. 1984, *The Church in Late Medieval Norwich, 1370–1532*. Toronto: Pontifical Institute of Mediaeval Studies.

TANNER, N. 1996, 'The Cathedral and the City', in Atherton et al. (eds.), 255–80.

TATTON-BROWN, T. 1984, 'Three Great Benedictine Houses in Kent: Their Buildings and Topography', *Archaeologia Cantiana* 100, 171–88.

TATTON-BROWN, T. 1989, *Great Cathedrals of Britain*. London: BBC Books.

TATTON-BROWN, T. 1991, 'The Buildings and Topography of St Augustine's Abbey, Canterbury', *J Brit Archaeol Assoc* 144, 61–91.

TATTON-BROWN, J. 1993, 'Building stone of Winchester Cathedral', in J. Crook (ed.), *Winchester Cathedral: Nine Hundred Years, 1093–1993*. Chichester: Phillimore, 57–68.

TATTON-BROWN, T. 1994, 'The Buildings of the Bishop's Palace and the Close', in M. Hobbs (ed.), *Chichester Cathedral: An Historical Survey*. Chichester: Phillimore, 225–46.

TATTON-BROWN, T., and MUNBY, J. (eds.) 1996, *The Archaeology of Cathedrals*. Oxford: University Committee for Archaeology Monograph 42.

TAYLOR, H., and TAYLOR, J. 1965, *Anglo-Saxon Architecture*. Vol. 1. Cambridge: Cambridge University Press.

THOMAS, P. 2002 unpub., 'The Opening of a Blocked Cupboard in the South Range of Norwich Cathedral Cloister'. Dean and Chapter Archive.

THOMAS, P. 2003 unpub., 'St Ethelbert Gate, Norwich Cathedral: A Report on the Standing Archaeology and Current Repairs'. Dean and Chapter Archive.

THOMAS, R. 1999, 'Feasting at Worcester Cathedral in the 17th Century: A Zooarchaeological and Historical Approach', *Archaeol J* 156, 342–58.

THOMPSON, M. W. 1995, *The Medieval Hall*. Aldershot: Scolar Press.

THOMPSON, M. W. 1996, 'Robert Willis and the Study of Medieval Architecture', in Tatton-Brown and Munby (eds.), 153–64.

THOMPSON, M. W. 1998, *Medieval Bishops' Houses in England and Wales*. Aldershot: Ashgate.

THOMPSON, M. W. 2001, *Cloister, Abbot and Precinct*. Stroud: Tempus.

THOMSON, D. 1980, 'Moulded or Stamped Brick', in *Medieval Sculpture from Norwich Cathedral*. Norwich: Sainsbury Centre for the Visual Arts, 40–44.

TILLYARD, M. 1987, 'The Documentary Evidence', in B. Ayers, 'Excavations at St Martin-at-Palace Plain, 1981', *East Anglian Archaeology* 37, 134–50.

TOLHURST, J. B. 1948, *The Customary of the Cathedral Priory Church of Norwich*. Henry Bradshaw Society 82.

TOULMIN SMITH, L. (ed.) 1870, *English Gilds*. Early English Text Society Original Series 40.

TRACY, C. 1990, *English Gothic Choir Stalls, 1400–1540*. Woodbridge: Boydell & Brewer.

TRINGHAM, N. J. 1990, 'The Cathedral and the Close', in M. W. Greenslade (ed.), *Victoria County History of Staffordshire*, vol. 14: *Lichfield*, Oxford: Oxford University Press.

TRISTRAM, E. W. 1935, 1936, 1937, 'The Cloister Bosses, Norwich Cathedral', *Friends of Norwich Cathedral Sixth [/Seventh/Eighth] Annual Report*, 6–13; 6–21; 12–49.

TRISTRAM, E. W. 1938, 'The Erpingham Gate', *Friends of Norwich Cathedral Ninth Annual Report* 9, 40–46.

TURNER, V. W. 1969, *The Ritual Process: Structure and Anti-Structure*. London: Routledge.

VEREY, D., and BROOKS, A. 2002, *The Buildings of England: Gloucestershire*, vol. 2: *The Vale and the Forest of Dean*. New Haven and London: Yale University Press.

VCH NORTHANTS, Victoria History of the Counties of England, 1906, *A History of Northamptonshire*. Vol. 2. London: Archibald Constable.

VCH NORFOLK, Victoria History of the Counties of England, 1906, *A History of Norfolk*. Vol. 2. London: Archibald Constable.

VIRGOE, R. 1996, 'The estates of Norwich Cathedral Priory, 1101–1538', in Atherton et al. (eds.), 339–60.

VOISY, D. 2003, 'An Archaeological Evaluation at Norwich Cathedral Slype and Chapter House', *Norfolk Archaeological Unit, Report no. 853.*

WALLIS, H. 2002a, 'Norwich Cathedral Refectory: Assessment Report and Updated Project Design', *Norfolk Archaeological Unit, Report no. 723.*

WALLIS, H. 2002b, 'Norwich Cathedral Refectory, Phase 3: Assessment Report and Updated Project Design', *Norfolk Archaeological Unit, Report no. 733.*

WALLIS, H. 2003, 'An Archaeological Excavation at Norwich Cathedral Hostry, Norfolk'. *Norfolk Archaeological Unit, Report no. 847.*

WALLIS, H. in press, 'Excavations on the Site of Norwich Cathedral Refectory, 2001–2003'. *East Anglian Archaeology*.

WARD, S. 2003, 'Dissolution or Reformation? A Case Study from Chester's Urban Landscape', in Gaimster and Gilchrist (eds.), 267–79.

WARREN, A. K. 1985, *Medieval English Anchorites and their Patrons*. Berkeley: University of California.

WARSOP, P., and BOGHI, F. 2002, 'Report on an Archaeological Watching Brief at Life's Green, Norwich Cathedral Close', *Norfolk Archaeological Unit, Report no. 741.*

WEBER, M. 1905 (1992), *The Protestant Ethic and the Spirit of Capitalism*, trans. T. Parsons. London: Routledge.

WHITELOCK, D. (ed.) 1930, *Anglo-Saxon Wills*. Cambridge: Cambridge University Press.

WHITTINGHAM, A. B. 1935 unpub., 'Excavations in the Close, Norwich, Summer 1934'. Norfolk Record Office: MC 186/50 648x4.

WHITTINGHAM, A. B. 1943 unpub., 'The Norman Refectory'. Norfolk Record Office: MC 186/50 648x4.

WHITTINGHAM, A. B. 1949, 'Plan of Norwich Cathedral Priory', *Archaeol J* 106, 86. Also published as a separate sheet in 1938, and amended in 1975.

WHITTINGHAM, A. B. 1951, 'Bury St Edmunds Abbey: The Plan, Design and Development of the Church and Monastic Buildings', *Archaeol J* 108, 168–87.

WHITTINGHAM, A. B. 1967 unpub., 'Norwich Cathedral Deanery'. Norfolk Record Office: MC186/50 648x4.

WHITTINGHAM, A. B. 1979, 'Norwich Saxon Throne', *Archaeol J* 136, 60–68.

WHITTINGHAM, A. B. 1980a, 'The Bishop's Palace, Norwich', *Archaeol J* 137, 364–8.

WHITTINGHAM, A. B. 1980b, 'The Carnary College, Norwich', *Archaeol J* 137, 361–4.

WHITTINGHAM, A. B. 1980c, 'The Deanery, Norwich', *Archaeol J* 137, 314.

WHITTINGHAM, A. B. 1980d, 'Gates of the Cathedral Close', *Archaeol J* 137, 316.

WHITTINGHAM, A. B. 1980e, 'Thompson College', *Archaeol J* 137, 80.

WHITTINGHAM, A. B. 1981, *Norwich Cathedral Bosses and Misericords*. Norwich: Norwich Cathedral.

WHITTINGHAM, A. B. 1985, 'The Development of the Close since the Reformation, with Notes on Properties in the Close', in G. A. Metters (ed.), *The Parliamentary Survey of Dean and Chapter Properties in and around Norwich in 1649*. Norfolk Record Society 51 (1988), 102–20.

WILLIAMS, J. F., and COZENS-HARDY, B. 1953, *Extracts from the Two Earliest Minute Books of the Dean and Chapter of Norwich Cathedral, 1566–1649*. Norfolk Record Society 24.

WILLIS, R. 1848, 'Description of the Ancient Plan of the Monastery of St Gall', *Archaeol J*
     5, 85–117.
WILLIS, R. 1868, 'The Architectural History of the Conventual Buildings of the Monastery
     of Christ Church in Canterbury', *Archaeologia Cantiana* 7, 158–83.
WINKLES, H. 1838, *Architectural and Picturesque Illustrations of the Cathedral Churches*. London:
     Effingham Wilson.
WOLLASTON, D. 1996, 'Herbert de Losinga', in Atherton et al. (eds.), 22–35.
WOOD, M. 1965, *The English Medieval House*. London: Bracken Books.
WOODMAN, F. 1996, 'The Gothic Campaigns', in Atherton et al. (eds.), 158–96.

Index